The Law
and Politics
of Abortion

The Law and Politics of Abortion

Edited by
Carl E. Schneider
Maris A. Vinovskis
University of Michigan

LexingtonBooks
D.C. Heath and Company
Lexington, Massachusetts
Toronto

Library of Congress Cataloging in Publication Data

Main entry under title:
    The Law and politics of abortion.

    Originally appeared in a special issue of the Michigan law review.
    Bibliography: p.
    Includes index.
    CONTENTS: Regan, D.H. Rewriting Roe v. Wade.—King, P.A. The
juridical status of the fetus.—Appleton, S.F. The abortion-funding cases and
population control. [etc.]
    1. Abortion—Law and legislation—United States—Addresses, essays,
lectures. I. Schneider, Carl, 1948-   . II. Vinovskis, Maris.
KF3771.A75L38   344.73'0419   79-3134
ISBN 0-669-03386-3   AACR1

Introduction copyright © 1980 by D.C. Heath and Company

Second printing, January 1982

Published simultaneously in Canada

Printed in the United States of America

International Standard Book Number: 0-669-03386-3

Library of Congress Catalog Card Number: 79-3134

Contents

Preface and Acknowledgments

These chapters originally appeared in a special issue of the *Michigan Law Review* and are being published here in order to reach a wider audience. Since many who will read these chapters do not have a legal background or may be unfamiliar with the recent abortion cases, we have greatly expanded the introduction to include a summary of the Supreme Court's decisions in this field.

The chapters in this book were solicited during Carl Schneider's tenure as editor of the *Review*, in collaboration with Maris Vinovskis, who was the guest coeditor of the special issue. Because of the inevitable, though regrettable, delays associated with assembling chapters from any group of scholars, the editing of this special issue was not completed until after Carl Schneider had left the *Review*. Therefore, we gratefully acknowledge our debt to the new staff of the *Review* for their invaluable labors for this project. That staff, and, in particular, Jeffrey S. Lehman, the new editor of the *Review*, edited these chapters with a zeal, discernment, and discretion which epitomized the tradition of law-review editing. Without their dedication and intelligence, this book could not have been prepared. Finally, we thank Margaret Zusky and the staff at Lexington Books, who skillfully produced this book so that it might be of some service to those who seek to understand the difficult issues its authors address.

Introduction

In *Roe* v. *Wade,* the Supreme Court decided an issue of such legal, social, and political importance that one might have supposed few legal scholars and even fewer student authors could resist writing about it. And, indeed, shortly after the Court spoke it was criticized by Richard Epstein in the *Supreme Court Review*[1] and by John Hart Ely in the *Yale Law Journal*[2] and was defended by Philip Heymann and Douglas Barzelay in the *Boston University Law Review.*[3] Thereafter, however, the constitutionality of criminal abortion statutes was the subject of few articles. This scholarly reticence is puzzling, not only because the decision was significant, but also because the consensus of legal academics seems to be that, whatever one thinks of the holding, the opinion is unsatisfying. And the reticence is the more puzzling because, legally and politically, abortion remains an unfinished topic: The Court continues to work out a series of subsidiary problems while Congress and state legislatures continue to question the correctness and desirability of the initial decision.

Six years after *Roe* v. *Wade,* then, it is time to appraise the Court's handling of the abortion issue and to place it in perspective. This book seeks to begin that task.

An important part of seeing *Roe* in perspective is seeing its relation to public sentiment. *Roe* invalidated almost universally adopted laws regulating an emotional issue; far beyond the average case, it was affected by, and sought to affect, public feeling. Justice Blackmun's opinion adduced "man's attitudes toward abortion," and Justice Rehnquist's dissent asked rhetorically whether the right to decide whether to have an abortion was "so rooted in the traditions and conscience of our people as to be ranked fundamental." And as Donald Regan comments in his chapter on *Roe,* "A good deal has been written recently on the idea that the Constitution should be interpreted in light of, or should be assumed to incorporate, 'conventional morality,' or 'community morality,' or some such." Without in any way supposing that public-opinion polls can by themselves define a people's ethos, we may find it helpful to see what those polls say about the state of public feeling.

When the Supreme Court first exercises its powers of judicial review in a controversial area about which the Constitution speaks only indirectly, the Court's political efficacy and even legitimacy are likely to be called into question. Hence another part of our task is to understand the political aspects of *Roe* v. *Wade.* Abortion reform was a fervently contested subject before the decision, and opponents of reform have vigorously tried to use the political system to restrict and reverse the effect of the Court's holding. Thus, for *Roe* as for *Brown* v. *Board of Education,* a central issue has been the Court's ability to secure political acceptance for its decision. We need to know therefore, what people thought about abortion before the Court acted. We need to understand whether and how the Court's decision altered popular sentiment. Finally, we may hope to learn something about the Court's institutional role by studying political reaction to the case.

These are not issues which lawyers are specially trained to handle, so, with the faith in interdisciplinary scholarship that springs eternal in the modern academic breast, we sought to consult the wisdom of the social sciences. Eric Uslaner and Ronald Weber examine public attitudes toward abortion before the decision in *Roe* and investigate changes the decision may have wrought in those attitudes. Vinovskis' analysis of voting behavior in the 1972 and 1976 presidential elections sheds light on the decision's political significance. That significance is further illuminated by his treatment of the major congressional reaction to *Roe* v. *Wade*—the Hyde Amendment's attempt to prohibit the use of federal funds for abortions.

It is also time to fit the decision into doctrinal perspective. We therefore solicited an article from Gregory Morgan that studies the state of abortion law before *Roe* and reads what was already inscribed on the tablet on which the Court was writing. Patricia King's investigation of the fetus's legal status clarifies a crucial part of *Roe*'s argument and speculates on its implications for related areas of law. Susan Appleton, dissecting the Abortion Funding Cases, treats one of the central debates that followed in *Roe*'s wake. Finally, Regan's chapter takes us back to the basic question: Was *Roe* rightly decided, and if so, on what grounds is it best rationalized?

We solicited these chapters from legal scholars and social scientists on the basis of their academic qualifications, without regard to their personal views on abortion. As a result, the contributions to this book reflect a variety of views of abortion and the law. Nevertheless, all of them point to the need for more scholarly research and discourse on abortion, both from lawyers and from social scientists. As the abortion debate continues, judges and legislators should be able to ask the academic community for wiser and fuller analyses that try to reconcile conflicting beliefs on this unsettled and unsettling issue.

Abortion Statutes in the Supreme Court: A Primer

Because the Supreme Court's abortion decisions have provoked deep-seated and widespread popular reactions, and because one of our purposes is to bring to bear the learning of two disciplines on the abortion controversy, we hope that this book will interest and be used by nonlawyers as well as by lawyers. But these chapters first appeared in a law review, and several were written for those versed in the law. Worse, these chapters treat an area of law in which the traditional process of reasoning is based on assumptions which may justly seem obscure to the layman. Further, because the quantity of the literature on the subject has not matched the importance of the issue, lawyers may well be unacquainted with at least some of the Court's decisions in the area.

Therefore, we present a summary of the basis for and holdings of those opinions in which the Supreme Court has ruled on aspects of the abortion issue. Since the precise language of a court's opinion is often important, and since we wish to convey the flavor as well as the facts of the Court's abortion decisions, we have quoted liberally from them. The reader should be warned, however, that this summary does not pretend to be analytically interesting; readers who are already familiar with the evolution of the right of privacy and the relation of that right to the abortion issue can safely pass this section by. Readers who simply wish to refresh their recollection of the Court's holdings in these cases may skip to the section entitled "The Antecedents of *Roe* v. *Wade*."

The Doctrine of Substantive Due Process

We begin with a précis of the legal background of the abortion controversy.[4] Until the late 1960s, abortion was almost entirely an issue for the states: in our federal system of government, states are the units of government primarily responsible for exercising what is called the "police power," that is, the power to make laws to protect the health, safety, and morals of the population. In the 1960s, although some states had begun to respond to reformers' pressures, most had statutes sharply limiting the circumstances in which women could obtain abortions.

Toward the end of the 1960s, the attack on such statutes moved to the federal courts. A federal court, however, may overturn a state statute only if a conflicting federal statute preempts the state statute, if the state statute infringes on an area of regulation in which Congress exercises exclusive authority, or if the state statute violates the federal Constitution. There was, as we have said, no conflicting federal abortion statute or congressional authority. Further, no provision of the Constitution expressly addresses the problem of abortions. The Fourteenth Amendment, however, forbids a state to "deprive any person of life, liberty, or property without due process of law."

For several reasons, the relevance of this passage to the abortion issue may not be instantly apparent. First, the Fourteenth Amendment was adopted after the Civil War in order to secure the civil rights of the recently freed slaves. Second, the language of the Fourteenth Amendment seems to be addressed only to the fairness of the *procedures* which must be followed before a state can deprive a person "of life, liberty, or property." Third, even if the phrase has substantive as well as procedural content, it is not self-evident that "life, liberty, or property" encompasses a woman's right to decide whether to have an abortion.

Nevertheless, the Supreme Court has not read the Fourteenth Amendment in the limited way which those three considerations might seem to make necessary. First, the breadth and strength of the Fourteenth Amendment's language have diminished the relevance of its historical origins. Second, as Justice Harlan observed,

> Were due process merely a procedural safeguard it would fail to reach those situations where the deprivation of life, liberty or property was accomplished by legislation which by operating in the future could, given even the fairest possible procedure in application to individuals, nevertheless destroy the enjoyment of all three. . . . Thus the guaranties of due process, though having their roots in Magna Carta's *"per legem terrae"* and considered as procedural safeguards "against executive usurpation and tyranny," have in this country "become bulwarks also against arbitrary legislation." [5]

Third, during the course of the Court's case-by-case evaluation of state laws, the phrase "life, liberty, or property" has, by the centuries-old process of judicial accretion, assumed considerable scope. Thus, Justice Harlan wrote, the "liberty" which the Fourteenth Amendment protects "is a rational continuum which, broadly speaking, includes a freedom from all substantial arbitrary impositions and purposeless restraints. . . ." [6]

This kind of imposing but vague formula, of course, hardly gives the Court the specific guidance one would like it to have (but which can rarely be achieved in any matter of real importance and which, consequently, the Constitution can rarely offer). We would like the Court to have this kind of guidance because the Court is something of an anomaly in a democratic society—it is the only non-elected branch of government. Thus the court must always steer between the Scylla of improvidently annulling laws written by the direct representatives of the people and the Charybdis of allowing to stand laws which destroy the liberties that the Constitution was written and the Court was created to protect. Individuals can and do disagree as to which wreck is preferable, and so the Court has inevitably interpreted what is called "substantive due process" in ways which have often been controversial.

In the late nineteenth century and into the 1930s, the Court announced and deployed the doctrine that "[t]he general right to make a contract in relation to his business is part of the liberty of the individual protected by the Fourteenth Amendment of the Federal Constitution." [7] However, the "right to contract" fell into growing disrepute as the Court used it to invalidate liberal economic and social reforms. For example, in the emblematic case of *Lochner* v. *New York,*[8] the Court found unconstitutional a law which, in an effort to mitigate the harmful effects of ambient flour dust and other conditions deleterious to the health of bakery employees, set their maximum working week at sixty hours. *Lochner* was the occasion of one of Justice Holmes' most famous dissents, in which he protested that "a constitution is not intended to embody a particular economic theory, whether of paternalism and the organic relation of the citizen to the State or of *laissez faire.*"[9] He wrote:

> I think that the word liberty in the Fourteenth Amendment is perverted when it is held to prevent the natural outcome of a dominant opinion, unless it can be said that a rational and fair man necessarily would admit that the statute proposed would infringe fundamental principles as they have been understood by the traditions of our people and our law.[10]

In the mid-1930s, after a fierce siege of New Deal legislation, the Supreme Court renounced substantive due process as a means of invalidating such economic and social legislation. By 1952, the Court could say, "Our recent decisions make plain that we do not sit as a super-legislature to weigh the wisdom of legislation . . . ."[11] However, to note here what will become apparent later, several *Lochner*-era cases involving *non*-economic rights seem to have survived the Court's repudiation of *Lochner*.

Before we discuss the Court's abortion decisions, we pause to discuss the analytic method which the Court uses in deciding substantive due process cases. The first question (and, as a practical matter, the determinative question) the Court asks is whether the right which the statute at issue infringes is a "fundamental" right. The test for a fundamental right has been variously described, for, as Justice Harlan said, "Due process has not been reduced to any formula. . . ."[12] Justice Harlan's own phrasing of the test, however, has been influential:

> The best that can be said is that through the course of this Court's decisions it has represented the balance which our Nation, built upon postulates of respect for the liberty of the individual, has struck between that liberty and the demands of organized society. . . . The balance of which I speak is the balance struck by this country, having regard to what history teaches are the traditions from which it broke. That tradition is a living thing.[13]

Justice Goldberg later added that judges

> must look to the "traditions and [collective] conscience of our people" to determine whether a principle is "so rooted [there] . . . as to be ranked fundamental." The inquiry is whether a right involved "is of such a character

that it cannot be denied without violating those 'fundamental principles of liberty and justice which lie at the base of all our civil and political institutions'. . . ."[14]

That a statute invades even a fundamental right does not, however, mean that the statute is unconstitutional, since the individual's interest in exercising a right (and society's interest in preserving fundamental rights) must be balanced against those societal interests the law was enacted to promote. The second stage of substantive-due-process analysis therefore directs the Court to examine the goals and means of the statute under attack. When a fundamental right is implicated, the statute is constitutional only if it is (1) necessary to serve a "compelling state interest" and (2) so narrowly drawn that it serves only legitimate state interests. When a fundamental right is *not* implicated, the statute needs merely to be rationally related to a permissible state interest. These tests notwithstanding, the Court's common practice in substantive-due-process litigation has been to find that, where the citizen's right is fundamental, the state interest is insufficient to overcome it; and where the right is not fundamental, the state interest justifies the statute. Therefore, the pivotal question has been whether the infringed right is fundamental.

The Antecedents of Roe v. Wade

In 1965, the Supreme Court in *Griswold* v. *Connecticut*[15] declared unconstitutional a statute which made it a criminal offense for anyone, married or not, to use contraceptives. In analyzing the "fundamental rights" aspect of the case, the Court for the first time identified a "zone of privacy created by several fundamental constitutional guarantees."[16] Among those guarantees were the First Amendment's implied right of association and the Fourth Amendment's express "right of the people to be secure in their persons, houses, papers, and effects, against unreasonable searches and seizures." The law affected a relationship—marriage—which lies within that zone of privacy: "Marriage is a coming together for better or for worse, hopefully enduring, and intimate to the degree of being sacred."[17] The law served the state's interests through means which "sweep unnecessarily broadly and thereby invade the area of protected freedoms."[18] The Court asked rhetorically, "Would we allow the police to search the sacred precincts of marital bedrooms for telltale signs of the use of contraceptives?" The Court answered rhetorically: "The very idea is repulsive to the notions of privacy surrounding the marriage relationship."[19]

Since *Griswold,* the Court has interpreted the "zone of privacy" as arising directly from the Fourteenth Amendment, rather than from a confluence of several constitutional provisions. However, *Griswold* remains important both because it was the Court's first real invalidation of that regime of ancient laws regulating sexual morality and because the right which those laws arguably infringe is still called the right of privacy. "Privacy" is a somewhat misleading word in this context, although it was a plausible choice in *Griswold,* which drew heavily on the Fourth Amendment and the enduring understanding that it guards citizens against government's invasions "of the sanctity of a man's home and the privacies of life."[20] The reader should bear in mind that the more the Court used the word "privacy," the less the Court meant the word in its ordinary sense—"seclusion from the sight, presence, or intrusion of others."

Griswold, we have seen, involved the use of contraceptives by married people. In 1972, the Court in *Eisenstadt* v. *Baird*[21] declared unconstitutional a statute which punished with up to five years in prison anyone (except a pharmacist upon a doctor's prescription) who distributed any article intending that it be used to prevent conception. The Court in *Baird* invoked the equal-protection clause of the Fourteenth Amendment, a clause which, as the Court has interpreted it, denies states "the power to legislate that different treatment be accorded to persons placed by a statute into different classes on the basis of criteria wholly unrelated to the objective of that statute."[22] In other words, the Court in *Baird* asked whether there was some reason married persons could be given contraceptives but unmarried people could not. The Court first decided that one possible reason—society's desire to prevent premarital sexual intercourse—was implausible, since the Court could not credit that that goal was actually a purpose of the law: "It would be plainly unreasonable to assume that Massachusetts has prescribed pregnancy and the birth of an unwanted child as punishment for fornication, which is a misdemeanor under Massachusetts General Laws. . . ."[23] The Court next decided that health considerations could not justify the different treatment of the married and the unmarried, since the effects of contraceptives on health are presumably identical for unmarried and married people. Finally, in a frequently quoted passage, the Court responded to the argument that the statute ought to be upheld on the ground that the state may believe that the very use of contraceptives is immoral:

> If under *Griswold* the distribution of contraceptives to married persons cannot be prohibited, a ban on distribution to unmarried persons would be equally impermissible. It is true that in *Griswold* the right of privacy in question inhered in the marital relationship. Yet the marital couple is not an independent entity with a mind and heart of its own, but an association of two individuals each with a separate intellectual and emotional makeup. If the right of privacy means anything, it is the right of the *individual,* married or single, to be free from unwarranted governmental intrusion into matters so fundamentally affecting a person as the decision whether to bear or beget a child.[24]

Roe *v.* Wade

"By 1950," Professor Mohr reports, "American public opinion considered abortion socially odious, and virtually no one in American society yet dared to call openly for its relegalization as an appropriate national practice."[25] However, as the 1960s wore on, attempts to liberalize state abortion laws emerged and, in 1967, were rewarded with the reform of Colorado's statute. By January 1973, seventeen other states and the District of Columbia had revised their abortion statutes.

Mohr suggests several reasons for the early success of the abortion-reform movement. In the 1960s, people in the United States began to notice and regret the overpopulation of the earth, and some came to see abortion as necessary to slow the population's growth. Mohr also reports "an increasing concern in the twentieth century for what was called the quality of life, as distinguished from biological life itself as an absolute."[26] If many of the indicia of life could artificially be maintained in what seemed a plainly lifeless body, was not human life more than simple biological life? One relationship of abortion to this concern was dramatically and sympathetically illuminated when Mrs. Robert Finkbine, who, while pregnant, had taken a drug (Thalidomide) which can cause the birth of deformed children, unsuccessfully sought an abortion in the United States and later flew to Sweden to have one. Mohr also points to the assertion of the modern feminist movement that women have a right to control their own bodies as well as to the medical profession's overwhelming approval—87 percent in 1967—of liberalized abortion policies. Nor were restrictive abortion laws easily enforced or universally respected—by the late 1960s, estimates of the annual number of illegal abortions ranged from 200,000 to 1,200,000. Illegal abortions could be humiliating and dangerous. So it was especially offensive to many Americans that legal abortions were more readily available to rich women than to poor, to white than to black.[27]

Nevertheless, it was not obvious in 1973 that abortion reform was an idea whose time had come. While public-opinion polls suggest there may have been a trend in favor of liberalized laws in the late 1960s, even by 1972 less than a majority of the country (46 percent) favored such changes.[28] Further, opponents of liberalized statutes organized in response to the success of the reformers, and, as the New York experience indicates, reforms often were won only narrowly and painfully. Nor were they always won. In 1972, for instance, Michigan voters rejected a referendum proposal to revise the state's abortion laws.

While the contests in state legislatures and referenda continued, however, state and lower federal courts were considering, and sometimes overturning, restrictive abortion statutes. In 1970 the pseudonymous Jane Roe filed a class-action suit seeking a declaratory judgment that Texas' abortion statutes were unconstitutional. Those statutes made it criminal to "procure an abortion'' unless the abortion was "procured or attempted by medical advice for the purpose of saving the life of the mother." On January 22, 1973, the Supreme Court handed down its decision in *Roe* v. *Wade*[29] and, by a vote of 7 to 2, pronounced those statutes unconstitutional.[30] The decision is of such importance that we recapitulate it in some detail.

Justice Blackmun's opinion for the Court opened with an acknowledgment "of the sensitive and emotional nature of the abortion controversy" and of the Court's obligation "to resolve the issue by constitutional measurement, free of emotion and of predilection."[31] The Court, Justice Blackmun said, bore in mind

> Mr. Justice Holmes' admonition in his now-vindicated dissent in *Lochner* v. *New York,* 198 U.S. 45, 76 (1905):
>
> > "[The Constitution] is made for people of fundamentally differing views, and the accident of our finding certain opinions natural and familiar or novel and even shocking ought not to conclude our judgment upon the question whether statutes embodying them conflict with the Constitution of the United States."[32]

After disposing of some preliminary matters, Justice Blackmun proceeded to a lengthy discussion of the history of abortion laws, the gist of which was that "the restrictive criminal abortion laws in effect in a majority of States today . . . are not of ancient or even of common-law origin. Instead, they derive from statutory changes effected, for the most part, in the latter half of the 19th century."[33] It is true that the Hippocratic oath does condemn abortion, but the oath merely "'echoes Pythagorean doctrines,' and '[i]n no other stratum of Greek opinion were such views held or proposed in the same spirit of uncompromising austerity.'"[34] It is true that, toward the end of antiquity, the oath became popular, since "[t]he emergent teachings of Christianity were in agreement with the Pythagorean ethic." It is true that the oath "'became the nucleus of all medical ethics' and 'was applauded as the embodiment of truth.'"[35] But since the oath "certainly was not accepted by all ancient physicians, . . . it is 'a Pythagorean manifesto and not the expression of an absolute standard of medical conduct.'"[36]

At common law, Justice Blackmun reported, "abortion performed before 'quickening'—the first recognizable movement of the fetus *in utero,* appearing usually from the 16th to the 18th week of pregnancy—was not an indictable offense,"[37] and it now appears "doubtful that abortion was ever firmly established as a common-law crime even with respect to the destruction of a quick fetus."[38] In 1803 the English Parliament passed Lord Ellenborough's Act, which "made abortion of a quick fetus, §1, a capital crime, but in §2 it provided lesser penalties for the felony of abortion before quickening. . . ."[39] In 1821 Connecticut adopted that part of the English act relating to a woman "quick with child," but it forbore to impose the death penalty. In 1828 New York made the abortion of an unquickened fetus a misdemeanor and the abortion of a quickened fetus second-degree manslaughter. New York excepted from its law abortions which "shall have been necessary to preserve the life of such mother, or shall have been advised by two physicians to be necessary for such purpose." Despite these early statutes, "[i]t was not until after the War Between the States that legislation began generally to replace the common law. . . . Gradually, in the middle and late 19th century the quickening distinction disappeared from the statutory law of most States and the degree of the offense and the penalties were increased."[40] In sum, the import of this historical excursus apparently was that "at common law, at the time of the adoption of our Constitution, and throughout the major portion of the 19th century, abortion was viewed with less disfavor than under most American statutes currently in effect."[41]

After surveying the present attitudes of the American Medical Association, the American Public Health Association, and the American Bar Association, Justice Blackmun assayed and found wanting three possible justifications of criminal abortion laws. First, such laws may discourage illicit sexual conduct. "Texas, however, does not advance this justification in the present case, and it appears that no court or commentator has taken the argument seriously."[42] Second, abortions can harm a woman's health. But antisepsis and modern techniques have made early abortions at least as safe as normal childbirth, and, "[c]onsequently, any interest of the State in protecting the woman from an inherently hazardous procedure, except when it would be equally dangerous for her to forgo it, has largely disappeared."[43] Third, the state has an interest in protecting prenatal life. Justice Blackmun acknowledged that people disagree as to when life actually begins, but "as long as at least *potential* life is involved, the State may assert interests beyond the protection of the pregnant woman alone."[44]

Justice Blackmun then undertook the pivotal section of his opinion, the section in which he replied to the question whether a woman has a "fundamental right" to an abortion. He began:

> The Constitution does not explicitly mention any right of privacy. In a line of decisions, however, going back perhaps as far as *Union Pacific R. Co.* v. *Botsford,* 141 U.S. 250, 251 (1891), the Court has recognized that a right of personal privacy, or a guarantee of certain areas or zones of privacy, does exist under the Constitution.[45]

Those cases apply only to rights which are "fundamental," and they

> also make it clear that the right has some extension to activities relating to marriage, *Loving* v. *Virginia;* procreation, *Skinner* v. *Oklahoma;* contra-

ception, *Eisenstadt* v. *Baird;* family relationships, *Prince* v. *Massachusetts;* and child rearing and education, *Pierce* v. *Society of Sisters, Meyer* v. *Nebraska.*[46]

Justice Blackmun then presented the crucial, if somewhat mysterious, sentence of the opinion:

> This right of privacy, whether it be founded in the Fourteenth Amendment's concept of personal liberty and restrictions upon state action, as we feel it is, or, as the District Court determined, in the Ninth Amendment's reservation of rights to the people, is broad enough to encompass a woman's decision whether or not to terminate her pregnancy.[47]

In the succeeding and apparently explanatory sentences Justice Blackmun described "[t]he detriment that the State would impose upon the pregnant woman by denying this choice altogether."[48] These detriments included medically diagnosable harm, psychological harm, the burdens of child care, the distress of an unwanted child, the difficulties of bringing an unwanted child into a family, and the stigma of unwed motherhood.

The Court did not identify the outer boundaries of the rather amorphous right of personal privacy. It did, though, warn that that right is not absolute and might have to yield to compelling state interests.

Before investigating the state's interests, Justice Blackmun paused to dismiss the argument that a fetus is a "person" within the meaning of the Fourteenth Amendment. This argument had to be considered, Justice Blackmun said, since "[i]f this suggestion of personhood is established, the appellant's case, of course, collapses, for the fetus' right to life would then be guaranteed specifically by the Amendment."[49] The Court diligently examined the references to "persons" in the Constitution and, after some thought, decided that "in nearly all these instances, the use of the word is such that it has application only postnatally."[50] Furthermore, the availability of abortion during the early nineteenth century confirmed the Court's conclusion that a fetus is not a "person" in the contemplation of the Constitution.

The opinion then returned to the mainstream of the compelling-state-interest problem:

> The pregnant woman cannot be isolated in her privacy. She carries an embryo and, later, a fetus. . . . The situation therefore is inherently different from marital intimacy, or bedroom possession of obscene material, or marriage, or procreation, or education. . . . [I]t is reasonable and appropriate for a State to decide that at some point in time another interest, that of health of the mother or that of potential human life, becomes significantly involved.[51]

But when was that "point in time" reached? Texas had argued in defense of its statute that life begins at conception and that therefore the state's interest is "compelling" throughout pregnancy. Justice Blackmun responded: "We need not resolve the difficult question of when life begins."[52] Although people give widely varying answers to that question, it can at least be said that, "[i]n areas other than criminal abortion, the law has been reluctant to endorse any theory that life, as we recognize it, begins before live birth. . . ."[53] Since the law has never recognized the unborn as persons "in the whole sense," Texas could not, "by adopting one theory of life, . . . override the rights of the pregnant woman that are at stake."[54]

This reasoning, though, did not necessarily establish the point at which the rights of the pregnant woman must yield to the state's interests. Justice Blackmun began to identify that point by announcing that "in the light of present medical knowledge," the first of the two interests—the interest in preserving the mother's health—becomes "compelling" at the end of the first trimester, since until that point an abortion may be safer than childbirth. Thus, during the first trimester, "the attending physician, in consultation with his patient, is free to determine, without regulation by the State, that, in his medical judgment, the patient's pregnancy should be terminated. If that decision is reached, the judgment may be effectuated by an abortion free of interference by the State."[55] And thus, after the first trimester, a state may regulate abortions *to the extent necessary to preserve the mother's health.*

The state's second interest—the interest in potential life—becomes compelling at viability (roughly the end of the second trimester), since the fetus then becomes capable of "meaningful life" outside the womb. Therefore, after viability the state may *prohibit* abortions altogether *unless the abortion is necessary to protect the mother's health or life.*

Since the Texas statute impermissibly prohibited abortions throughout pregnancy, the Court declared it unconstitutional. That holding, the Court said in conclusion, "is consistent with the relative weights of the respective interests involved, with the lessons and examples of medical and legal history, with the lenity of the common law, and with the demands of the profound problems of the present day."[56]

While they joined in Justice Blackmun's opinion for the majority, three members of the Court—Chief Justice Burger, Justice Douglas, and Justice Stewart—wrote concurring opinions expounding their own perspectives on the case. Chief Justice Burger's brief concurrence[57] stressed that the Texas law was harsh and that the holding was less sweeping than the dissenters seemed to believe. Justice Douglas' concurrence[58] argued for the breadth and precedential respectability of the right to privacy and concluded that "[e]laborate argument is hardly necessary to demonstrate that childbirth may deprive a woman of her preferred lifestyle and force upon her a radically different and undesired future."[59] Justice Stewart's concurrence[60] averred that, while the Court had explicitly pronounced the doctrine of substantive due process dead, cases like *Griswold* v. *Connecticut* had clearly resurrected it. Justice Stewart acquiesced in the fait accompli and addressed the problem of defining the scope of substantive-due-process rights by quoting Justice Frankfurter to the effect that "Great concepts like . . . 'liberty' . . . were purposely left to gather meaning from experience."[61] For a court, decisions are the stuff of experience, and Justice Stewart pointed to the "decisions of this Court [which] make clear that freedom of personal choice in matters of marriage and family life is one of the liberties protected by the Due Process Clause of the Fourteenth Amendment."[62] The right of the individual "to be free from unwarranted governmental intrusion into matters so fundamentally affecting a person as the decision whether to bear or beget a child"[63] necessarily includes a woman's right to decide whether to have an abortion:

> Certainly the interest of a woman in giving of her physical and emotional self during pregnancy and the interests that will be affected throughout her life by the birth and raising of a child are of a far greater degree of significance and personal intimacy than the right to send a child to private school protected in Pierce v. Society of Sisters or the right to teach a foreign language protected in Meyer v. Nebraska.[64]

Justice White and Justice Rehnquist dissented. Justice White's opinion[65] characterized the Court as deciding that "[d]uring the period prior to the time the fetus becomes viable, the Constitution of the United States values the convenience, whim, or caprice of the putative mother more than the life or potential life of the fetus. . . ."[66] Justice White could discover "nothing in the language or history of the Constitution to support the Court's judgment. The Court simply fashions and announces a new constitutional right for pregnant mothers and, with scarcely any reason or authority for its action, invests that right with sufficient substance to override most existing state abortion statutes."[67] In Justice White's belief, the Court should have left the issue it had decided to be resolved by the people acting through their state governments. The Court's failure to do so was "an improvident and extravagant exercise of the power of judicial review that the Constitution extends to this Court."[68]

Justice Rehnquist's dissent[69] criticized the Court's denomination of the fundamental right at issue in the case as the right of "privacy."[69] The Court used privacy, he said, in neither the ordinary sense of the word nor the special sense used by courts interpreting the Fourth Amendment's guarantee of freedom from unreasonable searches and seizures.

In any event, said Justice Rehnquist, the Court erred in applying the fundamental-rights/compelling-state-interest test, since "[t]he test traditionally applied in the area of social and economic legislation is whether or not a law such as that challenged has a rational relation to a valid state objective."[70] The test the Court applied leads to a "conscious weighing of competing factors . . . [which] is far more appropriate to a legislative judgment than to a judicial one"[71] and which leads the Court to repeat the mistakes it had repented having made in the era of *Lochner* v. *New York*. Thus, in *Roe* v. *Wade* the Court incorrectly identified the right to decide to have an abortion as "fundamental," yet a statute which, like U.S. abortion statutes, had been enacted by almost every state roughly a century ago surely did not conflict with any deeply rooted "traditions and conscience" of the people. Nor could the Court say that its result was contemplated by the framers of the Fourteenth Amendment, since at the time it was adopted at least thirty-six states or territories limited abortion.

Developments after Roe *v.* Wade

A landmark case like *Roe* v. *Wade* can dramatically shift the course of the law. But a single judicial decision, however dramatic, cannot by itself resolve a social issue as complex as the one the Court confronted in that case. Even Congress, which has the authority and time to write detailed and comprehensive legislation and which has among its members (or can consult) experts on any subject, cannot foresee and comprehend all the consequences and supplemental problems of one of its laws. And a court may not write legislation; rather it must, in principle at least, decide only the case which comes before it. Furthermore, when a decision provokes the kind of hostility which inevitably follows a case like *Roe* (or a case like the school-integration decision in *Brown* v. *Board of Education*), the Court must expect that some legislatures and courts will attempt to construe the decision so narrowly that it loses its vitality. Thus it was to be anticipated when *Roe* v. *Wade* was decided that the Court would accept and decide a series of cases which amplified and explicated the meaning of the Court's decision.

Doe v. Bolton. *Doe* v. *Bolton*,[72] the first of that series, was decided on the same day as *Roe* v. *Wade* in an opinion written by the author of *Roe*, Justice Blackmun. *Doe* concerned an abortion statute—Georgia's—which, in contrast to Texas' nineteenth-century law, was in its basics modeled on the abortion provision of a major proposal to reform American criminal law, the Model Penal Code. Georgia's statute forbade abortions except when they were necessary to preserve the woman's life or health, when the fetus was likely to be born with serious mental or physical defects, or when the pregnancy resulted from a rape (statutory or otherwise). Of course, on the principle of *Roe,* the law was unconstitutionally restrictive. But in *Doe* the

Court also considered several "procedural" provisions of the statute that limited the circumstances in which abortions could occur but which arguably survived *Roe*. It should be kept in mind that those provisions, like all the abortion statutes we discuss here, had to be evaluated in light of *Roe*'s holding that a woman has a fundamental right to decide free of governmental interference whether to have an abortion.

First, Georgia's statute required that abortions be performed only in hospitals accredited by the Joint Commission on Accreditation of Hospitals (JCAH). The Court, however, noted that Georgia allowed other kinds of surgery to be performed in hospitals not accredited by the JCAH and that the Model Penal Code contained no such provision. The Court held "that the JCAH-accreditation requirement does not withstand constitutional scrutiny in the present context. It is a requirement that simply is not 'based on differences that are reasonably related to the purposes of the Act in which it is found.'"[73] The Court added that

> the State must show more than it has in order to prove that only the full resources of a licensed hospital, rather than those of some other appropriately licensed institution, satisfy these health interests. We hold that the hospital requirement of the Georgia law, because it fails to exclude the first trimester of pregnancy . . . is also invalid.[74]

Second, the Georgia law required that even after a woman and her doctor had agreed that an abortion was medically appropriate, abortions be approved by a hospital-staff abortion committee. The Court again commented that the state's criminal law demanded such approval for no other surgery, and the Court concluded that the interposition of the hospital abortion committee was "unduly restrictive of the patient's rights and needs that, at this point, [had] already been medically delineated and substantiated by her personal physician."[75]

Third, Georgia's statute prohibited a physician from performing an abortion without the written concurrence of two other doctors who had independently examined the patient. Once more the Court observed that such concurrences were necessary for no other surgical procedure, and once again the Court decided that the "[r]equired acquiescence by co-practitioners has no rational connection with a patient's needs and unduly infringes on the physician's right to practice."[76]

Finally, the Georgia law set a residency requirement. The Court struck down that provision because it was insufficiently justified and because the Privileges and Immunities Clause of the Constitution protects the freedom to enter a state to seek medical services available there.[77]

Planned Parenthood of Central Missouri v. Danforth.[78] After the Court's decision in *Roe* v. *Wade*, many states rewrote their abortion statutes. These statutes, of course, accepted the basic holding of *Roe* v. *Wade*. However, they were generally passed at the behest of opponents of that decision, and many of the statutes were enacted to keep the number of abortions to a minimum: Legislators placed an elaborate array of civil and criminal hindrances in the path of a women who sought an abortion and the doctor who wished to perform one.[79] Thus, in 1974, Missouri passed a new abortion statute which contained a number of restrictive features. In *Planned Parenthood of Missouri v. Danforth,*[80] the Court weighed several provisions of that law.

First, the Court approved the statute's definition of viability as "that stage of fetal development when the life of the unborn child may be continued indefinitely outside the womb by natural or artificial life-support systems.[81] Denying a request that the state be compelled to define viability in terms of a specific number of weeks, the Court stated that it had "recognized in *Roe* that viability was a matter of medical judgment, skill, and technical ability," and that "it is not the proper function of the legislature or the courts to place viability, which essentially is a medical concept, at a specific point in the gestation period.[82]

Second, the Court upheld Missouri's requirement of a patient's informed, written consent to an abortion, even though Missouri made no such requirement for other surgical procedures. The Court referred to the difficulty and importance of the decision and the necessity that it be made knowledgeably, a goal the statute forwarded through permissible means.

The Court also let stand a provision of the statute which obliged doctors and health-care institutions to keep confidential records of the abortions with which they were concerned. While the Court suggested that some kinds of record-keeping requirements might interfere with the abortion decision or the doctor-patient relationship, this statute did not do so, and hence it withstood constitutional scrutiny.

Although the Court unanimously approved the above three provisions of the Missouri statute, it disapproved four others (though by a divided vote). For instance, the statute forbade abortions performed by saline amniocentesis after the first twelve weeks of pregnancy.[83] Under *Roe*, of course, restrictions on abortions are permissible after the first trimester if they reasonably relate to protecting the mother's health. Noting that saline amniocentesis was the technique then used in 68 to 80 percent of all abortions performed after the first trimester in the United States, and reading the record as indicating that other safe means were not readily available, the Court found the statute's prohibition of that technique "an unreasonable or arbitrary regulation designed to inhibit, and having the effect of inhibiting, the vast majority of abortions after the first 12 weeks."[84]

In respect to this issue, as to the other disapproved provisions, Justice White wrote a dissenting opinion in which he was joined by Chief Justice Burger and Justice Rehnquist.[85] Justice White adverted to evidence given in the district court to the effect that saline amniocentesis exposes women to severe complications and that the prostaglandin method is safer.[86] He said, "there is *no* evidence in the record that women in Missouri will be unable to obtain abortions by the prostaglandin method," and "[i]n any event, the point of [the provision] is to change the practice under which most abortions were performed under the saline amniocentesis method and to make the safer prostaglandin method generally available."[87]

The majority scrutinized and found constitutionally unsatisfactory a second section of the Missouri statute:

> No person who performs or induces an abortion shall fail to exercise that degree of professional skill, care and diligence to preserve the life and health of the fetus which such person would be required to exercise in order to preserve the life and health of any fetus intended to be born and not aborted. Any physician or person assisting in the abortion who shall fail to take such measures to encourage or to sustain the life of the child, and the death of the child results, shall be deemed guilty of manslaughter. . . . Further, such physician or other person shall be liable in an action for damages.[88]

The failing of the statute, the Court said, was that it did not specify "that such care need be taken only after the stage of viability has been reached."[89] Thus the provision "impermissibly requires the physician to preserve the life and health of the fetus, whatever the stage of pregnancy."[90]

Justice White's dissenting opinion retorted that this section of the statute would simply be without effect during the early stages of pregnancy, when the fetus could not possibly live outside the womb. In the only circumstances in which the section would be operative—when the fetus might be viable—the statute would be constitutional, "[s]ince the State has a compelling interest, sufficient to outweigh the mother's desire to kill the fetus, when the 'fetus . . . has the capability of meaningful life outside the mother's womb,' *Roe* v. *Wade*. . . ."[91]

Besides the provision requiring the woman's own written consent to the abortion, the statute included two third-party consent provisions. The first required the written consent of the woman's husband to an abortion, except when a doctor had certified the abortion was necessary to preserve the life of the mother. The Court conceded that a husband has a legitimate interest in his wife's pregnancy and in the fetus, and that the decision to have an abortion could profoundly affect the marital relationship. But the Court doubted that "the goal of fostering mutuality and trust in a marriage, and of strengthening the marital relationship and the marriage institution, will be achieved by giving the husband a veto power exercisable for any reason whatsoever or for no reason at all."[92] In any event, the Court thought it inaccurate to say that the provision encouraged the husband's "participation'' in the decision. Rather, since where there was disagreement, only the husband's wishes would prevail, it gave him a veto. Such an "absolute obstacle" to the woman's decision was held unconstitutional in *Roe*, and "[c]learly, since the State cannot regulate or proscribe abortion during the first stage, when the physician and his patient make that decision, the State cannot delegate authority to any particular person, even the spouse, to prevent abortion during that same period.''[93]

In dissent, Justice White thought it "truly surprising that the majority finds in the United States Constitution . . . a rule that the State must assign a greater value to a mother's decision to cut off a potential human life by abortion than to a father's decision to let it mature into a live child.''[94] Justice White rejected the majority's description of the statute as delegating to the father a power the state itself did not possess. Rather, the statute recognizes "that the husband has an interest of his own in the life of the fetus which should not be extinguished by the unilateral decision of the wife.''[95] The majority not only depreciated the father's interest; it exaggerated the mother's interests. When the Court in *Roe* described those interests, it "mentioned only the post-birth burdens of rearing a child.''[96] But Missouri had a law which forbade a woman to put her child up for adoption without her husband's consent. That plainly valid law represented "a judgment by the State that the mother's interest in avoiding the burdens of child rearing do not outweigh or snuff out the father's interest in participating in bringing up his own child.''[97] The wisdom of such a judgment is a matter "which a State should be able to decide free from the suffocating power of the federal judge, purporting to act in the name of the Constitution.''[98]

The Missouri statute further provided that a woman younger than eighteen years old could not obtain an abortion unless she had the written consent of a parent or unless the abortion was necessary to save her life. The state had attempted to justify this provision in terms of the traditional (and constitutionally approved) authority of parents over their children, but the Court doubted "that such veto power will enhance parental authority or control where the minor and the nonconsenting parent are so fundamentally in conflict and the very existence of the pregnancy already has fractured the family structure.''[99] In any event, this provision, like the spousal-consent provision, violated the teaching of *Roe* because "the State does not have the constitutional authority to give a third party an *absolute*, and possibly arbitrary, veto over the decision of the physician and his patient to terminate the patient's pregnancy, regardless of the reason for withholding the consent.''[100]

Justice White's dissent suggested that the parental-consent requirement served more than the state's interest in strengthening the family or the parent's interest in the abortion decision. The requirement, by keeping the minor from making a decision which was not in her own best interests, "vindicate[d] the very right created in *Roe* v. *Wade* . . . —the right of the pregnant woman to decide 'whether *or not* to terminate her pregnancy.'"[101] Such parental-consent requirements are simply the traditional way of protecting those who are too young to make mature decisions.

Justice Stevens also dissented from the Court's treatment of the parental-consent provision and argued that the requirement was entirely consistent with the holding in *Roe*. That holding simply established that the decision whether to have an abortion is important; but "even if it is the most important kind of a decision a young person may ever make, that assumption merely enhances the quality of the State's interest in maximizing the probability that the decision be made correctly and with full understanding of the consequences of either alternative."[102] A parental-consent requirement, Justice Stevens concluded, is a rational and permissible way of promoting that state interest.

The Abortion-Funding Cases. One of the most successful tactics of the opponents of *Roe* v. *Wade* has been to urge that, while a government may not pass criminal laws prohibiting women from having abortions, it can decline to use public funds to pay for abortions. Since abortions are disproportionately used by the less affluent, a government's decision to heed this advice could significantly lower the number of legal abortions performed in that jurisdiction. In 1976, after vigorous lobbying and before its members returned home to face elections, Congress enacted the Hyde Amendment as a rider to the 1977 fiscal-year budget of the Department of Health, Education, and Welfare. Congress has continued to enact a "Hyde Amendment," though with some variations, for each succeeding budget.[103] One version of it read:

> None of the funds provided for in this Act shall be used to perform abortions except where the life of the mother would be endangered if the fetus were carried to term; or except for such medical procedures necessary for the victims of rape or incest, when such rape or incest has been reported promptly to a law enforcement agency or public health service; or except in those instances where severe and long-lasting physical health damage to the mother would result if the pregnancy were carried to term when so determined by two physicians.[104]

The Supreme Court has not yet settled the constitutionality of the Hyde Amendment, but it will have the opportunity to do so in 1980, since it will then hear an appeal in *Harris* v. *McRae*, in which a lower federal court held the Hyde Amendment unconstitutional.[105]

Quite a few states have also passed laws which restrict, more or less severely, the availability of government funds for abortions. In the companion cases of *Beal* v. *Doe*[106] and *Mather* v. *Roe*,[107] the Supreme Court responded to such statutes.[108] In both cases, the Court voted 6 to 3 to sustain the states' attempts to do so. In both cases, Justice Powell wrote the majority opinion, and in both cases Justices Brennan, Marshall, and Blackmun dissented.

The only question before the Court in *Beal* was whether Title 19 of the Social Security Act required Pennsylvania to pay the costs of all legal abortions of Medicaid recipients, instead of paying for "medically necessary" abortions only. Since the Court was interpreting a statute and not the Constitution, it had simply to ascertain Congress' intent when, in 1965, it passed the Act. The Act provided: "A State plan for medical assistance must . . . include reasonable standards for . . . determining eligibility for and the extent of medical assistance under the plan which . . . are consistent with the objectives of this [Title]. . . ."[109] The Court interpreted this language as conferring "broad discretion" on the states and as requiring only that the state's standards be "reasonable" and "consistent with the objectives" of the Act.[110] Since in *Roe* v. *Wade* the Court had acknowledged the state's "valid and important interest in encouraging childbirth,"[111] the decision to subsidize only childbirth was not unreasonable. And "it is hardly inconsistent with the objectives of the Act for a State to refuse to fund *unnecessary*—though perhaps desirable—medical services."[112]

Justice Brennan wrote an opinion[113] for the three dissenting Justices which invoked the traditional rule of statutory construction that a statute should be interpreted so as to avoid raising unnecessary constitutional issues. Since the Court's reading of the statute raised equal-protection issues, Justice Brennan proposed another reading.

That reading took as the "very heart of the congressional scheme . . . that the physician and patient should have complete freedom to choose those medical procedures for a given condition which are best suited to the needs of the patient."[114] Justice Brennan quoted from a district court opinion: "'[A]bortion and childbirth, when stripped of the sensitive moral arguments surrounding the abortion controversy, are simply two alternative medical methods of dealing with pregnancy . . . .'"[115] It followed that Congress intended for the physician and patient to be free to choose between those "alternative medical methods."

Nor could the Court's construction of the statute be justified in terms of some affirmative policy. The state was not protecting its fiscal interests, since abortions are generally cheaper than childbirth; and the state was not protecting the mother's health, since elective abortions are now as safe as or safer than childbirth. Rather, in practical terms, the Court's construction condemned "penniless pregnant women to have children they would not have borne if the State had not weighted the scales to make their choice to have abortions substantially more onerous."[116]

In *Maher* v. *Roe,* the Court had before it a regulation of the Connecticut Welfare Department which provided that state Medicaid benefits could be provided for abortions in the first trimester only when they were medically (including psychiatrically) necessary. The Court had no doubt that a state need not pay for the medical expenses of indigents, but once a state has undertaken to do so, it must proceed constitutionally. Specifically, it must not violate the equal-protection clause of the Fourteenth Amendment.

The Court analyzes equal-protection claims in somewhat the way it analyzes substantive-due-process claims. It asks first whether a fundamental right has been infringed or whether a "suspect class" has been disadvantaged. If the answer to either question is yes, the statute must be justified by a compelling state interest. If the answer is no, the statute merely must rationally further a legitimate state purpose.

Justice Powell quickly concluded that the Connecticut regulation disadvantaged no "suspect class," since the Court has not accepted financial need as a sufficient condition for such a classification. Justice Powell then explained why the Court rejected the argument that the regulation impinged on the "fundamental right" expounded in *Roe* v. *Wade.* That case, he said, "did not declare an unqualified 'constitutional right to an abortion . . . .'" Rather, the right protects the woman from unduly burdensome interference with her freedom to decide whether to terminate her pregnancy."[117] The statute at issue in *Roe* v. *Wade,* for example, imposed *criminal* sanctions, and the consent provisions in the statute in *Danforth* set potentially absolute barriers in the path of a woman's decision. Here, however, the state had created no obstacles. Any obstacles an indigent woman encountered after the regulation was issued she would also have encountered in the absence of it. True, "[t]he State may have made childbirth a more attractive alternative, thereby influencing the woman's decision, but it has imposed no restriction on access to abortions that was not already there."[118]

Justice Powell asserted that this reasoning signaled no retreat from *Roe* v. *Wade,* since "[t]here is a basic difference between direct state interference with a protected activity and state encouragement of an alternative activity consonant with legislative policy."[119] He illustrated that difference by a comparison with *Meyer* v. *Nebraska* (in which the Court overturned a statute making it criminal to teach foreign languages to a child who had not completed the eighth grade) and to *Pierce* v. *Society of Sisters* (in which the Court found unconstitutional a statute requiring parents to send their children to public schools only.).[120] Justice Powell wrote:

Both cases invalidated substantial restrictions on constitutionally protected liberty interests: in *Meyer,* the parent's right to have his child taught a particular foreign language; in *Pierce,* the parent's right to choose private rather than public school education. But neither case denied to a State the policy choice of encouraging the preferred course of action.[121]

The state was free, in other words, to favor English by declining to teach German in its public schools and to favor public education by supporting only public schools. It followed that if a state did not have to justify with a compelling interest its decision to fund only public schools, neither did it have to justify in that way its decision to fund only normal childbirth.

Since the statute did not infringe a fundamental right, it had only to meet the lesser standard of justification, that is, to be rationally related to a permissible state interest. As in *Beal* v. *Doe,* the Court found with little discussion that encouraging childbirth was such an interest and that the regulation rationally forwarded it.

At the end of his opinion, Justice Powell responded to the protests of the dissenters that the decisions in the two cases imposed cruel choices on indigent pregnant women. His first response was that "'the Constitution does not provide judicial remedies for every social and economic ill.'"[122] His second response hearkened back to some of the considerations raised by the doctrine of substantive due process:

> [T]his Court does not strike down state laws "because they may be unwise, improvident, or out of harmony with a particular school of thought." . . . Indeed, when an issue involves policy choices as sensitive as those implicated by public funding of nontherapeutic abortions, the appropriate forum for their resolution in a democracy is the legislature. We should not forget that "legislatures are ultimate guardians of the liberties and welfare of the people in quite as great a degree as the courts."[123]

In an opinion for the three dissenters,[124] Justice Brennan attacked the Court's conclusion that the regulation did not impair a fundamental right and therefore that the compelling-state-interest test was not called into play. Justice Brennan rejected the Court's suggestion that only "absolute" obstacles to an abortion impair the fundamental right of *Roe* v. *Wade.* For example, on the same day the Court struck down the criminal statute in that case, it also struck down in *Doe* v. *Bolton* several procedural requirements which were in no way "absolute" bars to elective abortions. Nor could the obstacle in *Danforth* accurately be called "absolute," except "in the limited sense that a woman who was unable to persuade her spouse to agree to an elective abortion was prevented from obtaining one."[125] The Court had in *Carey* v. *Population Services International*[126] invalidated a New York law prohibiting the sale of contraceptives to children under sixteen years old, prohibiting anyone but a pharmacist from selling contraceptives, and banning advertisements for contraceptives. The Court had said in *Carey* that *Roe* v. *Wade, Doe* v. *Bolton,* and *Danforth* "establish that the same test must be applied to state regulations that burden an individual's right to decide to prevent conception or terminate pregnancy by substantially limiting access to the means of effectuating that decision as is applied to state statutes that prohibit the decision entirely."[127]

In short, by funding childbirths and abortions differently, the state regulation brought financial pressure on women who had a fundamental right to decide free from state interference whether to have an abortion. The regulation thereby infringed on that fundamental right, and thus the state should have been required to justify its action by identifying a compelling state interest.

Justice Marshall wrote a bitter dissenting opinion which applied to both *Beal* v. *Doe* and *Maher* v. *Roe.* The opinion opened:

> It is all too obvious that the governmental actions in these cases, ostensibly taken to "encourage" women to carry pregnancies to term, are in reality intended to impose a moral viewpoint that no State may constitutionally enforce. Since efforts to overturn [*Roe* v. *Wade* and *Doe* v. *Bolton*] have been unsuccessful, the opponents of abortion have attempted every imaginable means to circumvent the commands of the Constitution and impose their moral choices upon the rest of society.

> The present cases involve the most vicious attacks yet devised. . . . As the Court well knows, these regulations inevitably will have the practical effect of preventing nearly all poor women from obtaining safe and legal abortions.

> . . . I am appalled at the ethical bankruptcy of those who preach a "right to life" that means, under present social policies, a bare existence in utter misery for so many poor women and their children.[128]

In this opinion, as in many previous opinions, Justice Marshall criticized the dispositive quality of the Court's decision that the right implicated was not fundamental. He again urged on the Court an analysis in which it would assess several considerations together. Justice Marshall would have looked at the following considerations. First, the governmental benefit denied by the regulation—that is, the right to choose whether to bear a child—was of fundamental importance. Second, the regulation had a greatly disproportionate effect on the poor and the nonwhite, facts suggesting discrimination on the basis of wealth and race. Third, the state's interest in regulating first-trimester abortions had already (in *Doe* v. *Bolton*) been held too feeble to justify interference with the right to an abortion. Weighing all these factors, Justice Marshall believed, a court could conclude only that both the Pennsylvania and the Connecticut regulations violated the equal-protection clause.

Justice Blackmun also wrote a dissenting opinion (for both cases),[129] in which he was joined by his two dissenting colleagues. Like them, he believed that the two regulations simply accomplished indirectly what *Roe* v. *Wade* had said they could not do directly. He added:

> Neither is it an acceptable answer, as the Court well knows, to say that the Congress and the States are free to authorize the use of funds for nonthera-

peutic abortions. Why should any politician incur the demonstrated wrath and noise of the abortion opponents when mere silence and nonactivity accomplish the results the opponents want?[130]

Bellotti v. *Baird.* By 1979, the problem of teenage pregnancy had come to be seen as acute, and may well have given added urgency to the debate (to which *Danforth* had contributed) over parental-consent provisions of abortion laws. Although the overall rate of teenage fertility has decreased over the last twenty years, "nearly a million teenagers become pregnant each year and almost 600,000 of them have babies," and it has been estimated that "forty percent of all teenage girls will become pregnant as adolescents."[131] But what was perhaps more disturbing was that 39.5 percent of all teenage births in 1977 occurred among girls seventeen years old or younger, that 2 percent of all teenage births in that year occurred among girls under fifteen years old, and that the fertility of the very young has been increasing. Further, while there were 92,000 out-of-wedlock births to teenagers in 1960, there were 249,806 in 1977; 48.3 percent of the out-of-wedlock children in that year were born to teenagers. (And almost 90 percent of those children are now kept by the mother and not put up for adoption.)

In *Belotti* v. *Baird,*[132] the Court again joined in, but did not fully resolve, the debate over parental-consent laws by invalidating a Massachusetts statute. That statute, like the statute the Court had invalidated in *Planned Parenthood of Central Missouri* v. *Danforth,* required that an unmarried mother less than eighteen years old obtain parental permission to her abortion. Unlike the statute in *Danforth,* however, the Massachusetts statute provided that, "[i]f one or both of the mother's parents refuse such consent, consent may be obtained by order of a judge of the superior court for good cause shown, after such hearing as he deems necessary." As the Supreme Judicial Court of Massachusetts construed the statute, a minor could not seek judicial approval of an abortion before consulting her parents, and the judge making the decision could consider only the best interests of the mother.

Although the Court voted 8 to 1 to hold the statute constitutionally unsound, the majority divided, 4 to 4, in its reason for that holding. Justice Powell (for Chief Justice Burger, Justice Stewart, and Justice Rehnquist[133]) wrote an opinion which seemed designed to intimate to states that a constitutional parental-consent statute can be drafted.

Justice Powell observed that while minors have constitutional rights, their rights cannot be equated with those of adults. First, "the State is entitled to adjust its legal system to account for children's vulnerability and their needs for 'concern, . . . sympathy, and . . . paternal attention.'"[134] Thus juvenile courts may, in some respects, use different procedures than the Constitution demands be used to protect adults in criminal courts. Second, since minors sometimes lack mature judgment, the state may limit children's freedom to make choices which can have important consequences. For instance, state laws may limit minors' access to sexually oriented magazines, even though those magazines are not obscene by constitutional standards. "Third, the guiding role of parents in the upbringing of their children justifies limitations on the freedoms of minors."[135] As the Court had said in *Prince* v. *Massachusetts,* "It is cardinal with us that the custody, care and nurture of the child reside first in the parents, whose primary function and freedom include *preparation for obligations the state can neither supply nor hinder.*"[136] This

> tradition of parental authority is not inconsistent with our tradition of individual liberty; rather, the former is one of the basic presuppositions of the latter. Legal restrictions on minors, especially those supportive of the parental role, may be important to the child's chances for the full growth and maturity that make eventual participation in a free society meaningful and rewarding.[137]

Against that background of principle, Justice Powell said that since

> immature minors often lack the ability to make fully informed choices that take account of both immediate and long-range consequences, a State reasonably may determine that parental consultation often is desirable and in the best interest of the minor. It may further determine, as a general proposition, that such consultation is particularly desirable with respect to the abortion decision—one that for some people raises profound moral and religious concerns.[138]

However desirable such consultation, the extraordinary seriousness of the decision whether to have an abortion necessitated the holding in *Danforth* that the state may not give a parent an absolute veto over a minor's decision to have an abortion. Justice Powell then desribed his reconciliation of these conflicting state and individual interests: "[I]f the State decides to require a pregnant minor to obtain one or both parents' consent to an abortion, it also must provide an alternative procedure whereby authorization for the abortion can be obtained."[139]

The Massachusetts statute, of course, offered such an alternative: it provided for prompt and confidential judicial proceedings, and it allowed the judge to consider only the minor's best interests. Despite these safeguards, the statute was unconstitutional in two respects. First, a minor seeking to use the statute's provision for judicial approval of her abortion had to notify a parent of her wish. But since some parents might try to prevent the minor even from seeking a court's consent to an abortion, and since minors might well be vulnerable to parental pressure, "under state regulation such as that undertaken by Massachusetts, every minor must have the opportunity—if she so desires—to go directly to a court without first consulting or notifying her parents."[140] Second, as the Supreme Judicial Court of Massachusetts construed the statute, even if a judge determined that the minor herself was capable of making an informed and reasonable decision, the judge could still decide whether an abortion would be in her best interests. The Supreme Court ruled, however, that since "a constitutional right of unique character"[141] was implicated, a minor who *could* make such a decision had to be allowed to do so.

Justice Stevens, joined by Justices Brennan, Marshall, and Blackmun, wrote an opinion concurring in the Court's decision to invalidate the statute, but disagreeing with Justice Powell's reasons. Justice Stevens argued that the Court had failed to heed its decision in *Danforth*, from which the obligation to invalidate the statute followed *a fortiori*. *Danforth* had condemned absolute vetoes; that the Massachusetts statute ultimately gave such a veto to a judge instead of a parent was, if anything, less satisfactory. Justice Stevens wrote:

> The Constitutional right to make the abortion decision affords protection to both of the privacy interests recognized in this Court's cases: "One is the individual interest in avoiding disclosure of personal matters, and another is the interest in independence in making certain kinds of important decisions. . . ." It is inherent in the right to make the abortion decision that the right may be exercised without public scrutiny and in defiance of the contrary opinion of the sovereign or other third parties.[142]

Furthermore, asking the minor to go to court itself imposed a weighty burden, and asking the judge to use "the best interests of the minor" as the standard for decision gave too little useful guidance and too much scope to allow personal preferences to infect choices.

Justice White issued a short dissenting opinion[143] in which he noted that he had dissented in *Danforth* and which he concluded with these words:

> Until now, I would have thought inconceivable a holding that the United States Constitution forbids even notice to parents when their minor child who seeks surgery objects to such notice and is able to convince a judge that the parents should be denied participation in the decision.
>
> With all due respect, I dissent.[144]

Colautti v. *Franklin.* On April 11, 1974, over a year after *Roe* v. *Wade*, the Commonwealth of Massachusetts indicted Dr. Kenneth Edelin for manslaughter. The indictment stated "that [Dr. Edelin] did assault and beat a certain person, to wit: a male child described to the . . . Jurors as Baby Boy and by such assault and beating did kill the said person."[145] Dr. Edelin was the chief resident in obstetrics and gynecology at Boston City Hospital, an inner-city hospital. On October 3, 1973, after receiving the consent of his patient and her mother, he performed a hysterotomy on a seventeen-year-old girl who had, Dr. Edelin estimated, been pregnant for about twenty-two weeks. The fetus weighed between one pound five ounces and one pound eight ounces. It was for performing this abortion that Dr. Edelin was indicted.

Dr. Edelin was convicted after a trial which provoked attention among the public and anxiety among physicians. On appeal, his conviction was overturned by the Supreme Judicial Court of Massachusetts, which found that there was not sufficient evidence that Dr. Edelin's conduct had been "wanton" or "reckless." Nevertheless, the trial and the reaction to it suggested the effect which criminal penalties directed against doctors could have on the availability of abortions. Dr. Edelin's conviction foundered on the requirements of a manslaughter statute which had not been drafted with his case in mind. A number of states, however, have devised criminal statutes which are specifically designed to compel doctors to perform only those abortions which the Supreme Court says must be allowed and to compel them to attempt to save the life of the fetus.

In *Colautti* v. *Franklin,*[146] the Court examined a section of the Pennsylvania Abortion Control Act which provided:

> Every person who performs or induces an abortion shall prior thereto have made a determination based on his experience, judgment or professional competence that the fetus is not viable, and if the determination is that the fetus is viable or if there is sufficient reason to believe that the fetus may be viable, shall exercise that degree of professional skill, care and diligence to preserve the life and health of the fetus which such person would be required to exercise in order to preserve the life and health of any fetus intended to be born and not aborted and the abortion technique employed shall be that which would provide the best opportunity for the fetus to be aborted alive so long as a different technique would not be necessary in order to preserve the life or health of the mother.[147]

A person who failed to make such a determination or to exercise such a degree of care was "subject to such civil or criminal liability as would pertain to him had the fetus been a child who was intended to be born and not aborted."[148]

Justice Blackmun wrote an opinion for the six-member majority of the Court finding the statute unconstitutionally vague. He prefaced his opinion by saying that *Roe* v. *Wade, Doe* v. *Bolton,* and *Danforth* had emphasized that "viability" is a term the Court has purposely left to be medically defined and that the physician must be free to exercise his best medical judgment: "Viability is reached when, *in the judgment of the attending physician on the particular facts of the case before him,* there is a reason-able likelihood of the fetus' sustained survival outside the womb, with or without artificial support.''[149]

Justice Blackmun then recited the principle that a criminal statute is constitutionally void for vagueness when it ''''fails to give a person of ordi-nary intelligence fair notice that his contemplated conduct is forbidden by the statute,' . . . or is so indefinite that 'it encourages arbitrary and erratic arrests and convictions. . . .''''[150] Justice Blackmun noted that courts should look especially carefully at those allegedly vague statutes which may inhibit the exercise of constitutional rights.

Several fatal ambiguities afflicted the statute, Justice Blackmun said. First, the physician had to meet a prescribed standard of care ''if there is sufficient reason to believe the fetus may be viable.'' But ''sufficient rea-son'' from whose perspective? The attending doctor's? Or that of a cross-section of doctors in the community? Second, the statute used both the phrase ''is viable'' and the phrase ''may be viable.'' The syntax of the sen-tence and the fact that ''viable'' was defined elsewhere in the statute sug-gested that the phrases have different meanings. Consequently, the statute not only was vague, but it also established at least one definition of viability different from that of *Roe* v. *Wade* and *Danforth*. In short, the statute ''does not afford broad discretion to the physician. Instead, it conditions potential criminal liability on confusing and ambiguous criteria.''[151]

Justice Blackmun continued, ''The vagueness of the viability-deter-mination requirement . . . is compounded by the fact that the Act subjects the physician to potential criminal liability without regard to fault.''[152] True, the ''such civil or criminal liability'' language of the statute made applicable Pennsylvania's law of criminal homicide, and that law condi-tions guilt upon a finding of scienter. ''But neither the Pennsylvania law of criminal homicide, nor the Abortion Control Act, requires that the physi-cian be culpable in failing to find sufficient reason to believe that the fetus may be viable.''[153] Determining viability is a problematic undertaking, and no conclusion as to viability should have criminal consequences unless it was made in bad faith.

Finally, the standard-of-care provision was impermissibly vague. Jus-tice Blackmun wrote:

> [I]t is uncertain whether the statute permits the physician to consider his duty to the patient to be paramount to his duty to the fetus, or whether it requires the physician to make a ''trade-off'' between the woman's health and additional percentage points for fetal survival. . . . We hold only that where conflicting duties of this magnitude are involved, the State, at the least, must proceed with greater precision before it may subject a physician to possible criminal sanctions.[154]

Once again Justice White dissented, this time joined by Chief Justice Burger and Justice Rehnquist. In *Roe* v. *Wade,* he said, the Court had carefully defined viability to include the point at which a fetus is *potentially* able to survive, as well, of course, as the point at which the fetus would assuredly survive. By using the "may be viable" language, Pennsylvania was simply expressing its intention to regulate abortions throughout the entire period in which *Roe* v. *Wade* says the state has a compelling interest in the life of the fetus. Under Pennsylvania's law, "abortionists must not only determine whether the fetus is viable but also whether there is sufficient reason to believe that the fetus may be viable. If either condition exists, the method of abortion is regulated and a standard of care imposed."[155]

As to the scienter problem, Justice White responded that Pennsylvania's homicide statutes

> not only define the specified degrees of scienter that are required for the various homicides, but also provide that ignorance or mistake as to a matter of fact, for which there is a reasonable explanation, is a defense to a homicide charge if it negatives the mental state necessary for conviction.[156]

Finally, as to the standard-of-care provision, Justice White found it inconceivable that a doctor would be prosecuted for a good-faith mistake. If the Court entertained any doubt on this question, it should have directed the federal district court to abstain and to allow the state courts to construe Pennsylvania's homicide laws.

A Concluding Note

In the public turmoil over *Roe* v. *Wade,* it is easy to forget that the Court, in its conversations with state legislatures, has been cautious and rarely has erected absolute obstacles to the goals legislatures have pursued. For instance, although the Court has twice invalidated parental-consent statutes, four members of the Court have gone out of their way to show legislatures how they might draft a permissible statute, and a fifth, Justice White, has twice asserted that legislatures have already done so. Also, when the Court found Pennsylvania's standard-of-care law wanting, it said only that that law was too vague, not that its goal was impermissible. While the Court sometimes uses the comparatively inoffensive ground of vagueness to warn legislatures that a goal may be improper, it remains true that the Court made no effort to prohibit flatly standard-of-care legislation. Further, the Court has sustained the decisions of two states to restrict public funding of abortions. Finally, even *Roe* v. *Wade* itself is not immune from change, if only because medical progress might so advance the date of "viability" that a state could regulate abortions during a longer period of pregnancy.

January 1980

As this book went to press, the Supreme Court in *Harris* v. *McCrae* (June 30, 1980) upheld by a vote of 5 to 4 the so-called "Hyde Amendments" through which Congress has since 1976 limited the use of federal Medicaid funds for abortions. The most restrictive version of the Amendment provided that such funds could be used only where the life of the mother would be endangered if the fetus were carried to term or where the mother was a victim of rape of incest.

Relying principally on *Maher* v. *Roe*, the Court rejected substantive-due-process and equal-protection challenges to the Amendment. Justice Stewart wrote for the majority that a woman's right under *Roe* v. *Wade* to decide whether to have an abortion does not carry with it

> a constitutional entitlement to the financial resources to avail herself of the full range of protected choices . . . . [A]lthough government may not place obstacles in the path of a woman's exercise of her freedom of choice, it need not remove those not of its own creation. Indigency falls in the latter category.[157]

Justices Brennan, Marshall, Blackmun, and Stevens each wrote in dissent. In a characteristic passage, Justice Brennan said,

> By . . . injecting coercive financial incentives favoring childbirth into a decision that is constitutionally guaranteed to be free from governmental intrusion, the Hyde Amendment deprives the indigent woman of her freedom to choose abortion over maternity, thereby impinging on the due process liberty right recognized in *Roe* v. *Wade.*[158]

Notes

1. Epstein, *Substantive Due Process by Any Other Name: The Abortion Cases,* 1973 Sup. Ct. Rev. 159. A year later, the Supreme Court Review also published O'Meara, *Abortion: The Court Decides a Non-Case,* 1974 Sup. Ct. Rev. 337.

2. Ely, *The Wages of Crying Wolf: A Comment on* Roe v. Wade, 82 Yale L. J. 920 (1973).

3. Heymann and Barzelay, *The Forest and the Trees:* Roe v. Wade *and Its Critics,* 48 B.U. L. Rev. 765 (1973). Non-lawyers may have been less inhibited. See, *e.g.,* P. Ramsey, Ethics of the Edges of Life 3–142 (1978).

4. These matters are more thoroughly developed, *e.g.,* in Note, *Fornication, Cohabitation, and the Constitution,* 77 Mich. L. Rev. 252 (1978). For an extended discussion of substantive due process, see Tribe, Constitutional Law 427–455(1978; for an extended discussion of the right of privacy, see id. at 886–990.

5. Poe v. Ullman, 367 U.S. 497, 541 (1961) (dissenting).

6. 367 U.S. at 543.

7. Lochner v. New York, 198 U.S. 45, 53 (1905).

8. 198 U.S. 45 (1905).

9. 198 U.S. at 75.

10. 198 U.S. at 76.

11. Day-Brite Lighting, Inc. v. Missouri, 342 U.S. 421, 423 (1952).

12. Poe v. Ullman, 367 U.S. 497, 542 (1961) (dissenting).

13. 367 U.S. at 542.

14. Griswold v. Connecticut, 381 U.S. 479, 493 (concurring) (citations omitted).

15. 381 U.S. 479 (1965).

16. 381 U.S. at 485.

17. 381 U.S. at 486.

18. 381 U.S. at 485, quoting NAACP v. Alabama, 377 U.S. 288, 307 (1958).

19. 381 U.S. at 485–86.

20. Boyd v. United States, 116 U.S. 616, 630 (1886).

21. 405 U.S. 438 (1972).

22. Reed v. Reed, 404 U.S. 71, 75–76 (1971).

23. Eisenstadt v. Baird, 405 U.S. at 448.

24. 405 U.S. at 453 (emphasis original).

25. J. Mohr, Abortion in America 262–63 (1978) (paperback ed.).

26. Id. at 252.

27. Mohr discusses all these changes in detail at 246–63.

28. *See* Chapter 6, *infra.*

29. 410 U.S. 113 (1973). The Court's opinion is analyzed and criticized at length in Morgan, Roe v. Wade *and the Lesson of the Pre-*Roe *Case Law,* in this book, and alternative justification of the Court's holding in that case are explored in Regan, *Roe v. Wade: A Sheep in Wolf's Clothing?,* also in this book.

30. Roe v. Wade was not the Court's first abortion case. In United States v. Vuitch, 402 U.S. 62 (1971), the Court held that the District of Columbia's abortion statute, which prohibited abortions "unless the same were done as necessary for the preservation of the mother's life or health," was not unconstitutionally vague. The Court so held because it construed the statute as placing the burden of proving that the mother's life or health had not been endangered on the prosecution and as defining "health" to include both physical and psychological health.

31. 410 U.S. at 116.

32. 410 U.S. at 117.

33. 410 U.S. at 129.

34. 410 U.S. at 131–32, quoting L. Edelstein, The Hippocratic Oath 18 (1943).

35. 410 U.S. at 132, quoting L. Edelstein, The Hippocratic Oath 64 (1943).

36. 410 U.S. at 132, quoting L. Edelstein, The Hippocratic Oath 64 (1943).

37. 410 U.S. at 135. Mohr suggests that an important reason for the use of quickening was that there was no other reliable way of determining whether a woman was actually pregnant, since it was believed that menstrual cycles could also be interrupted by "blockages" which posed a genuine and serious threat to the woman's health. Mohr's able and absorbing book, *Abortion in America: The Origins and Evolution of National Policy* (1978), is distinctly the best treatment of its subject.

38. 410 U.S. at 136.

39. 410 U.S. at 136. The death penalty was removed from the statute in 1828.

40. 410 U.S. at 139.

41. 410 U.S. at 140.

42. 410 U.S. at 148.

43. 410 U.S. at 149.

44. 410 U.S. at 150.

45. 410 U.S. at 152. In *Botsford,* the Court held that a plaintiff in a civil action for a personal injury cannot be ordered to undergo a physical examination by a doctor which is designed to determine the extent of the plaintiff's injury. However, the Court explained in Sibbach v. Wilson & Co., 312 U.S. 1 (1941), that the Court's decision in *Botsford* relied on the ground that neither state statutes nor the common law gave a court authority to issue such an order. In *Sibbach,* the Court held that a provision of the Federal Rules of Civil Procedure legitimately authorized courts to issue such orders.

46. 410 U.S. at 152–53 (citations omitted). In the marvelously styled case of Loving v. Virginia, 388 U.S. 1 (1967), the Court invalidated Virginia's miscegenation statute. In the course of its opinion, the Court wrote, "The freedom to marry has long been recognized as one of the vital personal rights essential to the orderly pursuit of happiness by free men." 388 U.S. at 12.

Skinner v. Oklahoma, 316 U.S. 535 (1942), found violative of the equal-protection clause of the Fourteenth Amendment a law which provided for the sterilization of "habitual" criminals. Writing for the Court, Justice Douglas said in the course of what now seems a mild and cautious opinion,

We are dealing here with legislation which involves one of the basic civil rights of man. Marriage and procreation are fundamental to the very existence and survival of the race. . . . [S]trict scrutiny of the classification which a State makes in a sterilization law is essential, lest unwittingly, or otherwise, invidious discriminations are made against groups or types of individuals in violation of the constitutional guaranty of just and equal laws.

316 U.S. at 541.

Prince v. Massachusetts, 321 U.S. 158 (1944), upheld the conviction of a Jehovah's Witness who had violated child-labor laws by allowing her child to sell religious pamphlets on the public sidewalks. While the holding thus identified limits to the parent's right to bring up her child, the opinion contained language like the following:

It is cardinal with us that the custody, care and nurture of the child reside first in the parents, whose primary function and freedom include preparation for obligations the state can neither supply nor hinder. . . . And it is in recognition of this that these decisions have respected the private realm of family life which the state cannot enter.

321 U.S. at 166.

Pierce v. Society of Sisters, 268 U.S. 510 (1925), struck down an Oregon statute which required parents to send their children only to public schools. The Court thought it

entirely plain that the Act of 1922 unreasonably interferes with the liberty of parents and guardians to direct the upbringing and education of children under their control. . . . The fundamental theory of liberty upon which all governments in this Union repose excludes any general power of the State to standardize its children by forcing them to accept instruction from public teachers only.

268 U.S. at 534–35.

In Meyer v. Nebraska, 262 U.S. 390 (1923), the Court overturned the conviction of a man who had violated a law which forbade the teaching of a foreign language in any school to a child who had not completed the eighth grade. The Court noted that it had not "attempted to define with exactness the liberty" guaranteed by the Fourteenth Amendment, but that,

[w]ithout doubt, it denotes not merely freedom from bodily restraint but also the right of the individual to contract, to engage in any of the common occupations of life, to acquire useful knowledge, to marry, establish a home and bring up children, to worship God according to the dictates of his own conscience, and generally to enjoy those privileges long recognized at common law as essential to the orderly pursuit of happiness by free men.

262 U.S. at 399. Nebraska, however, had "attempted materially to interfere

with the calling of modern language teachers, with the opportunities of pupils to acquire knowledge, and with the power of parents to control the education of their own." 262 U.S. at 401.

47. 410 U.S. at 153.

48. 410 U.S. at 153.

49. 410 U.S. at 156–57. The Court did not discuss what the Fourteenth Amendment would require if a fetus were a person and the birth of the fetus would endanger the life of the mother.

50. 410 U.S. at 157.

51. 410 U.S. at 159.

52. 410 U.S. at 159.

53. 410 U.S. at 161. For a full treatment of the legal condition of the fetus, see chapter 2 *infra*.

54. 410 U.S. at 162.

55. 410 U.S. at 163. The Court's language seems to say plainly that the state may not regulate first-trimester abortions at all. That is certainly how Ely read the opinion. Ely, *The Wages of Crying Wolf,* 82 Yale L. J. 920, 921 & 942 n. 117 (1973). But that reading yields the absurd result that the state could not enforce even the elementary standards of cleanliness in the medical (sometimes surgical) procedure of an abortion that we hope it requires of Joe's Diner. The Court has since conceded as much: In Connecticut v. Menillo, 423 U.S. 9 (1975), the Court upheld the conviction of a non-physician under a Connecticut statute making criminal an attempted abortion by "any person." The Court explained that, while a state's interest in preserving the mother's health or protecting the fetus' life is not great enough to allow the state to restrict a woman's decision to have an abortion in the first trimester,

> the insufficiency of the State's interest in matternal health is predicated upon the first trimester abortion's being as safe for the woman as normal childbirth at term, and that predicate holds true only if the abortion is performed under conditions insuring maximum safety for the woman. Even during the first trimester of pregnancy, therefore, prosecutions for abortions conducted by nonphysicians infringe upon no realm of personal privacy secured by the Constitution against state interference.

423 U.S. at 11.

56. 410 U.S. at 165.

57. 410 U.S. at 207.

58. 410 U.S. at 209.

59. 410 U.S. at 214.

60. 410 U.S. at 167.

61. 410 U.S. at 169, quoting National Mutual Ins. Co. v. Tidewater Transfer Co., 337 U.S. 582, 646 (dissenting opinion).

62. 410 U.S. at 169. Justice Stewart listed Loving v. Virginia; Griswold v. Connecticut; Pierce v. Society of Sisters; and Meyer v. Nebraska. He directed readers to "see also" Prince v. Massachusetts and Skinner v. Oklahoma. For descriptions of all these cases except *Griswold,* see note 46 *supra.* For a description of *Griswold* see text at notes 15 to 20 *supra.*

63. 410 U.S. at 169–70, quoting Eisenstadt v. Baird, 405 U.S. 438, 453 (1972).

64. 410 U.S. at 170, quoting Abele v. Markle, 351 F. Supp. 224, 227 (Conn. 1972) (three-judge court) (citations omitted).

65. 410 U.S. at 221.

66. 410 U.S. at 221.

67. 410 U.S. at 221–22.

68. 410 U.S. at 222.

69. 410 U.S. at 171.

70. 410 U.S. at 173, citing Williamson v. Lee Optical Co., 348 U.S. 483, 491 (1955). See "The Doctrine of Substantive Due Process" *supra.*

71. 410 U.S. at 173.

72. 410 U.S. 179 (1973).

73. 410 U.S. at 194, quoting Morey v. Doud, 354 U.S. 456, 465 (1957).

74. 410 U.S. at 195.

75. 410 U.S. at 198.

76. 410 U.S. at 199.

77. "The Citizens of each State shall be entitled to aH Privileges and Immunities of Citizens in the several States." Art. IV, §2.

78. On the same day it decided *Danforth,* the Court also decided Singleton v. Wulff, 428 U.S. 106 (1976), and Bellotti v. Baird, 428 U.S. 132 (1976). We do not discuss *Wulff,* since it dealt with the matter of standing, an issue which has arisen frequently in abortion cases but which does not seem relevant to our purpose here. In Bellotti v. Baird, the Court had before it Massachusetts' parental-consent statute, which a three-judge district court had found unconstitutional. The Supreme Court held that the district court should have abstained from deciding the constitutional issue until the Massachusetts courts had had a chance to construe the statute in a constitutionally inoffensive way. Because the statute and a Supreme Judicial Court of Massachusetts interpretation of it subsequently came before the Court, we defer our discussion of it until the section entitled "The Abortion-Funding Cases," *infra.*

79. For example, in 1974, Pennsylvania passed its Abortion Control Act. Roughly summarized, that statute defined viability in a way arguably more limited than the Supreme Court's definition in Roe v. Wade; required the "informed consent" of the woman to the operation; required (in specified circumstance) spousal consent or parental consent; defined as second-

degree murder the intentional killing of a premature infant aborted alive; required abortionists to try to save the life of the fetus; prohibited abortions after viability except to save the life and health of the mother; forbade abortions except by a licensed physician in an approved facility; called for record-keeping and quarterly reports; prohibited soliciting or advertising with respect to abortions; barred the use of public funds for abortions except to preserve the life or health of the mother; authorized the Department of Health, Education and Welfare to write regulations for abortions and facilities where they are performed; and established criminal penalties for many violations of many of the law's provisions. This summary is drawn from the Supreme Court's description of the statute in Colautti v. Franklin, 439 U.S. 379 (1979).

80. 428. U.S. 52 (1976).

81. Quoted in 428 U.S. at 63.

82. 428 U.S. at 64. "In *Roe,* we used the term 'viable,' properly we thought, to signify the point at which the fetus is 'potentially able to live outside the mother's womb, albeit with artificial aid,' and presumably capable of 'meaningful life outside the mother's womb.' 410 U.S., at 160, 163." 428 U.S. at 63.

83. The law defined saline amniocentesis as a technique "whereby the amniotic fluid is withdrawn and a saline or other fluid is inserted into the amniotic sac for the purpose of killing the fetus and artificially inducing labor. . . ." Quoted in 428 U.S. at 87.

84. 428 U.S. at 79. The Court commented that the statute also seemed to outlaw the use of an apparently superior technique—prostaglandin instillation—which the dissent, 428 U.S. at 95–99, argued could and should be used instead of saline amniocentesis. See n. 85–87 and accompanying text *infra.*

85. 428 U.S. at 92. Justice Stevens wrote a separate opinion on this point, 428 U.S. at 101, with which Justice Stewart and Justice Powell agreed, 428 U.S. at 92. Justice Stevens said that a state could legitimately ban the less safe of two equally available abortion techniques, but that "the record indicates that when the Missouri statute was enacted, a prohibition of the saline amniocentesis procedure was almost tantamount to a prohibition of any abortion in the State after the first 12 weeks of pregnancy." 428 U.S. at 102.

86. Prostaglandins are "drugs that stimulate uterine contractibility, inducing premature expulsion of the fetus." Colautti v. Franklin, 439 U.S. 379, 399 (1979).

87. 428 U.S. at 97–98.

88. Quoted in 428 U.S. at 99.

89. 428 U.S. at 83.

90. 428 U.S. at 83.

91. 428 U.S. at 100, quoting Roe v. Wade, 410 U.S. at 113, 163 (1973).

92. 428 U.S. at 71.

93. 428 U.S. at 69. Justice Stewart joined in the Court's opinion, but he also wrote a concurring opinion in which he said he found that this issue presented "a rather more difficult problem than the Court acknowledges." 428 U.S. at 90. However, he agreed with the Court that "since 'it is the woman who physically bears the child and who is the more directly and immediately affected by the pregnancy . . . the balance weighs in her favor.'" 428 U.S. at 90, quoting 428 U.S. at 71.

94. 428 U.S. at 93.

95. 428 U.S. at 93.

96. 428 U.S. at 94.

97. 428 U.S. at 94.

98. 428 U.S. at 93.

99. 428 U.S. at 75.

100. 428 U.S. at 74 (emphasis added).

101. 428 U.S. at 94–95, quoting Roe v. Wade, 410 U.S. 113, 153 (1973) (emphasis added by Justice White).

102. 428 U.S. at 103.

103. *See* chapter 7 *infra.*

104. Section 210 of Pub. L. 95–480; 92 Stat. 1586, Oct. 18, 1978.

105. For a report on further developments in this case, see xxxviii *infra.*

106. 432 U.S. 438 (1977).

107. 432 U.S. 464 (1977).

108. For a response to the Court's response, see chapter 3 *infra.*

109. 42 U.S.C. 1396a(a) (1970 ed., Supp. V), quoted in 432 U.S. at 444.

110. 432 U.S. at 444.

111. 432 U.S. at 445.

112. 432 U.S. at 444–45 (emphasis original).

113. 432 U.S. at 448.

114. 432 U.S. at 450.

115. 432 U.S. at 449, quoting Roe v. Norton, 408 F. Supp. 660, 663 n. 3 (Conn. 1975).

116. 432 U.S. at 454.

117. 432 U.S. at 473–74.

118. 432 U.S. at 474.

119. 432 U.S. at 475.

120. See n. 46 *supra.*

121. 432 U.S. at 476–77.

122. 432 U.S. at 479, quoting Lindsey v. Normet, 405 U.S. 56, 74 (1972).

123. 432 U.S. at 479–80, quoting Williamson v. Lee Optical, 348 U.S. 483, 488 (1955), and Missouri, K. & T. R. Co. v. May, 194 U.S. 267, 270 (1904) (Holmes, J.).

124. 432 U.S. at 482.

125. 432 U.S. at 486.

126. 431 U.S. 678 (1977).

127. 431 U.S. at 688, quoted in 432 U.S. at 487.

128. 432 U.S. at 454–57 (citations omitted).

129. 432 U.S. at 462.

130. 432 U.S. at 463. On the same day it decided Beal v. Doe and Maher v. Roe, the Court decided Poelker v. Doe, 432 U.S. 519 (1977). There the Court, for the reasons explained in Maher v. Roe, found "no constitutional violation by the city of St. Louis in electing, as a policy choice, to provide publicly financed hospital services for childbirth without providing corresponding services for nontherapeutic abortions." 432 U.S. at 521. Justice Brennan, citing his dissent to Maher v. Roe, wrote an opinion, 432 U.S. at 522, for the three dissenters in which he said, "[I]t is clear that the city policy is a significant, and in some cases insurmountable, obstacle to indigent pregnant women who cannot pay for abortions in . . . private facilities." 432 U.S. at 523.

131. See generally Vinovskis, Adolescent Pregnancy: Some Historical Considerations (unpublished paper presented at the Conference on Women's History and Quantitative Methodology, Newberry Library, Chicago, July 5–7, 1979). Quotations in this paragraph are from that paper.

132. 443 U.S. 622 (1979).

133. In a brief concurring opinion, 443 U.S. at 651, Justice Rehnquist explained that he had not abandoned hope that the Court would reconsider its decision in *Danforth,* but that he joined Justice Powell's decision since "literally thousands of judges cannot be left with nothing more than the guidance offered by a truly fragmented holding of this Court." 443 U.S. at 652.

134. 443 U.S. at 635, quoting McKeiver v. Pennsylvania, 403 U.S. 528, 550 (1971) (plurality opinion).

135. 443 U.S. at 637.

136. 321 U.S. 158, 166 (1944), quoted in 443 U.S. at 638 (emphasis added by Justice Powell).

137. 443 U.S. at 638–39.

138. 443 U.S. at 640 (footnote omitted).

139. 443 U.S. at 643 (footnote omitted).

140. 443 U.S. at 647. Since, however, there is "an important state interest in encouraging a family rather than a judicial resolution of a

minor's abortion decision," the court "may deny the abortion request of an immature minor in the absence of parental consultation if it concludes that her best interests would be served thereby, or the court may in such a case defer decision until there is parental consultation in which the court may participate." 443 U.S. at 648.

141. 443 U.S. at 650.

142. 443 U.S. at 655 (citation omitted), quoting Whalen v. Roe, 429 U.S. 589, 599–600 (1977).

143. 443 U.S. at 656.

144. 443 U.S. at 657.

145. Quoted in Commonwealth v. Edelin, 359 N.E. 2d. 4, 9 (Mass. 1976). The Edelin case is discussed in Ramsey, Ethics at the Edges of Life (1978).

146. 439 U.S. 379 (1979).

147. Quoted in 439 U.S. at 380–81 n. 1. For a description of the whole statute, see n. 79 *supra*.

148. Quoted in 439 U.S. at 380–81, n. 1.

149. 439 U.S. at 388 (emphasis added).

150. 439 U.S. at 390 (citations omitted), quoting United States v. Harriss, 347 U.S. 612, 617 (1954), and Papachristou v. Jacksonville, 405 U.S. 156, 162 (1972).

151. 439 U.S. at 394.

152. 439 U.S. at 394.

153. 439 U.S. at 394–95.

154. 439 U.S. at 400–401.

155. 439 U.S. at 403.

156. 439 U.S. at 407.

157. Slip op. at 17. The Court also dismissed an argument that the Amendment contravened the Establishment Clause of the first amendment: "it does not follow that a statute violates the Establishment Clause because it 'happens to coincide or harmonize with the tenets of some or all religions.' *McGowan* v. *Maryland*, 366 U.S. 420, 422." Slip op. at 20.

158. Slip op. at 5.

PART I

THE LAW OF ABORTION

REWRITING *ROE v. WADE*

Donald H. Regan* †

Roe v. Wade is one of the most controversial cases the Supreme Court has decided. The result in the case — the establishment of a constitutional right to abortion — was controversial enough. Beyond that, even people who approve of the result have been dissatisfied with the Court's opinion. Others before me have attempted to explain how a better opinion could have been written.[1] It seems to me, however, that the most promising argument in support of the result of *Roe* has not yet been made. This essay contains my suggestions for "rewriting" *Roe v. Wade*.[2]

Ultimately, my argument is an equal protection argument. I shall suggest that abortion should be viewed as presenting a problem in what we might call "the law of samaritanism", that is, the law concerning obligations imposed on certain individuals to give aid to others. It is a deeply rooted principle of American law that an individual is ordinarily not required to volunteer aid to another individual who is in danger or in need of assistance. In brief, our law does not require people to be Good Samaritans. I shall argue that if we require a pregnant woman to carry the fetus to term and deliver it — if we forbid abortion, in other words — we are compelling her to be a Good Samaritan. I shall argue further that if we consider the generally very limited scope of obligations of samaritanism under our law, and if we consider the special nature of the burdens imposed on pregnant women by laws forbidding abortion, we must eventually conclude that the equal protection clause forbids imposition of these burdens on pregnant women. Some other potential samaritans whom there is better reason to burden with duties to aid are burdened less or in less

* Professor of Law, University of Michigan. A.B. 1963, Harvard University; LL.B. 1966, University of Virginia; B. Phil. 1968, Oxford University.—Ed.

† In writing this essay, I have been helped by numerous friends and colleagues: Barbara Adams, Elizabeth Axelson, Vince Blasi, Cheryl Helland, Doug Kahn, Rick Lempert, Gerry Rosberg, Joe Sax, Marianne Westen, Peter Westen, and Chris Whitman. I should also like to thank my research assistants, Lynn Helland and Brad Rutledge, whose contribution is most inadequately reflected in the footnotes, which I have intentionally kept rather sparse.

1. *E.g.*, Heymann & Barzelay, *The Forest and the Trees: Roe v. Wade and Its Critics*, 53 B.U. L. Rev. 765 (1973); Tribe, *Toward a Model of Roles in the Due Process of Life and Law*, 87 Harv. L. Rev. 1 (1973); Perry, *Abortion, the Public Morals, and the Police Power: The Ethical Function of Substantive Due Process*, 23 UCLA L. Rev. 689 (1976).

2. 410 U.S. 113 (1973).

objectionable ways, and still other potential samaritans whose situations are closely analogous to that of the pregnant woman are burdened only trivially or not at all. (I shall suggest a similar equal protection argument, based on the notion that abortion can be regarded as a problem in the law of self-defense, but I prefer the samaritanism argument and I shall give it much more attention.)

The argument I have just sketched will require a fairly lengthy development. In particular, it will require an extended (though far from complete) discussion of the law of samaritanism. It is worth explaining as well as I can in advance of the discussion why such an extended discussion is necessary. I do this not to justify my prolixity, but in hopes that the reader will be less likely to lose the thread of the larger argument.

The basic problem is that the situation of the pregnant woman is *sui generis*. If we regard the pregnant woman as a potential samaritan, there is no other potential samaritan whose situation is not in some important way distinguishable. This means that it is not possible to exhibit the sort of unjustified inconsistency of treatment that amounts to an equal protection violation just by comparing the pregnant woman with some other particular potential samaritan. Rather, it is necessary to survey the entire field of samaritan law, and to argue that laws forbidding abortion subject pregnant women to treatment which is at odds with the general spirit of samaritan law.

I have explained the necessity for a survey of samaritan law. Unfortunately, samaritan law is complicated. The basic and well-established common law principle is that one individual is not required to volunteer aid to another. But there are numerous exceptions to this principle recognized by the common law. There are also a number of exceptions and apparent exceptions to the principle created by statute. Because no single case is perfectly analogous to the case of the pregnant woman, we shall have to discuss a wide range of cases.

The uniqueness of the abortion case also creates problems when we get to the equal protection argument itself. I shall be compelled to sketch an approach to equal protection questions which justifies my rather unusual suggestion that laws forbidding abortion should be struck down, not because they treat pregnant women differently from the way we treat some other class of potential samaritans who are indistinguishable, but rather because they treat pregnant women in a way which is at odds with the general tenor of samaritan law.

It is perhaps worth noting that my equal protection argument will not turn simply on the fact that laws forbidding abortion seem aberrant when viewed against the background of samaritan law. I regard it as important that laws forbidding abortion impair constitutionally protected interests. (The interests I have in mind are *not* in "privacy" or in freedom of choice with regard to marriage, procreation, and child-rearing, but rather in non-subordination and in freedom from physical invasion.) I also regard it as important that laws forbidding abortion involve a classification which is at least somewhat suspect. These themes, which are familiar elements of the "new equal protection", will be developed further in Section III. The approach to equal protection I shall eventually sketch will differ somewhat from the Court's official doctrine on equal protection. Even so, it will represent not merely the approach I think the Court should take, but also, generally speaking, the approach I think they are taking.

Two final introductory points, on vocabulary. First, I have already referred to "laws forbidding abortion". Obviously there are a great variety of laws and possible laws forbidding abortion in at least some circumstances. What I mean by a "law forbidding abortion" is a law of the general type that was standard in the United States before the decision in *Roe*. I mean a law that forbids abortion in most circumstances, whether or not the law provides exceptions for cases involving rape, or for cases in which there is a substantial threat of death or serious physical harm to the pregnant woman, or whatever. Similarly, when I argue that laws forbidding abortion are unconstitutional, I do not mean that the state may not forbid abortion under any circumstances. I am arguing for something along the lines of what *Roe* guaranteed — freedom to choose abortion in the early stages (or before the final stage) of pregnancy. For the most part it will not be necessary to be more precise about the provisions of "laws forbidding abortion" or about the contours of the freedom for the woman I am defending. The second point on vocabulary is simply that for convenience I shall use the word "fetus" to refer to the conceptus at every stage of its development.

I. The Pregnant Woman As Samaritan

In this Section of the essay, I shall attempt to locate the abortion problem in the doctrinal landscape of samaritan law. Some readers will object that the abortion problem does not belong in that landscape at all, that I am looking at the wrong map. We usually think of samaritan problems as problems involving *omissions*. The established general principle that one does not have to volunteer aid (which I shall refer to as the "bad-samaritan principle") is normally thought of as equivalent to the notion that there is no liability for a failure to act. But the behavior of a woman who secures an abortion does not look like an omission. It looks like an act. So does the behavior of anyone who helps her. Perhaps the bad-samaritan principle is irrelevant. The first project for this part of the essay, then, is to explain why the abortion problem should be regarded as a problem in samaritan law.

Once we have established that we are looking at the right map, we shall attempt to orient ourselves with regard to some important landmarks, such as the established exceptions and apparent exceptions to the bad-samaritan principle. Two important propositions will appear. First, the abortion case is distinguishable in some significant respects from every other case in which a duty to aid is imposed. A respectable argument can therefore be made that if the pregnant woman is to be treated consistently with other potential samaritans, it is impermissible to impose on her even a trivially burdensome duty to aid. Many readers will not be persuaded by such an argument, however. They will believe that even if the pregnant woman is distinguishable from every other potential samaritan on whom duties to aid are imposed, still the cumulative force of the *similarities* of the abortion case to various other cases where duties are imposed makes it clear that the pregnant woman may be subjected to some burdens. That brings us to the second proposition: There is *no* other potential samaritan on whom burdens are imposed which are as extensive and as physically invasive as the burdens of pregnancy and childbirth. Even if the pregnant woman should be regarded as "eligible for compulsion to samaritanism" to some extent, she is by no means the most eligible member of the family of potential samaritans. It is not acceptable to subject her to specially extensive and specially invasive burdens, as laws forbidding abortion do.

By now every reader who has given any rein at all to his imagination will have thought up at least two or three objections to the claim that laws forbidding abortion are inconsistent with the general tenor of samaritan law. There are many possible objections to be dealt with, and I cannot deal with them all at once. In order that the reader shall not be distracted by impatience to know when I will deal with his particular objections, let

me indicate the order of treatment of the major topics in what
follows. First, I shall explain why abortion is a samaritanism
problem. Second, I shall examine the extent and nature of the
burdens imposed on women by anti-abortion statutes. I shall concentrate on the physical and psychological burdens of pregnancy
and childbirth, and I shall explain why I think these burdens are
more important to the *constitutional* argument concerning abortion than the burdens of child-rearing or the psychological cost
of giving up a child for adoption. (It is worth mentioning now that
one of the reasons laws forbidding abortion are not validated by
analogy to the "parenthood exception" to the bad-samaritan
principle is that the burdens of pregnancy and childbirth are
physically invasive in a way the burdens imposed on parents are
not. As I shall show, physical invasions are specially disfavored
by our common and constitutional law. I think this is not the only
distinction between the pregnant woman and the parent, but it
may well be the most important distinction for my purposes.)
Third, I shall explain why the pregnant woman is different from
every other potential samaritan on whom common-law duties to
aid are imposed, including the parent, the social host, the innocent or negligent creator of a dangerous situation, the samaritan
who voluntarily begins to give aid and may be forbidden to terminate the aid, and so on. In the process I shall explain why it is
not an adequate defense of laws against abortion that pregnancy
is "voluntary". Fourth, I shall distinguish the abortion case from
certain exceptions and apparent exceptions to the bad-samaritan
principle created by statute, notably the military draft. (The
draft involves burdens closely comparable to the burdens of pregnancy, but the draft, I shall argue, is *not* a problem in samaritan
law, however much it may seem so at first.) Finally, a few summary remarks will conclude this part of the essay.

A. *Is Samaritan Law Relevant?*

The bad-samaritan principle depends on a distinction between acts and omissions. It would exempt from all liability a
physically healthy adult who watched an unrelated child drown
in a foot of water, maliciously refusing to pull the child out. It
would not, however, permit the adult to hold the child under the
water. One might argue that the pregnant woman does not even
come within the general scope of the bad-samaritan principle
because aborting a fetus, or securing an abortion, is not an omission but a positive act, like holding the child under.

It is clear that from one perspective securing an abortion looks like a positive act. It should also be clear that from another perspective it does not. Carrying a fetus and giving birth are burdensome, disruptive, uncomfortable, and usually to some extent painful activities. In effect, the fetus makes continuing demands for aid on the woman who carries it. The fetus is not like a child being held under water, whose prospects would be satisfactory if the adult holding it under would merely go away. The fetus is much more like the child drowning on its own, who needs the adult bystander to rescue it. The principal difference between the demands of the fetus and the "demand" the child drowning on its own makes of an adult bystander is that the fetus's demands are much greater. If the adult bystander may refuse aid to the drowning child, then surely the same general principle (leaving aside the possibility of relevant exceptions to the principle, which will be discussed later) allows the pregnant woman to refuse aid to the fetus.

The point of the bad-samaritan principle is to establish that, as a general proposition, one does not have to give aid whenever another requires it. One can turn one's back on another's need, declining to subordinate one's own interests. One can choose not to be involved. When a woman secures an abortion in order to avoid the burdens imposed by an unwanted fetus, she is doing just what the bad-samaritan principle, in its standard applications, is designed to allow. It may seem odd to suggest that securing an abortion is really an "omission", but if we want the "act/omission"[3] distinction to reflect the values underlying the bad-samaritan principle, then that is how abortion ought to be viewed.

Suppose that a fetus and the pregnant woman carrying it were attached in such a way that the fetus could be removed without damaging it physically. The removed fetus would eventually die unless it was placed in some other womb, but it would come out of the original carrier's womb in just the same condition it was in inside. If this were the way pregnancy worked, it would be much easier to see that the general right of non-subordination or non-involvement embodied in the bad-samaritan principle would entitle the woman to remove the fetus at any time, unless she had waived or forfeited the right. It would be easier to see

---

3. The principle is discussed by Prosser in a section entitled "Acts and Omissions". W. Prosser, The Law of Torts § 56 (4th ed. 1971).

that the woman who did *not* remove an unwanted fetus was engaged in a continuing course of charitable conduct, which general samaritan law would permit her to terminate at any time. There are certain situations, to be discussed below, in which one who has started to give aid may not stop. But the general principle is that merely giving aid does not commit one to continuing it.

Now, pregnancy does not work the way I have suggested. It is not possible (at least at the stages of pregnancy where abortions are commonly done, and where they are safest and most desirable for the woman) to remove the fetus without making it inviable. This should make no difference to the conclusion that the woman is permitted by the bad-samaritan principle to remove the fetus. One reason it might be thought to make a difference is that the fetus which was removed without being damaged would have a chance of survival, if another willing carrier could be found in time, whereas the aborted fetus will certainly die. But the bad-samaritan principle protects even omissions that are certain to result in the death of the person denied aid. Unless the pregnant woman falls within some exception to the principle, the principle would permit her to remove the fetus without damaging it, assuming that were possible, even if it were known that the fetus would die because no other carrier could be found. Therefore the fact that the fetus is certain to die does not remove the woman from the scope of the principle.

It might be suggested that removing the fetus in a way which renders it inviable is more clearly an "act" than simply removing the fetus without damaging it. But this does not seem right. It may be that removing the fetus in a way which renders it inviable is likely to be a more complicated act, or a more difficult act. But it is no more an act. Like the mere removing, it is an act in one sense, but it ought to be viewed as an omission, or as part of a course of conduct amounting in overall effect to an omission, under the bad-samaritan principle. It is the only way, in the real world, for a pregnant woman to discontinue the burdensome course of aid to the fetus.[4]

---

4. Another possible objection to the argument in the text runs as follows: Removing-the-fetus-without-damaging-it and removing-the-fetus-and-rendering-it-inviable differ with respect to the actor's *intention.* In the latter case, but not the former, the death of the fetus is a *means* to the protection of the mother. Therefore, in the latter case but not the former the removal of the fetus is impermissible. This is the Doctrine of Double Effect. A great deal has been written about the Doctrine, and I shall not discuss it here. I do not think it has a place in moral reasoning, but that is beside the point. I also do not think it is part of American law, and that is very much to the point. In many situations, appeal

I have argued that abortion must be allowed if we are to respect the pregnant woman's interest in being free to refuse aid, an interest we protect for other potential samaritans. There are two possible counter-arguments, designed to show that we do not really value the potential samaritan's freedom to refuse aid as much as the existence of the bad-samaritan principle might suggest.

The first counter-argument involves the notion that we do not value the potential samaritan's freedom to be uninvolved — rather, we believe only that involvement should not be *legally compelled*. This suggestion strikes me as somewhat odd, but it is not incoherent. A full discussion of the suggestion would be interesting. For the present, however, it suffices to observe that this suggestion does not constitute a reason for thinking that abortion should be treated differently from other samaritan problems. The pregnant woman's involvement with the fetus she carries is not originally created by law, but if she does not desire the involvement, then, in the absence of laws forbidding abortion, she will have no difficulty terminating it. Laws forbidding abortion *compel* her continuing involvement just as much as a general law requiring one to be a Good Samaritan would compel the reluctant adult bystander to be involved with the drowning child.

The second counter-argument suggests that we do not really value either the potential samaritan's freedom to be uninvolved in every case *or* freedom from legally compelled involvement.

---

to the act/omission distinction may resemble argument based on the Doctrine of Double Effect, but the two sorts of argument are not the same, *see* Foot, *The Problem of Abortion and the Doctrine of the Double Effect*, in P. FOOT, VIRTUES AND VICES (1978), and the latter is not important in our law.

Anyone familiar with the literature on abortion will have assumed, correctly, that I owe the idea of the pregnant woman as samaritan to Judith Thomson's revelatory article, *A Defense of Abortion*, 1 PHILOSOPHY & PUB. AFF. 47 (1971). It is worth noting that Thomson does not unequivocally claim that securing an abortion should be viewed as an omission rather than as an act. Much of her essay seems to be based on this implicit premise, but when she addresses the issue directly, she apparently prefers to view abortion as an act of killing justified by principles regarding self-defense. I think a highly plausible argument can be made along these lines, and I shall devote a brief Section II to the self-defense argument. But I prefer to rely primarily on the bad-samaritan principle. I find it very plausible to view securing an abortion as a refusal-to-aid, and it is clear that our law allows refusals-to-aid for less weighty reasons than it requires for killing, even in self-defense. (In saying this, I do not mean to suggest that the reasons which may support an abortion are not weighty. They are.) One reason Thomson may have had for preferring the self-defense line does not concern me. For purposes of *moral* argument, which she was engaged in, it is much less clear that we accept the bad-samaritan principle than that we recognize a right of self-defense. But there is no doubt that the bad-samaritan principle is a principle of American law.

Instead, it is suggested, the bad-samaritan principle is a response to various difficulties in formulating legal rules requiring aid. In many situations where a person is in need of aid, there will be more than one potential samaritan. Each potential samaritan will be in a position to ask, "Why should I be the one to give aid?" Similarly, in many situations involving potential samaritans, it will be unclear just how much the samaritan ought to be required to do in the way of attempting a rescue, or whatever. Frequently, also, it will be difficult to establish a clear causal connection between the failure to give aid and the harm to the person who needed aid. It may seem that the bad-samaritan principle is a sort of *per se* rule designed to avoid all these difficulties by establishing a general, easily understood, and easily applied rule of non-liability. If so, it may also seem that the abortion case should be an exception to the *per se* rule. When a woman is pregnant and the fetus is in need of her continuing aid, there is no doubt who must provide the aid; there is no doubt what aid is required; and there will be no difficulty in identifying the woman's refusal of aid, if she has an abortion, as the cause of the harm to the fetus.

One answer to this argument is that even if the bad-samaritan principle were a *per se* rule of the sort described, it would not be clear that abortion cases should constitute an exception. There is no question about whose aid is required in the abortion case, and there is no question that a refusal of aid will be the cause of harm to the fetus. Nor is there doubt about what aid is required if the fetus is to survive. But the difficulty about the magnitude of aid which inclines us to a *per se* rule is not primarily the difficulty of deciding how much aid is required. It is the difficulty of deciding how much may justly be required of the potential samaritan. If we did not think there were limits to the aid that could justly be required, we could solve the "how much aid" difficulty by requiring the potential samaritan to do everything in his power that might conceivably be useful. As I shall show in the next Section, the burdens of pregnancy and childbirth are considerable, and they are burdens of a sort disfavored by our legal tradition. They are also far greater than the burdens imposed under exceptions to the bad-samaritan principle on any other potential samaritans, except (possibly) parents. The case for making an exception of the abortion situation would be problematic even if the *per se* analysis were correct and our commitment to the bad-samaritan principle were much weaker than the present scope of the principle suggests.

In any event, I do not think the bad-samaritan principle is adequately explained as a *per se* rule. I do not deny that some legal rules are of this type. Nor do I deny that for someone out of sympathy with the idea that an individual should be free to refuse aid, this sort of *per se* analysis may be the most appealing justification of the bad-samaritan principle available. But it is clear to me that if the difficulties we have mentioned were the only support for the bad-samaritan principle, the principle in its present broad form would not be part of the common law. There are many individual cases not involving abortion in which none of the difficulties mentioned is serious. If these difficulties were the only basis for the bad-samaritan principle, then instead of a flat rule we would consider the issue of samaritans' duties case by case and develop more specific rules. The uncertainty created would be no greater than that created by many hard-to-apply common law rules, and the gain in clarity about what we were doing would be considerable. The common law recognizes the bad-samaritan principle because it does value the freedom to refuse aid, to resist subordination even in trivial ways, to remain uninvolved. If this freedom is important, it is as important for the pregnant woman as for anyone else.

One final point should be mentioned in this Section. It will seem to some readers that even if the *woman's* act of securing an abortion can be viewed as an omission, the same cannot be said of the act of any doctor who assists her by performing the abortion. I agree that the doctor looks more "active" than the woman. That is not primarily because he performs the abortion while the woman suffers it. Rather it is because the doctor is not freeing *himself* from the fetus's demands for future aid, as the woman is freeing herself. The question, then, is whether the doctor is shielded from liability by arguments establishing the woman's freedom to refuse aid.

I do not know of any authority on whether a third party may assist a potential samaritan who needs help in refusing aid. The reason for the lack of authority is clear. It is only in the unusual case, like the abortion situation, that anything resembling a positive act is necessary for the samaritan to refuse aid. There is some law on third-party intervention in the context of the right of self-defense (or, from the point of view of the third party, the context of defense of others). In that context, the currently dominant view, and the view which is still gaining ground, is that third parties are entitled to intervene.[5]

For myself, I find it easy to conclude that if the woman is free to secure an abortion, the doctor should be able to help her. Although I find it easy to conclude this, I do not have much to say in support of my conclusion. I do have one observation. When abortion is forbidden by law, many women suffer severe injury or even death from illegal or self-induced abortions. If we assume that women should not be seeking abortions in the first place, it is possible to ignore this large cost, saying that the women have only themselves to blame. But it seems perverse to say that given the general tenor of samaritan law a woman ought to be permitted to refuse aid to the fetus, and yet to say that she may not receive assistance in this course when the assistance would avoid much suffering and when it is voluntarily offered and privately arranged.

B. *The Burdens Imposed By Laws Forbidding Abortion*

In this Section I shall discuss the nature and extent of the burdens imposed on women by anti-abortion laws. First I shall consider the extent of the physical burdens of pregnancy and childbirth. Then I shall argue that these burdens are of a *kind* that our law is ordinarily specially reluctant to impose on unwilling parties. Finally, I shall explain why these are the burdens most relevant to the *constitutional* status of abortion, even though there are other significant costs associated with or likely to result from an unwanted pregnancy.

1. *The Physical Burdens of Pregnancy and Childbirth*

It will be instructive to begin by listing what two obstetricians, writing for pregnant women and attempting not to alarm but to reassure them, call the "minor complaints" of pregnancy.[6]

First, complaints involving general inconvenience or discomfort: a tendency to faintness (generally limited to the first fourteen weeks); nausea and possibly vomiting (generally limited to the first fourteen weeks); tiredness (pronounced in the first fourteen weeks, then disappearing, to reappear near the end of preg-

---

5. *See, e.g.,* Restatement (Second) of Torts § 76 (1965); W. LaFave & A. Scott, Criminal Law § 54 (1972); ALI Model Penal Code § 3.05 (Proposed Official Draft 1962).

6. The discussion in the text is based on G. Bourne & D. Danforth, Pregnancy (rev. ed. 1975). I have not merely copied a list from that book; rather I have collected and arranged observations scattered throughout the book. To give specific citations would, however, pointlessly clutter these pages.

nancy); insomnia (difficulty going to sleep caused by inability in late pregnancy to find a comfortable position in bed, compounded by difficulty going back to sleep when wakened by a kicking fetus or by the need for frequent urination which accompanies pregnancy, also compounded by general disruption of the body's internal temperature-regulation mechanism); slowed reflexes; poor coordination; uncertainty of balance (caused by increase and redistribution of body weight); manual clumsiness in the morning (caused by swollen fingers and carpal-tunnel syndrome); shortness of breath following even mild exertion; and new aversions to certain foods or smells (especially fatty or spicy foods).

More specific complaints, still involving inconvenience or discomfort, are: tender breasts; stuffy nose; constipation; heartburn (different from nausea, and not limited to early pregnancy); nosebleeds; edema of the feet and ankles; a metallic taste in the mouth; special difficulty in curing any vaginitis that may occur; increased susceptibility to and difficulty of curing urinary tract infection; increased frequency of urination (quite apart from any urinary infection); occasional extreme urgency of urination (as the fetus bumps the bladder); and occasional stress incontinence from the same source. Many pregnant women also report more headaches than when they were not pregnant, though there is no apparent reason for this aside from the increased psychological stress of pregnancy.

Among complaints not merely uncomfortable but painful, some of which can be very painful indeed, we find: backache; costal-marginal pain (caused by the enlarged uterus pushing against the lower ribs); abdominal "round ligament" pain; abdominal muscle pain; pelvic ache; pelvic shooting pain (as the fetus bumps a nerve at the rim of the pelvis); foot and leg cramps; the different pain and leg cramps associated with varicose veins; hemorrhoids; pain and pins-and-needles in the wrist (carpal-tunnel syndrome); and mastitis. Finally, as a result of the general softening of ligaments during pregnancy, along with the extra weight and the loss of balance, there is an increased susceptibility to sprains and to aching feet.

The pregnant woman also experiences changes in her appearance: most obviously, the pronounced change in the shape of her body as a whole; consequent upon the change of body shape, an awkward gait and inability to wear her normal wardrobe; increased dryness of skin (for women with dry skin initially); thin, brittle, unmanageable hair; varicose veins (in the legs or the

vulva, and sometimes in pelvis, abdomen, or breasts[7]); swelling
of the face; changes in pigmentation (darkening of the nipples
and areolae; sometimes darkening of larger patches of the breast;
darkening of freckles or moles; the *linea nigra* from the pubic area
to the naval; the often blotchy "butterfly mask" or chloasma);
stretch marks (which result in part from avoidable excessive
weight gain, but which are not always avoidable).

Finally, as a result of hormonal changes, the pregnant
woman is likely to be at times markedly irritable, volatile in her
moods, or subject to periods of depression. She may also experience a loss of sexual desire.

After the period of pregnancy, there is the actual delivery of
the fetus. The days when a woman had a reasonable chance of
spending twelve hours or more in sweaty agony are happily gone.
But it is still true that for many women parturition is a thoroughly unpleasant and significantly painful experience. It can
also involve a major operation, with all the added risk and discomfort that entails, if the fetus is delivered by cesarean section.

I shall say nothing of the rare and dangerous complications
of a pregnancy and delivery, except to note that in all probability
full-term pregnancy and childbirth involve greater risks of death
to the mother than early abortion.[8]

Looking beyond delivery, some of the "minor complaints" of
pregnancy listed above persist for varying periods after parturition. There are also a few characteristic post-partum pains, such
as the discomfort caused by an episiotomy.

The permanent physical effects of pregnancy which are noticeable by anyone other than a doctor and which are genuinely
unavoidable appear to be few, perhaps limited to some stretch
marks, some darkening of the nipples and areolae, sometimes
varicose veins and hemorrhoids (which become more of a problem as the number of pregnancies the woman has been through
increases), and, when a cesarean is performed, the scar from that
operation. Beyond these effects, many women attribute to their
pregnancies such other permanent effects as weight gain, anemia,
constipation, skin damaged by dryness, damaged hair, sagging
breasts, weak bladder, and painful feet or back.

The truth may well be that avoiding all the avoidable permanent effects, and for that matter minimizing all the "minor com-

---

7. J. Greenhill & E. Friedman, Biological Principles & Modern Practice of
Obstetrics (1974).

8. *See* materials cited in Roe v. Wade, 410 U.S. 113, 149 n.44 (1973).

plaints", requires considerable self-indulgence during pregnancy. The woman who can rest in the afternoon, sleep two extra hours at night, persistently oil her dry skin, give her hair extra attention, not stay on her feet for too long at a time, eat small meals every two hours, never put off the urge to evacuate her bowels, religiously do her post-partum exercises, and so on, will suffer less discomfort and fewer lasting effects of pregnancy than the woman who cannot.

The ills of pregnancy, delivery, and beyond make an impressive list. To be sure, not every pregnant woman suffers all of these ills. Nor do those who are afflicted suffer them in equal degree or at all times during pregnancy. But most of the complaints I have listed are common ones. I suspect it is an unusually lucky woman who does not put up with enough pain, discomfort and disruption of appearance and emotional state to add up to a major burden. (We should perhaps remember that as a society we recoil from being a few pounds overweight, from living in a house where the temperature is below 70° even though we can afford sweaters, or from going to the dentist.)

It may seem that I must have got it wrong — that if having a child were as bad as I suggest, no woman would ever do it voluntarily. Alternatively, it has been suggested to me by colleagues (male) that the pain of childbirth is a "noble" pain, or that having a child is a "transcendent experience" in which the pain becomes a valued part of an incomparably valued whole. These suggestions completely and shockingly miss the point. I have no doubt that all the pain, discomfort, and annoyance of being pregnant and giving birth are worthwhile *if* one wants a child. I do not deny the existence of transcendent experiences, and I am prepared to believe that for some women carrying and delivering a child are just that. (I must say that I know other women, devoted and successful mothers, who say they would never go through pregnancy if one could get a child of one's own any other way.) But the question is not whether pregnancy is worthwhile, or whether it is a transcendent experience, for a woman who wants a child. The question is how burdensome it is for a woman who does *not* want a child.

The answer, clearly, is that for a woman who does not want a child, pregnancy is very burdensome indeed. It is worth mentioning that all of the pains and discomforts listed above are likely to be significantly aggravated when the entire pregnancy is unwanted. It is much easier to bear up under pain and inconvenience when they serve some end one has chosen than when they do not.

An unwanted pregnancy is vastly more burdensome than the actions required of potential samaritans under other exceptions to the bad-samaritan principle. Compare carrying and delivering an unwanted child to calling a doctor for an injured social companion,[9] or to warning the object of a death threat made by one's patient in psychotherapy,[10] or to letting a guest invited in for dinner stay the night,[11] and so on. Even setting aside the small risk of serious complications or death that is associated with pregnancy and with none of those other duties, there is no comparison at all. The one traditional exception to the bad-samaritan principle where the burdens bear comparison to the burdens of pregnancy is the parenthood exception. Even here, the burdens are of a different kind. Being a mother (of a child, not a fetus) does not alter the entire functioning of a woman's body the way being pregnant does. I shall say more about the importance of this point, and about other possible distinctions between the pregnant woman and the parent, later on.[12]

2. *The Disfavored Status of Physical Impositions*

In addition to imposing burdens greater than any of the recognized exceptions to the bad-samaritan principle (except possibly the parenthood exception), anti-abortion laws also impose burdens of a *kind* that is especially suspect in our law. We are traditionally very dubious about practices which involve direct

---

9. *See* Farwell v. Keaton, 396 Mich. 281, 240 N.W.2d 217 (1976).

10. *See* Tarasoff v. Regents of the Univ. of Calif., 17 Cal. 3d 425, 551 P.2d 334, 131 Cal. Rptr. 14 (1976).

11. *See* Depue v. Flatau, 100 Minn. 299, 111 N.W. 1 (1907).

12. There is some tension for the proponent of "women's rights" between the argument I am making here, emphasizing the burdens of pregnancy, and an argument made about cases like Cleveland Bd. of Educ. v. LaFleur, 414 U.S. 632 (1974), emphasizing the pregnant woman's ability to continue at her normal occupation almost to the point of delivery. The conflict is more apparent than real. First, there is an important difference between asking how great a burden we can impose on the woman for the benefit of the fetus and asking how great a burden the woman can bear while continuing at her usual job if she chooses. Second, the variation in the actual effects of pregnancy on different women works in the woman's favor in both cases. When considering what we can impose on women, we must surely consider, if not the worst possible case (where what we impose, by increasing the risk, is death), at least the worst situation to which a significant fraction of the women affected are involuntarily assigned. In the *LaFleur* situation, by contrast, it should suffice to require individual consideration of the woman's case if a significant fraction of pregnant women can carry on as teachers with their abilities in that role relatively unimpaired.

invasions of the body or the imposition of physical pain or extreme physical discomfort.

The clearest example is corporal punishment. Although the Supreme Court has never directly confronted the issue, Mr. Justice (then Judge) Blackmun wrote an opinion for the Eighth Circuit Court of Appeals in 1968 that apparently condemned any use of corporal punishment, even if specifically authorized by statute and judicial sentence.[13] Delaware, which was notorious in the 1960s as the only state which specifically provided for flogging, abolished that punishment in 1972. To my mind, the most plausible explanation of the Supreme Court's surprising decision in *Ingraham v. Wright*[14] that the eighth amendment does not apply in schools is that the Justices did not want either to eliminate corporal punishment in schools or to say that the eighth amendment allows corporal punishment.

More generally, decisions of both the Supreme Court and lower courts make it clear that punishment may not be too "physical". The Supreme Court has indicated that prisoners cannot be deliberately denied medical treatment,[15] and lower courts have held that such disciplinary methods as "strip cells" inadequately provided with hygienic facilities constitute cruel and unusual punishment.[16] In one specially interesting decision, a federal district court found a violation of the eighth amendment where prisoners on death row were denied exercise facilities.[17] There is no logical contradiction in requiring that prisoners awaiting death must be allowed to exercise, or in permitting capital punishment while we have effectively abolished corporal forms, but there is a mild paradox that says something about our attitudes towards pain and physical suffering.

In a different area, the result in *Rochin v. California*[18] was plainly determined by the Court's reaction to the physical brutality of the police and the invasive nature of stomach pumping. (Stomach pumping is not quite what it sounds like. It is accomplished by the introduction of an emetic into the stomach by a tube run through the nostrils and the esophagus. But it can be a distressing procedure, both because of the tube and because of

---

13. Jackson v. Bishop, 404 F.2d 571 (8th Cir. 1968).
14. 430 U.S. 651 (1977).
15. Estelle v. Gamble, 429 U.S. 97, 103 (1976).
16. *E.g.,* Wright v. McMann, 387 F.2d 519 (2d Cir. 1967).
17. Sinclair v. Henderson, 331 F. Supp. 1123, 1130-31 (E.D. La. 1971).
18. 342 U.S. 165 (1952).

the forced vomiting.) Later cases have established that physical searches — blood samples, mouth searches, rectal searches, perhaps even stomach pumping — are permissible in appropriate cases if carried out with decorum and procedural safeguards. But the few cases which have dealt with surgical searches (as for bullets) seem to draw a line between searches requiring only a superficial incision (permissible) and searches which involve going further into the body (disallowed).[19]

Other cases that demonstrate the judicial squeamishness about physical invasion, pain, and discomfort are the cases involving so-called "organic therapies" carried out in prisons or other custodial institutions. Organic therapies include psychosurgery, shock treatment, and aversive therapy with emetics or paralytics. There are many problems raised by the use of such therapies aside from the physical invasion or pain they involve. There are procedural issues about the need for medical authorization and supervision on each particular occasion of use; there are questions about the general efficacy of such therapeutic techniques; there are issues about the appropriateness of state-enforced "mind control". But the physically intrusive nature of the techniques is an important factor in the generally negative judicial reaction. One of the most persuasive opinions in the area is Judge Ross's opinion for the Eighth Circuit in *Knecht v. Gillman*.[20] The opinion is persuasive not because of exceptional analysis, but because it emphasizes that fifteen minutes to an hour of vomiting (as the result of an injection of apomorphine) is something known by all of us to be a "painful and debilitating experience".

In another area, a Pennsylvania court recently held that a healthy adult could not be compelled to be the donor for a bone-marrow transplant that represented the only realistic chance for the survival of his cousin, even though the transplant involved no significant risk to the donor.[21] So far as I am aware, the case is unique in confronting the question of compulsory organ donation, but a number of philosophers and lawyers have recently used compulsory organ donation as a hypothetical example of a practice clearly beyond the pale.[22] Evidence for the correctness of this

---

19. *Compare, e.g.*, Creamer v. State, 229 Ga. 511, 192 S.E.2d 350 (Ga. 1972), *cert. dismissed*, 410 U.S. 975 (1973), *with, e.g.*, State v. Haynie, 240 Ga. 866, 242 S.E.2d 713 (Ga. 1978). *See generally* United States v. Crowder, 543 F.2d 312 *(en banc)* (D.C. Cir. 1976), *cert. denied*, 429 U.S. 1062 (1977).

20. 488 F.2d 1136 (8th Cir. 1973).

21. McFall v. Shimp (unpublished, Ct. of Comm. Pleas, Allegheny County, Pa , Civil Division, July 26, 1978).

22. *E.g.*, R. Nozick, Anarchy, State, and Utopia 206-07 (1974); Kadish, *Respect for*

view can be found in decided cases in which judges have been very reluctant to permit organ donation by minors or incompetents, even to close relatives.[23]

It would be interesting to see a case in which the issue was presented of whether a parent has a duty to donate a needed organ to his or her child. My guess is that no duty would be found. To be sure, there are organ donations and organ donations. Donating an eye would not leave one blind, but it would significantly impair one's sight as well as increasing the risk of blindness if something happened to the other eye. Donating a kidney ordinarily has no effect at all so long as the other kidney remains intact. Donating bone marrow has only temporary effects, since the bone marrow regenerates. I would be surprised if any American court ordered even a parent-to-child bone-marrow transplant, an imposition which (not to forget our ultimate purpose) seems more defensible than forbidding abortion in every respect.

I do not claim that our disinclination to impose bodily invasion or physical pain overwhelms all other values. We require immunization against certain diseases for public schoolchildren. As noted previously, we allow physically invasive searches within limits. We may deny heroin to an addict in custody, causing the extreme discomfort and pain of a cold turkey withdrawal. Courts do sometimes approve the use of organic or aversive therapies. We are ambivalent about suicide and the "right to die", even where life may entail considerable pain or else dependence on highly invasive life-support machinery.

I say we are ambivalent about suicide and the right to die. There is the Karen Quinlan case,[24] holding that an irreversibly comatose patient has a right not to be kept alive by extraordinary means. But there is also the possibility that that unique decision is ahead of its time. There is the fact that abetting suicide is still a crime, in most or all states. But the explanation is in part that we are afraid the abettor may have exerted too much influence on the decision. Juries are notoriously reluctant to convict in appealing cases of abetting suicide or even of outright euthanasia of a terminal patient unable to kill himself.

Life and Regard for Rights in the Criminal Law, in Respect for Life in Medicine, Philosophy, and the Law 83, 93-94 (1977); L. Tribe, American Constitutional Law 918 (1978).

23. *E.g.*, Lausier v. Pescinski, 67 Wis. 2d 4, 226 N.W.2d 180 (Wis. 1975); *In re* Richardson, 284 So. 2d 185 (La. App. 1973).

24. *In re* Quinlan, 70 N.J. 10, 355 A.2d 647 (1976).

Even in the cases just mentioned, whenever a major invasion or infliction of pain is allowed (that is, in cases involving heroin withdrawal, aversive therapy, or the would-be suicide), there is a significant distinction from the abortion situation. The burdens, whatever they are, are at least arguably imposed for the subject's own good. In a day when many people think constitutional analysis should start from the views of John Stuart Mill, this may seem to make the impositions in question less defensible rather than more. But one can quite rationally take the following position: No man is his brother's keeper, and therefore the law should not require one individual to shoulder burdens for the sole benefit of a particular other. On the other hand, every man is assumed to want to pursue his own interests (except perhaps where he voluntarily chooses to help another), and therefore an individual who acts clearly contrary to his own interests, without thereby helping anyone else, must be incompetent, in which case his choice against his own interests need not be respected. The position I have just outlined may be oversimplified, but I think it is a fair sketch of the relevant part of our legal tradition.

We have wandered slightly from the main point of this Section, which is our reluctance to invade the body or to impose physical discomfort or pain. Let me conclude with three hypotheticals, not the ideal stuff of constitutional argument, but perhaps worth considering.

First, suppose that fetuses were freely transplantable from womb to womb at all stages of development, and suppose that we were confronted with a healthy, normal two-week fetus developing in the womb of a woman who was rapidly dying of some condition that would not affect the fetus until she died in a few days. Would we consider drafting another non-pregnant woman to carry the fetus, choosing her by lot and implanting the fetus, whether she wanted it or not, in her body, forbidding her to abort it?

Second, imagine that we had a machine we could hook a person up to which would cause the person to experience the sensations of a difficult and painful childbirth. Imagine also a completely innocent person who holds in his subconscious mind a piece of information that would allow the police to thwart a planned murder. This person is genuinely unable to recall the relevant information, but he would recall it with the encouragement of the childbirth-simulating-torture-machine. Would we allow a court to order that the person be hooked up to the machine involuntarily?

Finally, consider a simple burning building, with a child trapped inside. Would a court impose criminal liability on anyone, even the child's parent, who did not attempt to save the child at the risk of second-degree burns over one or two percent of his or her body?

In each of these situations, an innocent life can be saved by a physical invasion comparable to or less than pregnancy and delivery. In the third situation, even if the potential rescuer is specified to be the child's parent, liability is unlikely. In all other cases, the suggested imposition is unthinkable in the context of our legal system.

I am aware of arguments that can be made to distinguish these hypotheticals from the abortion case. One problem with the abortion case is that it is not exactly analogous to anything else. My hope is merely that these hypotheticals will help the reader to see what a striking departure abortion laws are from our usual commitment to the bad-samaritan principle and our usual reluctance to impose physical invasions or pain.

3. *Why the Physical Burdens Are Crucial*

So far I have concentrated on those interests of the pregnant woman which are invaded by pregnancy and delivery, including any post-partum or permanent effects of those physiological processes. The opinion in *Roe* and the principal scholarly defense of that opinion[25] give rather more prominence to the woman's interest in deciding how many children she will raise, and when she will have them. It is time for me to explain my relative unconcern with this "family-planning" interest.

To begin with, it may be doubted whether prohibiting abortion invades this "family-planning" interest at all. Ordinarily, the woman can give up a child she bears for adoption.[26] Now, even if the woman can give her child up for adoption, that does not mean that she can avoid post-partum injury to her interests of every kind. She can regulate the number of children she raises,

---

25. Heymann & Barzelay, *supra* note 1.

26. Because of legal restrictions or the unavailability of adoptive parents, this possibility may not always be available. For simplicity's sake, I shall write as if it were. Obviously, when it is not, prohibiting abortion *does* invade the woman's family-planning interest. Whether adoption is impossible often enough to make it clear on that ground that women's family-planning interests are importantly affected is an issue I shall not discuss. For reasons discussed in Section III.B. *infra*, the family-planning interest, even if it is impaired, would be better exploited by a samaritan-type argument than by the "balancing" approach of *Roe*.

and when she has them, but there may be significant psychological costs associated with giving a child away. There may be personal feelings of guilt over having "abandoned" the child, and there may also be family pressure (in favor of keeping the child) to resist and social disapproval to contend with. In effect, the woman faces, for each child she bears, a disjunctive burden. She must bear *either* the psychological costs of giving up her child *or* the burdens of actually raising the child.

If we adopt a relatively straightforward "balancing" approach to the constitutional problem of abortion — if we set out to identify the woman's interests, to identify the state's interests, and then (somehow) to balance — we must presumably put into the woman's side of this balance only the lesser of the two alternatives in the disjunctive burden described above (in addition, of course, to the burdens of pregnancy and delivery already discussed). Defenders of *Roe* ordinarily point to the number of women who keep and raise children they did not want, and assume that the two alternatives in question can be treated as equal for the purposes of constitutional analysis.

My approach, however, is not a balancing approach at all. I do not argue that the sum of the woman's interests in having an abortion outweighs the sum of the state's interests in forbidding it. I do rely in part on the magnitude of certain burdens imposed on the woman, but the magnitude of the burdens is relevant *not* because I want to compare those burdens to the social benefits achieved, but because I want to compare them to the burdens other potential samaritans are required to shoulder or allowed to shirk. The point of my argument is that the invasion of the woman's interests cannot be justified even on the ground that it is necessary to save the life of the fetus, so long as other potential samaritans more eligible for compulsion are allowed to refuse much less burdensome and less invasive life-saving aid.

Given the nature of my argument, I cannot deal with the disjunctive burden described above (involving *either* the costs of raising the child *or* the costs of giving it up) by saying that the two alternatives are about equally unattractive and the woman is as badly treated by being subjected to the disjunctive burden as she would be if she were straightforwardly required to keep and raise the child. The costs involved in giving up the child do not "count" under samaritan law in the same way that the burdens of raising the child would if that alternative were compelled. The costs of giving up the child are genuine costs, but they are not costs of giving aid. Once the child has been born and given away, the mother is free of duties to aid the child in any way. The mother may be made unhappy by the thought that she has abandoned the child, or whatever, but all sorts of laws make people unhappy without violating the bad-samaritan principle. I would say that *for purposes of samaritan analysis,* the effective weight of the lesser of the two alternatives in the disjunctive burden is zero, and the whole post-partum burden must therefore be regarded as irrelevant. The family-planning interest drops out entirely.[27]

The reader may wonder why, if samaritan analysis makes it impossible to consider the family-planning interests or the costs to the woman of giving the child up, I do not abandon the samaritan analysis in favor of some approach that would allow all the costs to the woman to be counted. The answer — which I will develop at greater length in Section III — is twofold. First, among the interests of the woman that are impaired by laws forbidding abortion, it is precisely the interests which count for purposes of samaritan analysis that can be shown to be given special status by the *Constitution*. Second, my approach, comparing the pregnant woman to other potential samaritans, avoids the necessity for a *de novo* weighing of the woman's interest in having an abortion against the state's interest in forbidding it, a weighing which I am not sure favors the woman.

Finally, the reader may be troubled by the fact that I emphasize interests of the woman which many women would not mention in explaining their desire for an abortion. Most women who want an abortion, asked why they want an abortion, would not begin their answer by describing the physical burdens of pregnancy and childbirth. There is a reason for this. The pregnant woman faces at least three possible courses: abortion, bearing and

---

27. Despite what I say in the text, if the vast majority of women would rather raise an unwanted child than give it up for adoption, then it could be argued that many women have no choice. They are compelled by their psychological make-up and by social pressures to undertake the burdens of parenthood once they have borne a child. If this is the situation, then perhaps the burdens of parenthood should count, for purposes of samaritan analysis, as being imposed by the prohibition of abortion. This possibility may be important to some readers. My own view is that a convincing argument for the woman can be based just on the physical burdens of pregnancy and childbirth. But for the reader who disagrees — and in particular for the reader who ends up thinking I have not adequately distinguished the pregnant woman from the parent or the military draftee — it may be that a convincing argument for the woman is possible if and only if the burdens of parenthood count as imposed by laws forbidding abortion. If they do count, there is no doubt that the total burdens imposed by anti-abortion laws are significantly increased.

raising the child, or bearing the child and giving it away. A full explanation for wanting an abortion must explain why both of the other courses are rejected. In everyday discussion, however, given that most women want to raise children, the question "Why do you want an abortion?" is likely to be intended as equivalent to "Why don't you want to raise that child?" It is natural, and appropriate, that the answer should focus on the difficulties associated with raising the child, as the answer (I assume) usually does. If the woman were pressed with a further question, "Why don't you bear the child and give it up for adoption?", I believe a high percentage of women would give prominent place in their responses to the burdens of pregnancy and childbirth I have described. I do not assert that these burdens would receive more emphasis than the psychological costs of giving the child away. But I am confident that, at this stage, unwillingness to suffer substantial pain and physical invasion for an individual with whom the woman desired no connection would be a significant factor in many women's explanations. That, I think, is enough to save my argument from the charge of being unrelated to what women really care about.

C. *Exceptions to the Bad-Samaritan Principle*

I turn now to the matter of comparing the pregnant woman to other potential samaritans who are required to give aid under standard exceptions to the bad-samaritan principle. It is worth repeating something I have said before: My object is not to show that by traditional standards the pregnant woman is indistinguishable from the totally uninvolved bystander who may refuse even the most trivial aid. The pregnant woman is not totally uninvolved. She is sufficiently involved that we could appropriately impose slight burdens of aid on her, if imposing slight burdens would do the fetus any good. Unfortunately, imposing slight burdens on her will not do the fetus any good. It is very large burdens or nothing. What I propose to show in this Section is that even if the pregnant woman is sufficiently involved to justify imposing some small duty of aid, she is still *less* "eligible for compulsion" than any of the other potential samaritans who figure in the standard exceptions to the bad-samaritan principle. Her situation is distinguishable, in ways that make her a less appropriate subject for compulsion, from the situation of every other potential samaritan on whom duties are imposed. If we consider in addition that the duties imposed on those other sa-

maritans are ordinarily trivial, both absolutely and in comparison
with the burdens of pregnancy and childbirth, it should become
clear why I suggest that laws forbidding abortion are out of line
with the general framework of samaritan law.

Two of the standard exceptions to the bad-samaritan principle can be disposed of quickly. One is the "statutory duty" exception. Any discussion of the bad-samaritan principle can be
expected to include the observation that there *is* a duty to aid if
some statute imposes such a duty. Now, statutes forbidding abortion are (on my analysis) statutes imposing a duty to aid. So it
might seem that the pregnant woman falls squarely within the
first standard exception we look at. But the statutory duty exception, considered as a *general* exception, is not relevant to our
purposes. The claim that there is a duty if some statute creates
such a duty assumes that the statute in question is constitutional,
whereas I am arguing precisely that anti-abortion statutes are
unconstitutional because they make an exception to the bad-
samaritan principle that is unacceptable given the general state
of samaritan law. It is relevant, of course, to compare anti-
abortion statutes, and the duty they impose, with other *specific*
duty-creating statutes and the duties they impose. Those other
statutes are part of the "general state of samaritan law". I shall
discuss some other statutory duties, including the draftee's duty
of military service, in Section D below.

The other standard exception to the bad-samaritan principle
that we can deal with summarily is the "contract" exception.
Duties to aid may be undertaken by contract. It might be suggested that when a woman marries, or perhaps when a woman has
sexual intercourse, she enters into an implied contract with her
husband or with the man involved to carry and deliver any conceptus that results. If there is such an implied contract, the fetus
can be regarded as a third-party beneficiary. We do not ordinarily
enforce contractual duties by criminal sanctions, but contractual
duties to aid the helpless can appropriately be so enforced in some
circumstances. The trouble with this argument, of course, is that
it is absurd to suggest that sex or marriage always carries with it
an implied promise to bear a child. Even among people who are
married, there are just too many who do not want children.[28] In

---

28. To be sure, we may say that marriage involves an implied promise to have children, *meaning* that unwillingness to beget or bear children is or ought to be a ground for
divorce. That is obviously quite a different matter. As to whether a husband's interest in
having a child ought, even in the absence of any contract, to entitle him to prevent his
pregnant wife from having an abortion, see Section III.B. *infra*.

arguing against the existence of an implied contract on the basis of what people want, I assume that we are talking about a contract implied "in fact". We sometimes imply contracts "in law" without caring what the parties want. If that possibility is relevant at all in the present context, it is under the heading of "status" exceptions to the bad-samaritan principle, to which I now turn.[29]

1. *Exceptions Based on Status or Relationship*

There are a number of cases in which a duty to render aid is based on the status of the potential samaritan, or on the relationship between the potential samaritan and the person in need of aid.[30] A common carrier has a duty to aid a passenger; the master of a ship has a duty to aid a member of his crew; a jailer must aid his prisoner. Others on whom duties to aid are imposed are innkeepers (*vis-à-vis* their guests), storeowners (*vis-à-vis* their customers), employers of all kinds (*vis-à-vis* their employees), schools (*vis-à-vis* their pupils), social hosts, spouses, and parents.

The situation of the pregnant woman can be distinguished from the situations of all these other potential samaritans on whom duties are imposed. In fact, in almost every case there is more than one significant ground of distinction. A ground of distinction which is common to all of the cases, however, is the degree of voluntariness of the assumption of the status or relationship on which the duty to aid is based. Every one of the statuses or relationships I have just named is entered into voluntarily. The condition (or status, or relationship with the fetus) of pregnancy is *not* chosen voluntarily by those women who, once pregnant, want abortions. Some readers may think the distinction just suggested is more apparent than real. I do propose to discuss it further. First, let us consider the extent to which pregnancy is voluntary.

---

29. The text ignores the possibility of an express contract to carry the fetus. Given problems of proof (unless we require such a contract to be in writing), and given the reluctance of the common law to grant specific performance of contracts for personal services, it is not clear that even an express contract ought to be enforceable. Certainly, however, a woman who has made an express contract to carry a fetus is a much more appropriate subject for compulsion than one who has not. Fortunately, we need not decide whether a woman should be allowed to bind herself by an express contract not to have an abortion. I am prepared to restrict the argument of this essay, and my conclusions, to women who have not made the attempt.

30. *See generally* RESTATEMENT (SECOND) OF TORTS §§ 314, 314A, 314B (1965); W. PROSSER, *supra* note 3, at 340-43; W. LaFave & A. Scott, *supra* note 5, at 184.

I think it may safely be assumed that most pregnancies *of women who want abortions* are not intentional.[31] Unintended pregnancies may occur for a variety of reasons. Many result from contraceptive failure. (If contraceptive methods of very high effectiveness, say 98%, were used carefully and consistently, there would be hundreds of thousands of pregnancies a year caused by contraceptive failure in a large population such as that of the United States.) Many more, probably, result from inept or inattentive use of contraceptives, or from occasional non-use. And many result from persistent non-use, caused by ignorance, laziness, the expense or disruptiveness of many contraceptive methods, pressure from male partners not to use contraception, and a variety of other possible psychological causes. In none of these cases has the woman who becomes pregnant chosen to be pregnant.

It might be argued, of course, that in every case where a woman becomes pregnant (except the case of rape), she has voluntarily done *something*. She has given in to pressure not to use contraception; or she has given in to her own laziness. If she has done neither of these things — if she is a victim of contraceptive failure despite responsible contraceptive use, or even if she is totally and excusably ignorant about methods of contraception — she has at least had sex. Assuming she is not so ignorant as to be unaware of the connection between intercourse and pregnancy, can she not be said to have assumed the risk of conception?

It is true that in every case in which a woman becomes pregnant (still excepting the case of rape), she has voluntarily had sex. Voluntariness, however, is something that admits of degrees. As Harry Wellington has pointed out, having sex may be more a matter of choice than eating, but it is an act to which most of us feel a strong compulsion.[32] It is clear to me that the choice to have

---

31. To be sure, there will be cases where the woman becomes pregnant intentionally and then changes her mind about having the child; but these cases will be comparatively rare. (If the practice of amniocentesis to determine the fetus's sex, followed by abortion of a fetus of the undesired sex, becomes more common, the case in question may not be so rare. That does not affect what I say in the remainder of this note.) In any case which is identifiably of this type, the case for denying the woman an abortion is very much stronger than in the usual case of a pregnancy which is unwanted from the beginning. Whether the case for denying an abortion is strong enough is a harder question. Some of the relevant considerations are canvassed later on, in the discussion of duties created by the voluntary commencement of aid, at pages 1598-1601. I think we can leave this unusual case unresolved without impairing the general argument.

32. Wellington, *Common Law Rules and Constitutional Double Standards: Some Notes on Adjudication,* 83 YALE L.J. 221, 308 (1973).

sex is ordinarily not as "voluntary" as the choice to be an inn-keeper, or a storeowner, or whatever.

It might be suggested that even if an innkeeper (for example) voluntarily chooses (in a strong sense of "voluntary") to be an innkeeper, he does not choose to be a good samaritan to his guests. He does not even choose that any of his guests shall ever need his aid (beyond room and board). All he *chooses* is to run the *risk* that some guest will have an accident or other misfortune which requires special aid. In other words, the innkeeper does just what the woman does when she has sex. He takes a risk. If the innkeeper may be compelled to be a samaritan when the event he does not want occurs, why not the woman as well?

This suggestion overlooks important differences between the innkeeper and the woman. The innkeeper may not want to be a good samaritan. But he actively invites the formation of the rela-tionship on which his duty of aid is based. The innkeeper wants guests. The woman does not want the fetus. What is true of the innkeeper is true of every other potential samaritan mentioned at the beginning of this Subsection (with the possible exception of the parent, to be discussed shortly). In some cases, the relation-ship which is the basis for the duty of aid is a relationship of some intimacy in which the potential samaritan chooses the *particular* individual with whom the relationship is to be formed. (I have in mind the relationship of spouse to spouse and of host to social guest.) This obviously makes it easier to accept the imposition of a duty to aid. Innkeepers, storekeepers, and so on, do not choose their guests or customers with such particularity. Even so, unlike the unwillingly pregnant woman, they actively seek the formation of the relationship. That is the point of their calling.

The reference to the innkeeper's "calling" suggests another observation. The innkeeper, the storekeeper, and so on, are all engaged in providing a service for pay. They are engaged in eco-nomic enterprise. That clearly contributes to the feeling that it is acceptable to impose duties of aid, to treat them as having "assumed the risk".[33] In fact, every potential samaritan on the list at the beginning of this Subsection (still excepting the parent) not only invites the formation of the relationship but *either* chooses the other party to the relationship with particularity *or* is engaged in an economic activity.[34]

33. W. PROSSER, *supra* note 3, at 339.
34. The claim in the text might be denied with respect to jails and *public* schools.

There is another respect in which all the potential samaritans discussed in this Subsection differ from the pregnant woman. All the relationships under discussion — of innkeeper to guest, shopkeeper to customer, parent to child, and so on — are relationships in which the second-named party would *expect* aid from the first. The potential samaritan in any of these categories who refuses aid will disappoint expectations which are likely to exist in fact and which we regard as reasonable. It might be suggested that the expectations exist only because of the legal duties to aid, but I think that suggestion is simply false. Even in the absence of legal duties, most innkeepers would aid guests who fell ill (both for humanitarian reasons and because it would be bad for business to refuse), most social hosts would aid their guests, and so on. Substantial expectations of aid would exist regardless of the legal rule, and one justification for the legal rule is that it protects these expectations. The fetus, in contrast, has no expectations to be protected. (Lest there be any doubt, I have been talking in this paragraph about psychological expectations, not "legal" expectations. The claim that the fetus has no expectations is not a *petitio principii*. It is, I believe, an empirical fact.)

Before we move on to compare the pregnant woman to the parent, let us summarize what we have established so far. There is undeniably *some* reason to regard the pregnant woman as "eligible for compulsion" for the benefit of the fetus. She has (except in the case of rape) voluntarily done an act which created the risk that her aid would be required. On the other hand, the pregnant woman seems a notably less apt candidate for compulsion than the other potential samaritans we have considered. Surely she should not be compelled to undertake greater burdens than they. And yet, so long as there are laws forbidding abortion, she is compelled to undertake much greater burdens than they. The aid required of innkeepers and the others is trivial. It is usually something on the order of calling a doctor or sending for medicine. As one of my colleagues put it, we speak easily of the innkeeper's duty to aid his guests, but we would hardly require an innkeeper to give up a kidney for transplanting into a guest whose kidneys had failed. That would be a duty comparable to

---

These cases are special for a different reason: the duties to aid, to the extent they are not imposed on individuals who are providing services for pay, are imposed on the *state*. Whatever value we attach to an individual's being free to refuse aid, we do not attach the same value to the state's having a similar freedom, especially where the relevant relationship, with the prisoner or the public school pupil, is not only "invited" but coerced.

the duty anti-abortion laws impose on the pregnant woman.

Probably the most troublesome comparison, for my argument, is the comparison between the pregnant woman and the parent. I have explicitly excepted the parent from some of the claims made in this Subsection about other potential samaritans whose duties are based on status or relationship. It is not true of all parents, as it is true of all innkeepers, that they have invited the relationship with their child. It is not true of any parents that they have chosen the particular individual with whom to establish the parent-child relationship; and it is true of very few parents, if any, that they have children primarily for economic reasons. In addition, the burdens of being a parent are considerably greater than the burdens of aid imposed on innkeepers and the like. All in all, it may seem that the parallel between the parent and the pregnant woman is very close.

There are, however, significant differences between the parent and the pregnant woman who wants an abortion, differences which make parenthood look much more "voluntary" than unwanted pregnancy. The woman who does not want to be a parent, or the couple who do not want to be parents, can give their child up for adoption. There are costs associated with giving the child up, as I have already noted. But if, as I have argued, these costs are not enough so that the burdens of parenthood count for purposes of samaritan analysis as being imposed on women by laws forbidding abortion, then neither are they great enough so that the burdens of parenthood cannot be avoided by parents.[35] It is much more plausible to view keeping the child as a voluntary assumption of the burdens of raising the child than to view having sex as a voluntary assumption of the burdens of pregnancy and childbirth.

We can make the same point in a slightly different way. It is true that the law imposes burdens of care on parents. It is also true that what we normally think of as "the burdens of parenthood" are very great. But it is not really true that the law imposes on parents all the "burdens of parenthood". Most parents assume most of the burdens voluntarily. They keep their child. They feed it, and care for it, generally speaking. What the law is likely to punish the parent for is some particular refusal of aid fairly local-

---

35. In years past, when giving the child up for adoption may have been harder to arrange than it is today, it was probably easier to arrange some informal "farming-out" of the child.

ized in time. (Even where the parent's failure is a long-term course of general neglect, the parent is arguably being punished as much for failure to enlist other assistance on the child's behalf as for anything else.) The parent, much more than the pregnant woman, creates the relationship with the child. The parent who refuses aid, much more than the pregnant woman who has an abortion, is like the samaritan who harms the object of his "assistance" by voluntarily embarking on a course of aid and then terminating it after other potential samaritans have turned their attention elsewhere, satisfied that the need is being met. (An extended comparison of the pregnant woman with the samaritan who volunteers aid and then terminates it is reserved for the next Subsection.)

Finally, it is worth emphasizing again that the burdens of parenthood, however great they are, are not as physically invasive as the burdens of pregnancy and childbirth. For better or worse, our tradition assigns special disvalue to the imposition of pain or extreme physical discomfort and to actual invasions of the body. I have suggested earlier, with my compulsory-organ-donation and burning-building hypotheticals, that we would stop far short of imposing on parents the sort of physical burdens anti-abortion laws impose on women.[36]

2. *Voluntarily Beginning Aid*

There is substantial authority for the proposition that one who voluntarily begins to aid another assumes certain duties.[37] The aid must be provided in a non-negligent manner, and in some circumstances the aid may not be terminated. It might be argued that a pregnant woman has embarked on a course of aid to the fetus which she may not terminate by an abortion.

The principal objection to this argument is that the pregnant woman has not "voluntarily" begun to aid the fetus. I have already discussed the degree of voluntariness of the woman's

---

36. As a last word on parenthood, it is worth noting that one sort of burden is arguably imposed on parents who are no more eligible for compulsion than unintentionally pregnant women. I have in mind support obligations imposed on fathers who did not want a child. I think the argument of this essay casts some doubt on the constitutionality of such support obligations. But for the reader who thinks such obligations are obviously constitutional (and I assume most readers will fall into this category), it should suffice to note that financial impositions of this sort are much less disfavored than the physical impositions involved in forbidding abortion.

37. RESTATEMENT (SECOND) OF TORTS §§ 323, 324 (1965); W. PROSSER, *supra* note 3, at 343-48.

choice. I have conceded that, except in the case of rape, her connection with the fetus is not totally involuntary. But in most cases the pregnant woman has not knowingly and intentionally offered the fetus any assistance at all. At most she has taken a small risk, and lost. All of the cases about "voluntarily beginning aid" involve potential samaritans who, unlike the pregnant woman, have knowingly and intentionally embarked on a course of assistance to someone in need.[38]

In addition, the cases where voluntarily beginning aid has been found to create a duty are ordinarily cases where the "aid" in question has left the recipient worse off, as where a landlord causes injury by performing negligently a repair he was not obligated to perform, or where a half-hearted samaritan terminates a rescue-in-progress short of completion after other potential rescuers have disappeared, thinking that matters were under control. When a pregnancy is terminated, however, the fetus is no worse off than it was before the only action of the woman that could possibly be construed as the beginning of aid, namely the sexual act as a result of which the fetus was conceived.

This "no worse off" argument may seem fanciful. I admit it is an argument many people are likely to be uncomfortable with. It nonetheless deserves to be taken seriously. The point is *not* just that the fetus is no worse off dead than alive.[39] The point is that the fetus which is conceived and then aborted is not made worse off *by the entire course of the woman's conduct.*[40] This is a signifi-

---

38. The discussion in the text may remind the reader of another traditional exception to the bad-samaritan principle, involving people who negligently or innocently create dangerous situations. That exception is the subject of the next Subsection.

39. Since the fetus does not have and has never had any conscious desire to live, I think it can be argued plausibly that it is not worse off dead than alive. But that is not the present point.

40. The reader who does take the argument in the text seriously may object that if the abortion causes pain to the fetus, then the fetus *is* made worse off by the woman's entire course of conduct. However, if we take account of the pain caused the fetus, we ought to take account also of the pleasures of its earlier life in the womb (a life for which many inhabitants of the harsher world outside reportedly pine). How we are to estimate the balance of pain and pleasure here I do not know. Conceivably the balance would weigh against a late saline abortion. In any event, early abortions, by whatever technique, can hardly cause the fetus much pain.

It might also be objected that in saying the fetus is no worse off having been conceived and aborted than if it had never been conceived at all, I am overlooking the possibility that the fetus has a soul. I do not claim much knowledge about the fortunes of fetal souls, but it seems to me that if the fetus has a soul, then it is better off (and therefore no worse off) for being conceived and aborted and spending eternity in Limbo, than if it had not been conceived at all.

cant distinction between the abortion case and most cases where
a duty is founded upon a voluntary undertaking to aid.

At this point, it might be suggested that there are certain
cases where a samaritan who begins a rescue may not terminate
it, despite the fact that his whole course of conduct leaves the
person in need of rescue no worse off. The *Restatement (Second)
of Torts* suggests in a comment that one who has pulled a drowning man halfway to shore with a rope might not be permitted
simply to drop the rope and walk away, even if no other potential
rescuer has been discouraged.[41] Similarly, the *Restatement* says
that one who has pulled another out of a trench filled with poison-
ous gas may not then throw him back in even though he is left
no worse off than before the rescue was begun.[42]

These cases both differ significantly from the abortion situation. As to the drowning man, the *Restatement* only surmises that
the half-hearted samaritan may not abandon the rescue. It may
seem obvious to many readers that the rescue may not be abandoned, but if so, I suspect it is because the picture that springs
to mind is of a relatively effortless pulling-to-shore. If we imagine
instead a rescue that requires a long-sustained and painful effort,
it should seem much less clear that the samaritan who has done
no harm and displaced no other rescuer may not quit. For the
benefit of any reader who thinks even the highly burdensome
rescue may not be terminated, it is worth noting that there is *still*
a significant difference between the drowning man and the fetus.
One of the reasons we would be appalled (in the case of the easy
rescue, perhaps only troubled in the case of the difficult rescue)
by the samaritan who abandoned the drowning man halfway to
shore is that the samaritan would have raised expectations in the
drowning man and then disappointed them. The fetus, as I have
observed before, has no expectations.

As to the samaritan who has pulled someone from a gas-filled
trench and may not throw him back, the point here is that once
the unfortunate is pulled from the trench, the rescue (or that part
of it) is complete. Throwing the person rescued back into the
trench is not in any sense a refusal to aid. Securing an abortion,
while it is in some respects a positive act like throwing the person
back into the trench, is the only way the pregnant woman can
deny future aid to the fetus. Indeed, it is the only way she can

---

41. RESTATEMENT (SECOND) OF TORTS § 323, comment e (1965).
42. RESTATEMENT (SECOND) OF TORTS § 324, comment g (1965).

deny very *burdensome* aid which, we should note once more, she never really volunteered in the first place.[43]

3. *Harm or Danger Caused By the Potential Samaritan*

There is authority for the proposition that one who injures another, or one who creates a situation which is dangerous to another, has a duty to take steps to minimize the injury or danger, even if it was innocently caused.[44] For example, it has been held that when a vehicle becomes disabled in a position where it blocks a highway, the driver of the vehicle, even though utterly free of fault, has a duty to set out flares or otherwise warn oncoming traffic.[45]

This exception to the bad-samaritan principle is distinctive. It contemplates a duty to aid where the potential samaritan has neither chosen to become involved with the person in need of aid nor invited the formation of a relationship. It might be suggested that the pregnant woman is analogous to the samaritan who innocently creates a dangerous situation. It might be suggested that the pregnant woman has put the fetus in a dangerous situation. Even if she is free of fault, may she not, like the driver of the disabled vehicle, be required to give aid?

There is a significant difference between the pregnant woman and the driver of the disabled vehicle, a difference we have already discussed in another context. If we allow a potential samaritan to refuse aid to someone he has harmed or endangered, he will have made the other worse off by his entire course of conduct. The pregnant woman who has an abortion, however, does not make the fetus worse off by her entire course of conduct. For all practical purposes, the abortion leaves the fetus in just the state it was in before it was conceived. Allowing a woman to have an abortion is therefore quite different from allowing a driver simply to walk away from a disabled vehicle blocking a highway on a foggy night.

---

43. It may seem that the "no worse off" aspect of my argument would tend to justify neonate infanticide. That claim can be rejected for either of two reasons. First, once the infant is born, the woman can refuse further aid with less cost to the infant simply by giving it up for adoption. Second, we can argue that the woman has waived her right to refuse aid sometime before the infant is born. I think a waiver argument is probably adequate to justify the Court's holding in *Roe v. Wade* that third-trimester abortions may be prohibited in most circumstances. *See* pages 1642-43 *infra*.

44. RESTATEMENT (SECOND) OF TORTS §§ 321, 322 (1965); W. PROSSER, *supra* note 3, at 342-43.

45. *E.g.*, Scatena v. Pittsburgh & New England Trucking, 2 Mass. App. Ct. 638, 319 N.E.2d 730 (1974).

The reader may wonder whether the "no worse off" idea is really as important as I suggest. It is a difference between the abortion case and the disabled vehicle case, but is it a difference that matters? We sometimes allow a person to escape liability even though he clearly makes another worse off, as where, through no fault of the driver, a vehicle goes out of control and kills someone instantly. If the driver in such a case escapes liability even though he makes his victim worse off, can the duty to aid in the disabled-vehicle case really be explained as simply a duty not to make the victim worse off?

I think the "no worse off" idea *is* important. Where an out-of-control vehicle kills someone instantly, the question of aid to the victim does not arise, because the harm happens all at once. Where the harm does not happen all at once, courts have apparently decided that the right to refuse involvement does not extend to a right to refuse aid to those one has made worse off, even innocently. To make someone worse off, or to put someone in a position where he is likely to be made worse off, is to become involved. The right to non-involvement can be regained only by undoing the damage one has done.

A corollary is that the right to non-involvement ought to be regained once the damage has been undone. Nothing in the cases involving danger innocently caused suggests that the potential samaritan must do more than undo the damage. If the pregnant woman who has an abortion leaves the fetus no worse off than before it was conceived, nothing in those cases suggests that a pregnant woman must instead carry the fetus and thereby confer on it a substantial net benefit.

I have discussed the duty to aid of a potential samaritan who has innocently caused harm or danger. There is a similar, and more firmly established, duty to aid when one has *negligently* caused harm or danger. Now, I have conceded the existence of a duty to aid even when the potential samaritan is innocent, and it might seem that I have therefore answered the strongest possible case against my position. I have eschewed reliance on the fact that many women who become pregnant are entirely innocent and would clearly be excused from any duty to aid that fell only on potential samaritans who *negligently* caused harm or danger. On the other hand, it could be argued that I have made things too easy for myself. It would not be surprising if potential samaritans who negligently caused harm or danger were subjected to more extensive duties of aid than potential samaritans who cause harm or danger innocently. If this were the case, and if it could be argued that most women who become pregnant unwillingly are at least negligent, then I would have made things easier than they should be. In fact, there is no evidence that greater duties are imposed on negligent than on innocent potential samaritans. Even if duties are imposed more consistently on the negligent, the burdens imposed are no greater. Accordingly (returning to my perennial final point), it is as true of the negligent potential samaritan as of the innocent potential samaritan that the duties of aid imposed on him are completely trivial compared to the burdens of pregnancy and childbirth.

4. *Erosion of the Bad-Samaritan Principle*

Scholars do not like the bad-samaritan principle, and they are eager to claim that the principle is being eroded away. Perhaps it is, but if so, then the erosion is very slow indeed.

Two recent cases that might be cited as evidence of erosion are *Tarasoff v. Board of Regents*[46] and *Farwell v. Keaton.*[47] In *Tarasoff,* the California Supreme Court held that a psychotherapist had a duty to warn a person against whom the therapist's patient made a death threat. In *Farwell,* the Michigan Supreme Court said a teenage boy had a duty not to abandon in a parked car a friend who was unconscious from a beating by other boys, suffered during a night of drinking and "cruising" in search of female companionship.

Farwell may represent a slight extension of traditional duties to aid, but the relationship of participants in a social "joint venture" is closely analogous to the relationship of host and guest. Most importantly, the relationship is undertaken knowingly and voluntarily. In addition, there is an element of reciprocity in the relationship that is absent in most samaritan cases. This is a case where the court might plausibly find that a bilateral contract to give minor aid is implied "in fact".

Tarasoff appears unusual at first because the duty found by the court runs to a party not directly involved in the relationship that gives rise to the duty. But the case is not really very striking. There is clear precedent for duties to third parties in cases where the potential samaritan has a more extensive duty to control the behavior of another — for example the duty of a jailer to prevent the escape of his prisoners, or of an employer to control his em-

---

46. 17 Cal. 3d 425, 551 P. 2d 334, 131 Cal. Rptr. 14 (1976)
47. 396 Mich. 281, 240 N.W.2d 217 (1976).

ployees.[48] The fact that a psychotherapist does not have a full-fledged duty to control his patient should not prevent us from recognizing, in the duty to warn, a weaker analogue. It is relevant that the role of psychotherapist, like the role of jailer or employer, is undertaken voluntarily and, ordinarily, for pay.

I cannot discuss every case which might be cited as evidence that the bad-samaritan principle is disappearing. I think there is little persuasive evidence for this proposition. In any event, even scholars who see the rule weakening are thinking of its application to cases where the burdens on the potential samaritan are trivial. Thus Prosser suggests that the bad-samaritan principle may erode to the point where "the mere knowledge of serious peril, threatening death or great bodily harm to another, which an identified defendant might avoid *with little inconvenience,* creates a sufficient relation . . . to impose a duty of action."[49] Or more recently, Marshall Shapo: "I have evolved as a working principle that one has a duty to aid others in situations in which hazardous conditions necessitate assistance for the preservation of life and of physical integrity, and in which one possesses the power to expend energy in that task without serious inconvenience or possibility of harm to herself."[50]

Whatever else may be said of the supposed duty of a woman to carry a fetus, it is not a duty that can be discharged "with little inconvenience" or even "without serious inconvenience or possibility of harm".

D.   *Statutory Duties*

A variety of statutes create duties to act for the benefit of others and therefore create either exceptions or apparent exceptions to the bad-samaritan principle. As I have noted previously, the truth of the general proposition that statutes may create duties to aid does not undermine my argument against laws forbidding abortion, because the general proposition presupposes that the statutes in question are constitutional. However, since my argument is an equal protection argument, based in part on the claim that pregnant women are treated worse than other potential samaritans, it is important to compare laws forbidding abortion with other specific statutes or statutory schemes imposing duties to act.

---

48. W. Prosser, *supra* note 3, at 349-50.
49. *Id.* at 343 (emphasis added).
50. M. Shapo, The Duty to Act: Tort Law, Power, and Public Policy 69 (1977).

The most arresting statutorily created exception (or, as I
think, apparent exception) to the bad-samaritan principle is the
military draft. (Though the draft is not currently in force, there
is talk of reinstituting it, and its *constitutionality* is not currently
doubted, which is the key fact for our purposes.) One of my principal themes has been that the burdens imposed on pregnant
women by laws forbidding abortion are significantly greater than,
and different in kind from, the burdens imposed on other potential samaritans. The only potential samaritans who are subjected
to burdens at all comparable to the burdens of pregnancy and
childbirth are parents (whom I have already discussed) and military draftees.

Now, we could attempt to distinguish laws forbidding abortion from the military draft by reference to the nature of the
burdens imposed in the two cases. We could suggest that the
burdens of pregnancy and childbirth, even if not greater than the
burdens imposed on draftees, are more constitutionally objectionable. They involve invasions of the body, and they more directly
touch on the specially sensitive area of sexual intimacy.[51] This
does not seem to me a sufficient ground of distinction between
anti-abortion laws and the draft.

Draftees are likely to be subjected to a good deal of forced
exercise under unpleasant and demanding conditions. For many,
this will result in considerable discomfort and even pain. To be
sure, the draftee is not compelled to allow another person to grow
inside his body, and it might be argued that the pains of military
training make the body a more versatile and useful instrument
for varied physical activities, while pregnancy makes the
woman's body less adapted to physical activities other than
carrying a fetus. But these differences do not alter the fact that
compulsory military service involves a considerable *physical* invasion.

As to the suggestion that forbidding abortion touches on a
zone of special intimacy, that is true, but I am not certain the
draft is so different. The draftee is presented with a new group of
associates he has no hand in picking. He will eat with them, sleep
in close proximity to them, share bathroom facilities with them,
and spend most of his leisure time with them. Intimate associa-
tional interests of the draftee are strongly affected. Even as to sex,

---

51. For a suggestion along these lines, see Gerety, *Redefining Privacy*, 12 HARV. C.R.-
C.L. L. REV. 233, 275 n.153 (1977).

the draftee is taken away from whatever sexual relationships or
patterns of sexual behavior he has established for himself in his
civilian life and he is thrown into a new society that is likely to
have and to enforce by considerable social pressure expectations
regarding both what he shall say about sex and what he shall do
about it. Remembering that the draftee's tour of duty normally
lasts two years while the pregnant woman's lasts nine months, I
am not persuaded that the burdens of pregnancy and childbirth
are clearly greater than, or importantly different in kind from,
the burdens of military conscription.[52]

To my mind, the crucial difference between the pregnant
woman denied an abortion and the military draftee is this: The
woman is being required to aid a specific other individual (the
fetus); the draftee is not. Rightly or wrongly, our tradition distinguishes between obligations to aid particular individuals and obligations to promote a more broadly based public interest. (This,
incidentally, is why the draft is only an *apparent* exception to the
bad-samaritan principle. The bad-samaritan principle applies
only when aid to specific individuals is in issue.)

In the opinion that established the constitutionality of the
draft, the unanimous Court gave most of its attention to a federalism question — whether the power to conscript belonged to
Congress or to the states.[53] The Court gave the thirteenth amendment issue, which is the relevant issue for our purposes, short
shrift. That issue is discussed explicitly only in the final paragraph of the opinion:

> Finally, as we are unable to conceive upon what theory the
> exaction by government from the citizen of the performance of his
> supreme and noble duty of contributing to the defense of the rights
> and honor of the nation, as the result of a war declared by the great
> representative body of the people, can be said to be the imposition
> of involuntary servitude in violation of the prohibitions of the Thir-
> teenth Amendment, we are constrained to the conclusion that the
> contention to that effect is refuted by its mere statement.[54]

If the Justices were genuinely unable to conceive how the
draft could be said to impose involuntary servitude, they were
deficient in imagination. But the point of their rebuttal is clear.

---

52. The text notwithstanding, a *possible* argument to the effect that the burdens
imposed by laws forbidding abortion are greater than the burdens imposed by the draft
was suggested in note 27 *supra*.

53. Selective Draft Law Cases, 245 U.S. 366 (1918).

54. 245 U.S. at 390.

It does not offend the traditions of a free people to require citizens to perform their "supreme and noble duty of contributing to the defense of the rights and honor of the nation". When the nation calls and the public welfare is at stake, the citizen must respond.

In answer to the suggestion that the draftee serves a public interest while the pregnant woman denied an abortion serves only the interest of the fetus, it might be argued that every interest protected by state power becomes *ipso facto* a public interest. There is something to this. I am protected by law against gratuitous physical assault, and that suggests that in some sense there must be a public interest in so protecting me. Still, the public interest involved is ultimately based on my private interest in physical integrity. Similarly, if the prohibition on abortion is justified on the ground that the fetus has a right to life (as it commonly is these days), then the ultimate public interest is in protecting the private interest of the fetus. This public interest is not enough to justify compelling the pregnant woman to carry the fetus. The reason is that in *every* potential samaritan case there is a public interest in protecting the person in need of aid which is precisely analogous to the public interest in saving the fetus. We cannot rely on this public interest in the abortion situation and ignore it elsewhere.

The draft appeals to a more public, or more general, public interest — in national security. It simply does not present the same issue as abortion. There is a difference between the idea that an individual is not his brother's keeper, which underlies the bad-samaritan principle, and the idea that a citizen owes nothing to society at large.[55]

If the difference between the draft and laws forbidding abortion is what I have suggested, then laws forbidding abortion might well be constitutional if they were justified on grounds other than the right to life of the fetus. In particular, it seems that

---

55. It may seem that the distinction between public interest and private interest, which I rely on in the text, is a weak reed on which to base a constitutional argument. The idea that private property can be taken only for "public use" has arguably not been a significant limitation on the power of eminent domain. The idea that government can regulate only businesses "affected with a public interest" is as dead as any constitutional doctrine can hope to be. A full-scale discussion of the public/private distinction, while interesting, would take us far beyond a reasonable scope for this essay. Whatever the difficulty of drawing the line in other contexts, it seems to me there is an intuitively arresting difference between making someone serve in the military, in defense of interests which are plainly public if any are, and making someone carry a fetus, for the benefit of the fetus or the child it might become.

if there were a genuine national commitment to population growth, abortion could be prohibited in furtherance of that commitment. This will strike some readers as a curious and unacceptable conclusion, but it is a conclusion I am prepared to accept. We do sometimes require great sacrifices in the public interest. The draft is the most extreme example. If it were necessary to require women to bear children in the pursuit of a goal similar to national security, I see no reason why that sacrifice could not be required.

In addition to the duty of military service, there are many other statutorily created duties to act for the benefit of others. There are duties to fight forest fires, to work on public roads, to submit to quarantine for infectious disease, to be a witness or a juror. There is the lawyer's duty to serve some indigent clients without compensation, the duty of the master of a ship to rescue at sea,[56] the duty of children to contribute to the support or medical expenses of impoverished parents. Although this list is not exhaustive, I believe a discussion of these representative duties will suffice.

The first thing to say about all of these statutory duties is that they impose burdens very much lighter than the burdens of pregnancy and childbirth. Just as the parenthood exception to the bad-samaritan principle is the only common law exception which resembles laws forbidding abortion in the magnitude of the burdens imposed, so the draft, which I have already discussed, is the only statutory exception or apparent exception which is comparable in this respect.

Every one of these statutory duties differs from the duty to carry a fetus (imposed by laws forbidding abortion) in other ways as well. The duties to fight forest fires, to work on public roads, and to submit to quarantine are, I believe, no longer of great practical importance. Also, like the duty to be a witness or a juror, they all involve *public* service — they are not duties to aid specific other individuals, but rather duties to benefit the community at large. The duty of the lawyer to serve indigent clients might also be regarded as a duty of public service, promoting the public interest in seeing justice done. If this "public" interest seems too closely tied to the private interest of the lawyer's client (since the lawyer does work *for* his client in a way the witness and the juror do not), we can also observe of both the lawyer's duty

---

56. 46 U.S.C. § 728 (1976).

and the duty of the master of a ship to rescue at sea that these duties are attached to activities ordinarily undertaken for pay. Furthermore, the lawyer and the ship's master are required to render services of *kinds* that they have shown a general willingness to render by their choice of occupation. The same cannot be said of the unwillingly pregnant woman. With regard to the last statutory duty, the duty of children to support impoverished parents, I have always had doubts about the constitutionality of statutes imposing such a duty. People do not choose their parents; they do not even choose to *have* parents. Many states have statutes imposing duties of filial support, but the constitutionality of such statutes has never been passed on by the Supreme Court.[57] Even if such statutes are constitutional, they are distinguishable from laws forbidding abortion. The burdens imposed by filial support statutes, while significant, are monetary. Also, I assume that anyone inclined to defend filial support statutes would rely on the claim that the child was merely repaying the parent for benefits received, a claim which cannot be made in the abortion case.

E. *Final Comments*

I have argued that abortion is a problem in samaritan law, and I have compared the situation of the pregnant woman with the situations of other potential samaritans and others (such as draftees) who are not strictly speaking potential samaritans (because it is not other *individuals* who require their aid) but who are compelled to act for the benefit of persons besides themselves. As I have noted, the situation of the pregnant woman has no perfect analogue. There is no other case in which noninvolvement on the part of the potential samaritan requires something that looks so much like a positive act; and there is no other case in which the potential samaritan has contributed to the existence of a relationship with the person in need of aid with just the same degree of voluntariness. Expanding on the last point, I have conceded that by having sex the pregnant woman has (except in the case of rape) done *something* that gives us *some* reason to compel her to aid the fetus. On the other hand, the pregnant

---

57. The closest the Court has come was to vacate, with a request for clarification on whether there was an adequate state ground, a California Supreme Court decision that such a statute was *un*constitutional under the federal Constitution, or under the California constitution, or both. Department of Mental Hygiene v. Kirchner, 380 U.S. 194 (1965).

woman has not done as much to establish a relationship with the fetus as has the parent to establish a relationship with her child, the voluntary rescuer to establish a relationship with the object of the rescue, or even the innkeeper to establish a relationship with his guest. If we bear in mind that no other potential samaritan is required to bear burdens as physically invasive as the burdens of pregnancy and childbirth, and if we bear in mind also that no other potential samaritan (with the possible, but doubtful,[58] exception of the parent) is subjected to burdens remotely comparable in magnitude to the burdens imposed on the pregnant woman, we conclude that laws forbidding abortion are at odds with the general spirit of samaritan law.[59]

One final point. When I suggest that the woman should not be compelled to subordinate her interests to those of the fetus, I sometimes meet with the response: "But if she is allowed to have an abortion, the fetus is subordinated. It is just a question of who shall be subordinated to whom." In a sense, of course, this is correct. There is a conflict of interest between the woman and the fetus, and someone is going to lose. But that is true in every samaritan situation. There is a conflict between the distressed party's need for aid and the potential rescuer's desire not to give it. The point is that our law generally resolves this conflict in favor of the potential samaritan. When a woman is pregnant, it is the fetus that needs aid and the woman who is in a position to give it. If the conflict between the woman and the fetus is to be resolved consistently with the resolutions of the most closely analogous cases, the woman must prevail.

---

58. *See* discussion at pages 1597-98 *supra*.

59. An issue I have not mentioned is whether, in view of the greater responsibility for the fetus of the woman who has sex without taking measures against conception, a state could make access to abortion conditional on responsible contraceptive use. In theory, this suggestion has considerable appeal. But there are difficulties. Many women are excusably ignorant concerning contraceptive methods. Perhaps before the state makes contraceptive use a prerequisite to abortion it must do a better job of contraceptive education. Also, there are significant side effects from many contraceptive methods. If, as I have argued, the woman who conceives and then has an abortion does not make the fetus worse off by her entire course of conduct, it is not clear that the woman should be required to run any risk to herself in order to avoid these consequences to the fetus. Most significantly, the invasions and uncertainty involved in *enforcing* a rule that conditioned abortion on responsible contraceptive use would be extreme. More could be said on this topic, but since no state has attempted to condition abortion on contraceptive use, no more need be said in this essay.

II.   ABORTION AS SELF-DEFENSE

I have already mentioned that for those who cannot bring themselves to view removing a fetus from a woman's body as an omission for purposes of the bad-samaritan principle, there is another possibility. We can concede that the woman who has an abortion actively kills the fetus but argue that she acts in self-defense. We can view the woman who secures an abortion as merely resisting the fetus's unjustified attack on her person.

Obviously the fetus is not like a willful attacker knowingly bent on murder or mayhem. But, despite the absence of much authority, it seems clear that the privilege of self-defense extends beyond a privilege to resist willful attacks. Surely we would recognize a privilege to defend oneself against an assailant one knew to be insane, even though such an assailant would be free of any criminal liability.[60] Indeed, I have no doubt that we would recognize a privilege to defend oneself against an attacker whose conduct could not even be regarded as volitional.[61] Suppose, for example, one found oneself cabined in a very small space with someone who was seized by wild convulsions while holding a sharp cleaver.

There are limits, of course, to the situations in which one can harm an innocent person to avoid harm to oneself. If someone begins to shoot at me, I cannot seize a completely uninvolved bystander and use him as a shield. If I find myself and another non-swimmer on a boat that is foundering, I cannot throw him off to save myself. The question is, where does abortion fall on this spectrum?

It may help to recall some facts about the early stages of fetal life. The fetus begins as a zygote, inside the woman but unattached. It is not until days later that it adheres to the uterine wall, then burrows into the endometrium, sprouts chorionic villi, and grapples onto the woman's insides. Once attached, it sends out its own hormone signals, which trigger the enormous changes pregnancy works on the woman's body.[62] The woman simply is not pregnant until the blastocyst latches on and commandeers the woman's metabolism. On this account, the fetus may seem

---

60. *See* ALI MODEL PENAL CODE § 3.04, comment 5 (Tent. Draft No. 8, 1958). The *Restatement (Second) of Torts* takes no position on this question. *See* RESTATEMENT (SECOND) OF TORTS §§ 64 (caveat), 66 (caveat) (1965).

61. *See* Kadish, *supra* note 22, at 68.

62. *See generally* J. GREENHILL & E. FRIEDMAN, *supra* note 7, at 25-29.

less "active" than the violent insane attacker or even than the
person in convulsions brandishing a cleaver, but the fetus is not
at all like an uninvolved bystander. The fetus is involved with the
woman carrying it, and it is the fetus's presence and nothing else
that threatens harm to the woman. Nor does the fetus seem like
the second occupant of a foundering boat. The difference, of
course, is that the woman *is* the boat. Perhaps the closest analogue of abortion would be a case where two persons are in an
ocean together without any boat at all, swimming or treading
water. One tires first and begins in a delirium to cling to the
other. Surely the one being clung to may disentangle himself and
save himself if he can.[63]

There may be some special wrinkles to self-defense against
innocent attackers. First, the *Restatement (Second) of Torts* suggests that there may be a duty to retreat before using force
against an innocent attacker in cases where retreat would not be
required if the attack were willful.[64] But there is never a duty to
retreat except where the harm threatened can be avoided by re-
treating. There is no escape from the burdens of pregnancy save
abortion. Second, there may be no privilege to defend oneself
against an innocent attacker if one has provoked or invited the
attack.[65] I have noted previously that (except in the case of rape)
the pregnant woman has done *something* which made her pregnancy more likely, indeed which made it possible. But at least if
the woman has attempted to avoid pregnancy, she can hardly be
said to have invited the fetus's attack any more than one invites
attack by walking near a mental hospital where one knows there
are some violent inmates. Finally, it could be suggested that even
if there is a privilege to defend oneself against an innocent attacker, there is no privilege to defend a third person against an
innocent attacker, since that involves choosing between two innocents without being impelled by the desire for self-preservation.
(The defense-of-third-persons problem arises because women
need the assistance of doctors to have safe abortions.) Suffice it
to say in response that after early vacillation, our law now generally recognizes privileges to defend third persons wherever they

---

63. Surely also the stronger swimmer may disentangle himself from the weaker, even
if he could carry the weaker swimmer to safety but only at the cost of serious injury to
himself caused by the extra exertion and prolonged exposure to stressful conditions.
64. RESTATEMENT (SECOND) OF TORTS § 64, comment b (1965).
65. *See* ALI MODEL PENAL CODE § 3.04(2)(b)(i) (Proposed Official Draft 1962).

are privileged to defend themselves.[66] Surely the asymmetry between the innocent attacker and the innocent attacked is reason
enough to allow third persons to intervene on behalf of the latter.
Surely if a woman can defend herself against the fetus, a doctor
may help.[67]

I have saved for last the most troublesome question raised by
the self-defense analysis. On this analysis, the woman is killing
the fetus. How does one answer the suggestion that, provided the
mother's life is not at stake, the privilege of self-defense is lost
because abortion involves excessive force?

Observe first that abortion does not involve force which is
excessive in the sense of being greater than necessary to avoid the
threatened harm. The woman cannot be spared the burdens of
pregnancy without killing the fetus. It might be suggested that if
the post-partum interests of the woman are ignored on the ground
that they can be avoided by giving the child up for adoption, then
the burdens of *late* pregnancy and delivery can be avoided without killing the fetus by removing the viable fetus during the last
trimester. But this is a dangerous operation for the woman, surely
involving a sufficient risk of death or serious bodily harm so that
she can defend herself against the prospect by removing the fetus
earlier. The question, then, is whether abortion is excessive in the
sense that the harm to the woman involved in a normal pregnancy and delivery is just not great enough to justify killing the
fetus.

According to the Model Penal Code, deadly force may be
used to defend oneself against death, serious bodily harm, rape,
or kidnapping.[68] We must consider whether, in cases where the
risk to the woman's life is minimal, the burdens of pregnancy and
childbirth can be assimilated either to serious bodily harm or to
rape. To my mind, there is a good case on both counts.

The Model Penal Code, although it talks of "serious bodily

---

66. *See* materials cited in note 5 *supra.*

67. Model Penal Code provisions making self-abortion a lesser crime than abortion-
on-others and forbidding aid-to-suicide even though suicide is not a crime. ALI MODEL
PENAL CODE §§ 230.3, 210.5 (Proposed Official Draft 1962), are *not* examples of rejecting
intervention by third parties even though the act of the "principal" is innocent. The
authors of the Model Penal Code plainly do not approve of either self-abortion or suicide.
They treat them as lesser crimes or as no crime at all for reasons of common sense and
efficient administration.

68. ALI MODEL PENAL CODE § 3.04 (2)(b) (Proposed Official Draft 1962). *Cf.*
RESTATEMENT (SECOND) OF TORTS § 65 (1965) (allowing the use of deadly force in self-
defense against a threat of death, serious bodily harm, or ravishment).

harm", never defines it. It does define "serious bodily injury", used in analogous contexts in such a way as to suggest that the phrases are intended to be equivalent, as "bodily injury which creates a substantial risk of death or which causes serious, permanent disfigurement, or protracted loss or impairment of the function of any bodily member or organ."[69] The comments to the *Restatement (Second) of Torts* also indicate that the permanent or protracted loss of function of any important member or organ counts as serious bodily harm.[70]

What a woman suffers from pregnancy is a protracted impairment of function of her body as a whole. It does not seem particularly plausible to view her as losing the function of *a* member or *an* organ. If it were important to identify *an* organ, we could specify several whose functioning is altered during pregnancy: the pituitary and the hypothalamus, for example. But the real point is that the woman's entire hormonal system and consequently her entire body are altered. Aside from the pain and discomfort of being pregnant, any activities that demand grace, flexibility, balance, coordination, muscle tone, or significant physical exertion are likely to be impossible for the last half of the pregnancy. Surely for an athlete or a dancer, the last four months of pregnancy would involve protracted loss of important bodily functions. And even for the woman who is not primarily an athlete or a dancer, sports or dancing or comparable physical activities may be very important.

It is interesting to note that one of the comments in the *Restatement (Second) of Torts* includes an illustration which strongly implies that a broken arm is serious bodily harm.[71] The illustration in question does not *say* that a broken arm is serious bodily harm, because the primary object of the illustration is not to define serious bodily harm but rather to indicate the legal effect of a mistake on the part of the attacker about the extent of harm he is likely to cause. Nor does the illustration specifically say that deadly force can be used to avoid the broken arm, since what force can be used depends in part on how much force is actually necessary in the circumstances. However, the illustration appears in connection with the basic section on the use of deadly force in self-defense, and it would lose its point if it were not intended that a broken arm should represent a higher level

---

69. ALI MODEL PENAL CODE § 210.0(3) (Proposed Official Draft 1962).
70. RESTATEMENT (SECOND) OF TORTS § 63, comment b (1965).
71. *Id.* § 65, Illustration 2.

of harm than the harm which justifies the use of non-deadly force. It seems to me that, so far as one can compare these things, a broken arm and pregnancy involve similar interferences with normal physical activity.

There will be those who suggest that pregnancy does not represent any "impairment" or "loss of function". This suggestion seems plausible because there is a sense in which pregnancy is "normal" while a broken arm is not. Even for a woman who wants to be pregnant, however, pregnancy entails a significant interference with normal activities. To say that pregnancy is "normal" in some sense, and even often desired, is not to say that it imposes no costs. Furthermore, as I have said before, the proper point of view in this discussion is the point of view of the woman who does *not* want to be pregnant. For her the pregnancy represents a major burden without redeeming benefits.

Two further objections may be made against my suggestion that an unwanted pregnancy is serious bodily harm justifying the use of deadly force in self-defense. First, it might be suggested that the force used to repel an attack must always be proportionate to the harm threatened, and that even if pregnancy constitutes serious bodily harm, it cannot be avoided at the cost of the death of the fetus. This objection ignores the fact that, in formulating many sorts of rules, our law tends to divide physical harms into two categories. One category is death-or-serious-bodily-injury. The other category is harms less than death-or-serious-bodily-injury. Whatever some people might like, our law does not take the position that death is in a class by itself.[72] Unquestionably one can kill in self-defense in order to avoid some harms less than death. Surely one can kill to avoid being made a quadriplegic. Surely one can kill to avoid being made a paraplegic. Surely one can kill to avoid being blinded. There is, of course, a line-drawing problem. But we frequently operate on the assumption that there is *one* line, between death-or-serious-bodily-injury and everything less.

It might still be said, however, that before something can count as serious bodily injury it must involve a substantial *risk* of death. It is probably true that most cases where an attacker threatens serious bodily injury involve a significant risk of death, and it may be that this is one reason why we assimilate serious

---

72. Our law does *sometimes* take the position that death is in a class by itself, as in formulating the law of murder. But it does not treat death as special in all contexts

bodily injury to death. But I think it is not true that before something can count as serious bodily harm it must involve a risk of death. The Model Penal Code and the *Restatement* both say quite explicitly that serious bodily injury is injury which involves *either* substantial risk of death *or* protracted loss of an important physical function. The broken arm illustration, noted above, involves no risk of death (and pregnancy does, though not a risk so substantial that I would argue pregnancy was serious bodily harm on that account alone).

Let us consider now whether pregnancy can be assimilated to rape, which is generally understood to justify the use of deadly force in self-defense. Why is rape so appalling that a woman may kill to avoid it? Being raped is likely to be painful. Given the habits of rapists as a class, being raped also involves a significant risk of death. Being raped involves an intrusion into the most intimate parts of the body. Being raped may create fears and anxieties that interfere with the victim's normal sexual relations. Finally, being raped is humiliating because the victim's body is being used, treated purely as a physical object.

Everything I have just said about rape is true also of pregnancy imposed by prohibitions on abortion. Pregnancy is painful. It involves a significant risk of death. It represents an intrusion into the most intimate parts of the woman's body. It is likely to interfere directly with sexual relations while it continues (during the latter part of the pregnancy), and the fear of pregnancy, if abortion is not available, is likely to make sexual relations less satisfactory even after the pregnancy is over. Finally, the woman who is compelled to carry a fetus she does not want is in effect being used as an incubator. She is being used as a physical object quite as much as the victim of rape.

There are differences, of course. Being raped may make a woman fearful every time she goes out into the street. Indeed, it may make her fearful *everywhere,* whether or not she is one of those victims so unfortunate as to be raped in their homes. Unwanted pregnancy, in contrast, makes the victim fearful only of sex. (Remember, however, that being fearful of sex may poison a great deal more of one's life than just the time spent in intercourse.) Also, it may be that the statistical risk of death associated with rape is greater than that associated with pregnancy. So far, I should say, we have mentioned differences of degree that do not amount to differences in kind for present purposes.

One who objects to the comparison of pregnancy with rape

is much more likely to think there is an intrinsic horror to rape that is absent from pregnancy. Does it not make a difference that the rapist, unlike the fetus, is a full-sized, visible, malevolent, *active* attacker?

At this point, it is difficult to know what to say. For a start, anyone who attempts simply to deny that there is an intrinsic horror to unwanted pregnancy lacks either imagination or compassion. Here both the woman's feelings of being used during the pregnancy and her dismay at the consequent choice between actually raising the child and giving it up for adoption are plainly relevant. Also, if rape involves a malevolent, active attacker who uses the victim's body, laws forbidding abortion involve the requisitioning of the woman's body by the state. Is it clearly worse to be treated as an object by one deviant individual than to be relegated to the status of a broodmare (for this is how the pregnant woman may well view the matter) by society at large?

Two final points. First, we are discussing, in this section, self-defense against an *innocent* attacker. The general rules of self-defense allow the use of deadly force to avoid serious bodily harm or rape, and I have argued previously that we would allow the use of deadly force to avoid serious bodily harm at the hands of an innocent attacker. But it might be thought that rape is different, that the injury from rape depends more on the hostility of the attacker. It might therefore be suggested that deadly force cannot be used on the innocent rapist or, by extension, on the fetus. There is something in this suggestion. Imagine a woman being raped by a man whom she knows is suffering from the insane delusion that she is his wife, who enjoys resisting and being taken by force. (We can make the attacker more sympathetic by supposing that he actually has such a wife and that his delusion concerns only the identity of the woman he is attacking.) Would this woman be permitted to kill her assailant, if necessary? Certainly the case is harder than that of the ordinary "sane" rapist. To my mind the case is less strong from the woman's point of view than the case of pregnancy imposed by laws against abortion. Yet I believe that if the case arose a privilege to use deadly force would be found.

Finally, it might be suggested that all the normal rules about self-defense assume the impossibility of deliberation — that, at least to the extent these rules allow deadly force to be used for any other purpose than to avoid death, they represent a concession to the way imperfect human beings will behave in emergencies. The fetus is unique among "attackers" in that it allows its victim time to reflect; and it could be argued that the woman should decide, on reflection, to submit to the fetus's intrusion and the attendant costs so long as her own life is not at stake. I have no decisive response to this argument, but I do not find it convincing. I admit that the justification for the use of deadly force in response to non-deadly force seems weaker when there is time to reflect. On the other hand, comparison of the law of self-defense with the law of voluntary manslaughter and of duress makes it clear that the right of self-defense is not *merely* a concession to predictable human weakness. The law of self-defense is shaped in part by the notion that there is an asymmetry between attacker and attacked (even when the attacker is innocent) which justifies the attacked in protecting himself or herself even in some cases where the cost to the attacker is greater than the harm from which the attacked is spared.

III. THE CONSTITUTIONAL ARGUMENT

I have spent quite a number of pages trying to show that if we viewed abortion as a problem in samaritan law, or if we viewed it as a problem in the law of self-defense, abortion would be allowed. It is time now to say more about the constitutional argument I think my observations support. I shall treat explicitly only the constitutional argument suggested by the discussion of samaritan law. An argument that is similar in outline could be based on the law of self-defense, but I find the samaritan argument more persuasive. Enough of what I say about the samaritan argument would carry over to the self-defense argument that a separate treatment of the latter is unnecessary. Having spelled out the constitutional argument, I shall comment briefly on two further topics: (1) the advantages of my argument over the Court's actual argument in *Roe,* and (2) the consequences of my argument for other problems in the general area.

A. *The Nature of the Argument*

John Hart Ely has rightly insisted that constitutional arguments ought to be based on values that can be inferred from the text of the Constitution, the thinking of the Framers, or the structure of our national government.[73] The argument against laws

---

73. Ely, *The Wages of Crying Wolf: A Comment on Roe v. Wade,* 82 YALE L.J. 920 (1973).

prohibiting abortion is based on three such values: non-subordination, freedom from physical invasion, and equal protection. Before I specify the precise nature of the argument, let me say a few words about the first two of the values just mentioned.

The non-subordination value that is implicit in the bad-samaritan principle of the common law is also at the core of the thirteenth amendment. The thirteenth amendment speaks not merely of slavery, but of "involuntary servitude". In numerous cases,[74] the Supreme Court plainly viewed peonage as a form of involuntary servitude, and not just as a vestige of slavery which Congress may prohibit on a theory like that of *Jones v. Mayer.*[75] The objection to peonage is best summed up in one of the early decisions, by then Associate Justice Hughes: "The plain intention [of the thirteenth amendment] was to abolish slavery of whatever name and form . . .; to make labor free, by prohibiting that control by which the personal service of one man is disposed of or coerced for another's benefit which is the essence of involuntary servitude."[76] Unwilling pregnancy is not slavery in the fullest sense, nor does it involve labor of the sort Hughes was referring to; but it certainly involves the disposition and coercion of the (intensely) personal service of one "man" for another's benefit.[77]

The second value, freedom from physical invasion or imposed physical pain or hardship, is embodied in the eighth amendment and also plainly counts among those fundamental values of our society which are traditionally subsumed under fifth and fourteenth amendment due process. The due process clauses are vague, and it might be objected that to say something is subsumed under the due process clauses is not really to name a connection with any recognized constitutional value at all. That may be true in some cases, where the claim that something comes under the due process clauses is a novel one. But there is nothing novel about the claim that the due process clauses speak to the

74. *E.g.,* Taylor v. Georgia, 315 U.S. 25 (1942); Bailey v. Alabama, 219 U.S. 219 (1911).
75. Jones v. Alfred H. Mayer Co., 392 U.S. 409 (1968).
76. Bailey v. Alabama, 219 U.S. 219, 241 (1911).
77. Peonage is not less objectionable when it is "voluntarily" entered into. Pollock v. Williams, 322 U.S. 4, 24 (1944). Nor is peonage less "involuntary servitude" because it is not a permanent status. (Peonage contracts apparently tended to be open-ended, the effective term being "until the laborer pays back his advance". In *Pollock,* the Court overturned a conviction secured less than three months after the laborer received his advance. In Bailey v. Alabama, 219 U.S. 219 (1911), there was a definite term of one year.) On both counts, compare an unwanted pregnancy which the woman is forbidden to termi nate.

matter of physical maltreatment.[78]

It may be that an adequate constitutional argument against abortion statutes could be based on these two values alone. The non-subordination value is not enough to prevent all impositions of duties to aid, as many of the exceptions to the bad-samaritan principle, involving trivial impositions, make clear. Similarly the physical integrity value is not enough to prevent all physical invasions, nor even all serious physical invasions, as the example of the draft and perhaps the example of medically proven and carefully supervised aversive therapies make clear. But the woman who is prevented from terminating her pregnancy can appeal simultaneously to both of these values. There is no other case, I believe, in which the law imposes comparable physical invasion and hardship as an obligation of samaritanism. We might plausibly suggest that imposing such invasion and hardship for the benefit of a third person is flatly inconsistent with our nation's fundamental traditions.

There are two difficulties with this suggestion. First, I am not certain that laws imposing comparable impositions more uniformly would be, or should be, held unconstitutional. If a state altered the bad-samaritan principle by statute, creating an obligation to undertake even physically dangerous rescues, I would be disinclined to say that the new statute was unconstitutional. Nor am I confident that the Court would invalidate it. Similarly, if a state passed a statute requiring parents to donate needed organs to their children (where this would not endanger the life of the parent), I am not certain that the statute would be, or should be, held unconstitutional. If these hypothetical statutes *would* be held unconstitutional (and I am sure some readers will think they would be), then statutes forbidding abortion should be held unconstitutional for the same reasons. But if these hypothetical statutes would not be unconstitutional, then abortion statutes cannot be held unconstitutional just on the basis of the values so far considered.

The second difficulty with the argument under consideration (to the effect that, equal protection aside, laws forbidding abortion violate our fundamental traditions with regard to non-subordination and physical integrity) is the fact that statutes forbidding abortion had, until *Roe*, been on the books in all states for many years. This history does not conclude the constitutional

---

78. *See, e.g.*, Rochin v. California, 342 U.S. 165 (1952).

question. On occasion, the Court has overturned a great deal of history. But the Court has rarely overturned as much history all at once as it did in *Roe v. Wade.* That surely ought to give us pause.

I do not say, of course, that history is entirely on the side of those who would defend abortion statutes. The values of non-subordination and freedom from physical invasion are very much a part of our history. Although arguments nominally based on our "fundamental traditions" often have little to do with our traditions, fundamental or otherwise, that is not true of the "fundamental traditions" argument I have suggested.

On the other hand, there is no logical reason why our traditions forbidding subordination of one individual to another, or forbidding physical invasions, should not recognize exceptions. It is not implausible to suggest that one of the exceptions our traditions recognize is for laws prohibiting abortion. That is why I do not find the pure "fundamental traditions" argument sufficient.

We need to bring in the equal protection value. We need to argue that even if those parts of our tradition which forbid subordination or physical invasion have historically included an exception for abortion laws, the exception is impermissible. It creates an inequality that is inconsistent with an even more fundamental part of our tradition, reflected in the equal protection clause and the due process clause of the fifth amendment. It is no accident, I think, that the greatest inroads on history (that is, the most sweeping invalidations of existing legal arrangements) have come in equal protection decisions like *Reynolds v. Sims*[79] and *Brown v. Board of Education.*[80] For all of our failures in the pursuit of equality, and for all of our (justifiable) uncertainty about just what equality means, there are few values, perhaps none, with deeper roots in our traditions or a firmer hold on our imaginations than the value of equal treatment under law.

Some readers may doubt that the value underlying the equal protection clause is relevant to the abortion problem. Anti-abortion statutes do not look like the sort of statute that normally raises equal protection issues. The state does not draw a line between blacks and whites, or between women and men, and treat the two classes differently. The state does not even draw a line between optometrists and opticians and say the former may

79. 377 U.S. 533 (1964).
80. 347 U.S. 483 (1954).

offer services which the latter may not.[81] The state simply says that no one may have an abortion. It is true that only some people want abortions. But so long as the state denies abortions to everyone who wants them, there does not seem to be a problem of the equal protection variety.

To see the equal protection problem, we must look at abortion in a broader context. Life in society produces many situations in which one individual is in a position to give needed aid to another individual. That is to say, life in society offers many opportunities to be a good or bad samaritan. The objection to an anti-abortion statute is that it picks out certain potential samaritans, namely women who want abortions, and treats them in a way that is at odds with the law's treatment of other potential samaritans. Women who want abortions are required to give aid in circumstances where closely analogous potential samaritans are not. And they are required to give aid of a *kind* and an *extent* that is required of no other potential samaritan.[82]

The preceding paragraph, sketchy as it is, is enough to reveal that the equal protection argument I am suggesting is nonstandard in two respects. First, I do not claim that the situation of the woman who wants an abortion has any perfect analogue among the situations of other potential samaritans. The abortion case is unique in requiring us to view what is in some sense an act as being, for purposes of samaritan law, an omission. The abortion case also differs from every other case except that of parenthood in that the woman has, by her prior behavior, contributed to the creation of the fetus which needs her assistance.

I argued in the course of the discussion of samaritan law that the woman seeking an abortion falls somewhere on a spectrum of eligibility for compulsion to be a samaritan, a spectrum that runs from the totally uninvolved bystander at one end to the parent at the other. I do not assert that the pregnant woman is placed under greater burdens than other potential samaritans who are precisely as eligible for compulsion. It is not clear just where on the spectrum the pregnant woman belongs. Rather, I suggest that the burdens imposed on the pregnant woman are out of line with the general treatment of other potential samaritans *all along the spectrum*. There are some cases in which other potential samari-

---

81. *See* Williamson v. Lee Optical Co., 348 U.S. 483 (1955).

82. Recall that the draft, which might seem to provide a counterexample, is not a true samaritan case at all.

tans who might be viewed as less eligible for compulsion are none-theless compelled. But the burdens they are compelled to assume are incomparably less than the burdens of pregnancy. Parents, who are the most eligible potential samaritans, are placed under heavy burdens. But even these burdens are not physically inva-sive in the way that pregnancy is, and no state imposes on parents (or, I think, would impose if a case came up) the burdens that would be most comparable to the burdens of pregnancy, such as the burdens of a genuinely dangerous rescue or of compulsory organ donation.[83]

I said earlier that there were two respects in which my equal protection argument is non-standard. One respect, which I have been discussing, is the lack of any precise analogue for the preg-nant woman. The other respect, which is related but distinct, is that the argument goes so far afield for its comparisons. Laws which classify on the basis of race or sex, or which draw lines between opticians and optometrists or between advertising on a truck for the owner's business and advertising for someone else's,[84] suggest equal protection issues to anyone. But most peo-ple, unprompted, do not connect the abortion problem and the problem of samaritanism. It may seem that courts should not look so far afield. There are enough equal protection problems presented on the faces of statutes without looking for problems in imaginative comparisons. As Justice Douglas said in *Railway Express Agency v. New York*, "[T]he fact that New York City sees fit to eliminate from traffic this kind of distraction [certain advertising on the sides of trucks] but does not touch even

---

83. As a matter of logic, it might seem that the strongest part of my argument is the comparison of the woman seeking an abortion with the parent. Should I not simply say that the woman seeking an abortion, who is less eligible for compulsion than the parent, is subjected to greater burdens (or at least greater burdens of the particular physically invasive sort that are specially disfavored) and leave it at that, eschewing comparison with any other potential samaritans? There are three reasons for not doing this. First, the most telling comparisons between the woman seeking an abortion and the parent are in a sense hypothetical. I *assume* that parents are not required to rescue their children from burning buildings or to donate organs. Certainly there are no statutes or cases imposing such obligations. But then, so far as I know, there are no statutes or cases specifically rejecting such obligations either. There is simply no explicit authority. Second, parents do bear heavy burdens, of a general sort, even if they are subjected to less in the way of physical invasion than the pregnant woman. Finally, since the pregnant woman is not precisely analogous to any other potential samaritan, but is somewhere in the middle of the spectrum of eligibility for compulsion, it seems foolish to drop from the argument the fact that in virtually all cases where obligations of samaritanism are imposed, the burdens are trivial.

84. *See* Railway Express Agency v. New York, 336 U.S. 106 (1949).

greater ones in a different category, such as the vivid displays on Times Square, is immaterial. It is no requirement of equal protection that all evils of the same genus be eradicated or none at all."[85] I shall refer to the notion that courts should not concern themselves, in equal protection analysis, with comparisons so far-ranging as that between the pregnant woman and other potential samaritans as the "too far afield" objection to my argument.

We now have before us two questions: (1) What do we make of the "too far afield" objection? In other words, should the Court even consider an argument which proceeds by comparing the pregnant woman and other potential samaritans? (2) If the argument merits consideration, does it justify the conclusion that laws prohibiting abortion are unconstitutional? It might seem that the first question is logically prior to the second and should be disposed of first. Whatever the logic of the matter, the considerations relevant to the two questions overlap considerably. Because the second question is of a more familiar sort than the first, I propose to begin with the second question. Let us hold the "too far afield" objection in abeyance and attack the substantive issue.

If there were a non-controversial general theory of equal protection, all we would need to do at this point would be to apply the general theory to the case of abortion. Unfortunately, there is no non-controversial theory. Even more unfortunately, I do not have a general theory to suggest. Still, given the uncertain state of equal protection theory, it seems desirable to say something on a general level before turning to the specific problem at hand.

What I propose to do is to describe some features I think an acceptable general theory is likely to have. My list of general features will be in some degree controversial, but I think it will establish enough common ground between me and a sufficient number of readers that I can then proceed to a meaningful discussion of the abortion problem. I would emphasize that little of what I shall say on the general level is original. Nor will it be necessary for the reader to accept everything in my general remarks to find elements of the specific argument about abortion persuasive. Finally, I would observe that within the tolerance of this schematic presentation, I think I shall be describing both what courts ought to be doing in the equal protection area and what the Supreme Court is doing. (What the Court is doing is

---

85. 336 U.S. 106, 110 (1949).

somewhat different, in my view, from what the majority of Justices say they are doing.)

For a start, I approve of the "new equal protection" to this extent: I think it is appropriate to subject different laws to different levels of judicial "scrutiny". Actually, to say one law deserves more scrutiny than another may mean two quite different things. It may mean that judicial resources are more appropriately spent in reviewing the law which deserves more scrutiny, or it may mean that that law should be held to a higher standard of justification in terms of its tendency to promote significant state interests. The Court has generally concentrated on the second meaning, ignoring the first so far as theory goes. (They have not ignored it in their traditionally unexplained decisions regarding choice of cases.) Ordinarily, considerations that tend to justify heightened scrutiny in the sense of greater judicial attention will also tend to justify it in the sense of requiring a stronger justification for the law, and vice versa. But there may be some situations in which special judicial attention is called for, but not a requirement of special justification. As it turns out, this distinction between different ways of giving special scrutiny is of limited relevance to the present problem. I shall have scant occasion (though I shall have some occasion) to mention the distinction in what follows.

Although I accept the idea of different levels of scrutiny, I do not think the Court's official "two-tier" model is satisfactory. I agree with those Justices and commentators who think the Court is not actually applying such a model.[86] Instead of regarding all classifications as either suspect or innocent, the Court seems to perceive a range of classifications of varying degrees of suspectness. Race is thoroughly suspect, along with national origin or ethnicity. Sex and illegitimacy are somewhat suspect, but not as suspect as race. Alienage is probably still somewhat suspect, though the question is confused by the federalism aspects. Similarly, there is a range of rights — some more fundamental, some less. The right to vote is fundamental, but not quite so fundamental is the right to vote by absentee ballot.[87] The right of a criminal

---

86. *E.g.*, San Antonio Indep. School Dist. v. Rodriguez, 411 U.S. 1, 70-137 (1973) (Marshall, J., dissenting); Craig v. Boren, 429 U.S. 190, 211-14 (1976) (Stevens, J., concurring); Gunther, *The Supreme Court, 1971 Term — Foreword: In Search of Evolving Doctrine on a Changing Court: A Model for a New Equal Protection*, 86 HARV. L. REV. 1 (1972)

87. *See* McDonald v. Board of Election Commrs., 394 U.S. 802 (1969). *But see* O'Brien v. Skinner, 414 U.S. 524 (1974).

defendant to certain assistance in his defense is fundamental. The right to education is apparently fundamental up to a point, but not fundamental or certainly less fundamental thereafter.[88] Marriage and divorce seem both to be "somewhat" fundamental.[89]

Although I do not endorse all the Court's decisions about which classifications are suspect (and to what degree) and about which rights are fundamental (and to what degree), I regard the general approach the Court seems to be following as the correct one. I approve of "variable suspectness", "variable fundamentality", and consequent "variable scrutiny".

I do *not* think the eventual scrutiny should be just a matter of vetting the law in issue for an appropriate degree of "goodness of fit" between means and ends. We could build a theory in which the suspectness of classifications and the fundamentality of rights were appealed to only as the basis for selecting an appropriate level of review for the "goodness of fit". But that is not the sort of theory I have in mind. The mere use of suspect classifications imposes costs. Any impairment of fundamental rights is a cost. Differential impairment of different persons' fundamental rights is a special cost. These costs must be justified by what is achieved by the law under review. A law that is perfectly designed to achieve an insufficiently important end is still unacceptable.

It may seem that what I have sketched so far is a "balancing" approach to equal protection. We throw into the scales on the individual's side the costs imposed by the use of suspect classifications or by the impairment of fundamental rights. These costs will of course vary with the degree of suspectness of the classification or the degree of fundamentality of the right involved. We throw into the scales on the government's side the benefits achieved by the law, which depend upon the weightiness of the state interest and the degree to which the law promotes the interest. Then we "balance".

This sketch of the process is not entirely off the mark, but it is incomplete or misleading in two respects. First, and most important, talk of balancing suggests that *any* interests of the individual are eligible to be labeled "fundamental" and put into the scales against the law. One of the unsatisfactory aspects of the

---

88. *See* San Antonio Indep. School Dist. v. Rodriguez, 411 U.S. 1, 36-37 (1973).

89. As to marriage, *compare* Zablocki v. Redhail, 434 U.S. 374 (1978), *with* Califano v. Jobst, 434 U.S. 47 (1977); as to divorce, *compare* Boddie v. Connecticut, 401 U.S. 371 (1971), *with* Sosna v. Iowa, 419 U.S. 393 (1975).

Court's opinion in *Roe v. Wade* (which is not, of course, an equal protection opinion but which does deal with "fundamental rights") is that it lists a variety of interests belonging to a pregnant woman that laws against abortion may impair, but it gives very little attention to the question of which of these interests are actually protected by the Constitution. Under the scheme I have in mind, rights would be regarded as fundamental or classifications as suspect only if the rights in question were protected, or the classifications disfavored, by the Constitution or by constitutionally based values as developed in our legal tradition. (Incidentally, it seems to me that if we try to identify fundamental rights and suspect classifications by reference to our constitutional tradition, it is almost inevitable that we should end up with "variable fundamentality" and "variable suspectness". It would be a poor tradition indeed, and not ours, which recognized only two degrees of importance of rights, or only two degrees of acceptability of classifications.)

The second reason the "balancing" sketch above is misleading is that it suggests that once the Court has decided to take an equal protection question seriously, there is no further room for deference to the legislature. Obviously deference to legislative judgment is not something that is easily defined or quantified, but I think some deference is appropriate even in cases where specially protected rights or specially disfavored classifications are involved.

I prefer to think of my suggested approach to equal protection as a "reasonable American legislature test". According to this test, an inequality of treatment imposed by the law is unconstitutional if and only if it is one that a reasonable American legislature could not countenance. The reference to *reasonableness* (which is something more than mere rationality) captures the balancing aspects of the approach, the role of specially protected rights and specially disfavored classifications. The reference to the reasonable *American* legislature reminds us that decisions about what rights and classifications raise special problems are to be made on the basis of our constitutional tradition. Finally, the formulation of the test in terms of the behavior of a reasonable American *legislature* emphasizes that even when dealing with fundamental rights or suspect classifications, legislatures must have some leeway.

Labels, for all their usefulness, can be misleading. Although I have attempted to explain my choice of the phrase "reasonable

American legislature test", there is some danger that the phrase will create precisely the wrong impression. I do *not* suggest that the Court should try to decide what it would do if it were the legislature. The question is not what the "ideally reasonable" legislature *would* do, but rather what a "humanly reasonable" legislature (steeped in and concerned for our national traditions) *could* do. A law is constitutional, under this test, if a reasonable American legislature *could* pass it or fail to repeal it. The relationship I envision between the Court and the legislature is somewhat like the relationship between a trial judge and trial jury.

Another aspect of the theory I am now outlining deserves mention. Legislative *purpose* is important. The Court may have gone slightly too far in its unqualified pronouncements about the importance of purpose in recent cases,[90] but basically it is on the right track. Suspect classifications are suspect in considerable part because of the "badge of inferiority" aspect, and because they are specially resented. A classification that is neutral (nonsuspect) on its face but that produces effects significantly describable in terms of some non-neutral (suspect) classification does *not* have the same "badge of inferiority" aspect unless the apparently neutral classification was chosen by the legislature with a bad purpose, that is, as a surrogate for an impermissible classification.

Justice Stevens is right to remind us that bad effects are often the best evidence of bad purpose.[91] And Paul Brest is right to suggest that *indifference* to bad effects may sometimes be so extreme as to count as bad purpose.[92] (This is especially likely to be the case where what is in issue is the legislature's failure to repeal or modify a scheme that was adopted with innocent purposes, but that now produces bad effects.) But as a general proposition, where the only objection to a statute is that it has bad effects (in terms of suspect classifications), the legislature's innocent purpose ought to protect the law from being held unconstitutional.

This treatment of purpose is also suggested, to my mind, by the label of the "reasonable American legislature test". It may be that an ideal legislature would never pass a law that had a dispar-

---

90. Washington v. Davis, 426 U.S. 229 (1976); Village of Arlington Heights v. Metropolitan Hous. Dev. Corp., 429 U.S. 252 (1977); Personnel Admr. v. Feeney, 99 S. Ct. 228 (1979).

91. Washington v. Davis, 426 U.S. 229, 253-54 (Stevens, J., concurring).

92. Brest, *The Supreme Court, 1975 Term — Foreword: In Defense of the Anti-discrimination Principle*, 90 HARV. L. REV. 1, 14-15 (1976).

ate impact on a class protected against purposeful discrimination
without weighing the special costs such a disparate impact
would impose by aggravating historic disadvantages. But unless
the disparate impact is extreme, it is enough for the humanly
reasonable legislature to avoid, or to weigh carefully, the explicit
use of suspect classifications and to refrain from using apparently
neutral classifications with the *purpose* of discriminating.[93]

So much for my outline of an equal protection theory. The
approach I suggest will strike many readers as unacceptably
"unprincipled". I concede that the "reasonable American legislature test" does not lend itself to mechanical application. On the
other hand, it should not be taken as a license for unbridled
judicial interference with legislative decisions. The court applying this test should be constrained both by attention to our tradition and by deference to legislative decisions. Those constraints
can be real even though they are not precisely definable nor their
effects on judicial decision precisely measurable. Furthermore,
within the context of a fairly loose general theory, it is still possible for judges to tell us a great deal about why individual cases
strike them as they do, and why different cases strike them differently. Candid discussion by judges along these lines may tell us
more about both the judges' thinking and our traditions than
discussions concerning the application of some purportedly mechanical test. The "reasonable American legislature test" may do
little more than emphasize that there is no mechanical test in the
equal protection area. But it is better to have a vague "test" that
captures the right idea than a precise test that captures some
wrong idea.

---

93. Just as legislative purpose is relevant, so is legislative process. That is, whether
a law is constitutional may in some cases appropriately turn on what the legislature
thought about in passing it, and on how hard they thought about it. There are at least
two reasons for this. First, a legislative judgment about what is required by our constitutional tradition is entitled to some deference. How much deference the judgment is entitled to in any particular case depends in part on how thoroughly considered it was (if it
was made explicitly at all). Second, and probably more important, the legislature is
entitled to rely on any empirical proposition that an American legislature could reasonably accept. The fact that a legislature has acted on a particular empirical proposition is
always *evidence* that a reasonable legislature could accept it. But the strength of this
evidence varies with the amount and nature of the consideration given by the legislature
to the empirical proposition in question. Although I think there are probably objections
to the legislative process behind many abortion statutes — particularly regarding the
extent to which significant constitutional interests have been overlooked — I shall not rely
on process arguments in this essay. Deficiencies of process can be cured. But even careful
legislative reconsideration would not answer the objections to abortion laws detailed
below.

It is time to return to the abortion problem and to explain why abortion laws are specially problematic and why, ultimately, they should be held unconstitutional. In the process I shall expand implicitly on some of the features of my general approach to equal protection. I shall continue to hold the "too far afield" objection (the objection that my comparison of the pregnant woman to other potential samaritans ranges too far afield for an equal protection argument) in abeyance for the present.

First, it is important that the inequality of treatment between pregnant women and other potential samaritans touches on the constitutional values of non-subordination and freedom from physical invasion. A woman who is denied an abortion is compelled to serve the fetus and to suffer physical invasion, pain, and hardship. As already noted, it can be argued that the Constitution prohibits this imposition outright, without regard to any inequality of treatment. I have said that I do not find this argument persuasive. But the fact that such an argument can plausibly be made surely means that any inequality of treatment we can point to becomes harder to justify. Inequalities with regard to interests given specific constitutional protection are likely to be more costly, in terms of our community value structure, to the relatively disadvantaged parties than inequalities involving other interests. For this reason, and also because of the apparent hypocrisy of guaranteeing a full measure of the constitutionally sanctioned interest for some people but not for others, inequalities with regard to such interests are likely to be specially resented by the disadvantaged parties. If these inequalities are both specially costly and specially resented, that is surely some reason for the Court to look at them carefully and to require special justification for them.

I have indicated that subjective resentment on the part of the individuals disadvantaged is a significant element in equal protection analysis. It might be suggested that even women who want abortions do not resent the specific inequality (between the treatment of them and other potential samaritans) that I focus on. There is some truth in this. The precise comparison between pregnant women and other potential samaritans is not a standard one. On the other hand, it is clear that there is a great deal of resentment among women of laws forbidding abortion. (That many women do not feel this resentment does not strike me as important. Many women *do* feel it.) Furthermore, it is clear that a good deal of the resentment is based on a feeling among women that they are being used in a way no one else, or almost no one else, in our society is ever used. The perception on the part of women that they are being used — more specifically that their bodies are being taken over by the state for the benefit of third persons — in a way which is at odds with our society's general practices is sufficient, to my mind, to constitute resentment of the inequality I rely on.

Other reasons for the Court to give the abortion problem special attention are related to the suspect classification idea. Only women need abortions. Parents of both sexes might be required to undertake physically dangerous rescues, or to donate organs, and people of both sexes find themselves in most of the standard potential-samaritan situations. But the one potential samaritan who is singled out for specially burdensome treatment is a potential samaritan who must, given human physiology, be female. Why is this important?

First, any inequality that flows from an unchosen and unalterable characteristic is likely to be specially resented. It also works against the idea, deeply rooted in our culture, that people ought to be masters of their own destinies, at least within the limits of legally acceptable behavior that apply to everyone. Since pregnancy happens only to women, and since no one has any choice about whether to be a woman, susceptibility to pregnancy (and to being in the position of wanting an abortion) is a nonchosen characteristic. (It is not an unalterable characteristic, since a woman might have herself sterilized, but this method of altering the characteristic itself involves a significant physical invasion.)

It might be objected that even if susceptibility to pregnancy is an unchosen characteristic, pregnancy itself is not, and that laws attaching unpleasant consequences to pregnancy therefore do not interfere with women's controlling their own destinies. Even if such laws are resented, the objection continues, the resentment is unjustified. Now, many pregnancies are not chosen in the fullest sense. They are the result of accident, of carelessness, or whatever. I assume this is true of the vast majority of pregnancies which the women involved want to terminate by abortion. What the objector presumably means, when he says that pregnancy is not unchosen, is that the woman *could* avoid pregnancy (leaving rape out of account) by eschewing sexual intercourse. This is true. Women could avoid becoming pregnant. But the only method of avoiding pregnancy with certainty requires, for many people, extraordinary self-denial. The availability of sexual abstinence as a means of avoiding pregnancy does

not, to my mind, eliminate the force of the suggestion that pregnancy is often sufficiently "unchosen" so that laws specially
disadvantaging pregnant women limit women's control of their
lives, are justifiably resented, and deserve more-than-minimal
judicial attention.[94]

Another reason for heightened equal protection scrutiny of
abortion laws is that women (and perhaps pregnant women especially) have suffered from a history of discrimination in our society. They have suffered not just from occasional laws counter
to their interests, but from an extensive pattern of discriminatory
laws and social practices. This makes them suspicious and resentful (and justifiably suspicious and resentful) of any particular
inequality, however it is supposed to be justified. It is certainly
worth investing some extra judicial resources in review of laws
that impose inequalities tied to sex in order to allay this suspicion
and resentment. It is probably worth requiring more-than-
minimal substantive justification for such laws, both to minimize
resentment and to avoid adding to the continuing burdens resulting from past injustices whose effects have not been entirely elim-
inated. An inequality that would be tolerable against a background of equal treatment may be intolerable when it is an extra
burden imposed on top of other disadvantages.[95]

It is worth adding that, at the level of statistical generalities,
the women who suffer most from prohibitions on abortion are
likely to be the same women who have suffered most from other
sorts of discrimination or injustice. I have in mind both poor
women and women who want to pursue careers outside the home.
These two groups of women have suffered from distinct but overlapping injustices in our past, and they have probably both suffered more than the adequately-provided-for woman whose life
has focused primarily on her family.

It might be suggested that the "suspect classification" elements in the argument just presented should all be discounted
because there is (or may be) no legislative *purpose* to disadvan-
tage women. I have indicated previously that innocent purpose is
relevant principally in cases where we are confronted with bad
effects of a classification which is not suspect on its face. Now the
inequality created by abortion laws is not expressly an inequality
between women and men. It is between pregnant persons and

---

94. The claim that pregnancy is "unchosen" for present purposes is refined somewhat
in the discussion at pages 1633-34 *infra*.
95. *See* Brest, *supra* note 92, at 10-11.

others. But pregnancy is much more closely connected with sex, both empirically and in our habits of thought, than are, say, educational qualifications[96] or wealth[97] with race. Classification in terms of pregnancy is sufficiently like classification explicitly in terms of sex, especially when we remember the costs of definitively avoiding pregnancy, that classification in terms of pregnancy should be regarded as significantly suspect regardless of legislative purpose.

Of course, to say that classification in terms of pregnancy should be regarded as significantly suspect is not to say that all laws disadvantaging pregnant women should be held unconstitutional. For example, I tend to think that *Geduldig v. Aiello,*[98] in which a California disability insurance plan for private employees disabled by an injury or illness not covered by workmen's compensation was upheld by the Court even though the plan excluded normal pregnancies from coverage, was rightly decided. Without discussing *Geduldig* extensively, it may help to illustrate the approach to equal protection I have in mind if I explain why a reasonable American legislature could regard the scheme at issue in *Geduldig* quite differently from the statute at issue in *Roe.*

First, no established constitutional interest was impaired in *Geduldig.* The supposed "right to procreate" is not inferrable from the text, historical background, or structure of the Constitution. In this respect it differs from the interests in non-subordination and in freedom from physical pain and invasion. Even if we say that there is a constitutionally protected interest in procreation (citing the ninth amendment, the fourteenth amendment privileges and immunities clause, and *Skinner v. Oklahoma*[99]), that interest is not impaired by denying disability benefits in connection with pregnancy in the same way that the interests in non-subordination and physical integrity are impaired by laws forbidding abortion.

Furthermore, the choice to be pregnant is much more likely to be a fully voluntary choice in the *Geduldig* context than in the abortion context. Most women who want abortions did not want to be pregnant in the first place. But I assume it is still the case that most children in this country are wanted, which is to say that

96. *See* Washington v. Davis, 426 U.S. 229 (1976).
97. *See* Village of Arlington Heights v. Metropolitan Hous. Dev. Corp., 429 U.S. 252 (1977).
98. 417 U.S. 484 (1974).
99. 315 U.S. 535 (1942).

most women who are pregnant and do *not* want an abortion *did* want to be pregnant. To be sure, I am now generalizing. I am ignoring cases such as the woman who did not want to be pregnant but who rejects abortion for moral reasons. But the likelihood that the relevant pregnancy is voluntary is very different in *Roe* and *Geduldig*. Also, it is more appropriate to rely on generalizations, even if we know there are exceptions, when we are justifying features of an insurance scheme that allocates monetary benefits among a group of employees, than to do so when we are justifying direct state interference with individual decisions. To a considerable extent the real question in *Geduldig* is whether those employees who do not want (additional) children shall subsidize, indirectly, those who do.

This discussion of the difference in "voluntariness" of the pregnancies involved in *Roe* and in *Geduldig* suggests a refinement of the claim that classification in terms of pregnancy should be assimilated to classifications in terms of sex. Perhaps we should say that classifications in terms of pregnancy are just as suspect as classifications in terms of sex for purposes of justifying the expenditure of resources in judicial review, but that whether they are as suspect for purposes of raising the level of required substantive justification for the law in question depends on just how "voluntary" are the pregnancies affected.

Before I attempt to say where all of this leaves us, let me point out an argument I have *not* made. I have not suggested that laws against abortion deserve special judicial scrutiny because women are politically powerless or because most legislators are male. That argument is not persuasive in this context. Both sides in the abortion controversy have been well organized politically. Further, many of the opponents of abortion are women. This is simply not an issue to which the partial exclusion of women from the political process is relevant. Generally speaking, the reasons I have suggested for special judicial concern about abortion do not depend on the political powerlessness of women as a class. On the contrary, they show why legislators should not be able to hide behind the claim that because many women oppose abortion the sex-specificity of the burdens of unwanted pregnancy is irrelevant.

It is time to take stock. In view of the considerations I have mentioned, could a reasonable American legislature pass or fail to repeal a statute forbidding abortion? I think the answer is "No." I am certain that most legislatures would defend laws against abortion on the ground that they protect human life (or

potential life). This is certainly the most promising defense of
such laws. But, in the context of our legal system, the defense is
inadequate. The inequality between the treatment of pregnant
women and the treatment of other potential samaritans who are
not required to undertake burdens (often very much smaller burdens) in order to save life is too great. The inequality trenches on
two distinct constitutionally protected interests — the interest in
non-subordination and the interest in freedom from serious physical invasion. In addition, the inequality disadvantages a class
that is defined by a non-chosen characteristic (whether sex or
unwanted pregnancy) and that has suffered from a history of
discrimination. This is more than any reasonable American legislature would tolerate.

An argument that might be made on the other side runs as
follows: As a society we simply discount the pain and invasion of
pregnancy, as compared to other pains of comparable intensity
or invasions of similar extent. We view pregnancy as special,
either because so many women undertake it voluntarily, or because it is a "natural" part of the process of continuing the
species, or both.

I do not deny that there is a tendency to view pregnancy as
special and to devalue accordingly the pain and invasion it involves. I suggest that this tendency is one that reasonable American legislators, looking squarely at the question properly formulated, would overcome. The fact that many women willingly undertake the burdens of pregnancy, for reasons of their own, is no
reason to discount the burdens as they affect women to whom
they are unwelcome. Similarly, the fact that some women must
bear children if the nation is to continue is no reason to impose
the burdens of pregnancy on women who are unwilling, so long
as there is an adequate supply of volunteers.

It might also be suggested that a reasonable American legislature would remember and be swayed by a fact that has somehow been pushed from center stage in my analysis, namely, that
a *life* is at stake.[100] This objection depends on a common assumption that preserving life is the highest value in our tradition. But
the assumption is either stated too broadly or simply wrong. The
equal protection argument I have made about abortion could not
be made were it not that in many *other* cases involving potential
samaritans our legal system prefers values such as non-

---

100. I shall explain in Section III.B. *infra* why I think we must accept the proposition
that a life is at stake *for purposes of constitutional argument about abortion laws.*

subordination and physical integrity to the value of preserving life. It is simply not possible to claim that in our system preserving life takes precedence over everything else.

Finally, it might be suggested that a reasonable American legislature would (or at least *could*) reject my argument at its very first step, the step where I decide that securing an abortion counts as an omission in the context of samaritan law. For purposes of constitutional analysis, viewing my entire argument through the lens of the reasonable American legislature test, I think this first step is the most problematic. It seems clear to *me* that if we want to be faithful to the spirit of our law regarding samaritanism, we must conclude that securing an abortion is more an omission than an act. But, just because the degree of deference due a contrary legislative judgment is not precisely quantifiable, I am not completely comfortable asserting a proposition (which I do nonetheless assert) that is essential to my argument, namely the proposition that any reasonable American legislature would, on reflection, see this matter as I do.

I do not claim to have established beyond doubt that laws against abortion deny equal protection. There are limits to how far logic and analysis can carry us. If the ultimate test in the equal protection area is whether a reasonable American legislature could have passed (or in some cases, could fail to repeal) a particular law, then there comes a point at which the judgment of persons imbued with and sensitive to our traditions is worth more than hypotheticals and distinctions.

In effect, the Court in *Roe* decided that a reasonable American legislature could *not* have passed (or failed to repeal) most state abortion laws. To be sure, the Justices did not explain themselves in this way. To my mind, they did not even explain as well as they might have why abortion laws presented a hard constitutional question — why they were not obviously constitutional. But I have tried to explain why abortion laws *do* present a hard question. Against that background, the most important fact about the decision in *Roe* is that seven Justices, including some not known for their activist tendencies, were impelled to strike down abortion laws even though they must have realized that their arguments were not very persuasive. In this case, given the nature of the issue, the fact that the Court held abortion laws unconstitutional is evidence for the proposition that they *are* unconstitutional, even though the Constitution does not simply mean what the Court says it means.

Of course, the Court's decision would be stronger evidence

(to my mind) if the Court had cast its argument about why abortion was a hard question in the terms of this essay. If the Court must exercise judgment, it is better that it exercise its judgment on properly formulated questions. If the Court had decided there was no general "right of privacy" and no right inferrable from the Constitution to decide how many children to bear, and if it had formulated the question in my equal protection terms, it is possible that it would have upheld abortion laws. If so, then the decision in *Roe* should be reconsidered. But my guess is that the Justices would have answered my question the same way they answered their own. And my judgment is that they would have been right. If one considers dispassionately the question, "Could a reasonable American legislature, remembering the constitutionally protected interests impaired by abortion laws, focusing on the inequality of treatment between some potential samaritans and others, and bearing in mind all the other considerations we have mentioned, pass or fail to repeal a law forbidding abortion?", I think the correct answer is "No."

There is one final matter to be dealt with. We have yet to answer the "too far afield" objection, the claim that courts simply should not entertain equal protection arguments which depend on such far-ranging comparisons as that between abortion and other samaritan problems. I can think of four possible arguments against such far-ranging comparisons: (1) Allowing such comparisons expands vastly, and unacceptably, the number of laws subject to equal protection scrutiny. (2) Allowing such comparisons raises issues too subjective and formless to be appropriate for judicial decision. (3) Striking down a law on the basis of such a comparison suggests implicitly a criticism of the legislature, which criticism may be undeserved. If the comparison is too unusual, the legislature may not have been at fault in failing to take it into account. (4) Inequalities that are revealed only by far-reaching comparisons are unlikely to be resented in the same way as traditional, immediately apparent inequalities. They therefore do not impose the same social costs or call for as much judicial solicitude.

These arguments are not without substance. They suggest that a degree of circumspection may be appropriate where far-reaching comparisons are suggested. But they do not, to my mind, justify a general refusal to consider such comparisons. Nor do they weigh strongly against considering the comparison I suggest in the abortion case.

As to the idea that far-ranging comparisons will cause new

equal protection issues to spring up everywhere, it is a sufficient answer that other aspects of the approach I suggest — the attention to tradition in defining specially protected interests and specially disfavored classifications, and the general deference to the legislature — will limit the number of problems which need to be taken seriously and will limit results overturning legislative choices. In the abortion case, as we have seen, two specially protected interests are impaired by an inequality of treatment involving a specially disfavored classification.

As to the idea that far-ranging comparisons give rise to questions that are too subjective, the answer is that every serious equal protection problem eventually reduces to a question that is subjective in the same sense. I say "subjective in the same sense" advisedly, since the ultimate question is *not* "subjective" in the strongest sense in which that term is commonly used. Ultimately, every equal protection problem comes down to a question about whether some law is or is not consistent with our legal tradition. There is no mechanical way for a judge to answer such a question. However, the conscientious judge who attempts to answer such a question is doing something quite different from attempting to decide whether the law before him comports with his own sense of justice. Also, even if the ultimate question is subjective in some significant sense, the example of this essay demonstrates (I hope) that argument and analysis are important in identifying the precise contours and context of the ultimate decision about what our tradition allows.

As to the suggestions that far-ranging comparisons will require the courts to consider inequalities which legislatures reasonably overlooked and which no citizen is troubled by, I think the answer is that some far-ranging comparisons will have more force than others. The comparison of the pregnant woman with the potential samaritan is not yet a commonplace of legal or public discussion of the abortion issue. But my experience is that most people, once introduced to the comparison, see that it is a significant and troublesome comparison. It is easy to overlook, but it is not easy to put aside as fanciful or irrelevant, once it is noticed. Even if legislatures have not noticed this comparison, I suggest that any reasonable American legislature would be persuaded by the comparison to repeal abortion laws once the comparison was brought to its attention. If that is so, then it is appropriate for courts to strike down abortion laws on the basis of the comparison without waiting for legislative reconsideration. No serious criticism of legislatures is implied.

With regard to the claim that members of the public, or women in particular, are not disturbed by this specific comparison, I have explained previously why many women's manifest resentment of abortion laws is based on considerations closely related to the equal protection argument of this essay, even if the considerations have not been articulated in quite the same way.

In sum, whatever we may think of other arguments based on far-ranging comparisons, the argument I have suggested against abortion laws cannot be brushed aside on the ground that it ranges too far afield.

B. *The Consequences of the Argument*

In this final Section, I shall comment very briefly on why I regard my argument as stronger than the Court's argument in *Roe* and on what it would mean for other cases involving abortion or "privacy" generally if my argument were adopted.

The Court's argument in *Roe* posits a "right of privacy" that is "broad enough to encompass a woman's decision whether or not to terminate her pregnancy".[101] The Court's argument has been elaborated in the scholarly literature by Heymann and Barzelay,[102] who infer constitutional protection for the woman's interest in having an abortion from a series of cases running from *Meyer v. Nebraska*[103] to *Eisenstadt v. Baird.*[104] According to Heymann and Barzelay, these cases establish a "realm of private decision as to matters of marriage, procreation and child rearing".[105] Unfortunately, as John Hart Ely has pointed out, the cases relied on are a rag-tag lot.[106] Most of them either claim to be or are best understood as being primarily about something other than "marriage, procreation and child-rearing". It is not clear that they add up to anything at all, especially when one remembers other cases in which colorable claims concerning marriage, procreation, or child-rearing have received short shrift.[107]

My argument, unlike the Court's, appeals to constitutional values — non-subordination, freedom from physical invasion,

---

101. 410 U.S. at 153.
102. Heymann & Barzelay, *supra* note 1.
103. 262 U.S. 390 (1923).
104. 405 U.S. 438 (1972).
105. Heymann & Barzelay, *supra* note 1, at 769.
106. Ely, *supra* note 73, at 931-32 n.79.
107. *E.g.*, Sosna v. Iowa, 419 U.S. 393 (1975) (marriage, or actually divorce); Dandridge v. Williams, 397 U.S. 471 (1970) (procreation); Baker v. Owen, 423 U.S. 907 (1975), *summarily affg.* 395 F. Supp. 294 (M.D.N.C. 1975) (child-rearing).

and equal protection — which are firmly established. I do not
claim that my argument generates the result in *Roe* by unassail-
able logical deduction from unimpeachable premises. Constitutional argument does not work that way. I do claim that my
argument is better grounded than the Court's in what are undeniably constitutional values.

The Court's argument not only relies on a right to make
decisions about "marriage, procreation and child rearing", but
it also relies heavily on what I have referred to as the post-partum
"family-planning" interests. In enumerating the costs to the
woman of being denied an abortion, the Court emphasizes costs
associated with actually *raising* the child.[108] However, it is not
appropriate to count all of these costs even in a "balancing"
process unless we are persuaded (as I am not) that the psychological cost to a woman of giving up a child for adoption is as great
as the cost of rearing an unwanted child. (We should remember
also that what is relevant is not the cost to a woman who wants
a child of being compelled to give it up once it is born, but rather
the cost of parting with the child for a woman who did not want
it in the first place. The woman may be ambivalent at all stages,
and being compelled to bear the child and then give it up, instead
of aborting it, may make the feelings of attachment to the child
harder to deny. Even so, this is an aspect of the problem where
remembering the relevant viewpoint, which is that of the mother
who does *not* want a child, seems to make the cost smaller rather
than greater.) My argument, as I have explained, does not rely
on these "family-planning" interests.

Perhaps the greatest advantage of my argument is that it
makes it possible to avoid the question of whether the fetus is,
or may be treated by the state as, a person. Justice Blackmun
claims at one point that the Court need not decide "when life
begins".[109] But his general argument, which during the first two
trimesters prefers the woman's "right of privacy" over the state's
interest in protecting "potential life", seems plainly to assume
that the fetus is *not* a person until the point of viability (at the
earliest).[110] Indeed, Blackmun elsewhere suggests that if the fetus
were a person within the meaning of the fourteenth amendment,
the woman's claim to an abortion would be foreclosed by the

---

108. 410 U.S. at 153.
109. 410 U.S. at 159.
110. *See, e.g.,* 410 U.S. at 163.

Constitution itself.[111]

On the last point, I think Blackmun is mistaken. Even if the fetus were a person for purposes of the fourteenth amendment, it would not follow that abortion was forbidden by the Constitution or that states were required by the Constitution to have laws forbidding abortion. The people who need the assistance of potential samaritans in ordinary samaritan cases are persons under the fourteenth amendment, and yet the general common law bad-samaritan principle is not unconstitutional. (Similarly, the fact that fourteenth amendment persons are killed does not vitiate the ordinary law of self-defense.)

Although I think Blackmun is mistaken about what would follow from a holding that the fetus is a person under the fourteenth amendment, I think he is right that the fetus is not a person under the fourteenth amendment.[112] That, however, is not enough to justify his refusal to treat the fetus as a person for purposes of weighing the interests affected by the Texas abortion statute. The fourteenth amendment does not say that the fetus is a person, but neither does the fourteenth amendment say that a state may not decide to regard the fetus as a person, if the state so chooses.

It is essential to Blackmun's argument that he brush aside the state's attempt to regard the fetus as a person. As far as I can see, there is no adequate constitutional justification for this brushing aside. My argument, unlike Blackmun's, does not depend on refusing to allow the state to regard the fetus as a person. Everything I have said is consistent with the assumption that the fetus is a person. Other persons are allowed to die when potential samaritans are authorized by the bad-samaritan principle to deny aid. The personhood of the fetus, even if it be conceded, is not an adequate reason (indeed it is no reason at all) for treating the pregnant woman differently from other potential samaritans.

A similar but more general point in favor of my argument is that it is not a "balancing" argument.[113] Even after the Court decides that the fetus may not be treated by the state as a person (during the first two trimesters), the Court must still balance the woman's "right of privacy" against the state's interest in protecting *potential* human life. It is far from clear that this balance favors the woman. Whether or not the cases from *Meyer* to

---

111. 410 U.S. at 156-57.
112. 410 U.S. at 158.
113. *See* pages 1589-90 *supra.*

Eisenstadt establish a right of family-related freedom-of-choice, none of those cases involves a state interest remotely like the interest in protecting "potential" but *already conceived* human life. Accordingly none of those cases establishes or even suggests that the right of family-related freedom-of-choice is weighty enough to overcome the state's interest in forbidding abortion.

My argument, on the other hand, does not require any such balancing by the Court. I doubt that it is correct to regard the bad-samaritan principle and the right of self-defense as based on "balancing" at all, but even if they are, the balancing is already done when those doctrines are accepted. Whether or not the interests in physical integrity and non-involvement "outweigh" the interest in human life, our law leaves no doubt that they prevail over it (and *a fortiori* over the interest in potential life) in the relevant contexts.

Finally, my argument justifies more clearly than the Court's argument the Court's conclusion that abortion may not be forbidden even in the third trimester when the life or health of the mother is at stake.[114] If the problem is ultimately one of balancing, as the Court's opinion suggests, it is not clear why the state's compelling interest (as the Court describes it) in protecting the potential life of a fetus already capable of "meaningful life outside the mother's womb"[115] (in the Court's phrase) is outweighed even by the woman's life, much less by her health. On my approach, however, the matter is clear. Even the reader who rejects my general conclusions must admit that there is no other case in which we would even consider requiring one individual to sacrifice his life or health to rescue another.

Since I have suggested that my argument provides a better justification than the Court's for the result in *Roe,* it is worth asking whether my argument justifies *all* of the result. In particular, does it justify drawing a line at the end of the second trimester, after which abortion may be generally forbidden? To be sure, the burdens of pregnancy and delivery that will be avoided by an abortion diminish as the pregnancy advances. Even so, an abortion by induced labor early in the third trimester would spare the woman two months of advanced pregnancy plus the difference between the pain and discomfort of a full-term delivery and the lesser pain and discomfort of an easier, earlier-induced delivery.

---

114. 410 U.S. at 163-64.
115. 410 U.S. at 163.

The burdens avoided by even a third-trimester abortion are distinctly greater than the burdens imposed by other exceptions to the bad-samaritan principle.

I think the Court's line between the second and third trimesters can be justified on the ground that the woman who allows her pregnancy to reach the third trimester without having an abortion (assumed to be permissible in the first two trimesters) has waived her right of non-involvement with the fetus. Surely by the end of the second trimester a woman has had knowledge of her pregnancy long enough to have had a reasonable time to think through the difficult issue of whether she wants an abortion. There is a genuine state interest in encouraging decision at the earliest reasonable opportunity, even if it is only the interest in avoiding the greater dismay of many members of the public at late abortions.[116]Admittedly, this argument does not tell us precisely where the "waiver" line should be. But if we consider the possibilities for denial by the woman early in the pregnancy, the difficulty of the issue for many women, and, on the other hand, the desirability of some clear line so long as it is not too early, a line at the beginning of the third trimester seems a reasonable solution.[117]

Since *Roe,* the Court has dealt with a number of subsidiary issues involving abortion — procedural requirements,[118] parents' consent requirements,[119] husband's consent requirements,[120] public funding,[121] and so on. With the possible exception of the cases on public facilities and public funding, these cases largely involved state attempts to forbid abortion by indirection. Generally speaking, my argument leads to the same results in these cases

---

116. The text may seem inconsistent with the earlier suggestion, made in discussing the military draft, that there is no genuinely "public" interest in forbidding abortion. If there is sufficient public interest to support a requirement that the woman decide whether to have an abortion by a certain time, why may not the abortion be forbidden on the basis of the same interest? A full answer to this question would require an extensive discussion of constitutional "waiver" theory. I shall not give a full answer. The short answer is that I think certain public interests may be enough to require an individual to make a decision and stick by it even though those interests are not enough to compel a particular decision and may not even count towards compelling a particular decision.

117. Actually, it seems to me that a reasonable American legislature could probably put the "waiver" line *somewhat* earlier. But I cannot be sure of that without looking more carefully than I have at the mechanics of arranging abortions for women in various circumstances.

118. *E.g.,* Doe v. Bolton, 410 U.S. 179 (1973).

119. *E.g.,* Planned Parenthood v. Danforth, 428 U.S. 52 (1976).

120. *E.g.,* Planned Parenthood v. Danforth, 428 U.S. 52 (1976).

121. *E.g.,* Maher v. Roe, 432 U.S. 464 (1977).

that the Court has reached. To the extent that there is more to
these cases than mere striking down of attempts to avoid *Roe,* my
argument may explain the Court's results marginally better than
the Court's argument does.

For example, the step from saying the state may not forbid
an abortion when the woman and her husband both want it (or
when there is no husband in the picture) to saying the state may
not forbid an abortion when the woman wants it and her husband
does not is not quite so simple on Blackmun's approach as Blackmun claims.[122] After all, if the whole issue is one of balancing,
might it not be that the state's interest, which is less than the
interest of the woman or of the woman and her husband together
when they are aligned, is greater than the *difference* between the
interests of the woman and her husband when they are opposed?
Indeed, given the weightiness of the state's interest and the similarity of the woman's interests to her husband's (especially while
the Court emphasizes the "family-planning" aspect rather than
the physical burdens of pregnancy), is it not quite likely? On my
approach, however, it is clear that the state can no more make
the unwilling woman serve the fetus and her husband than it can
make her serve the fetus alone.

As to the issue of parents' or judges' consent to abortion for
minors, this is a difficult problem. It is far from obvious that a
statute which was well calculated to encourage identification of
the minor's best interests (a statute, that is, which was not a mere
anti-abortion statute in disguise) would deserve to be struck
down. But again, if the Court is committed to striking down such
statutes (and this is much less certain after *Bellotti II*[123] than it
seemed before), the justification seems somewhat stronger on my
approach than on the Court's. The interests of the woman which
my approach makes central (interests in avoiding physical burdens) are more easily appreciated and weighed by a minor than
the comparatively abstract family-planning interests emphasized
by the Court.

With regard to the public facilities and public funding cases,
there is also little to choose between the Court's approach and
mine. I tend to think the Court decided these cases correctly,
though I shall not argue for that view here. My approach may

---

122. *See* Planned Parenthood v. Danforth, 428 U.S. 52, 69 (1976): "[T]he State
cannot delegate authority to any particular person, even the spouse, to prevent abortion
[when the State alone may not prevent it]."

123. Bellotti v. Baird, 99 S. Ct. 3035 (1979).

make the correctness of the decisions a bit clearer than the Court's. The Court's approach more easily suggests a fundamental right of the woman to have an effective choice whereas my approach emphasizes that what is objectionable is the state's compelling the woman to serve the fetus, a compulsion which is absent once abortion is no longer forbidden.

It is when we look at problems not involving the right to abortion that the difference between my approach and the Court's becomes striking. One noteworthy feature of my argument is that it is asymmetric. Unlike Blackmun's argument, it provides no support for a right to bear children. I regard this as an advantage. There may be a right of some sort to bear children, but such a right does not find much support in the *Meyer*-to-*Eisenstadt* line of cases (aside from some quotable language here and there). The right, if it exists, must be founded rather on the sort of argument Harlan advanced in his *Poe v. Ullman* dissent,[124] and it must, I think, be an incident of marriage.

Looking beyond procreation, there is a considerable literature suggesting that a broad "right of privacy" was established in *Roe*. The Court's language certainly encouraged this belief. Yet litigants who have tried to persuade the Supreme Court to implement the right of privacy outside the abortion area have generally been disappointed. Consider *Doe v. Commonwealth's Attorney*,[125] in which the Court summarily affirmed a decision upholding Virginia's sodomy statute. It is far from obvious why something called the "right of privacy", which encompasses the right to bring about the death of a fetus in a clinic serving the public, should not encompass the right of consenting adults to engage in the nonviolent sexual behavior of their choice in private. It *is* obvious, however, that my argument in support of *Roe*, based on the bad-samaritan principle or the self-defense analogy, says nothing at all about the right to engage in homosexual (or heterosexual) relations. The argument I suggest in justification of *Roe* is much more closely tied to the specific problem of abortion than is the Court's argument. My argument therefore seems more in line with the Court's later decisions in the "privacy" area.

ENVOI

If I had been writing an essay about moral philosophy instead

---

124. 367 U.S. 497, 539-55 (1961) (Harlan, J., dissenting).
125. 425 U.S. 901 (1976), *summarily affg.* 403 F. Supp. 1199 (E.D. Va. 1975).

of about constitutional law, I would have made the argument in favor of abortion turn centrally on the proposition that a fetus is not a person. I would *not* have relied on the proposition that there is no general duty to aid a person in serious danger even when one can do so at trivial cost to oneself. I would not have appealed to any notion that corporal punishment is impermissible, nor indeed would I have given the same negative weight to physical invasions generally that I do in the present essay. I would not have claimed that there is a right to kill an innocent rapist. However, I have not been writing about moral philosophy. I have been writing about American constitutional law. For reasons I cannot explain here, I think the projects are quite different.

Sometimes the argument of this essay seems to me an adequate constitutional justification of the result in *Roe*. Sometimes it does not. (My principal nagging doubt is about the very first step of the argument, when viewed from the constitutional perspective. I think the general thrust of samaritan law requires that securing an abortion be treated as an omission in that context. Indeed, I have no doubt on that point. But might not a reasonable American legislature simply disagree?) Adequate or not, the argument I have presented almost always seems to me the best justification of the result in *Roe* that I know of.

THE JURIDICAL STATUS OF THE FETUS: A PROPOSAL FOR LEGAL PROTECTION OF THE UNBORN

Patricia A. King*

What claims to protection can be asserted by a human fetus? That question, familiar to philosophy and religion, has long haunted law as well. While the philosophical and theological issues remain unresolved, and are perhaps unresolvable,[1] I believe that we can no longer avoid some resolution of the legal status of the fetus. The potential benefits of fetal research,[2] the ability to fertilize the human ovum in a laboratory dish,[3] and the increasing awareness that a mother's activities during pregnancy may affect the health of her offspring[4] create pressing policy issues that raise possible conflicts among fetuses, mothers, and researchers. This Article probes the juridical status of the fetus, assessing what it should be in the light of recent developments in case law,[5] legislation,[6] medicine, and technology.[7]

---

* Associate Professor of Law, Georgetown University Law Center; B.A. 1963, Wheaton College; J.D. 1969, Harvard Law School. [The author is presently a Fellow of the Institute of Society, Ethics, and the Life Sciences and a Resident Scholar at the Joseph and Rose Kennedy Institute of Ethics and was formerly a member of the National Commission for the Protection of Human Subjects of Biomedical and Behavioral Research.] —Ed.

1. The moral status of the fetus has been extensively discussed. *See generally* D. CALLAHAN, ABORTION: LAW, CHOICE AND MORALITY (1970); THE MORALITY OF ABORTION: LEGAL AND HISTORICAL PERSPECTIVES (J. Noonan ed. 1970) [hereinafter cited as MORALITY OF ABORTION]; THE PROBLEM OF ABORTION (J. Feinberg ed. 1973); Wertheimer, *Understanding the Argument,* 1 PHIL. & PUB. AFF. 67 (1971).

2. In 1974 Congress passed the National Research Act, which established the National Commission for the Protection of Human Subjects of Biomedical and Behavioral Research. The National Commission was given a mandate to investigate and study research involving the living fetus, and to recommend whether and under what circumstances such research should be conducted or supported by the Department of Health, Education, and Welfare. National Research Act, Pub. L. No. 93-348, § 213, 88 Stat. 342 (1974). Congress was concerned that unconscionable acts involving the fetus might have been performed in the name of scientific inquiry.

3. *See All About That Baby,* NEWSWEEK, Aug. 7, 1978, at 66; *The First Test-Tube Baby,* TIME, July 31, 1978, at 58.

4. *See* note 154 *infra* and accompanying text.

5. *See, e.g.,* Roe v. Wade, 410 U.S. 113 (1973).

6. *See, e.g.,* the following statutes and regulations, all of which regulate fetal research: National Research Act, Pub. L. No. 93-348, § 213, 88 Stat. 342 (1974) (congressionally mandated moratorium on research on the living human fetus); HEW Additional Protections Pertaining to Research, Development, and Related Activities Involving Fe-

Section I reviews the Supreme Court's landmark decision in *Roe v. Wade*[8] and assesses its helpfulness in defining fetal status. I contend that, while the Court's opinion leaves many issues unresolved,[9] it provides a sketchy base upon which to construct a definition. *Roe* is useful because it relies on the biological stages of fetal development, especially viability, rather than attempting a philosophical determination of when human life begins. I argue, however, that *Roe* furnishes inadequate guidance for reconciling fetal interests with conflicting interests of the mother. In particular, it fails to illuminate the resolution of arguable claims on behalf of the previable fetus. Should fertile women be permitted to work in environments that might endanger the health of their offspring? In attempting *in vitro* fertilization, followed by transfer of the fertilized ovum into a mother's womb, should the physician be able to use several eggs and discard those fertilized ova that are not implanted?[10] Moreover, *Roe* fails to define adequately what protection should be afforded viable fetuses before birth. Does *Roe* permit abortion of a viable fetus when the mother asserts that continued pregnancy would cause her great mental anguish?[11]

---

tuses, Pregnant Women, and Human in Vitro Fertilization, 45 C.F.R. §§ 46.201-211 (1978); ARIZ. REV. STAT. ANN. § 36-2302 (West Supp. 1978); CAL. HEALTH & SAFETY CODE § 25956 (West Supp. 1978); ILL. ANN. STAT. ch. 38, §§ 81-18, -26, -32 (Smith-Hurd 1977); IND. CODE ANN. § 35-1-58.5-6 (Burns 1977); KY. REV. STAT. § 436.026 (1975); LA. REV. STAT. ANN. § 14:87.2 (West 1974); ME. REV. STAT. tit. 22, § 1593 (Supp. 1978); MASS. ANN. LAWS ch. 112, § 12J (Michie Law. Co-op 1975); MINN. STAT. ANN. § 145.422 (1973); MO. ANN. STAT. § 188.035 (Vernon Supp. 1979); N.D. CENT. CODE §§ 14-02.2-01, -02 (Supp. 1977); 35 PA. STAT. ANN. tit. 35, § 6605 (Purdon 1974); S.D. COMP. LAWS ANN. § 34-23A-17 (1976); UTAH CODE ANN. § 76-7-310 (1978).

7. *See* note 3 *supra; see also* text at notes 123-33 *infra.*

8. 410 U.S. 113 (1973).

9. This Article does not address the problems of constitutional interpretation raised by *Roe*. These issues have been explored in several excellent articles. *See, e.g.,* Ely, *The Wages of Crying Wolf: A Comment on Roe v. Wade,* 82 YALE L.J. 920 (1973); Heymann & Barzelay, *The Forest and the Trees: Roe v. Wade and Its Critics,* 53 B.U. L. REV. 765 (1973); Tribe, *The Supreme Court, 1972 Term — Foreword: Toward a Model of Roles in the Due Process of Life and Law,* 87 HARV. L. REV. 1 (1973).

10. The Ethics Advisory Board of the Department of Health, Education, and Welfare studied this research and has issued a report and recommendations concerning the conditions under which such research should be conducted and supported. 44 Fed. Reg. 35,033 (1979).

11. The Court in *Roe* stated that "[i]f the State is interested in protecting fetal life after viability, it may go so far as to proscribe abortion during that period, except when it is necessary to preserve the life or health of the mother." 410 U.S. at 163-64. However, the Court did not explain what it meant by "health."

Two years earlier, the Court faced this issue in United States v. Vuitch, 402 U.S. 62 (1971). In *Vuitch* the Court held that a District of Columbia statute prohibiting abortion

Section II examines the historical reliance on birth as the point at which legal protection vests in the developing human. I contend that that reliance was due to the perceived significance of birth as the moment at which a developing human became capable of independent existence, not to any special importance of physical separation. Since a fetus today becomes capable of independent existence — viable — before birth, I argue that the law should recognize fetal claims to legal protection.

Section III compares fetuses with newborn children, identifying relevant similarities and differences. Like children, fetuses may develop into rational adults. I contend that the ability to interact with humans other than the mother — possessed by children but not by fetuses — is not a relevant distinction. This contention is supported by an examination of society's treatment of the interests of the dead.

Section IV studies whether fetuses at all stages of development should have the same protection and concludes that they should not. Previable fetuses should remain legally distinguishable from viable fetuses. I argue that the viability criterion strikes a fair balance between the competing interests of developing and mature humans.

Section V examines the practical implications of choosing viability as a developmental stage of special significance for legal protection. It responds to some of the difficulties created by a standard that shifts with medical technology and shows them inadequate to overcome the logical and ethical arguments in favor of the viability criterion.

---

except as "necessary for the preservation of the mother's life or health" was not unconstitutionally vague. 402 U.S. at 68, 72. Although the Court did not define health, it said, on the basis of dictionary definition, that the term included mental health. 402 U.S. at 72.

Justice Douglas, however, disagreed. He felt that the imprecision of the term "health" made the statute unconstitutionally vague. He illustrated the lurking ambiguities by posing the following questions:

May [the doctor] perform abortions on unmarried women who want to avoid the "stigma" of having an illegitimate child? Is bearing a "stigma" a "health" factor? Only in isolated cases? Or is it such whenever the woman is unmarried?

Is any unwanted pregnancy a "health" factor because it is a source of anxiety?

Is an abortion "necessary" in the statutory sense if the doctor thought that an additional child in a family would unduly tax the mother's physical well-being by reason of the additional work which would be forced upon her?

Would a doctor be violating the law if he performed an abortion because the added expense of another child in the family would drain its resources, leaving an anxious mother with an insufficient budget to buy nutritious food?

Is the fate of an unwanted child or the plight of the family into which it is born relevant to the factor of the mother's "health"?

402 U.S. at 76 (Douglas, J., dissenting in part). These questions remain unanswered.

I. *Roe v. Wade* REEXAMINED

Jane Roe, unmarried and pregnant, wanted an abortion.
Because her life was not threatened by continuing pregnancy, she
could not get an abortion legally in her home state of Texas.[12]
Moreover, she could not afford to travel to another jurisdiction for
a legal abortion.[13] She therefore sued on behalf of herself and all
similarly situated women. Roe contended that she had a constitutionally guaranteed right of privacy that included the right to
terminate her pregnancy.[14] In defense of its statutes, Texas contended that it could protect fetal life constitutionally from the
time of conception, and that Roe therefore had no right to an
abortion.[15] A three-judge district court panel held that the Texas
criminal abortion statutes were void on their faces, but they abstained from granting the plaintiff's request for an injunction.[16]
Roe appealed to the Supreme Court,[17] Texas cross-appealed, and
the Court had to determine the constitutionality of the Texas
statutes.

The Court agreed with Roe that a woman has a constitutional right of privacy that "is broad enough to encompass [her]
decision whether or not to terminate her pregnancy."[18] Yet the
Court emphasized that the state might have "important" and
"legitimate interests" that could limit that right. Mind you, not
any interest would do — the interest had to be a " 'compelling
state interest.' "[19] Nonetheless, the woman's right of privacy was
definitely qualified.

The issue was thus whether the state had any "compelling"
interests that could justify criminal abortion statutes. The Court

---

12. 410 U.S. at 113, 120.
13. 410 U.S. at 120.
14. 410 U.S. at 129.
15. 410 U.S. at 156.
16. 410 U.S. at 122.
17. Plaintiff Doe and intervenor Hallford also appealed from a denial of the injunction. Plaintiff Doe alleged that she was married, suffered from a disorder, had been
advised by her physician to avoid pregnancy, and on medical advice had discontinued use
of birth control pills. She alleged that she would desire a legal abortion should she become
pregnant. The district court dismissed her complaint because she did not have standing.
This action was upheld by the Supreme Court. 410 U.S at 129. Hallford was a licensed
physician who sought to intervene in Roe's action. He alleged that he had been arrested
for violation of the statutes at issue and that two prosecutions were pending against him.
The district court found that Hallford had standing to sue. The Supreme Court reversed,
410 U.S. at 126-27, relying on its decisions in Samuels v. Mackell, 401 U.S. 66 (1971), and
Younger v. Harris, 401 U.S. 37 (1971).
18. 410 U.S. at 153.
19. 410 U.S. at 154, 155.

engaged in a lengthy examination of the historical bases for such
statutes. It observed that three justifications could be offered
— discouraging immoral conduct, safeguarding the health of
pregnant women, and protecting fetal life[20] — but quickly dismissed the first justification because Texas had not proffered it,
and because neither courts nor commentators had ever considered it seriously.[21]

The second justification, paternalistic concern for the safety
of pregnant women, grew from the historical dangers of the abortion technique. The information available to the Court regarding
the safety of contemporary abortion procedures was contradic-
tory. Roe, relying on data about abortions in New York City,
argued that mortality rates for childbirth are higher than mortality rates for induced abortions.[22] *Amici* supporting Texas laws
challenged the reliability of the New York data and pointed to
evidence showing higher abortion mortality rates when abortions
are performed late in pregnancy.[23] In the face of these conflicting
presentations, the Court concluded that abortions can be performed more safely today than when criminal abortion laws were
first enacted,[24] and that, at least at some stages of pregnancy,
modern abortions are as safe as childbirth.

The *Roe* Court held that the state's interest in protecting a
woman's health becomes compelling — at the point where the
risk of death from an abortion is not less than the risk of death
from a normal childbirth, roughly the end of the first trimester
of pregnancy.[25] After that point, "a State may regulate the abor-

---

20. 410 U.S. at 147-52.
21. 410 U.S. at 148.
22. Brief for Appellants at 30-32, Roe v. Wade, 410 U.S. 113 (1973).
23. Motion and Brief Amicus Curiae of Certain Physicians, Professors and Fellows
of the American College of Obstetrics and Gynecology in Support of Appellees at 32-40,
Roe v. Wade, 410 U.S. 113 (1973). Amici pointed out that most abortions in Eastern
Europe were performed in the first trimester of pregnancy and that fact might account
for the very low mortality rates of those countries. They further contended that higher
mortality rates in Western and Northern Europe might be the result of the performance
of abortions after the first trimester. *Id.* at 39. Appellants also argued that abortion was
without significant psychiatric sequellae. Brief for Appellant, *supra* note 9, at 33-34. This
assertion was also contested. Motion and Brief Amicus Curiae of Certain Physicians,
supra, at 55-58.
24. 410 U.S. at 149.
25. 410 U.S. at 163. The Court's reasoning indicates that the state's compelling
interest in the woman's health is dependent upon mortality data. If the data changed,
presumably the point at which the state's interest would attach would also change. Recent
data suggest that mortality from abortions during the first 12 weeks of pregnancy is
declining while mortality associated with childbirth is increasing. This suggests that some

tion procedure to the extent that the regulation reasonably relates
to the preservation and protection of maternal health.''[26] Before
that point, the state's interest in her health is insufficient to
override the woman's decision in consultation with her physician.[27]

The third justification for criminal abortion statutes, the
state's interest in protecting prenatal life,[28] was potentially the
most complex. The medical and scientific data before the Court
were inconclusive on all the details of fetal development, except
for general consensus that a fetus has a separate genetic identity
at or soon after conception.[29] On the other hand, the common law
had traditionally been stingy in awarding rights to the unborn,
and where it had grudgingly made such awards, it had, with few

---

second trimester abortions may be safer than childbirth, and thus, a state's compelling
interest in the mother's health would not justify legislation until later in pregnancy.
Tietze, *New Estimates of Mortality Associated with Fertility Control*, 9 FAMILY PLAN.
PERSPEC. 74 (1977).

26. 410 U.S. at 163. The Court had a somewhat narrow view of what constituted
appropriate implementations of that compelling state interest in maternal health after the
first trimester. As examples, the Court would have permitted

requirements as to the qualifications of the person who is to perform the abortion;
as to the licensure of that person; as to the facility in which the procedure is to be
performed, that is, whether it must be a hospital or may be a clinic or some other
place of less-than-hospital status; as to the licensing of the facility; and the like.

410 U.S. at 163.

The Court, however, did not convincingly explain why the state does not have a
similar interest in maternal health during first trimester abortions. Presumably, the state
is interested in licensure and quality of facilities whenever its citizens undergo surgery.
The reliance on comparative mortality rates between normal childbirth and first trimester
abortion does not justify the absence of all regulation in the first trimester, although it
might justify a lesser degree of regulation.

27. 410 U.S. at 163. The consultation requirement constitutes a minimal regulation
for first trimester abortions, ensuring only that abortions are performed under safe conditions. By precluding other regulation of first trimester abortions, the Court may have been
trying to prevent state interference with a woman's interests during the first three months
of pregnancy. That hope, however, was soon shattered. In the year after *Roe*, many state
legislatures enacted restrictive legislation. *See* Moss, *Abortion Statutes After Danforth:
An Examination*, 15 J. FAM. L. 537 (1976-1977).

The Court itself has subsequently conceded that states may otherwise restrict a
woman's access to abortion. For example, Missouri's statute requiring the written consent
of the woman as well as certain recordkeeping requirements for hospitals and physicians
was held to be constitutional. Planned Parenthood v. Danforth, 428 U.S. 52, 65-69, 79-81
(1976). The decision of the Court in Maher v. Roe, 432 U.S. 465 (1977), holding that the
failure of states to pay abortion expenses while paying costs related to childbirth was not
a violation of the equal protection clause, also burdens a woman's decision to seek an
abortion. *See* Beal v. Doe, 432 U.S. 438 (1977); Poelker v. Doe, 432 U.S. 519 (1977).

28. 410 U.S. at 150.

29. For an overview of fetal development, see text at notes 123-29 *infra*.

exceptions, made them contingent upon the fetus's live birth.[30] The Court first held that "the word 'person,' as used in the Fourteenth Amendment, does not include the unborn."[31] But the Court did not and could not stop there. Texas was arguing that, whether or not a fetus was a " 'person' as used in the Fourteenth Amendment," the state could take a legitimate, even compelling interest in its well-being. After noting that in other areas of the law, legal protection vests at the moment of birth, the Court equivocated on a central issue:

> We need not resolve the difficult question of when life begins. When those trained in the respective disciplines of medicine, philosophy, and theology are unable to arrive at any consensus, the judiciary, at this point in the development of man's knowledge, is not in a position to speculate as to the answer.[32]

That statement was more than a little disingenuous. Only a few pages later, the Court did decide "when life begins," at least for the purpose of limiting the moment at which a state may bestow full legal protection. The Court held that a state acquires a compelling interest in the potential human life of the fetus at the moment the fetus becomes viable — "potentially able to live outside the mother's womb, albeit with artificial aid."[33] After that time, a state may prohibit all abortions that are not necessary to protect the life or health of the mother.[34]

Later in this Article, I will suggest that the *Roe* decision's indirect implications regarding legal protection of fetal interests — indirect because they express those interests as those of the state rather than of the fetus — are justifiable in history and in reason. Before doing so, it is useful to discuss some of the ambiguities and logical flaws that weakened the *Roe* opinion.

One ambiguity rests with the Court's definition of viability. The statement that a fetus is "potentially able to live" can be interpreted in at least two ways. It could be merely a contingent prediction: the fetus is now alive and will continue to live unless something alters its environment. Viability in this sense depends

---

30. 410 U.S. at 161-62. The Constitution of the United States does not discuss the time at which a developing entity acquires rights, and nothing indicates that the founders intended "person" to include the unborn. No court had so assumed. Furthermore, every state, including Texas, had statutorily endorsed some abortions through exceptions to its criminal abortion provisions. 410 U.S. at 157-58.

31. 410 U.S. at 158.

32. 410 U.S. at 159.

33. 410 U.S. at 160 (footnote omitted).

34. 410 U.S. at 162-63.

on a continuing, unaltered relationship between mother and child. But viability has a second meaning: the level of developmental maturity at which a fetus will continue to live and develop even if physically separated from its mother. Clearly the Court intended this latter sense, which includes the possibility that artificial aid might be needed. It referred to a specific stage of development (twenty-four to twenty-eight weeks)[35] and refused to recognize a compelling state interest in potential human life before then.[36] If the Court intended "viable" to be understood in the first sense, it would have had to recognize a compelling state interest at the moment of conception, since from that time on fetuses are "potentially able to live" *if* they are not separated from their mothers.

The comment that viability "is usually placed at about seven months (28 weeks) but may occur earlier,"[37] created a second ambiguity. Undoubtedly the Court wished to reflect present knowledge of premature survival rates. Although most fetuses are capable of surviving at twenty-eight weeks, some fetuses are not able to survive independently until some later point, and a few fetuses survive as early as twenty-four weeks after conception.[38] The moment when a particular fetus can survive is affected by such factors as race, medical care, nutritional health of the mother and fetus, genetic composition, and availability of neonatal facilities.[39] General predictions about fetal survival do not consider these personal traits; at best, they describe only the typical case, and suggest a range of probability rather than a specific developmental point. But although the Court's range of weeks may have been an accurate generalization about available

---

35. 410 U.S. at 160.

36. 410 U.S. at 163.

37. 410 U.S. at 160.

38. 410 U.S. at 160. Some commentators have suggested that viability should be linked to weight as well as gestational age. *See* Behrman & Rosen, *Report on Viability and Nonviability of the Fetus,* in RESEARCH ON THE FETUS: APPENDIX 12-1, 12-6, 12-9 (Natl. Commn. for the Protection of Human Subjects of Biomedical and Behavioral Research ed. 1975) (HEW Publication No. (OS) 76-128). *See also* Gordon, *Neonatal and "Perinatal" Mortality Rates by Birth Weight,* 2 BRIT. MED. J. 1202 (1977); Stewart, Turcan, Rawlings, & Reynolds, *Prognosis for infants weighing 1000 g or less at birth,* 52 ARCHIVES OF DISEASE IN CHILDHOOD 97 (1977) [hereinafter cited as Stewart].

39. *See* Noonan, *An Almost Absolute Value in History,* in MORALITY OF ABORTION, *supra* note 1, at 52; North & McDonald, *Why Are Neonatal Mortality Rates Lower in Small Black Infants Than in White Infants of Similar Birth Weight?,* 90 J. PEDIATRICS 809 (1977) (suggests black babies are genetically endowed with greater capacity to survive than whites, and females are more likely to survive than males).

medical information, it left unsettled whether a state's compelling interest attaches at twenty-four weeks — when it is possible, but not likely, that the individual fetus can survive — or at whatever point the fetus can in fact survive, but in no event later than twenty-eight weeks.[40]

The Court's *Roe* discussion contains further ambiguities. It includes a statement that the state's compelling interest in potential life attaches at viability "because the fetus then presumably has the capability of meaningful life outside the mother's

---

40. The Supreme Court has reexamined the definition of viability in two subsequent cases. In Planned Parenthood v. Danforth, 428 U.S. 52 (1976), the Court sustained the constitutionality of a Missouri statute's definition of viability: "Viability [is] that stage of fetal development when the life of the unborn child may be continued indefinitely outside the womb by natural or artificial life-supportive systems." Mo. ANN. STAT. § 188.015(3) (Vernon Supp. 1975). The Supreme Court held that the Missouri definition was compatible with the definition of viability in *Roe*. 428 U.S. at 63. In fact, said the Court,
one might argue . . . that the presence of the statute's words "continued indefinitely" favor, rather than disfavor, the [challengers], for, arguably, the point when life can be "continued indefinitely outside the womb" may well occur later in pregnancy than the point where the fetus is "potentially able to live outside the mother's womb."
428 U.S. at 64. The Court apparently believed that the Missouri abortion statute did not cover the entire area of permissible regulation (24-28 weeks), but apparently regulated only abortions of fetuses with an estimated gestational age of 28 weeks or longer.

The Court has recently made another effort to clarify its concept of viability. In Colautti v. Franklin, 439 U.S. 379 (1979), the Court held unconstitutional on grounds of vagueness a Pennsylvania statute that subjected a physician to criminal penalties for failure to conform to a statutorily prescribed standard of care following a determination that the fetus "is viable" or "may be viable." 439 U.S. at 381. The Court found two problems with the statute. First, it did not clarify whether the physician's determination would be judged by a subjective or objective standard, or a mixture of the two. Second, the Court was not sure whether the phrase "may be viable" incorporated *Roe's* viability standard or whether the phrase referred to a period prior to viability. 439 U.S. at 391.

To the first concern, the Court stated that the determination of viability was a subjective assessment to be made by the attending physician. However, the Court appears to have changed the *Roe* definition of viability in stating: "Viability is reached when, in the judgment of the attending physician on the particular facts of the case before him, there is a reasonable likelihood of the fetus's sustained survival outside the womb, with or without artificial support." 439 U.S. at 388. The apparent departure from *Roe* was noted in the dissenting opinion of Justice White. He argues that *Roe* used the term "potentially able" and for that reason the *Roe* definition of viability "reaches an earlier point in the development of the fetus than that stage at which a doctor could say with assurance that the fetus *would* survive outside the womb." 439 U.S. at 402 (emphasis in original).

Second, the Court considered whether the phrases "may be viable" and "viable" had different meanings. Pennsylvania argued that the two phrases meant the same thing. 99 S. Ct. at 684. The Court rejected that contention, finding two possible interpretations for the distinction. Under either interpretation, the Court found the statute ambiguous and therefore unconstitutionally vague. 439 U.S. at 393-94.

womb."[41] What did the Court mean by the word "meaningful"? Did it mean that human life must have some special, unarticu-
lated quality before it is entitled to protection by the state? Did it mean that fetuses with genetic diseases are excluded from the domain of legitimate state interests? This seems unlikely. Even at the time of *Roe,* it was usually possible to diagnose genetic disease before the twenty-four to twenty-eight week period used by the Court,[42] and there was nothing special about the twenty-four to twenty-eight period for purposes of diagnosis. Moreover, the greatest strides in development of prenatal diagnostic techniques have been made since the *Roe* decision.[43] It is far more likely that the Court meant the word "meaningful" to exclude only the class of fetuses that lack the minimal integrative physiological equipment and therefore could not survive for a significant period of time — more than a few minutes — if separated from their mothers by existing medical techniques.[44]

Although the *Roe* Court took a reasonable position on fetal status, its holding stood upon notably weak reasoning. The Court chose viability as the critical point in fetal development "because presumably the fetus has the capability of meaningful life outside the mother's womb."[45] As Professor Ely eloquently observed, "the Court's defense seems to mistake a definition for a syllogism"[46]: the definition of viability for a syllogism demonstrating that a compelling interest arises at viability. The Court found that, until a fetus is viable, neither it nor the state has a compelling interest that can override the constitutionally protected rights of the mother to obtain an abortion. After viability, except where the life and health of the mother are at issue, the state can vindicate its interests in fetal life and deny a woman an abortion. The Court offered no justification for this conclusion, perhaps because any justification would have exposed the thinness of its claim that it was taking no position on when life begins.

The remainder of this Article examines the suitability of the *Roe* framework for resolving legal and public policy issues involv-

---

41. 410 U.S. at 163.

42. Omenn, *Prenatal Diagnosis of Genetic Disorders,* 200 SCIENCE 952 (1978).

43. *Id.*

44. Humans with severe malformations of the central nervous system, such as those without brains (anencephaly), severe and grotesque multiple system malformations (cyclops), and severe fetal asphyxia or anoxia would not be considered biologically viable. Behrman & Rosen, *supra* note 38, at 12-26.

45. 410 U.S. at 163.

46. Ely, *supra* note 9, at 924.

ing the unborn. I believe that although the opinion was inadequately reasoned, its framework is broadly acceptable if properly
modified and rooted in the reasons developed below.

II. The Reasons for the Traditional Live Birth Requirement for Granting Legal Protection

A. *The Historical Perspective*

At the time *Roe* was decided, the case law typically bestowed
legal protection at birth, a determination that suggests at least
two possible explanations: only then was the fetus physically separate from the mother, and only then was the fetus traditionally
capable of surviving independently of the mother.[47] The cases are
unclear about which of those explanations was more central,
largely because there was no reason to decide. Live birth was an
adequate and uncomplicated standard, and courts rarely needed
to discuss its significance.

Yet two types of cases provide clues to the value underlying
the live birth standard. The first type involves a premature infant
who exhibits some signs of life, but who expires shortly after
birth. The second type involves an infant born after a normal
gestation period, but who expires before all physical connections
to the mother have been severed.

Although few early American cases concerned premature
births, the first case to consider whether one may inherit through
a stillborn child, *Marsellis v. Thalhimer,*[48] discussed the problem
of prematures in dictum. The question presented was whether a
widow, pregnant at the time of her husband's death, could inherit
the share of her husband's estate allocable to her unborn child,
when that child was subsequently stillborn. The law was clear
that, had the fetus been born alive, it would have taken the
share.[49] A child born alive qualifies for an inheritance even if it

---

47. This Article stresses capability rather than actual independence. Even a newborn
is not actually independent; it would die without the care of others. Actual ability to feed
and clothe oneself only occurs well after birth.

48. 2 Paige Ch. 24 (N.Y. 1830).

49. The historical use of live birth is traced from Roman law to the present in 4 R.
Pound, Jurisprudence § 127, at 384-94 (1959). The civil law principle, later adopted by
the common law, was that fetal existence was a legal fiction used to protect fetal interests
in property until live birth occurred. *Id.* at 387-90. Louisell takes a different view. He
asserts that all of these cases accidentally involve live-born children. He argues: "Under
such circumstances it is understandable, but really gratuitous and superfluous, for the
court to observe that the child must have been born alive. The observation is only dictum;
it does not necessarily require a different result in those cases where the observation is

was only a fetus *in utero* at the testator's death. What was unclear was whether another person could benefit from the existence of a fetus *in utero* that was not subsequently born alive. After examining the civil law, the source of the rule permitting inheritance by a child who was *in utero* at the death of the testator,[50] the *Marsellis* court concluded that "children born dead, or in such an *early state of pregnancy as to be incapable of living, although they be not actually dead at the time of their birth,* are considered as if they had never been born or conceived."[51] Thus, a third party could not inherit through a stillborn child; a live birth of a mature baby was necessary to secure property interests. The dictum also suggests that a person claiming through a premature child had to prove that the child was capable of continued existence.[52] Since *Marsellis,* other cases[53] have reinforced its implications that the live birth criterion was important not as a sign of physical separation, which could occur at any time during the gestational period, but as verification of a capacity for continued life.

Cases involving fetuses born after a full gestation period, but who died before they were completely separated from their mothers, offer other clues. In *State v. Winthrop,*[54] the issue was whether the killing of such a fetus was homicide — the killing of a person. The trial court instructed the jury as follows:

> If the child is fully delivered from the body of the mother, while the after birth is not, and the two are connected by the umbilical cord, and the child had independent life, *no matter whether it has*

---

inappropriate." Louisell, *Abortion, The Practice of Medicine and the Due Process of Law,* 16 UCLA L. Rev. 233, 237 (1969).

50. 2 Paige Ch. at 40.

51. 2 Paige Ch. at 41 (emphasis added).

52. In civil law, a child born within the first six months after conception was presumed incapable of living. This presumption had to be rebutted before these newborns could inherit and transmit property to others. 2 Paige Ch. at 41.

53. *E.g.,* Tomlin v. Laws, 301 Ill. 616, 618, 134 N.E. 24, 25 (1922); Swain v. Bowers, 91 Ind. App. 307, 316-17, 158 N.E. 598, 601-02 (1927); Harper v. Archer, 12 Miss. (4 S. & M.) 99, 109 (1845); In re Will of Wells, 129 Misc. 447, 457, 221 N.Y.S. 714, 725 (Sur. Ct. 1927); Kimbro v. Harper, 113 Okla. 46, 49, 238 P. 840, 842 (1925). Whether a living but previable fetus *ex utero* can be the subject of homicide remains undecided. An early case illustrates the difficulty in determining whether death was caused by the previability itself or by the criminal assault. "Want of hair, nails, &c. or other circumstances of premature birth, must be evidence in favor of the prisoner [indicted for the murder of her child]. Circumstances of maturity, marks of violence, &c. are evidence against her." Pennsylvania v. McKee, 1 Addison 1 (Allegheny County Ct. Pa. 1791). *But see* Morgan v. State, 148 Tenn. 417, 421, 256 S.W. 433, 434 (1923) (if the fetus is criminally injured while previable and dies of its injuries after birth, the offense constitutes homicide).

54. 43 Iowa 519 (1876).

breathed or not, or an independent circulation has been established or not, it is a human being . . . .[55]

Because that instruction looked solely to the fact of physical expulsion in defining personhood, the Supreme Court of Iowa reversed.[56] According to the court, the instruction "would tell the jury . . . that they might find independence of life in utter disregard of the conditions in which alone, it could exist."[57] The high court held that potential independence was not enough; the state needed to show actual independence in order to sustain a conviction for homicide.[58] Thus, the state had to prove that the victim had an independent circulation, that the umbilical cord had been severed, and that the newborn had breathed on its own[59] before the killing. To be a "person," the infant needed to be capable of survival; mere physical separateness was not determinative.

Other cases agree with *Winthrop's* view of when a fetus becomes a person and reject mere physical separation in favor of other factors, factors suggesting a capacity for continued independent life. The indices of live birth that courts have used include independent circulation,[60] severance of the umbilical cord,[61] and physical expulsion from the uterus.[62] Secondary signs have also been offered, such as vocal cries[63] and heartbeat.[64] The most widely used criterion, however, has been independent respiration.[65]

B. *The Effect of Recent Medical Advances on the Case Law*

Two developments in medicine have eroded the adequacy of

---

55. 43 Iowa at 520 (emphasis in original).
56. 43 Iowa at 521.
57. 43 Iowa at 521.
58. 43 Iowa at 521-22.
59. 43 Iowa at 521-22.
60. Shedd v. State, 178 Ga. 653, 654-55, 173 S.E. 847, 847 (1934); State v. O'Neall, 79 S.C. 571, 573, 60 S.E. 1121, 1122 (1908); Morgan v. State, 148 Tenn. 417, 420-21, 256 S.W. 433, 434 (1923).
61. Shedd v. State, 178 Ga. 653, 655, 173 S.E. 847, 848 (1934); Morgan v. State, 148 Tenn. 417, 420-21, 256 S.W. 433, 434 (1923).
62. *See* Wallace v. State, 7 Tex. Crim. 570, 573 (1880) (total expulsion required).
63. Allen v. State, 128 Ga. 53, 57 S.E. 224 (1907). The transcript of the trial record is discussed in Shedd v. State, 178 Ga. 653, 656, 173 S.E. 847, 848-49 (1934). *But see* State v. Osmus, 73 Wyo. 183, 194, 276 P.2d 469, 472 (1954) ("Not every baby cries when born").
64. People v. Chavez, 77 Cal. App. 2d 621, 623, 176 P.2d 92, 94 (1947).
65. Jackson v. Commonwealth, 265 Ky. 295, 296, 96 S.W.2d 1014, 1014 (1936); State v. O'Neall, 79 S.C. 571, 572, 60 S.E. 1121, 1122 (1908); Morgan v. State, 148 Tenn. 417, 419, 256 S.W. 433, 433 (1928); Harris v. State, 28 Tex. Crim. 308, 309, 12 S.W. 1102, 1103 (1889).

the live birth criterion. First, as the *Roe* Court acknowledged, modern biological studies have verified that the fetus is *genetically* a separate entity from a point at or near conception.[66] Second, advances in medicine have made it possible for a fetus that is too young for normal birth to survive apart from its mother.[67] These developments directly called into question the selection of live birth as *the only* relevant moment for distributing legal protection.

The verification and acceptance of the fetus's genetic separation from the mother at or near conception significantly influenced tort law. As early as 1946, the court in *Bonbrest v. Kotz*[68] awarded damages to a child for injuries suffered *en ventre sa mere*.[69] The court specifically rejected the contention that a fetus is only a "part" of its mother and therefore not entitled to an independent claim, calling such notion "a contradiction of terms." By 1967, every state had followed *Bonbrest's* lead and permitted recovery for fetal injury if the fetus was subsequently born alive.[70]

---

66. *See* notes 123-29 *infra* and accompanying text.

67. *See* note 133 *infra*.

68. 65 F. Supp. 138 (D.D.C. 1946).

69. Dietrich v. Inhabitants of Northampton, 138 Mass. 14 (1884), was the first American case to consider whether a fetus injured *in utero* and born alive could recover from a negligent defendant. This case involved a woman who miscarried after falling on a negligently maintained highway. The infant was previable and lived for a few minutes before dying. The court, in an opinion by then-Judge Holmes, stated that a child subsequently born alive would have no cause of action for injuries sustained while *in utero,* because the child did not have independent existence apart from the mother. 138 Mass. at 16. This was the law until *Bonbrest v. Kotz* was decided. However, the *Dietrich* position was challenged as early as 1900 in a dissenting opinion in Allaire v. St. Luke's Hosp., 184 Ill. 359, 56 N.E. 638 (1900). This case involved the negligent operation of an elevator in which the pregnant mother was a passenger. The fetus was injured while viable. The majority followed *Dietrich,* but a dissent by Judge Boggs argued persuasively that fetuses injured while viable and subsequently born alive should be able to recover. 184 Ill. at 368-74, 56 N.E. at 640-42.

70. W. Prosser, Handbook of the Law of Torts § 55 (4th ed. 1971). Courts also quickly established that live birth followed closely by death would not preclude a cause of action under a wrongful death statute. *Id.*

Courts disagree whether a fetus must be viable at the time of injury to recover. In Bonbrest v. Kotz, 65 F. Supp. 138 (D.D.C. 1946), the fetus was viable and some courts retained that requirement. However, where the injured fetus is born alive there seems to be little point in drawing an arbitrary line about when injury must occur. If the objective of recovery is to compensate a living person who bears injuries caused by another's negligence, the timing of the injury is irrelevant. For a listing of states still adhering to viability and those who have abandoned it, see Comment, *Negligence and the Unborn Child: A Time for Change,* 18 S.D. L. Rev. 204, 204 n.7, 213 n.74 (1973). Since the date of that publication, Florida has abandoned the viability requirement. Day v. Nationwide Mut. Ins. Co., 328 So. 2d 560 (Fla. Dist. Ct. App. 1976).

The second modern medical development — a fetus's ability to exist independently of its mother at about twenty-eight weeks — helped some courts even before *Roe* to award fetuses full legal protection at the moment of viability.[71] *Verkennes v. Corniea,*[72] decided in 1949, initiated this trend: it was the first case to allow recovery for injuries to a viable fetus that resulted in stillbirth. The Supreme Court of Minnesota reasoned, "There is no question here about the viability of the unborn child, or its capacity for a separate and independent existence . . . . [W]here independent existence is possible and the life is destroyed through a wrongful act a cause of action arises."[73] By relying on a capacity criterion — a finding that the fetus was capable of continued independent existence — the court endorsed the view that I discussed above: capacity was the key reason for the traditional reliance on birth. Because the fetus was sufficiently mature to grow and develop even if separated from its mother, the court saw no reason to treat it differently from a newborn infant. The view first expressed in

---

71. The recognition of the fetus as a separate entity has led some commentators to argue that it should be entitled to legal protection from a point at or near conception. *See e.g.,* Noonan, *supra* note 39; Ramsey, *Reference Points in Deciding About Abortion* in MORALITY OF ABORTION, *supra* note 1, at 60. This was the point selected by the West German Constitutional Court in holding a permissive abortion statute unconstitutional. Judgment of Feb. 25, 1975, Bundesverfassungsgericht, 39 BVerfGE 1. (An English translation appears in Gorby & Jonas, *West Germany Abortion Decision: A Contrast to Roe v. Wade,* 9 J. MAR. J. PRAC. & PRO. 551, 605 (1976)).

The special reliance in tort law on the fact that the fetus is genetically separate from the mother from conception is causing current difficulty. In suits seeking recovery for preconception injuries where the fetus is born alive, it is argued that no duty is owed to one not yet in being. These suits involve negligent conduct which occurs prior to the conception of the child. The injury occurs to the parent(s), but they are not harmed. The harm attaches to the fetus at conception. These injured children will be unable to recover if it is required that the fetus be a separate entity at the time of the negligent conduct. Such a result seems unjust. The traditional elements of the tort of negligence can be applied to allow recovery. "If there is a human life, proved by subsequent birth, then that human life has the same rights at the time of conception as it has at any time thereafter. There cannot be absolutes in the minute to minute progress of life from sperm and ovum to cell, to embryo to foetus, to child." Zepeda v. Zepeda, 41 Ill. App. 2d 240, 249-50, 190 N.E.2d 849, 853 (1963), *cert. denied,* 379 U.S. 945 (1964).

In at least one case a cause of action for a preconception injury has been permitted. In Renslow v. Mennonite Hosp., 40 Ill. App. 3d 234, 351 N.E.2d 870 (1976), the plaintiff's mother had been given two blood transfusions when she was thirteen. These transfusions were the wrong blood type and caused sensitization of her blood. This was discovered eight years later through routine testing of her blood while she was pregnant with the plaintiff. Since the plaintiff's life was in danger, labor was induced. The plaintiff was born, but suffered injuries including permanent damage to the brain and nervous system.

72. 229 Minn. 365, 38 N.W.2d 838 (1949).

73. 229 Minn. at 370-71, 38 N.W.2d at 841.

Verkennes has now been adopted in a substantial number of states.[74]

The criminal law of at least one state has developed similarly.[75] In *Keeler v. Superior Court*,[76] the Supreme Court of Cali-

---

74. Alabama: Eich v. Town of Gulf Shores, 293 Ala. 95, 300 So. 2d 354 (1974); Connecticut: Gorke v. LeClerc, 23 Conn. Supp. 256, 181 A.2d 448 (1962); Hatala v. Markiewicz, 26 Conn. Supp. 358, 224 A.2d 406 (1966); Delaware: Worgan v. Greggo & Ferrara, Inc., 50 Del. 258, 128 A.2d 557 (1956); District of Columbia: Simmons v. Howard Univ., 323 F. Supp. 529 (D.D.C. 1971) (mem.); Georgia: Porter v. Lassiter, 91 Ga. App. 712, 87 S.E.2d 100 (1955); Illinois: Chrisafogeorgis v. Brandenburg, 55 Ill. 2d 368, 304 N.E.2d 88 (1973); Indiana: Britt v. Sears, 150 Ind. App. 487, 277 N.E.2d 20 (1971); Kansas: Hale v. Manion, 189 Kan. 143, 368 P.2d 1 (1962); Kentucky: Rice v. Rizk, 453 S.W.2d 732 (Ky. 1970); Maryland: State ex rel. Odham v. Sherman, 234 Md. 179, 198 A.2d 71 (1964); Massachusetts: Mone v. Greyhound Lines, Inc., 368 Mass. 354, 331 N.E.2d 916 (1975); Michigan: O'Neill v. Morse, 385 Mich. 130, 188 N.W.2d 785 (1971); Minnesota: Verkennes v. Corniea, 229 Minn. 365, 38 N.W.2d 838 (1949); Mississippi: Rainey v. Horn, 221 Miss. 269, 72 So. 2d 434 (1954); Nevada: White v. Yup, 85 Nev. 527, 458 P.2d 617 (1969); New Hampshire: Poliquin v. MacDonald, 101 N.H. 104, 135 A.2d 249 (1957); Ohio: Stidam v. Ashmore, 109 Ohio App. 431, 167 N.E.2d 106 (1959); Oklahoma: Evans v. Olson, 550 P.2d 924 (Okla. 1976); Oregon: Libbee v. Permanente Clinic, 268 Or. 258, 518 P.2d 636 (1974); Rhode Island: Presley v. Newport Hosp., 117 R.I. 177, 365 A.2d 748 (1976); South Carolina: Fowler v. Woodward, 244 S.C. 608, 138 S.E.2d 42 (1964); Todd v. Sandidge Constr. Co., 341 F.2d 75 (4th Cir. 1964) (South Carolina law); Washington: Moen v. Hanson, 85 Wash. 2d 597, 537 P.2d 266 (1975) (en banc); West Virginia: Baldwin v. Butcher, 155 W. Va. 431, 184 S.E.2d 428 (1971); Wisconsin: Kwaterski v. State Farm Mut. Auto. Ins. Co., 34 Wis. 2d 14, 148 N.W.2d 107 (1967).

The following states expressly deny recovery under wrongful death statutes for injury to the fetus *in utero* that results in stillbirth: Arizona: Kilmer v. Hicks, 22 Ariz. App. 522, 529 P.2d 706 (1974); California: Justus v. Atchison, 19 Cal. 3d 564, 565 P.2d 122, 139 Cal. Rptr. 97 (1977); Florida: Stern v. Miller, 348 So. 2d 303 (Fla. 1977); Iowa: McKillip v. Zimmerman, 191 N.W.2d 706 (Iowa 1971); Louisiana: Wascom v. American Indem. Corp., 348 So. 2d 128 (La. App. 1977); Missouri: State ex rel. v. Sanders, 538 S.W.2d 336 (Mo. 1976) (en banc); Nebraska: Egbert v. Wenzl, 199 Neb. 573, 260 N.W.2d 480 (1977); New Jersey: Graf v. Taggert, 43 N.J. 303, 204 A.2d 140 (1964); New York: Endresz v. Friedberg, 24 N.Y.2d 478, 248 N.E.2d 901, 301 N.Y.S.2d 65 (1969); North Carolina: Cardwell v. Welch, 25 N.C. App. 390, 213 S.E.2d 382, *cert. denied,* 287 N.C. 464 (1975); Pennsylvania: Marko v. Philadelphia Transp. Co., 420 Pa. 124, 216 A.2d 502 (1966); Tennessee: Hamby v. McDaniel, 559 S.W.2d 774 (Tenn. 1977); Virginia: Lawrence v. Craven Tire Co., 210 Va. 138, 169 S.E.2d 440 (1969).

Two states, however, have indicated that they would allow recovery for injuries resulting in stillbirth even without proof that the fetus was viable when the injury occurred. *See* Presley v. Newport Hosp., 117 R.I. 177, 188-89, 365 A.2d 748, 753 (1976) (dictum stating that recovery would be allowed for previable injury resulting in subsequent stillbirth); Porter v. Lassiter, 91 Ga. App. 712, 87 S.E.2d 100 (1955) (allowing recovery for injury to a woman one and one-half months pregnant which resulted, after quickening, in a stillborn infant at four and one-half months).

75. Most states required live birth to convict an offender of homicide for the infliction of fatal prenatal injuries. *See, e.g.,* Keeler v. Superior Ct., 2 Cal. 3d 619, 470 P.2d 617, 87 Cal. Rptr. 481 (1970); State v. Cooper, 22 N.J.L. 52, 54 (1849); State v. Dickinson, 23 Ohio App. 2d 259, 263 N.E.2d 253 (1970), *affd.,* 28 Ohio St. 2d 65, 275 N.E.2d 599 (1971); Morgan v. State, 248 Tenn. 417, 256 S.W. 433 (1928).

In People v. Chavez, 77 Cal. App. 2d 621, 626, 176 P.2d 92, 94 (1947), the court said

fornia held that a viable fetus was not a human being within the meaning of the state homicide statute. The California legislature responded by revising the general homicide statute to read: "Murder is the unlawful killing of a human being, *or a fetus,* with malice aforethought."[77] In 1976, a court of appeals in California construed the revised statute in a case involving the death of a fetus twelve to fifteen weeks in development.[78] Such a fetus was "previable": it had not reached the stage where it was capable of living independently of its mother. In construing the statute the court concluded that its protection was coextensive with the capability for independent human life, and thus existed only from the point of viability.[79]

Thus, birth was traditionally the point at which the fetus was entitled to full legal protection of its interests *because birth was once synonymous with viability.* Now that the concepts are distinct, courts have begun to abandon birth as the central criterion in both tort and criminal law. The next Sections of this Article analyze the arguments for retaining birth as the event that heralds legal protection and the related question of whether the law

that a child killed while being born could be the subject of homicide. The court's statement, however, was dictum since it affirmed the defendant's conviction on the ground that there was sufficient evidence to support jury findings that the child was born alive and removed from the mother.

Louisiana by statute makes criminal "killing a child during delivery" by the "intentional destruction, during parturition of the mother, of the vitality of life of a child in a state of being born and before actual birth, which child would otherwise have been born alive." LA. REV. STAT. ANN. § 14.87.1 (West 1974).

In a few states killing a fetus before it was quick constituted a lesser crime than manslaughter. *See* Evans v. People, 49 N.Y. 86 (1872); Foster v. State, 182 Wis. 298, 196 N.W. 233 (1923). Other cases that outlawed abortion from conception forward did not equate abortion with murder. *See, e.g.,* State v. Reed, 45 Ark. 333 (1885); Smith v. State, 33 Me. 48 (1851); State v. Elliott, 206 Or. 82, 289 P.2d 1075 (1955). However, some states did make illegal abortion a felony. *See* State v. Reed, 45 Ark. 333, 334 (1885) (prequickening attempted abortion a felony; postquickening attempt a misdemeanor); Smith v. State, 33 Me. 48, 57 (1851) (felony if intent to destroy fetus, otherwise a misdemeanor).

76. 2 Cal. 3d 619, 470 P.2d 617, 87 Cal. Rptr. 481 (1970).
77. CAL. PENAL CODE § 187 (West Supp. 1979) (emphasis added).
78. People v. Smith, 59 Cal. App. 3d 751, 129 Cal. Rptr. 498 (1976).
79. 59 Cal. App. 3d at 757, 129 Cal. Rptr. at 502. A California court recently affirmed a conviction for the murder of a viable fetus between 22-24 weeks in development. People v. Apodaca, 76 Cal. App. 3d 479, 142 Cal. Rptr. 830 (1978). The defendant was convicted of murder in the second degree against the fetus, and rape and assault against the mother. The court held that multiple punishment was warranted because each conviction "was [for] a crime of violence against a different victim: the murder was a crime against the fetus, while the rape was a crime against [the mother]." 76 Cal. App. 3d at 493, 142 Cal. Rptr. at 840.

should provide the same protection to fetuses at different stages of development.

III. THE CASE FOR RECOGNIZING LEGAL PROTECTION FOR THE UNBORN: THE ANALOGIES TO CHILDREN AND TO THE DEAD

To determine whether the unborn should be able to claim legal protection, we must ascertain what qualities determine who is entitled to such protection. The United States Constitution only protects "persons."[80] At least since the passage of the post-Civil War Amendments, all born of human parents have been regarded as persons.[81] The Constitution protects persons by granting them rights that the state must respect. But not all persons have the same rights.[82] For example, public officials, soldiers, and prisoners have constitutional rights, but they may have fewer rights than citizens at large. Moreover, although two persons may have similar rights, the law does not always permit them to assert those rights in identical ways.[83] The differences between the legal rights of adults to make reproductive decisions and those of children illustrate that fact of American life.

Competent adults may, subject to compelling state interests, determine whether and under what circumstances they will reproduce.[84] The Supreme Court has stated: "If the right of privacy

---

80. U.S. CONST. amends. V, XIV § 1. *Cf.* Dred Scott v. Sandford, 60 U.S. (19 How.) 393, 451-52 (1856) (denying rights to blacks after holding that blacks are mere property).

81. *See generally* U.S. CONST. amends. XIII-XV. These amendments, ratified between 1865 and 1870, were designed primarily to protect fundamental rights of blacks who had recently been emancipated from years of slavery and treatment as something less than human. *See* Dred Scott v. Sandford, 60 U.S. (19 How.) 393 (1856). Today, however, these amendments protect all humans of any race. *See* Regents of the Univ. of Cal. v. Bakke, 438 U.S. 265, 289-95 (1978) (opinion of Powell, J.).

Apart from the questions of who is a human, or of how we determine who is a member of the species, there is the more interesting question of what, if anything, distinguishes humans from some of the more intelligent animals. One of the characteristics thought to distinguish humans from animals has been the ability to communicate through language. This distinction may become blurred, however, since there is evidence that some animals can be taught language skills. *See* Hayes, *The Pursuit of Reason*, N.Y. Times, June 12, 1977, § 6 (Magazine) at 21. This in turn raises the issue of whether some animals ought to have rights. *See* Feinberg, *The Rights of Animals and Unborn Generations*, in PHILOSOPHY AND ENVIRONMENTAL CRISIS 43, 45-51, 55-57 (W. Blackstone ed. 1974).

82. Children, for example, do not have the right to trial by jury in juvenile delinquency hearings. McKeiver v. Pennsylvania, 403 U.S. 528 (1971).

83. *See* text at notes 92-104 *infra.*

84. Carey v. Population Servs. Intl., 431 U.S. 678, 687-89 (1977) (plurality opinion); Griswold v. Connecticut, 381 U.S. 479 (1965). In *Griswold* the Court invalidated a Connecticut statute prohibiting distribution of contraceptives to married couples. The Court stated that a zone of privacy, emanating from the Bill of Rights, encompasses the marital

means anything, it is the right of the *individual,* married or single, to be free from unwarranted governmental intrusion into matters so fundamentally affecting a person as the decision whether to bear or beget a child."[85] This recognition of rights pertaining to childbearing began with *Griswold v. Connecticut,*[86] a case addressing married persons' use of contraceptives. The recognition continued with *Eisenstadt v. Baird*[87] (contraception), *Roe v. Wade*[88] (abortion) and *Planned Parenthood v. Danforth*[89] (abortion), and it culminated recently in *Carey v. Population Services International.*[90] In *Carey,* the Court invalidated a statute that permitted only licensed pharmacists to distribute nonprescription contraceptives:

> *Griswold* may no longer be read as holding only that a State may not prohibit a married couple's use of contraceptives. Read in light of its progeny, the teaching of *Griswold* is that the Constitution protects individual decisions in matters of childbearing from unjustified intrusion by the State.[91]

Children, too, have constitutional rights entitling them to make reproductive decisions.[92] However, the cases hold that the state may regulate the child's right to make decisions about re-

---

relation. 381 U.S. at 484-86. That zone of privacy can be regulated only upon a showing of compelling state interest. Despite the Court's denial, *Griswold* extends the substantive due process approach adopted by the Court in Lochner v. New York, 198 U.S. 45 (1905). For a discussion of the right to privacy and substantive due process, see Tribe, *supra* note 6; Ely, *supra* note 6.

85. Eisenstadt v. Baird, 405 U.S. 438, 453 (1972).

86. 381 U.S. 479 (1965) (the Court struck down a Connecticut statute banning the use of contraceptives by married people).

87. 405 U.S. 438 (1972) (right of access to contraceptives the same for single and married individuals).

88. 410 U.S. 113 (1973).

89. 428 U.S. 52 (1976).

90. 431 U.S. 678 (1977) (plurality opinion).

91. 431 U.S. at 687. The Court distinguished the right to privacy from a more expansive notion of a right to autonomy that might, for example, protect homosexual relations between consenting adults. As Justice Goldberg stated in his *Griswold* concurrence, "[T]he Court's holding today . . . in no way interferes with a State's proper regulation of sexual promiscuity or misconduct." 381 U.S. at 498-99. *See also* Carey v. Population Servs. Intl., 431 U.S. at 694 n.17; 431 U.S. at 702-03 (White, J., concurring in part and concurring in the judgment). It has been argued persuasively, however, that the right of privacy as used in *Roe* embraces the notion of autonomy rather than traditional notions of privacy. *See, e.g.,* Friendly, *The Courts and Social Policy: Substance and Procedure,* 33 U. MIAMI L. REV. 21, 35-36 (1978); Note, *Roe and Paris: Does Privacy Have a Principle?,* 26 STAN. L. REV. 1161 (1974).

92. *See* Carey v. Population Servs. Intl., 431 U.S. 678, 693 (1977) (minors have a right to privacy that protects procreation).

productive matters more extensively than it may an adult's right.[93] The issue is not whether children are capable of having rights in all respects equivalent to those of adults,[94] but rather whether the state's interest in regulating the activites of children may permit it to limit those rights more than it limits those of adults. The issue "is a vexing one, perhaps not susceptible to precise answer."[95] Although the Supreme Court has overturned statutes prohibiting persons from distributing contraceptives to minors under the age of sixteen[96] and statutes requiring parental consent to abortion for unmarried women under eighteen,[97] those decisions also suggest that the state may regulate a child's right to make reproductive decisions more extensively than an adult's right. *Carey,* which invalidated New York's blanket prohibition of contraceptive sales to minors,[98] did not foreclose less burdensome restrictions on such sales and did not give minors a full constitutional right to have sexual relations.[99] In *Bellotti v.*

---

93. *See* Planned Parenthood v. Danforth, 428 U.S. 52, 74 (1976) (the state may subject minors' constitutional rights to greater regulation than that permissible for adults).

94. The Supreme Court has often held that specific constitutional guarantees extend to minors as well as adults. *See, e.g., In re* Winship, 397 U.S. 358 (1970) (proof beyond a reasonable doubt required in delinquency hearing); *In re* Gault, 387 U.S. 1 (1967) (extending the due process clause to juvenile delinquency hearings and specifically requiring notice of charges, right to counsel, and a right to cross examination); Haley v. Ohio, 332 U.S. 596 (1948) (plurality opinion) (due process requires suppression of minor's involuntary confession). *But see* McKeiver v. Pennsylvania, 403 U.S. 528 (1971) (refusing to extend right of trial by jury to juvenile delinquency hearings).

95. Carey v. Population Servs. Intl., 431 U.S. at 692 (plurality opinion).

96. Carey v. Population Servs. Intl., 431 U.S. 678 (1977).

97. Planned Parenthood v. Danforth, 428 U.S. 52 (1976).

98. 431 U.S. at 91-96 (plurality opinion). The decision in *Carey* is a majority opinion except upon the issue of prohibiting the distribution of contraceptives to minors under the age of 16. That portion of the opinion, referred to in the text, is a plurality opinion written by Justice Brennan and joined by Justices Stewart, Marshall, and Blackmun. Justice White concurred in the judgment on this issue because he found that the state had not demonstrated that the prohibition against distribution of contraceptives to minors had a deterrent effect on premarital intercourse. 431 U.S. at 702. Justices Powell and Stevens based their concurrences in part on the statute's unconstitutional prohibition of distribution of contraceptives to married females between the ages of 14 and 16. 431 U.S. at 707-08 (Powell, J., concurring in part and concurring in the judgment); 431 U.S. at 713 (Stevens, J., concurring in part and concurring in the judgment).

99. The concurring opinions to that part of the opinion in *Carey* declaring the statute unconstitutional emphatically make that point. Justice Stevens, in a statement with which Justice White explicitly concurred, 431 U.S. at 702-03, wrote: "Indeed, I would describe as 'frivolous' appellees' argument that a minor has the constitutional right to put contraceptives to their intended use, notwithstanding the combined objection of both parents and the State." 431 U.S. at 713. Justice Powell stated that the New York statute was unconstitutional because "this provision prohibits parents from distributing contra-

Baird,[100] the Court held unconstitutional a Massachusetts statute that did not permit a mature minor to make an independent decision about abortion and required parental consultation and notification for all minors. However, four Justices suggested that a court could determine that an abortion was not in the best interests of an immature minor.[101]

Both adults and children, then, may claim constitutional protections. On what basis do we distinguish the scope of their respective rights? Why, in the area of reproductive decisions, do we treat children differently from adults?[102] Traditionally there has been concern for a minor's ability to evaluate risks. Some states protect children from the risks associated with medical procedures by declaring that children are incapable of consenting to those procedures.[103] States have also limited a child's right to engage in other activities, such as driving, making contracts, and purchasing alcoholic beverages. These restrictions all manifest the state's concern for a child's ability to make mature judgments.[104]

While protecting the child from the consequences of immature decisions, the state has played an active role in rearing children, especially in matters that might contribute to a child's future ability to make judgments. State laws on compulsory education and on rehabilitation of juvenile delinquents are two ex-

---

ceptives to their children, a restriction that unjustifiably interferes with parental interests in rearing their children." 431 U.S. at 708.

100. 99 S. Ct. 3035 (1979). In Planned Parenthood v. Danforth, 428 U.S. 52 (1976), all of the Justices indicated that a requirement of parental consultation might well be constitutional. Justice Stewart believed the Missouri statute to be unconstitutional primarily because of the absolute limitation that it created to a minor's access to abortion. However, citing *Bellotti,* he held open the possibility that a requirement only of parental consultation, as opposed to parental consent, would be constitutional. 428 U.S. at 90-91 (Stewart, J., concurring). The remaining Justices would have upheld the Missouri requirement of parental consent and would have undoubtedly have held the less restrictive requirement of parental consultation constitutional as well. 428 U.S. at 95 (White, J., with Burger, C.J., & Rehnquist, J., concurring in part and dissenting in part) (parental consent furthers valid state interest in ensuring that unmarried minor makes abortion decision in her own best interests); 428 U.S. at 103 (Stevens, J., concurring in part and dissenting in part) (parental consent maximizes probability that abortion decisions will be made with full understanding of consequences).

101. 99 S. Ct. at 3050.

102. In *Bellotti* Justice Powell offered three reasons: "the peculiar vulnerability of children; their inability to make critical decisions in an informed, mature manner; and the importance of the parental role in child-rearing." 99 S. Ct. at 3043.

103. Pilpel, *Minors' Rights to Medical Care,* 36 ALB. L. REV. 462, 463-64 (1972).

104. *See* Planned Parenthood v. Danforth, 428 U.S. at 102-93 (Stevens, J., concurring in part and dissenting in part).

amples of state efforts toward that end. Such efforts presume that a child must be carefully instructed and educated in order to assume adult responsibilities, and that during the education period it must be protected from the adverse consequences of its own behavior and from the harmful actions of others. Competent adults are not afforded similar nurture and protection. It is thought that they possess a level of maturity and capability for rational action that children lack. They are presumed capable of making responsible, mature, and reasoned decisions, fully appreciating the possible consequences.

If children cannot make rational decisions, why do we give them any rights at all? We do so to increase the likelihood that they will be regarded as persons rather than property.[105] Giving children rights also makes it easier for the state to protect them from the harmful acts of parents or third parties. Long ago, the Supreme Court said, "It is in the interest of youth itself, and of the whole community, that children be both safeguarded from abuses and given opportunities for growth into free and independent well-developed men and citizens."[106] Ultimately, it may be this last trait that truly motivates courts and legislatures to give children rights — the potential to grow into mature, competent, well-developed adults.[107] Although we realize that they are "not possessed of that full capacity for individual choice" that is essential to exercise of the broadest rights,[108] we know that children are

---

105. *See* Areen, *Intervention Between Parent and Child: A Reappraisal of the State's Role in Child Neglect and Abuse Cases,* 63 GEO. L.J. 887 (1975). Areen traces the history of child abuse and neglect and points out, for example, that children were forced to be indentured servants both in England and the United States. *Id.* at 894-903. That suggests that children were treated like property.

106. Prince v. Massachusetts, 321 U.S. 158, 165 (1944).

107. Feinberg argues that beings must have interests if they are logically to be subjects of rights. He suggests that interests are composed of conations ("conscious wishes, desires, and hopes; or urges and impulses; . . . or latent tendencies, direction of growth, and natural fulfillments"). Feinberg, *supra* note 81, at 49. Interests are necessary because a right-holder must be capable of being represented (a being cannot be represented if it has no interest), and because a right-holder must be capable of being a beneficiary in its own person. In the usual case a right-holder is a normal adult human being. Feinberg contends that children are also right-holders because they have interests, or in the case of newborns because they have a capacity to acquire interests. Emerging interests are sometimes in need of protection, otherwise they might never come into existence. These interests may be protected by representatives. He further argues that the same principle can be extended to the unborn. The unborn a day prior to birth are "not strikingly different" from the newborn in the first hour after birth. *Id.* at 62. In a later article, he argues that the unborn have no right to be born. Feinberg, *Is There a Right to Be Born?,* in MORAL PHILOSOPHY: PROBLEMS OF THEORY AND PRACTICE 346 (J. Rachels ed. 1976).

108. Ginsberg v. New York, 390 U.S. 629, 649-50 (1968) (Stewart, J., concurring in the result).

potentially capable, and we nurture that potentiality.

The unborn are like children in their potentiality to become rational adults. Notwithstanding the *Roe* holding that the unborn are not persons within the meaning of the fourteenth amendment, that critical similarity between fetuses and children is convincing evidence for giving fetuses and children at least some legal protection. Neither fetuses nor newborn infants are capable of making rational judgments; both can develop that capacity. Professor Feinberg has remarked that a newborn infant "lacks the traits necessary for the possession of interests, but he has the capacity to acquire those traits, and his inherited potentialities are moving quickly toward actualization even as we watch him."[109] The identical statement could be made of the unborn.[110]

What differences there are between a fetus and a newborn are not of the sorts that the law has found material in awarding legal protection. Although it is true that the newborn infant is conscious and the fetus is not, comatose adults do not forfeit their constitutional rights. Not even the most arguably relevant difference between the newborn and the unborn — the ability to interact with other humans — is persuasive. Birth is certainly the point at which other humans see, touch, and communicate with the developing infant. But is there something unique about the characteristic of human interaction that should prevent recognition of legal protection at some earlier point in human development? I would argue not. Both the dead and the unborn lack that capacity to interact, yet the law respects the interests of the deceased; the incapacity to interact should be no greater barrier to legal protection for the unborn.

A brief digression to probe the forms and purposes of legal deference to the dead will prove enlightening. At first, the idea that the dead deserve legal protection seems strange. Physically, after all, they are mere decaying matter. They are incapable of

---

109. Feinberg, *supra* note 81, at 62. The argument that beings have rights because they have the potential to be competent adults raises disturbing questions, however, with respect to the severely mentally retarded and the mentally disabled. We can argue that to the extent that they are potentially curable they should have rights. However, it might be extremely difficult to regard some humans as potentially curable — those in irreversible comas, for example. Should these beings have rights? I am inclined to think not. I hasten to add that the fact that perhaps they should not have rights does not imply that they are to be treated cavalierly. There may be many reasons we should treat them as though they had rights. For Feinberg's discussion of this issue, see *id.* at 60-61.

110. The legal rights of children must often be asserted by representatives, because that is the only practical means of assuring that those rights will be protected. The same principle could extend to the unborn.

making promises or of fulfilling responsibilities.[111] Yet, in a
significant sense, they may be said to rule from the grave. This
is especially true in property law; where testamentary disposi-
tions change the lives of the living according to the whims of those
no longer with us.[112] And it is true elsewhere in the law as well.
For the most part, the wishes of the deceased concerning disposition of his corpse prevail, even though at English common law the
corpse was not property[113] and was therefore not subject to testamentary direction.[114] In the United States, the strict English rule
has been relaxed to the extent that, although there is no commercial property right in a dead body and it is not part of a decedent's
estate,[115] a "quasi property" right exists.[116] In some states a person's right to ordain the manner of disposition of his own body
has been specifically conferred by statute.[117] The general Ameri-

---

111. For example, at common law death ended the contract. RESTATEMENT OF
CONTRACTS §§ 35 (1)(d), 48 (1932).

112. Blackstone argues that the ability to pass title to property is not a natural right.
He writes: "[T]here is no foundation in nature or in natural law why a set of words upon
parchment should convey the dominion of land . . . ." 2 W. BLACKSTONE, COMMENTARIES*
2. However, Blackstone concedes that humans have always been permitted to devise
property.

> [T]he universal law of almost every nation (which is a kind of secondary law of
> nature) has either given the dying person a power of continuing his property, by
> disposing of his possession by will; or, in case he neglects to dispose of it, or is not
> permitted to make any disposition at all, the municipal law of the country then
> steps in, and declares who shall be the successor . . . .

Id. at * 10-11. In the United States, the Supreme Court has stated that although validly
created wills will be enforced, enforcement is not necessarily a matter of constitutional
rights. Irving Trust Co. v. Day, 314 U.S. 556, 562 (1942). Contra, Nunnemacher v. State,
129 Wis. 190, 108 N.W. 627 (1906).

113. In re Estate of Johnson, 169 Misc. 215, 217-20, 7 N.Y.S.2d 81, 83-86 (Sur. Ct.
1938).

114. The prevailing concept of the human body was a temple for the Holy Spirit, from
which a person's soul was temporarily separated at death. It would have been repugnant
to common law society to attach to such a holy vessel the commercial values that attend
legal property rights. In re Estate of Johnson, 169 Misc. 215, 218, 7 N.Y.S.2d 81, 84 (Sur.
Ct. 1938). Therefore, until the time of Henry VIII, the place and manner of burial were
controlled by the ecclesiastical courts. See Groll & Kerwin, The Uniform Anatomical Gift
Act: is the Right to a Decent Burial Obsolete?, 2 LOY. CHI. L.J. 275, 275 (1971). Bodies,
according to law and custom, were buried intact in the community churchyard. Any
attempt by the decedent to control the manner of his burial by testamentary direction
failed because the body was not "property." Id. at 275-76.

115. Fidelity Union Trust Co. v. Heller, 16 N.J. Super. 285, 290, 84 A.2d 485, 487
(1951).

116. Diebler v. American Radiator & Standard Sanitary Corp., 196 Misc. 618, 620,
92 N.Y.S.2d 356, 358 (1949).

117. The New York statute, which made it a crime to interfere with the decedent's
wishes for his own burial, was repealed upon enactment of the Uniform Anatomical Gift
Act, 1970 N.Y. Laws ch. 466, § 2.

can rule is that, while the decedent's wishes or directives concerning his interment are not technically testamentary and legal compulsion may not necessarily attach to them, they are entitled to respectful consideration and have been allowed great weight.[118]

The terms of the Uniform Anatomical Gift Act[119] also respect the wishes of the deceased. That Act provides that any individual of sound mind and eighteen years or more of age may donate all or part of his body for transplant or for medical research by testamentary directive or by execution of a properly attested nontestamentary document,[120] even over opposition by his family.[121]

Why have we so frequently respected the deceased's desires concerning their remains, enforced their promises, and permitted their desired disposition of property? As living, existing persons we have many interests, most of which we can assert while we remain alive. But some interests cannot be asserted and fulfilled during our lifetimes; they must survive death if they are to be recognized and enforced. Yet, our legal system protects them. Does that protection imply that the dead have rights? Are we protecting those interests for the exclusive benefit of the dead? Probably not. Do we do it for the good of us all? Probably so. Most of us desire assurance that our wishes about the world we shall leave behind are recognized. We wish to take care of our families. We wish to leave nothing to certain people. It is a continuation of the responsibilities we assumed while living. By recognizing the

---

118. In disputes between executors or administrators attempting to carry out the decedent's directions and decedent's next-of-kin having other plans for interment, courts have held that the wishes of the deceased for the disposition of the remains are paramount to all other considerations. *E.g., In re* Estate of Henderson, 13 Cal. App. 2d 449, 57 P.2d 212 (1936); *In re* Harlam, 57 N.Y.S.2d 103 (1945); *In re* Herskovits, 183 Misc. 411, 48 N.Y.S.2d 906 (1944); *In re* Estate of Eichner, 173 Misc. 644, 18 N.Y.S.2d 573 (1940). Even when the decedent's testamentary directives contravene the religious beliefs of his family (*e.g.,* where a Jewish decedent leaves instruction that he should be cremated), courts still have often upheld the wishes of the deceased. *See generally In re* Herskovits, 183 Misc. 411, 412, 48 N.Y.S.2d 906, 907 (1944); *In re* Estate of Johnson, 169 Misc. 215, 7 N.Y.S. 81 (1938).

A majority of courts, however, refuse to allow a body, once buried, to be exhumed. *E.g.,* Yome v. Gorman, 242 N.Y. 395, 403, 152 N.E. 126, 128 (1926). Moreover, since a decision in disputes between a decedent's executor and surviving relations is an exercise of equitable powers, the courts have not hesitated to violate the decedent's directions where the directives offend the court's conception of family responsibility or community interest. *See* Herold v. Herold, 16 Ohio Dec. 303, 3 Ohio N.P. (n.s.) 405 (C.P. Butler Co. 1905).

119. Codifications for all participating jurisdictions are collected in Groll & Kerwin, *supra* note 114, at 290 n.49.

120. Uniform Anatomical Gift Act §§ 2(10), 4(a).

121. *See* Uniform Anatomical Gift Act §§ 2(a), 4(a).

claims of all dead people, we hope that our own desires will be accorded similar respect and deference. Giving legal protection to the dead thus serves two purposes. It gratifies people who are now alive by encouraging their present hopes that their own preferences will be satisfied after they are gone. Moreover, it affirms the importance to our society of human life generally: continued respect for the wishes of those who were once persons bolsters respect for the wishes of those who are still persons.

What relevance does consideration of the interests of the deceased have to the interests of the unborn? First, it makes clear that ability to interact with other humans is not a prerequisite for recognizing legal protection in our society. Second, the reasons that motivate our society to protect the dead have analogies in the realm of the unborn. Corresponding with the gratification felt by mature adults at the thought that their own wishes will be significant after they die is a gratification at the thought that their wishes were significant even before they were born. They can thereby escape whatever insecurity may be aroused by the notion that at one time in their prenatal existences they were deemed wholly undeserving of legal respect. Similarly, it can bolster societal appreciation of human life generally, by assuring that at no time during the development of any person alive today was that person wholly beyond legal concern.

To say that a fetus should have legal protection is not to delineate the contours of that protection.[122] It does not imply that the protection must be coextensive with that given children, any more than newborns must have rights equivalent to those of teenagers. I assert only that the unborn fetus, the newborn child, and the mature adult are all at different stages of development, and the fact that a fetus is not conscious or socially responsive should not preclude all legal protection.

---

122. The problem of choosing where on the continuum of human potentiality we wish to acknowledge significant legal protection is analogous to the issue of how far into the future we want to permit the wishes of the dead to control disposition of property. From the earliest times, the common law sought to balance the power to bind land indefintitely against the desire for free alienability of property. The Rule Against Perpetuities, first announced in The Duke of Norfolk's Case, 22 Eng. Rep. 931 (Ch. 1682), attempted to strike a balance between these competing concerns. The Rule is, without doubt, somewhat arbitrary and is certainly difficult to understand and apply, but it does attempt a balance between competing, equally valid concerns. For an interesting account of the Rule and its origins, see Haskins, *Extending the Grasp of the Dead Hand: Reflections on the Origins of the Rule Against Perpetuities,* 126 U. PA. L. REV. 19 (1977).

IV. What Legal Protection for the Unborn? The Case for
Distinguishing Between the Previable and the Viable Fetus

Even if, as has been argued above, there is no justification
for denying the unborn all legal protection, we must still confront
another problem: Should we give the same degree of legal protection to all humans at every stage of development, or should we
recognize some specific point on the continuum of potentiality at
which the legal protection becomes substantially greater than it
was before? This problem is particularly acute when the interests
of a fully matured individual conflict directly with those of a
human at an earlier stage of biological development. In such a
situation, it is impossible to resolve the conflict satisfactorily
without subordinating the interests of one of the parties. For example, should the interests of a fertilized ovum be accorded the
same, lesser, or greater legal protection than those of an infertile
woman who desires to have a child through a procedure that
involves fertilization outside of the womb? In such a procedure,
physicians may destroy unused fertilized ova in an effort to im-
pregnate the mother. In my view, the fetus should not be entitled
to the same degree of protection at every stage of development.
We should distinguish between the legal protection afforded the
viable and the previable fetus just as we once distinguished between legal protection furnished before and after birth.
     In exploring the contours of a revised view of legally cogniza-
ble fetal interests, we should consider the available medical and
biological data concerning human development. Current medical
understanding indicates that the meeting of sperm and ova results in the creation of a zygote possessing a totally independent
genetic package of twenty-three chromosome pairs.[123] Within a
week of fertilization, the zygote implants itself in the uterine
wall[124] — a significant event, because only after implantation can
we diagnose pregnancy.[125] "Twinning," and occasionally recombi-

123. *See* Hellegers, *Fetal Development*, 31 Theo. Stud. 3, 3-4 (1970). This article is
a particularly vivid and nontechnical description of fetal development which highlights
stages of development and the importance that has been attached to them historically.
     124. *Id.* at 6. Normally, implantation occurs in the endometrium, the lining of the
uterine cavity. However, extrauterine implantation sometimes occurs, most commonly in
the fallopian tubes, resulting in an ectopic pregnancy.
     125. *Id.* at 7. Pregnancy can be diagnosed at this stage by chemical tests that measure
hormones secreted to stop the menstrual cycle. However, these chemicals tests indicate
only that pregnancy has probably occurred. The positive signs of pregnancy are: "(1)
identification of the fetal heartbeat separately and distinctly from that of the mother; (2)
perception of active fetal movements by the examiner; and (3) recognition of the fetus

nation, takes place[126] during the first fourteen days after fertilization. This suggests that although fertilization creates a new genetic grid, conception occurs over an extended time period. Moreover, fertilization does not necessarily indicate that genetic individuality has been accomplished. Thus, it may be impractical to recognize legal protection on the entire continuum of fetal existence if for no other reason than that we are not sure when "existence" begins.

Early fetal development continues through the eighth week of pregnancy, after which all organs of the fetus exist in rudimentary form and we can detect readable but not understandable brain activity. Subsequent development consists of growth and maturation of structures formed during the embryonic period.[127] Somewhere between the twelfth and sixteenth weeks, "quickening" — fetal movement perceptible to the mother — occurs.[128] Given current medical knowledge and technology, the fetus is viable[129] somewhere between the twentieth and twenty-eighth weeks.

In addition to better information about the stages of fetal development, modern science has acquired knowledge that is useful to prevent, ameliorate, or cure some fetal disabilities. We should also consider that information carefully in evaluating fetal interests. It suggests that some fetal interests deserve some legal protection at all stages of development. We have developed new and better methods of caring for neonates (infants four weeks old or younger).[130] Greater numbers of prematures are surviving, and

radiologically or sonographically." J. PRITCHARD & P. MACDONALD, WILLIAMS' OBSTETRICS 204 (15th ed. 1976). Menstrual extraction, the morning-after pill, and the intrauterine device, commonly used as contraceptives, might technically be considered "abortifacients" since they interrupt pregnancy before it can be diagnosed.

126. Hellegers, supra note 123, at 4.

127. See J. PRITCHARD & P. MACDONALD, supra note 125, at 89.

128. Id. at 212. In the early criminal law, this was a significant point before which abortion was sometimes permitted. Later criminal abortion statutes prohibited abortion from conception. Since quickening is a matter of maternal perception rather than fetal development, it has no modern legal significance.

129. Hellegers, supra note 123, at 8-9. Hellegers asserts that the fetus between the 20th and 28th weeks may have approximately a 10% chance of survival. This view is not universally accepted. Behrman and Rosen report that a worldwide survey revealed that no infant weighing less than 601 grams and less than 24 weeks in gestational age has survived. Behrman & Rosen, supra note 38, at 12-9.

130. See Brans, Advances in Perinatal Care: 1970-1980, 19 J. REPRODUCTIVE MED. 111 (1977). Brans discusses the significant advances in selected areas — hemolytic disease, hyperbilirubinemia, maternal diabetes, hyaline membrane disease, nutrition of the tiny premature neonate, infections, and monitoring mother-child interaction.

they are surviving at earlier periods of development.[131] We have also developed a variety of techniques for observing individual fetuses. It is possible, for example, to detect and accurately diagnose *in utero* some disabilities and anomalies resulting from genetic conditions.[132] We can determine the sex of the fetus, hear fetal heartbeats, diagnose multiple fetuses, and obtain an outline of fetal structure.[133] Indeed, recent research has garnered so much knowledge about the fetus and its environment that we can view the fetus as a "second patient."[134]

We are only beginning to develop the capacity to administer therapy to fetuses *in utero*. One noteworthy achievement treats Rh incompatibility between mother and fetus: we can now give transfusions to the fetus *in utero*.[135] Current research suggests that administering certain drugs to mothers can prevent or minimize respiratory distress in newborns.[136] Moreover, contemporary

131. *See* Manniello & Farrell, *Analysis of United States neonatal mortality statistics from 1968 to 1974,* 129 AM. J. OBSTETRICS & GYNECOLOGY 667 (1977). That article analyzes neonatal statistics with specific reference to changing trends in major casualties. The authors conclude that the data show a fall in the annual newborn mortality rate from 16.1 to 12.3 per 1000 births. *Id.* at 669. They attribute this decline to advances in perinatology. *Id.* at 673. *See also* Stewart, *supra* note 38. That article concludes that provided intensive care methods are available, the prognosis for infants weighing less than 1000 grams is better than in the past. *Id.* at 103. However, the costs of providing for perinatal intensive care are high. One investigator reports a $40,000 figure per infant less than 1000 grams. Pomerance, Ukrainski, & Ukra, *The Cost of Living for Infants ≤ 1000 Gms. at Birth, abstracted in* 11 PEDIATRIC RESEARCH 381 (1977). These high costs suggest that guidelines should be developed concerning problems such as when to withdraw intensive perinatal care.

132. *See* Omenn, *supra* note 42. The most common technique employed is amniocentesis. Amniocentesis involves the insertion of a needle through the abdominal wall into the amniotic sac to withdraw amniotic fluid. The fluid and fetal cells found in the fluid are analyzed to detect the presence of genetic diseases. Currently most chromosomal anomalies and more than 60 inborn errors of metabolism can be identified through that technique. Littlefield, Milunsky, & Atkins, *An Overview of Prenatal Genetic Diagnosis,* in BIRTH DEFECTS 221 (1974). Other techniques are visualization of the fetus by a fetoscope, radiography and ultrasound, and sampling of fetal and maternal blood. For an explanation of these techniques and their current level of development see Omenn, *supra* note 42.

133. *See* J. PRITCHARD & P. MACDONALD, *supra* note 125, at 204-05, 537-40, 274-77.

134. This is a relatively new concept for medicine. Until about 25 years ago the mother was regarded as the patient. The fetus was regarded as another maternal organ. The physician, therefore, always acted in the best interests of the mother, believing that doing so was in the best interest of the unborn. *See* J. PRITCHARD & P. MACDONALD, *supra* note 125, at 265.

135. *See id.* at 809-11.

136. *See* Liggins & Howie, *The Prevention of RDS by Maternal Steroid Therapy,* in MODERN PERINATAL MEDICINE 415 (L. Gluck ed. 1974); Liggins & Howie, *A Controlled Trial of Antepartum Glucocorticoid Treatment for Prevention of the Respiratory Distress Syndrome in Premature Infants,* 50 PEDIATRICS 515 (1972).

animal research is expected to develop additional therapeutic techniques.[137]

This review of the medical data suggests a number of points in fetal development at which one might recognize a strong claim for significantly increasing the legal protection given a developing human. I would argue that, absent powerful countervailing considerations, the point selected should reflect the fundamental principles underlying the present legal system — principles that warrant revised rules to keep pace with recent medical advances.

As I noted earlier, the law has traditionally considered the acquisition of a capacity for independent existence to be the significant point in human development. Traditionally, birth was the point at which the capacity criterion was satisfied. Today viability precedes birth, and therefore birth is no longer the event most appropriately satisfying the capacity criterion.[138] Viability is preferable to birth, because, as we saw earlier, there is no relevant difference between a viable fetus and a newborn.[139] Explicit substitution of viability for birth as the point at which important legal protections vest would not establish a new principle. It would adhere to the traditional principle, invoking a more precise formulation of the standard in response to modern medical information and capabilities.

---

137. Investigators are removing primate fetuses from the womb, performing complicated neurosurgery, replacing the fetuses, and delivering them at term. It is hoped that such research will increase knowledge about nervous system damage in humans. *Primate Neurobiology: Neurosurgery with Fetuses,* 199 SCIENCE 960 (1978).

138. An analogous change is occurring in the determination of when a person is legally dead. The traditional criterion for determining whether death has occurred was cessation of the heartbeat. Modern medicine has made it possible, however, artificially to sustain the heart even while the patient is in an irreversible coma. *See* Capron & Kass, *A Statutory Definition of the Standards for Determining Human Death: An Appraisal and a Proposal,* 121 U. PA. L. REV. 87, 89 (1972). In light of this achievement, our reliance on cessation of the heartbeat to indicate death has been seriously challenged. As a consequence, new criteria for determining death have been proposed. *See* Ad Hoc Committee of the Harvard Medical School to Examine the Definition of Brain Death, *A Definition of Irreversible Coma,* 205 J.A.M.A. 337 (1968); Task Force on Death and Dying, Institute of Society, Ethics and the Life Science, *Refinements in Criteria for the Determination of Death: An Appraisal,* 221 J.A.M.A. 48 (1972). Adoption of new criteria has not meant that our concept of dying has changed. It means only that we must consider new medical data and new technological innovations in determining when death occurs.

139. One court permitting recovery for injury to a viable stillborn infant stated:
Suppose . . . viable unborn twins suffered simultaneously the same prenatal injury of which one died before and the other after birth. Shall there be a cause of action for the death of the one and not for that of the other? Surely logic requires recognition of causes of action for the deaths of both, or for neither.
Stidham v. Ashmore, 109 Ohio App. 431, 434, 167 N.E.2d 106, 108 (1959).

But we should not content ourselves with the law's traditional application of a capacity criterion. Before applying that
criterion in the light of new developments, we must ask why it is
an appropriate standard. Why should it be preferred to another
principle, such as genetic individuality? Traditional acceptance
alone is inadequate justification. I would argue that we should
continue to use the capacity criterion because it represents a
careful balance among powerful, complex, and perplexing societal concerns.

Society is naturally prone to protect most securely the interests of its most mature and responsible members. This instinct
reveals itself whenever the interests of those members conflict
with the interests of less mature or less responsible citizens. Preferring the interests of a "remote" potentiality in cases of conflict
would be perceived as an intolerable incursion on the interests of
the fully matured. Accordingly, we tend to favor the interests of
parents over the interests of children when those interests collide.

Yet society has never wholly disregarded the interests of
those less mature. It has always sought to strike a fair balance
and has typically done so at that point in development where the
entity shows a significant likelihood of becoming a mature, contributing member. That point has, logically, been the moment at
which the entity is capable of independent existence — the capacity criterion. The criterion is thus a rational one — it represents a societal commitment to bestowing rights on those likely
to contribute to its advancement. It naturally follows the societal
instinct for self-perpetuation. It explains the early common law
property rule that one had to be alive at the time of a testator's
death to inherit; otherwise no one would fulfill the feudal responsibilities.[140] Similarly, modern law gives rights to artificial entities
such as corporations only when they are capable of bearing responsibilities.[141]

Thus, the capacity criterion is a rational principle, and the
viability standard is a rational application of that principle to the

---

140. *In re* Peabody, 5 N.Y.2d 541, 158 N.E.2d 841, 186 N.Y.S.2d 265 (1959). The court
stated:

> Because of the necessity in medieval England always to have available a living
> person who could be charged with the performance of feudal duties, the common
> law developed the rule that a remainder estate was destroyed if the heir or devisee
> was not alive when the prior estate came to an end.

5 N.Y.2d at 546, 158 N.E.2d at 844, 186 N.Y.S.2d at 269.

141. *See* Trustees of Dartmouth College v. Woodward, 17 U.S. (4 Wheat.) 518, 636
(1819).

modern world. Yet that should not obscure the arguments in Section IV above: Although principal rights should be bestowed at viability, the previable fetus should still receive some protection. Where the protectable interests of fully mature members do not conflict with those of less mature members, there is no justification for ignoring the latter's claims. The *Roe* opinion was correct in recognizing a state's legitimate interest in protecting the previable fetus. In tort, property, and criminal law, when that interest does not oppose a protected interest of the mature mother, the state should not hesitate to vindicate it.

V. Some Implications of the Viability Criterion

I have argued that medical data and common law theory strongly support a viability criterion as one of central significance. There is today no inherent legal obstacle to giving viable fetuses legal protection fully equivalent to that given the newborn. But is it practical? Will it help to resolve disputes between fetuses and mothers? Or between fetuses and third parties?

The first difficulty with the viability criterion is the extraordinary complexity of determining a particular fetus's viability.[142] Estimates of gestational age have a two-week margin of error. Moreover, even if we could always determine precisely the gestational age of a fetus, that datum would not be sufficient to tell us whether the fetus was in fact viable.[143] To apply the viability

---

142. The Supreme Court acknowledged that complexity in *Colautti v. Franklin:* As the record in this case indicates, a physician determines whether or not a fetus is viable after considering a number of variables: the gestational age of the fetus, derived from the reported menstrual history of the woman; fetal weight, based on an inexact estimate of the size and condition of the uterus; the woman's general health and nutrition; the quality of the available medical facilities; and other factors. Because of the number and the imprecision of these variables, the probability of any particular fetus' obtaining meaningful life outside the womb can be determined only with difficulty.
439 U.S. 379, 395-96 (1979) (footnote omitted).

143. Indeed, between the 20th and 28th weeks there is no reliable technique to make the determination of viability. *See* Kass, *Determining Death and Viability in Fetuses and Abortuses, in* Research on the Fetus: Appendix, *supra* note 38, at 11-1, 11-15. A competent examiner using a stethoscope can detect a heartbeat that suggests fetal life and age at approximately 20 weeks of pregnancy. Even *ex utero,* determining viability is not entirely free of difficulty. One author suggests that a fetus *ex utero* is to be considered viable if it shows all five of the following signs: (1) spontaneous muscular movement, (2) response to external stimuli, (3) elicitable reflexes, (4) spontaneous respiration, and (5) spontaneous heart function. *Id.* Behrman suggests that a fetus is viable *ex utero* if it has a minimum number of basic intergrative physiologic functions. In 1975 he listed the following: (1) perfusion of tissues with adequate oxygen and the prevention of the increasing accumulation of carbon dioxide and/or lactic and other organic acids, and (2) neuro-

criterion in today's world we must resort to estimates of the probability of viability drawn from statistics on premature births. Using those estimates, we must then create a rebuttable legal presumption of viability or nonviability associable with each gestational age. The presumption chosen is vitally important, for in many cases it will not be feasible to marshal the evidence necessary to rebut it.

In *Roe,* the Court said that viability usually occurs at twenty-eight weeks, adopting what it believed to be the consensus of the medical profession that at least 40-50% of fetuses born at twenty-eight weeks of gestation survive.[144] But the Court did not stop there. It acknowledged that some fetuses beat the odds and survive at fewer than twenty-eight weeks of gestational age, possibly as early as twenty-four weeks. As I mentioned above, this left interpreters of the *Roe* opinion with a difficult ambiguity — when did the Court intend the presumption of viability to arise? At twenty-eight weeks, when most fetuses survive, or at twenty-four weeks, when some fetuses survive?

I would contend that states should be permitted to assert a compelling interest in potential life at the earliest point at which there has been verified fetal survival — at twenty-four weeks under *Roe.*[145] Such an assertion would certainly be within the

---

logic regulation of the components of the cardiorespiratory perfusion function, of the capacity to ingest nutrients, and of spontaneous and reflex muscle movements. Behrman & Rosen, *supra* note 38, at 12-26. He suggests, however, that these functions cannot be reliably assessed in all cases. He argues that there is a correlation of these functions with gestational age and weight. Delivered infants weighing less than 601 grams and/or less than 24 weeks gestational age should be considered nonviable. At this stage signs of life, such as a beating heart, pulsation of the umbilical cord, etc., are not adequate in and of themselves to indicate the presence of the basic minimum functions. *See id.*

144. *See* Behrman & Rosen, *supra* note 38, app. A at 12-51. Their study has comprehensive data on premature survival rates by gestational age. Although this study does not represent a statistical sampling of total world, U.S., or Canadian births, it represents the best available data at the time the study was done. The study shows the percent of survivors among those born at 28 weeks is 46.2%.

145. "Verified" means substantiated in the manner that new medical information is substantiated by acceptance and publication in an established medical journal. Earliest verified survival refers to survival in the United States. Historically, American physicians have been held to a standard of practice in a particular locality. *See* W. PROSSER, *supra* note 70, § 32 at 164. However, accreditation of medical schools, better methods of communication and transportation, and availability of medical literature, and consultation have contributed to a breakdown of the locality rules. In some jurisdictions the locality rule has been entirely discarded. *Id.* There of course will be babies who will not live although born well after the earliest verified survival because viability is in part a function of available medical resources, and these babies will not be born in or near hospitals with the resources to keep them alive. *See* text at note 39 *supra.* In the future, earliest verified survival will ideally be determined by some national body, applicable in the entire United States, and

language of *Roe*. Moreover, it would be consistent with the reasons for giving fetuses legal protection in the first place. If we want to ensure that no human being is denied fair consideration by entitling every fetus to legal protection as soon as it is viable, then we should err on the safe side by protecting all who might have such an entitlement. In fact, given the margin of error in estimating gestational age, one could at least argue for a compelling state interest in any potential human estimated to be within two weeks of the age of the youngest fetus known to have survived. Especially when we know that the concerned mature persons have had a chance to protect their interests earlier in pregnancy, we should draw the line to maximize protection for those who may be viable.[146]

Despite the logic of such an approach, the Supreme Court's post-*Roe* opinions strongly suggest that statutes adopting a presumption at twenty-four weeks would be unconstitutional.[147] In *Planned Parenthood v. Danforth*[148] the Court stated, "[I]t is not the proper function of the legislature or the courts to place viability at a specific point in the gestation period. [T]he determination of whether a particular fetus is viable is, and must be, a matter for the judgment of the responsible attending physi-

subject to periodic review. *See* text at notes 163-64 *infra*. This national body might decide to take into account survival data from other countries in arriving at a national standard of viability for the United States. Information from foreign countries was taken into account by the National Commission when making its recommendations concerning fetal research. *See* Behrman & Rosen, *supra* note 38, at 12-2, 12-4.

146. Because our ability to sustain life earlier in gestation will probably move faster than common acceptance of this information by physicians, legislatures, and courts, perhaps a state should be able to create a zone in which we have no verified fetal survival but in which abortion is prohibited. Kass argues that we should treat every fetus with an audible heartbeat (which occurs at about twenty weeks) as if it were viable, although some will not be. *See* Kass, *supra* note 143, at 11-14. The National Commission adopted this approach in its report. It recommended that the "possibly viable infant," who is likely to be between 20 and 24 weeks and between 500 and 600 grams, could be involved in research only under stringent conditions. NATL. COMMN. FOR THE PROTECTION OF HUMAN SUBJECTS OF BIOMEDICAL AND BEHAVIORAL RESEARCH, RESEARCH ON THE FETUS: REPORT AND RECOMMENDATIONS 75 (1975) (HEW Publication No. (OS) 76-127).

147. The Court has never considered a carefully drafted statute or a statute that incorporated the *Roe* definition of viability. At least one state legislature attempted to prohibit abortion on demand 24 weeks after conception. This statute was declared unconstitutional in Floyd v. Anders, 440 F. Supp. 535 (D.S.C. 1977) (three judge panel), *vacated and remanded per curiam*, 440 U.S. 445 (1979). "Because the District Court may have reached this conclusion on the basis of an erroneous concept of 'viability' which refers to potential, rather than actual, survival of the fetus outside the womb," the Court remanded in light of Colautti v. Franklin, 439 U.S. 379 (1979). The Court also suggested that the district court give further consideration to abstention.

148. 428 U.S. 52 (1976).

cian."[149] The Court expressly affirmed this view in *Colautti v. Franklin*.[150] Thus, a reading of *Roe, Danforth* and *Colautti* might suggest that the states' compelling interest in potential life arises clearly at twenty-eight weeks, and earlier only if an individual physician so determines.[151]

If that is how the Court intends to resolve the problem of determining individual viability, its approach is not convincing. The medical profession is not of one mind concerning the conclusion that the fetus does not have a reasonable likelihood of survival until twenty-eight weeks. Some would argue that the point of reasonable likelihood of survival occurs earlier. In the Court's own words,

> [E]ven if agreement may be reached on the probability of survival, different physicians equate viability with different probabilities of survival, and some physicians refuse to equate viability with any numerical probability at all. In the face of these uncertainties, it is not unlikely that experts will disagree over whether a particular fetus in the second trimester has advanced to the stage of viability.[152]

The Court's extraordinary deference to the medical profession regarding what constitutes a reasonable likelihood of survival seems unwarranted. Physicians do have some competence to tell us the probabilities of survival at each stage of development. They do not, however, have peculiar competence to decree that a specific probability of survival is the critical one for determining when a state's interest in potential life becomes compelling. That decision is important to all of society.

Moreover, the Court's apparent refusal to permit states to assert a compelling interest at the earliest moment of known fetal survival sacrifices the objectivity and ease of administration which that system offers. Under the Court's system, a physician could reasonably abort a fetus that other physicians consider viable. All physicians called upon to estimate the odds will do so subjectively under circumstances that make it impossible to ignore the powerful motives of the parties. One must question the justice of imposing such a difficult question of values on a profes-

---

149. 428 U.S. at 64.

150. 439 U.S. 379 (1979).

151. Under the Court's position presumably the physician could determine that a fetus older than 28 weeks was not viable. The physician might however have a difficult time sustaining that position if the finding were contested.

152. 439 U.S. at 396 (footnote omitted).

sion that neither wants to answer it nor is especially competent to do so.

Although I have stressed the importance of the presumption of viability or nonviability, the manner of rebutting it should not be ignored. The question of a fetus's viability often arises when it is delivered stillborn after a traumatic event that occurred near the time of viability. For example, a fetus might be injured through another's negligence during the twenty-sixth week of pregnancy. After stillbirth, the question might arise of whether a wrongful death suit on its behalf could be brought in those states that require that the fetus be viable when injured. Under my approach, it would be presumed viable from the twenty-fourth week onward. To rebut the presumption, a doctor would have to examine the fetus after birth to find peculiar characteristics known to affect the time of viability. The difficult factual issue need not be any tougher than those already presented by efforts to separate the birth process from the moment of birth.

A second problem with giving full legal protection at viability stems from the fetus's physical attachment to the mother. Given this fact, how should we resolve conflicts between the interests of mothers and of viable, attached fetuses? The Court in *Roe* suggests that the mother's interest predominates, at least when her life and health are at stake.[153] It offered no justification for this value preference and did not attempt to reconcile it with the fact that a state's compelling interest in potential life otherwise attaches at viability. Moreover, it offered no guidance for other conflicts of interests, such as where a mother's treatment of her own body might hurt her unborn child. If it could be demonstrated that the intake of alcohol or drugs during pregnancy is likely to harm the fetus, could we prohibit a pregnant mother from drinking or taking drugs?[154] These are difficult issues, which should perhaps be distinguished according to whether the fetus is viable or previable.

I submit that the Court in *Roe* was not justified in assuming that the mother's interest in her life or health predominates over

---

153. *See* Roe v. Wade, 410 U.S. 113, 163-64 (1973).

154. Current research suggests that there is a relationship between maternal use of alcohol and fetal abnormality. *See* Ouellette, Rosett, Rosman, & Weiner, *Adverse Effects of Maternal Alcohol Abuse During Pregnancy*, 297 NEW ENG. J. MED. 528 (1977). At least one female has been indicted for child abuse for giving birth to a child addicted to heroin. *In re* Baby X, No. 77-1557 (6th Jud. Cir. Oakland Cty., Mich.). However, another case has held that a mother cannot be punished in such circumstances. Reyes v. Superior Court, 75 Cal. App. 3d 214, 141 Cal. Rptr. 912 (1977).

the identical interests of the viable fetus. The interests of mother and viable fetus should be weighed equally in resolving conflicts between them. We should strike a fair balance between their competing interests[155] on an issue-by-issue basis, considering the gestational age of the fetus, the severity of possible harm to the fetus, and the severity of possible harm to the mother's interests. If continued pregnancy threatens a mother's life[156] or health[157] at a time when her unborn child is viable, we should first consider separating them by a procedure designed to minimize the risks to both. Such a step is often difficult and is sometimes impossible, but in situations of clear danger to the mother, it may prove the fairest reconciliation of their competing interests. In other circumstances, that reconciliation might go more directly against the interests of the mother. It may require her to submit to activities she finds objectionable, such as blood transfusions, where they are necessary to save the life of the unborn fetus.[158] In such a case, that seems an appropriate balance between the mother's nonabsolute right to free exercise of religion and the fetus's life-or-death concern.

Where the mother's personal activities — smoking, drinking, using medication, or working, to give a few examples — endanger the fetus, resolution of conflicts should consider how much control the mother actually has over her actions, the severity of possible damage to the fetus, the nature of the conduct engaged in,

---

155. Some will argue that this approach places too great a constraint on a woman's right to terminate her pregnancy. This is true only if termination of pregnancy means that a woman is entitled to a method of termination that will result in a dead fetus. There seems to be no justification for permitting termination of pregnancy after viability by a method likely to kill the fetus. We do not permit infanticide. There seems to be no logic in permitting the death of an entity that, like the newborn, is capable of living independently of its mother, on the ground that it has not been physically detached from the mother. We are simply extending the rationale behind proscriptions against infanticide to viable but unborn entities. Since viability will probably continue to occur earlier in pregnancy, at some future point some fetuses may be viable very early in the gestational period. If that event comes to pass, it may also become possible to separate mothers and fetuses upon request at minimal risk to both.

156. It appears that there are relatively few instances where continued pregnancy implies certain death for the mother. The threat to her life is relative and may depend on whether she has the financial resources to permit her to be hospitalized, to hire domestic help, etc. See Ryan, *Humane Abortion Laws and the Health Need of Society,* 17 W. Res. L. Rev. 422, 430 (1965).

157. Health is a difficult concept to define. See note 11 supra.

158. See Raleigh Fitkin-Paul Morgan Mem. Hosp. v. Anderson, 42 N.J. 421, 201 A.2d 537, cert. denied, 377 U.S. 985 (1964). In this case, the court ordered that a blood transfusion should be administered contrary to a woman's religious beliefs as a Jehovah's Witness, if needed to save the life of her unborn 32-week-old fetus.

and the invasion of the mother's interests. For example, if the
mother were a heroin addict, the newborn could be born addicted
— a serious injury. Her conduct would be involuntary, but her use
of heroin illegal. It would certainly be justifiable to compel her
to undergo treatment; we might even consider more severe sanctions.[159] If society may punish an addict for giving drugs to her
children, it may consistently punish her for causing her unborn
child to become addicted.[160] The more difficult cases involve
smoking, drinking, or working in environments hazardous to fetuses. Perhaps resolution of those conflicts ought to turn on the
risk of harm to the fetus. We should consider how likely it is that
the risk will come about and the severity of damage if it occurs.
Such conflicts may be difficult. But certainly the difficulty is not
sufficient to force a retreat from the viability criterion or to warrant disregarding the fetus whenever a mother asserts some interest in her own lifestyle or health.

Viability poses another dilemma. It is not biologically fixed
at some permanent time.[161] It will arrive earlier in gestation as

---

159. *But see* Colautti v. Franklin, 439 U.S. 379, 386 n.7 (1979) (prior to viability, state
may not impose criminal sanctions to protect fetal life).

160. I do not suggest here that the mother should be punished rather than treated in
such circumstances. However, persons have often been punished for involuntary behavior
and a similar result here would be consistent with that legal tradition.

161. Viability has been criticized as a criterion for that reason. *See* Krimmel & Foley,
*Abortion: An Inspection Into the Nature of Human Life and Potential Consequences of
Legalizing its Destruction*, 46 U. CIN. L. REV. 725, 741-42 (1977). Some commentators
have emphasized biological properties. Some argue for conception as the most relevant
point in fetal development, because it dates the creation of a unique genetic makeup.
See Noonan, *supra* note 39, at 57. Others select a period up to fourteen days after conception or when we are assured that individualization has occurred. This point was selected
by the Constitutional Court of West Germany. *See* note 71 *supra*. Still others select viability. *See* Engelhardt, *The Ontology of Abortion*, 84 ETHICS 217, 228-30 (1974). Another
view suggests that, rather than looking to a point in fetal development such as viability
in defining when full legal protection is appropriate, we should look to the presence or
absence of certain unique human characteristics, though there is little consensus as to
what those characteristics should be. Some examine the degree of social and personal
concern invested in an entity in defining when life begins. *See id.* at 230-32. Others
emphasize the entity's intellectual and cognitive functions. *See* Lederberg, *A Geneticist
Looks at Contraception and Abortion*, 67 ANNALS INTERNAL MED., SUPP. 7, at 26 (1976).
Still others emphasize the possession of self-consciousness or a capacity for self-
consciousness. *See* Fletcher, *Indicators of Humanhood: A Tentative Profile of Man*,
HASTINGS CENTER REPORT, Nov., 1972, at 1. These approaches share the same defect. Since
they are all the product of philosophical views and social influences prevalent in different
sectors of society at any given time, they are subject to prejudicial and subjective applications. In the past, such approaches have justified unjust treatment of persons based upon
color, racial, sexual, religious, or cultural difference. By excluding blacks from the slave
owners' definition of human (based upon "scientific" data of biological inferiority that
often was falsified), the slave owners were able to rationalize slavery. *See* A. ROSE, THE

new and better techniques are developed for sustaining existence outside the womb. The Supreme Court noted this possibility in *Danforth* when it stated: "[W]e recognized in *Roe* that viability was a matter of medical judgment, skill, and technical ability, and we preserved the flexibility of the term."[162] It is precisely the fact that viability is not forever fixed in time that gives rise to the strongest criticism of its use as a criterion. Some would object to granting legal protection at different moments in the gestational period for different generations; such critics would prefer to choose an unvarying point in fetal development. But since viability strikes a balance of competing interests with a standard that applies fairly to all humans, striking that balance at different times for different people is not morally offensive. And viability is not subject to the type of arbitrariness that lurks in vague formulations of "personhood." It is a biological concept that would minimize the possibility of discriminatory treatment of different human lives.

The shifting moment of viability would not create an undue problem under the standard for establishing the viability presumption that I espoused above. It is relatively easy to keep track of the age of the youngest known successful birth and to advance it with each new "miraculous" premature survival. Nonetheless, it would create difficulties in assessing the appropriate way to rebut that presumption in an individual case. Surely the standards for that assessment will have to be revised periodically in light of new medical knowledge and advances. Who should make that revision and who should have the responsibility for verifying the earliest known survival? The National Commission for the

---

NEGRO IN AMERICA 31-36 (1956). Such justifications even permeated the Supreme Court in the *Dred Scott* decision, where it stated:

> [T]he right of property in a slave is distinctly and expressly affirmed in the Constitution. The right to traffic in it, like an ordinary article of merchandize and property, was guarantied [*sic*] to the citizens of the United States . . . . And no word can be found in the Constitution which gives Congress a greater power over slave property, or which entitles property of that kind to less protection than property of any other description.

Dred Scott v. Sandford, 60 U.S. (19 How.) 393, 451-52 (1856). Blacks in America are not the only persons discriminated against because of supposed biological inferiority. The Chinese in America and the Jews in Europe as well as others have suffered similar fates. *See* People v. Hall, 4 Cal. 339, 404-05 (1854) (Chinese, as well as blacks, excluded from testifying in action where any party is white because marked by nature as inferior and incapable of progress of intellectual development beyond a certain point); International Military Tribunal: Nuremberg 14 Nov. 1945 - 1 Oct. 1946 Trial of the Major War Criminals.

162. Planned Parenthood v. Danforth, 428 U.S. 52, 64 (1976).

Protection of Human Subjects of Biomedical Behavioral Research has recommended giving a federal agency responsibility for monitoring new developments.[163] Legislatures and courts could then be guided by that agency's reports. Another possibility would be to give some organized arm of the medical profession responsibility for issuing guidelines that summarize the most recent knowledge about the specific factors affecting viability. This would be a less satisfying resolution, however, for such guidelines would operate without the imprimatur of government approval. If the responsibility were lodged in a government agency, all interested concerns, including the medical profession, could participate in the formulation of the guidelines.[164]

The shifting moment of viability suggests another possible concern. Physicians currently can diagnose certain genetic conditions and complications *in utero* in time to perform an abortion under *Roe* standards.[165] If viability were to move to an earlier point in gestation, abortion of a defective fetus might not be allowed. Yet the problem is really not new. Whether one may kill a human, either because it will enjoy a quality of life below some minimal level or because its parents do not wish a severely handicapped child, is not a question peculiar to the use of viability as a standard.[166] We should treat viable, defective fetuses in the same way we treat defective newborns. The problem, in short, should be viewed as one of euthanasia and not one uniquely affecting legal protection of fetuses.

A final potentially troublesome aspect of viability is that it is a moment in development whose achievement is not readily apparent to lay persons, or even to physicians. This problem also afflicts the current debate over shifting the traditional legal definition of death, which looks to heartbeat cessation, to a definition that looks to brain activity. Neither brain death nor viability is

---

163. NATL. COMMN. FOR THE PROTECTION OF HUMAN SUBJECTS OF BIOMEDICAL AND BEHAVIORAL RESEARCH, *supra* note 146, at 5, 75.

164. Note, however, that suggestions for new criteria for determining death originated with nongovernmental groups. *See* note 156 *supra*.

165. *See* note 132 *supra*.

166. Some commentators who look to the possession of certain unique characteristics in defining when life begins have been forced to consider the legality of infanticide as well as that of abortion. Some would allow infanticide in some circumstances. *See, e.g.,* J. FLETCHER, THE ETHICS OF GENETIC CONTROL 152-54; 185-87; Tooley, *Abortion and Infanticide,* 2 PHIL. PUB. AFF. 37 (1972). Other commentators reach different conclusions. Paul Ramsey, for example, advises against the abortion of defective fetuses but supports a withdrawal of medical treatment that would lead to the fetus's death. Ramsey, *supra* note 71, at 97-100.

readily understood. Moreover, there is often lay resistance to the use of criteria that are technologically determined and can be used only by professionals. This is more a political problem than a legal or ethical one. We are therefore fortunate that, as a practical matter, the need to determine the point of viability, just as the need to use brain death definitions, is infrequent. In most abortion cases, we will have a termination of the pregnancy long before viability. In most other cases there will be a live birth. Achievement of live birth will adequately prove a separate and independent existence, to the satisfaction of professional and lay persons alike.

VI. Conclusion

Most legal and philosophical literature about the fetus concerns abortion, and in recent years moral philosophers have thought the critical preliminary issue in resolving the morality of abortion to be whether the fetus is a person. In Roe v. Wade, the Supreme Court also approached the abortion issue through the question of personhood. The Court held that the fetus is not a person, a holding that has been criticized for inadequate analysis.

I submit that whether the fetus is a "person" is irrelevant to whether it should have legal protection. The personhood debate has only obscured the decisive issues. The juridical status of developing humans has historically depended upon their capacity for a separate and independent existence. It is not necessary to abandon that traditional understanding; we must only revise its application in the context of greater scientific knowledge. Today, capacity to have independent existence points to viability instead of birth as the determinative moment in development. There are no serious legal problems to recognizing legal protection of viable fetuses equal to that already afforded newborns. The standard presents some problems that birth does not, but none that is sufficiently serious to challenge the thesis that all fetuses merit some protection and that viable fetuses merit all protection currently given the newborn infant.

THE ABORTION-FUNDING CASES AND POPULATION CONTROL: AN IMAGINARY LAWSUIT (AND SOME REFLECTIONS ON THE UNCERTAIN LIMITS OF REPRODUCTIVE PRIVACY)

*Susan Frelich Appleton**

Betty Boe v. Abbot Abraham, President of the City Council of New Gotham, New Gotham State, et al.

United States Court of Appeals, Special Circuit**

June 20, 1979

Before ADAMS, BAKER, CARSON, DANIEL, and EVERETT, Senior Circuit Judges.

ADAMS, Senior Circuit Judge.

Two issues are before us today: (I) the meaning of the term "medically necessary" in a public hospital's charter and (II) the constitutionality of state action that provides free medical treatment to indigent pregnant women seeking an abortion but denies them such assistance for prenatal care and childbirth. On the basis of recent Supreme Court authority, we find that such action violates neither the hospital's charter nor the United States Constitution.

The city of New Gotham, a large and crowded metropolis, owns and operates one hospital, which, pursuant to its charter, provides "medically necessary services" free of charge for the

---

* Associate Professor, Washington University School of Law. A.B. 1970, Vassar College; J.D. 1973, University of California, Berkeley.— Ed.

The author gratefully acknowledges the assistance of Sonya M. Davis and Patricia A. Greenfield, students at the Washington University School of Law, and the helpful comments on earlier drafts of this paper provided by Robert G. Dixon, Jr., Daniel Noyes Kirby Professor of Law, and Professors Jules B. Gerard, Patrick J. Kelley, and Ronald M. Levin of the Washington University School of Law.

** The United States Court of Appeals, Special Circuit, last sat in 1965 in order to decide *Jones & Smith v. Town of New Harmony. See* Bittker, *The Case of the Checker-Board Ordinance: An Experiment in Race Relations,* 71 YALE L.J. 1387 (1962). With Professor Bittker's permission and this author's acknowledged debt to his article, the same judges — now senior circuit judges eager to resolve another fictitious controversy — have reconvened to decide the instant case. Any apparent changes in judicial personalities or writing styles may be attributed to the passage of time and the annual succession of law clerks.

city's indigent residents.[1] Alarmed by the recent dramatic increase in New Gotham's population, particularly among the poor, and by the resulting drain on public services,[2] the City Council of New Gotham, whose members are duly elected by the city's residents, has enacted a number of measures designed to encourage population control, consistent with the campaign promises of several councilmen.[3] Among these measures is a policy directive requiring the public hospital to cease providing all medical services related to prenatal care and childbirth. Instead, a physician on the hospital staff is to instruct every woman seeking medical care there in connection with pregnancy that an abortion[4] is available at any time throughout her pregnancy.[5]

In accordance with a longstanding staffing practice, the doctors and medical students at the public hospital's obstetrics-gynecology clinic are drawn from the faculty and student body of the New Gotham Medical School, known nationwide for its work in population control and related fields; as a result, the medical

---

1. The hospital is a municipal hospital established under the laws of New Gotham State and a city ordinance "for the reception of persons requiring relief during temporary sickness." As an "acute short term general hospital," it does not provide indefinite or custodial treatment. All residents of the city of New Gotham are entitled to in-patient admission for any surgical or other procedure which the hospital permits and for the performance of which it has the proper facilities. Although any city resident may have any such procedure or treatment performed at the hospital for a specified charge, under its charter the hospital is to provide all "medically necessary" services at no cost for those residents who meet the hospital's standards of indigency. Under these standards, an indigent person or family is one who falls below the federally defined poverty level. See 45 C.F.R. §§ 1060.2-1, .2-2 (1978) (poverty income guidelines). For a description of a similar municipal hospital, see Hathaway v. Worcester City Hosp., 475 F.2d 701 (1st Cir.), stay of mandamus denied, 411 U.S. 929 (1973).

2. Though New Gotham is crowded in comparison to other urban areas of roughly the same size and in recent years has experienced fiscal difficulties, there is no evidence that either of these problems has approached an emergency condition. Instead, the principal concern is that the city has too many inhabitants to be able to provide the "quality of life" that a majority of its residents desire.

3. The policy and practice at issue in this case constitute only part of a series of measures undertaken by New Gotham for the purpose of promoting population control. The city has, for example, also established throughout the metropolitan area a number of abortion clinics and family planning agencies operating independently of the public hospital.

These measures were among those included in the "quality of life" platform espoused by all of the winning candidates for the City Council in the last municipal election.

4. Neither the New Gotham policy directive nor the physicians on the hospital staff make a distinction between so-called "therapeutic" and "nontherapeutic" abortions; regardless of any particular indigent woman's physical or emotional reaction to her pregnancy, termination is available as described.

5. The legislature of New Gotham State, in which the city of New Gotham is located, also eager to encourage reduced reproduction, has repealed all criminal abortion statutes from the state's penal code, thus legalizing all abortions whenever performed.

personnel who are asked to comply with the policy directive
strongly support its aims.

Immediately before the filing of this lawsuit, plaintiff Betty
Boe, an indigent resident of New Gotham, consulted a physician
on the public hospital staff who informed her that she was approximately six weeks pregnant and that the hospital would provide her with an abortion free of charge at any time during her
pregnancy. Boe proceeded unsuccessfully to seek free prenatal
care at the public hospital.[6] Because she still wishes to receive
prenatal care, to carry the pregnancy to term, and to give birth
to the child, but lacks the financial wherewithal to do so, she
brought this action alleging a violation of the hospital's charter
and challenging the constitutionality of the policy directive and
hospital staffing practice that together preclude her from obtaining the desired treatment free of charge.[7] Following a trial to
the court, the trial judge found for defendants and dismissed the
complaint with prejudice; Boe appeals.

I

Boe first argues that the policy in question violates the public
hospital's own charter, under which the hospital is to provide the
indigent with all care that is "medically necessary."[8] We disagree.[9]

---

6. All parties stipulate that during her initial visit to the hospital Boe was assured
that her request for free childbirth and postpartum treatment would likewise be denied.
At the time this appeal was argued, one month ago, Boe's attorney reported that she was
beginning the seventh month of her pregnancy, that she still desired to deliver rather than
abort, that she met the hospital's standards of indigency, that she remained unable to pay
for the desired services herself, and that she had not found any alternative means for
obtaining such medical treatment without cost. On the basis of these undisputed facts,
there is no question that this lawsuit satisfies the case or controversy requirement of article
III of the Constitution.

7. Boe filed this civil rights action, on behalf of herself and all others similarly situated, under 42 U.S.C. § 1983 (1976) and 28 U.S.C. § 1343 (1976). Her complaint named
as defendants Abbot Abraham, the presiding member of the City Council of New Gotham,
as well as the other members of the Council, and Dr. Clyde Carver, the Director of the
Department of Health and Hospitals and Hospital Commissioner of New Gotham
[hereinafter referred to collectively as "New Gotham" or "the city"]. Boe sought, in the
words of her complaint, declaratory and injunctive relief against "the existence, application, implementation, and enforcement of express and implied policies, rules, regulations,
procedures, and practices barring, thwarting, limiting, and infringing the provision by the
public hospital of New Gotham of free medical treatment related to prenatal care and
childbirth for the indigent residents of the city." For a similarly worded complaint, see
Doe v. Poelker, 515 F.2d 541 (8th Cir. 1975), revd. per curiam, 432 U.S. 519 (1977).

8. See note 1 supra.

9. By itself, the construction of the hospital's charter would not present a federal

The United States Supreme Court recently confronted a related issue in *Beal v. Doe,* 432 U.S. 438 (1977), where it was asked to construe Title XIX of the Social Security Act,[10] which requires states participating in its federally funded medical assistance program for needy persons to formulate "reasonable standards" for determining the extent of assistance to be provided, consistent with the objectives of the Act.[11] Pursuant to this requirement, Pennsylvania had adopted regulations allowing such assistance for abortions only where certified by physicians to be "medically necessary."[12] Elective or nontherapeutic abortions were thus excluded from coverage. A majority of the Court found the regulations to be within the broad discretion accorded to the states by the Act, reasoning that "it is hardly inconsistent with the objectives of the Act for a State to refuse to fund *unnecessary* — though perhaps desirable — medical services." 432 U.S. at 444-45 (emphasis in original).

Dissenting, Mr. Justice Brennan pointed out that an implicit corollary of the majority's analysis was that medical services for childbirth would likewise fall outside the scope of "medically necessary" treatment if the state were to provide nontherapeutic abortions for its needy women. 432 U.S. at 451-52.[13] He reasoned that "[p]regnancy is unquestionably a condition requiring medi-

---

question appropriate for our consideration. We nonetheless have pendent jurisdiction to decide the question, because of the close relationship between this issue and plaintiff's federal constitutional challenge. UMW v. Gibbs, 383 U.S. 715 (1966). In view of the strong policy disfavoring the unnecessary resolution of constitutional questions, we address it first, as did the district court below. *See* Hagans v. Lavine, 415 U.S. 528, 546-47 (1974). *See also* Hathaway v. Worcester City Hosp., 341 F. Supp. 1385, 1388 app. (D. Mass. 1972), *revd. on other grounds,* 475 F.2d 701 (1st Cir.), *stay of mandamus denied,* 411 U.S. 929 (1973). In addition, because of the continuing progression of plaintiff's pregnancy and the consequent need to resolve this case as expeditiously as possible, we decline to exercise our discretionary authority to abstain until a state court construction of the charter is available. *See also* Zbaraz v. Quern, 572 F.2d 582, 587 (7th Cir. 1978); Hathaway v. Worcester City Hosp., 475 F.2d at 705.

10. Title XIX of the Social Security Act, 42 U.S.C. §§ 1396-1396k (1976 & Supp. I 1977), establishes the Medicaid program under which participating states may provide federally funded medical assistance to needy persons. *See* 432 U.S. at 440.

11. 42 U.S.C. § 1396a(a)(17) (1976).

12. *See* 432 U.S. at 441-42 n.3. The purpose of the federal statute is to "[enable] each State, as far as practicable under the conditions in such State, to furnish . . . medical assistance on behalf of [those] whose income and resources are insufficient to meet the costs of *necessary medical services.*" 42 U.S.C. § 1396 (1976) (emphasis added). *See* 42 U.S.C. § 1396a(a)(10)(C)(i) (1976).

13. Mr. Justice Brennan stated that, under the Court's analysis, "therapeutic" abortions, like care accompanying live births, would also not constitute "necessary medical services" if elective abortions were available. 432 U.S. at 451-52 (Brennan, J., dissenting). Using this logic, prenatal care would be "unnecessary" under similar circumstances.

cal services . . . . Treatment for the condition may involve medical procedures for its termination, or medical procedures to bring the pregnancy to term, resulting in a live birth." 432 U.S. at 449. Given the two mutually exclusive alternatives for responding to pregnancy,[14] it is clear that Mr. Justice Brennan is correct: the availability of one kind of medical procedure — in the instant case, abortion — necessarily renders the other — childbirth — unneeded.

Relying upon a line of reasoning employed by a majority of the United States Supreme Court and the elaboration of that reasoning offered by Mr. Justice Brennan, we therefore conclude that the implementation of the challenged policy directive by the New Gotham public hospital does not contravene that hospital's obligation under its charter to provide at no cost to the indigent all treatment that is "medically necessary."

II

Boe's complaint also raises questions of the right of privacy,[15] due process of law,[16] and equal protection.[17] Relying on *Griswold v. Connecticut*, 381 U.S. 479 (1965), and *Eisenstadt v. Baird*, 405 U.S. 438 (1972), she claims first that the ninth amendment's reservation of rights to the people[18] shields from state intrusion

---

14. " '[A]bortion and childbirth, when stripped of the sensitive moral arguments surrounding the abortion controversy, are simply two alternative medical methods of dealing with pregnancy . . . .' " 432 U.S. at 449 (quoting Roe v. Norton, 408 F. Supp. 660, 663 n.3 (D. Conn. 1975), *revd. sub nom.* Maher v. Roe, 432 U.S. 464 (1977)).

15. *See, e.g.*, Carey v. Population Servs. Intl., 431 U.S. 678, 684-85 (1977); Whalen v. Roe, 429 U.S. 589, 599-600 (1977); Planned Parenthood v. Danforth, 428 U.S. 52, 60 (1976); Roe v. Wade, 410 U.S. 113, 152-53 (1973); Griswold v. Connecticut, 381 U.S. 479, 485-86 (1965). *See generally* Dixon, *The Griswold Penumbra: Constitutional Charter for an Expanded Law of Privacy?*, 64 MICH. L. REV. 197 (1965); Henkin, *Privacy and Autonomy*, 74 COLUM. L. REV. 1410 (1974); McKay, *The Right of Privacy: Emanations and Intimations*, 64 MICH. L. REV. 259 (1965); Silver, *The Future of Constitutional Privacy*, 21 ST. LOUIS U. L.J. 211 (1977).

16. *See, e.g.*, Carey v. Population Servs. Intl., 431 U.S. 678, 684 (1977); Cleveland Bd. of Educ. v. LaFleur, 414 U.S. 632, 639-40 (1974); Roe v. Wade, 410 U.S. 113, 152-53 (1973); Tribe, *The Supreme Court, 1972 Term — Foreword: Toward a Model of Roles in the Due Process of Life and Law*, 87 HARV. L. REV. 1 (1973). *See also* Moore v. City of East Cleveland, 431 U.S. 494, 500-04 (1977) (plurality opinion).

17. *See, e.g.*, San Antonio Indep. School Dist. v. Rodriguez, 411 U.S. 1, 16-17 (1973). *See also* Eisenstadt v. Baird, 405 U.S. 438, 446-47 (1972); Skinner v. Oklahoma, 316 U.S. 535, 541-43 (1942).

18. *See* Stanley v. Illinois, 405 U.S. 645, 651 (1972); Griswold v. Connecticut, 381 U.S. 479, 488-93 (1965) (Goldberg, J., concurring). *See also* Roe v. Wade, 410 U.S. 113, 153 (1973).

her "decision whether to bear or beget a child."[19] She asserts
further that a similar right of privacy, rooted in the fourteenth
amendment's protection of personal liberty and explicitly recognized by the Supreme Court in *Roe v. Wade*, 410 U.S. 113, 153
(1973),[20] renders unconstitutional New Gotham's action, which,
she argues, injects the government impermissibly into a private
realm of decision.[21] Finally, Boe contends that the policy directive
and staffing practice of the public hospital create a suspect classification, distinguishing indigent women seeking to abort from
those seeking to carry their pregnancies to term,[22] that jeopardizes
her fundamental right to procreate;[23] because Boe claims that
defendant officials of New Gotham have failed to demonstrate
any compelling state interest or emergency situation justifying
the policy in question, she alleges a violation of the fourteenth
amendment's guarantee of equal protection of the laws.[24]

Although the general constitutional principles that Boe in-
vokes may be correct in the abstract, as current opinions of the
United States Supreme Court demonstrate,[25] they do not invalidate the official action she challenges here, for they do not control

19. Eisenstadt v. Baird, 405 U.S. 438, 453 (1972). The Court used similar language
in Carey v. Population Servs. Intl., 431 U.S. 678, 686 (1977).

20. *See* note 16 *supra.*

21. *See* Whalen v. Roe, 429 U.S. 589, 599 & n.24, 600 & n.26 (1977); Tribe, *supra* note
16, at 11; Comment, *A Taxonomy of Privacy: Repose, Sanctuary and Intimate Decision*,
64 CALIF. L. REV. 1447, 1466-69 (1976).

22. *See also* Skinner v. Oklahoma, 316 U.S. 535 (1942).

23. Skinner v. Oklahoma, 316 U.S. 535, 541 (1942). She also claims that the city
invidiously discriminates between nonindigent women who can afford to purchase medical
care for childbirth and indigent women who cannot. *See* Boddie v. Connecticut, 401 U.S.
371 (1971); Douglas v. California, 372 U.S. 353 (1963); Griffin v. Illinois, 351 U.S. 12
(1956).

24. If Boe successfully shows that the challenged policy either establishes a suspect
classification or infringes a fundamental right, then she is entitled to invoke the standards
of a mode of equal protection review described as "strict" judicial scrutiny. *See, e.g.,* San
Antonio Indep. School Dist. v. Rodriguez, 411 U.S. 1, 16-17 (1973); Korematsu v. United
States, 323 U.S. 214, 215 (1944). Such analysis shifts the burden of proof from the party
challenging the classification and requires the party seeking to uphold it to demonstrate
that it is necessary to further a compelling state interest and that there are available no
less onerous alternatives for achieving that objective. 411 U.S. at 16-17. *See also* Gunther,
*The Supreme Court, 1971 Term — Foreword: In Search of Evolving Doctrine on a
Changing Court: A Model for a Newer Equal Protection*, 86 HARV. L. REV. 1 (1972);
Developments in the Law — Equal Protection, 82 HARV. L. REV. 1065, 1087-131 (1969).

The compelling state interest test is likewise applied outside the equal protection
context in cases where protected rights or liberties are infringed by state action that does
not necessarily classify at all. *E.g.,* Carey v. Population Servs. Intl., 431 U.S. 678, 686
(1977); Roe v. Wade, 410 U.S. 113, 154-56 (1973). *See also* 410 U.S. at 173 (Rehnquist, J.,
dissenting).

25. *See* Maher v. Roe, 432 U.S. 464, 470-71 (1977) (equal protection); Carey v. Population Servs. Intl., 431 U.S. 678, 684-85 (1977) (privacy and due process).

on the facts of this particular case. We base our conclusion on the holdings, language, and reasoning employed by the Supreme Court in its recent decisions in *Beal v. Doe,* 432 U.S. 438 (1977), *Maher v. Roe,* 432 U.S. 464 (1977), and *Poelker v. Doe,* 432 U.S. 519 (1977).

The facts of those cases are not complex and make clear their pertinence to the controversy before us:

In *Beal,* 'which we summarized above,[26] a majority of the Court, reasoning that elective abortions are not "medically necessary," found no violation of the Social Security Act in Pennsylvania's refusal to extend Medicaid coverage to nontherapeutic abortions. In reaching that conclusion, the Court emphasized that, even though under *Roe v. Wade,* 410 U.S. 113 (1973), governmental interests favoring childbirth are not sufficiently compelling before fetal viability[27] to justify a proscription of abortions, such interests are of adequate legitimacy and force throughout pregnancy to support state action designed to encourage a woman to carry to term. 432 U.S. at 445-46.

The Court developed that reasoning further in two other cases decided the same day. In *Maher v. Roe,* 432 U.S. 464 (1977), a majority of the Court[28] ruled that the statutory interpretation announced in *Beal* does not violate the Constitution and that, therefore, states participating in the Medicaid program established by Title XIX of the Social Security Act are not constitutionally compelled to finance nontherapeutic abortions when they choose to pay medical expenses for childbirth. The Court thus rejected the contention that such an allocation of public funds violates the equal protection clause of the fourteenth amendment by discriminating against those indigent women who choose to exercise the constitutional right to abort instead of carrying their pregnancies to term.[29] Expanding upon the analysis employed in

26. *See* text at notes 10-14 *supra.*
27. Roe v. Wade, 410 U.S. 113, 163-65 (1973). The Court in *Roe* defined a viable fetus as one "potentially able to live outside the mother's womb, albeit with artificial aid." 410 U.S. at 160.
28. In *Beal* and *Maher,* Justice Powell wrote opinions for a majority composed of himself, Chief Justice Burger, and Justices Stewart, White, Rehnquist, and Stevens. Chief Justice Burger, though joining in the majority opinion in *Maher,* submitted a separate concurrence in that case. 432 U.S. at 481. The main opinion in *Poelker v. Doe* was published as a per curiam for the same six members of the Court.
The dissenters in all three cases — Justices Brennan, Marshall, and Blackmun — filed a number of separate opinions. 432 U.S. at 448 (Brennan, J.); 432 U.S. at 454 (Marshall, J.); 432 U.S. at 462 (Blackmun, J.); 432 U.S. at 482 (Brennan, J.); 432 U.S. at 522 (Brennan, J.).
29. Plaintiffs in *Maher* had argued that, under *Roe v. Wade,* states are required to

Beal, the majority explained that, although *Roe v. Wade* and its progeny may foreclose a state from creating an "absolute obstacle"[30] to abortion, particularly during the first trimester, those cases do not inhibit the democratic[31] adoption of policies and practices favoring one response to the condition of pregnancy, childbirth, over the alternative, abortion.[32]

Poelker v. Doe, 432 U.S. 519 (1977), the third case decided that day, applied the constitutional principle articulated in *Maher* to validate both a policy directive of Mayor John Poelker of St. Louis, Missouri,[33] and a staffing practice of one of St. Louis's city-owned hospitals[34] that together operated to prohibit nontherapeutic abortions in that public facility.[35] While observing that the mayor's personal opposition to abortion was legally irrelevant, the Supreme Court found significant the St. Louis voters' approval of policies preferring childbirth to abortion, ex-

---

accord equal treatment to both abortion and childbirth. 432 U.S. at 470.

30. 432 U.S. at 473 (quoting Planned Parenthood v. Danforth, 428 U.S. 52, 70-71 n.11 (1976) (emphasis deleted)).

31. 432 U.S. at 480.

32. The Court emphasized the distinction between an "absolute obstacle," *see* note 30 *supra,* or "unduly burdensome interference with [the] freedom to decide whether to terminate [a] pregnancy," 432 U.S. at 474, on the one hand, and an official "value judgment," 432 U.S. at 474, "state encouragement," 432 U.S. at 475, or "policy choice," 432 U.S. at 477, favoring childbirth, on the other. While the former (which includes criminal penalties and withdrawals of *all* welfare benefits to those exercising the right in question, 432 U.S. at 474 n.8) must be justified by a compelling state interest, *see* 432 U.S. at 475-76, the latter (which includes refusals to subsidize the protected activity, 432 U.S. at 474 n.8) needs only to be rational in order to pass constitutional muster, 432 U.S. at 478. In developing this contrast, the Court noted by analogy that, even though parents have a constitutionally protected right to choose to educate their children in private schools, a state may nonetheless encourage the selection of public school education by making it the more attractive alternative through state funding. 432 U.S. at 476-77. Similarly, the Court contrasted penalties on the exercise of a constitutional right, *e.g.,* the right to travel interstate, with failure to subsidize that right for the indigent, *e.g.,* the failure to provide free bus fares. 432 U.S. at 474-75 n.8. While the Constitution may prohibit the former, it does not require the latter. 432 U.S. at 474-75 n.8. *See also* D____ R____ v. Mitchell, 456 F. Supp. 609 (D. Utah 1978). The Court has continued to employ the "undue burden" language in subsequent analysis. *See* Bellotti v. Baird, 99 S. Ct. 3035, 3046, 3050, 3051 (1979) (plurality opinion).

33. The directive barred the performance of all abortions in the public hospitals absent a threat of grave physiological injury or death to the mother. 432 U.S. at 520.

34. For several years, the obstetrics-gynecology clinic at the city hospital in question had drawn its staff from the faculty and students at the St. Louis University School of Medicine, a Jesuit-operated institution opposed to abortion. 432 U.S. at 520.

35. In *Poelker,* plaintiff's challenge to the policy directive and staffing practice had been "cast . . . in an equal protection mold," 432 U.S. at 520, by the court below, which had struck down this official action as invidious discrimination against women who cannot afford to obtain abortions at private hospitals, as distinguished from those who can. 432 U.S. at 520.

pressed in their election of Poelker. 432 U.S. at 521. Whatever the
right acknowledged in *Roe v. Wade,* the Court found no constitutional violation in a city's implementation of the policy choices
of its electorate, even if such choices might, as a practical matter,
hinder the exercise of that right.[36]

Although the precise issues before the Court in those cases,
the abortion-funding cases, are the mirror image of those presented here, we think the broad governmental discretion approved in *Beal, Maher,* and *Poelker* amply supports the value
judgments reflected in the New Gotham public hospital directive
and staffing practice. In those cases, the majority's repeated affir-
mation of the constitutional validity of a state or local government's expression and implementation of policy preferences favoring childbirth[37] intimates that official policy preferences for
precisely the opposite goal would be equally acceptable, at least
from a constitutional perspective.[38] Thus, when the Supreme
Court notes that governmental concerns falling short of compelling state interests afford sufficient constitutional support for refusal to provide abortions at public expense,[39] it suggests that
less-than-overriding governmental concerns would likewise justify excluding treatment for prenatal care and childbirth from
welfare coverage[40] — precisely the path chosen by New Gotham.

Similarly, when the Court explains that official value judgments fostering childbirth are appropriately determined on a
democratic basis,[41] it authorizes an electorate to favor an allocation of public funds that promotes abortion instead. Surely, if
voters are to have a choice, the courts must allow them to consider the available alternatives. Here, the collective will of the

---

36. The Court stressed that Mayor Poelker "is an elected official responsible to the
people of St. Louis," 432 U.S. at 521, whose "policy of denying city funds for
[nontherapeutic] abortions . . . is subject to public debate and approval or disapproval
at the polls." 432 U.S. at 521.

37. *See* Maher v. Roe, 432 U.S. at 474-77; Poelker v. Doe, 432 U.S. at 521. *See also*
Beal v. Doe, 432 U.S. at 445-46.

38. Nowhere in the abortion-funding cases does the majority limit its reasoning to
policy preferences favoring childbirth; it simply presents a series of broad and general
reasons for upholding types of state action that, in those cases, happen to favor the value
of childbirth. The analysis used is sufficiently open-ended to control in a situation in
which abortion is selected as the preferred value instead. *See* Bolner & Jacobsen, *The
Right to Procreate: The Dilemma of Overpopulation and the United States Judiciary,* 25
LOY. L. REV. 235, 254-55 (1979).

39. *E.g.,* Maher v. Roe, 432 U.S. at 477.

40. *See* note 38 *supra.*

41. *See, e.g.,* Beal v. Doe, 432 U.S. at 447-48 n. 15; Maher v. Roe, 432 U.S. at 480;
Poelker v. Doe, 432 U.S. at 521.

residents of New Gotham is apparent from their election to the
City Council of candidates advocating population control.[42] Particularly pertinent here is the Court's specific observation in
Maher that one sort of reason that might prompt valid state
action deviating from "a position of neutrality between abortion
and childbirth" would be "legitimate demographic concerns."
432 U.S. at 478 n.11. Such language is certainly broad enough to
encompass New Gotham's very real concerns regarding the size
of its population and its resulting efforts to limit procreation.[43]

In short, even if we concede that Boe and others similarly
situated have a fundamental right, secured by the fourteenth
amendment and embraced within the constitutionally protected
zone of privacy, to decide whether to carry their pregnancies to
term or to abort,[44] and even if, as we assume, New Gotham's
interest in curbing population growth is not of a "compelling"
character,[45] still we find no constitutional violation. Like the state
action challenged in *Beal, Maher,* and *Poelker,* the actions of the
defendants here do not obstruct absolutely or burden unduly the
exercise of the asserted right.[46] Notwithstanding the policy directive and staffing practice of the public hospital, Boe may still
obtain the medical treatment she seeks. The city's policy preferences do not compel her to terminate her pregnancy now or at any
other time. To paraphrase the language of the Supreme Court,

> [t]he State may have made [abortion] a more attractive alterna-
> tive, thereby influencing the woman's decision, but it has imposed
> no restriction on access to [childbirth] that was not already there.
> The indigency that may make it difficult — and in some cases,
> perhaps, impossible — for some women to [carry their pregnancies
> to term and deliver their children] is neither created nor in any
> way affected by the [city's] regulation.

---

42. See text at note 3 *supra.*

43. The demographic concerns in *Maher* were not so clearly apparent; the majority
in that case never explained whether or not a desire to combat underpopulation was, in
fact, responsible for Connecticut's policy preference favoring childbirth. *But see* 432 U.S.
at 489 n.* (Brennan, J., dissenting). *Cf.* Young Women's Christian Assn. v. Kugler, 342
F. Supp. 1048, 1074 (D.N.J. 1972) (pre-*Roe* abortion bar successfully challenged; court
rejects state's purported interest in fostering population growth "especially in a densely
populated and heavily urbanized state like New Jersey, with its attendant demographic,
economic, sociological and ecological problems").

44. See notes 19-21 *supra* and accompanying text.

45. See note 2 *supra.* New Gotham, though emphasizing the importance of its concerns regarding overpopulation, has conceded that its interests are not now of the same
magnitude as those that have been adjudged "compelling" under the fourteenth amendment. *See* Regents of the Univ. of Calif. v. Bakke, 438 U.S. 265, 314 (1978) (Powell, J.);
Korematsu v. United States, 323 U.S. 214 (1944).

46. See note 32 *supra.*

Maher v. Roe, 432 U.S. at 474. There is no controlling authority, moreover, for the proposition suggested by Boe that her indigency somehow places her within a "suspect class."[47] As the Supreme Court has observed, it has never held that "financial need alone identifies a suspect class for purposes of equal protection analysis." 432 U.S. at 471.

Of course, even though a state may have considerably broader power to encourage actions deemed to be in the public interest than it does to interfere directly with protected activity,[48] we must still determine whether the official action challenged here satisfies "the less demanding test of rationality that applies in the absence of a suspect classification or the impingement of a fundamental right." 432 U.S. at 478.[49] We conclude that New Gotham has met that test.

First, as we noted earlier, "legitimate demographic concerns about [a state's or city's] rate of population growth" are sufficient to support governmental "departure from a position of neutrality between abortion and childbirth." 432 U.S. at 478 n.11.[50] The parties have stipulated that there has been a recent increase, albeit one short of crisis proportions, in the population of New Gotham; the voters' election to the City Council of candidates who campaigned on platforms of population control demonstrates public awareness of this phenomenon and public desire to mitigate this trend.[51]

Nor is the policy in question irrational as it relates to the health of New Gotham's pregnant residents. As the Supreme Court pointed out several years ago, abortions during early pregnancy by competent licensed physicians are now "relatively safe" and the risks to women undergoing such abortions "appear to be as low as or lower than . . . for normal childbirth." *Roe v. Wade*, 410 U.S. 113, 149 (1973).[52] Even with respect to abortions performed after the first trimester, the maternal mortality rate in

---

47. *See* notes 22-24 *supra* and accompanying text.
48. Maher v. Roe, 432 U.S. 464, 476 (1977).
49. *See* Dandridge v. Williams, 397 U.S. 471, 485 (1970).
50. *See also* Moore v. City of East Cleveland, 431 U.S. 494, 499-500 (1977) (plurality opinion) (preventing overcrowding, minimizing traffic and parking congestion, and avoiding undue financial burden on city's schools are legitimate goals); Village of Belle Terre v. Boraas, 416 U.S. 1, 9 (1974) (land-use restrictions designed to promote quiet, family values, and clean air are legitimate).
51. *See* note 3 *supra* and accompanying text.
52. Though New Gotham provides free abortions in later pregnancy as well, *see* note 5 *supra* and accompanying text, any woman choosing to abort may obtain such treatment as early during her pregnancy as she wishes.

childbirth exceeds the maternal mortality rate from abortions. *See Planned Parenthood v. Danforth,* 428 U.S. 52, 77 (1976).

Similarly, New Gotham's bona fide financial concerns make this policy a reasonable one. As Mr. Justice Blackmun has observed, "the cost of a nontherapeutic abortion is far less than the cost of maternity care and delivery, and holds no comparison whatsoever with the welfare costs that will burden the State for the new indigents and their support in the long, long years ahead." *Beal v. Doe,* 432 U.S. 438, 463 (1977) (Blackmun, J., dissenting).[53]

For these reasons, we reject Boe's constitutional challenges to the manner in which New Gotham has chosen to operate its public hospital.

Judges BAKER and CARSON concur; Judge DANIEL concurs in an opinion to be filed at a later time.

EVERETT, Senior Circuit Judge, dissenting.

I respectfully dissent.

I

I would find the policy directive inconsistent with the hospital's charter. Prenatal care and medical services incident to childbirth are "medically necessary" because, in today's world, that happens to be the way pregnancies are treated. That is not to say, as Justice Brennan implies in *Beal v. Doe,* 432 U.S. 438, 449-52 (1977), that pregnancy is a disease or that prenatal care and delivery are among the "cures" therefor;[1] it is simply to point out a

---

53. *See* Zbaraz v. Quern, 469 F. Supp. 1212, 1218 & n.8 (N.D. Ill.) (comparative costs of state-funded abortion and state-funded childbirth), *probable jurisdiction noted sub nom.* Williams v. Zbaraz, 100 S. Ct. 447 (1979). *But see* Hardy, *Privacy and Public Funding: Maher v. Roe as the Interaction of Roe v. Wade and Dandridge v. Williams,* 18 ARIZ. L. REV. 903, 927-32 (1976).

****

1. The reasoning used by Justice Brennan in dissent in *Beal* and relied upon by the majority in this case is unsound. Abortions performed to terminate pregnancies that jeopardize a woman's life or health are clearly distinguishable from other abortions. Given that distinction, the *Beal* majority's interpretation of "medically necessary" cannot be reduced to the absurdity that Justice Brennan asserts; where a pregnancy does not present risks to life or health, an abortion is no different from any other elective, nonnecessary medical procedure, unless, of course, pregnancy itself is to be considered a disease that must be "cured" in every case by some sort of medical treatment. Although there appears to be no universally accepted definition of "disease," *see generally The Concept of Health,* 1 THE HASTINGS CENTER STUDIES No. 3, 1973, there is substantial authority for excluding pregnancy from the reach of that term, whatever the precise boundaries of its meaning. *See, e.g.,* Gilbert v. General Elec. Co., 375 F. Supp. 367, 375 (E.D. Va. 1974) ("pregnancy is not a disease, as that term is commonly understood"), *aff'd.,* 519 F.2d 661 (4th Cir.

fact of American life in this decade.[2] "The pregnancy of the
mother, absent miscarriage, inevitably and biologically terminates in the birth of the child, a process which today at least
requires medical attention and assistance." *Roe v. Norton*, 522
F.2d 928, 941 (2d Cir.) (Mulligan, J., concurring in part and
dissenting in part), *on remand*, 408 F. Supp. 660 (D. Conn. 1975),
revd. sub nom. Maher v. Roe, 432 U.S. 464 (1977). The availability of free abortions for indigent women does not alter this general
fact although, for any given woman who elects to interrupt the
natural biological course of her pregnancy by abortion, childbirth
will not occur. But such cases tell us nothing about medical necessity in general, nor do they provide a meaningful basis for
analyzing those situations in which no abortion is performed.[3]

1975), *revd. on other grounds*, 429 U.S. 125 (1976); Geduldig v. Aiello, 417 U.S. 484, 500
n.4 (1974) (Brennan, J., dissenting) (pregnancy is a physiological process causing a variable degree of disability on an individual basis); Cleveland Bd. of Educ. v. LaFleur, 414
U.S. 632, 652 (1974) (Powell, J., concurring) ("pregnancy is a normal biological function"); T. STEDMAN, STEDMAN'S MEDICAL DICTIONARY, 401, 1134 (4th Unabr. Lawyers' ed.
1976) (defining "disease" as "[m]orbus; illness; sickness; an interruption, cessation, or
disorder of body functions, systems, or organs" but defining "pregnancy" as "[g]estation;
fetation; cyesis; cyophoria; graviditas; gravidity; the state of a female after conception
until the birth of the baby"). And just as pregnancy itself is not a disease, childbirth, the
would-be "alternative" to abortion, is not "treatment" for pregnancy. *See, e.g., id.* at
1473 ("treatment" defined as "[t]herapeutics; therapy; the medical or surgical care of a
patient; the institution of measures or the giving of remedies designed to cure a disease").
Though childbirth restores a pregnant woman to a nonpregnant state and though, today,
it is always accompanied by medical attention and assistance, *see* note 2 *infra*, it is not
in itself a medical procedure at all but rather the inevitable and biological end of a
pregnancy in which no abortion, spontaneous or induced, has occurred. In short, childbirth simply "happens," whether a doctor is present or not. *See* Klein v. Nassau County
Medical Center, 347 F. Supp. 496, 500 (E.D.N.Y. 1972), *vacated and remanded*, 412 U.S.
925 (1973).
    See generally Chalmers, *Implications of the Current Debate on Obstetric Practice*,
in THE PLACE OF BIRTH 44, 47-48 (1978); Antler & Fox, *The Movement Toward a Safe
Maternity: Physician Accountability in New York City, 1915-1940*, 50 BULL. HIST. MED.
569, 571-72 (1976).
    2. Periodic medical attention throughout pregnancy and during and immediately
following childbirth is now accepted practice and has contributed significantly to the
decreased maternal and infant mortality rate in this country. *See* A. GUTTMACHER, PREG-
NANCY, BIRTH, AND FAMILY PLANNING 86-89, 335 (1973); *Obstetrical Practices in the United
States: Hearing Before the Subcomm. on Health and Scientific Research of the Senate
Comm. on Human Resources*, 95th Cong., 2d Sess. 36-37 (1978) (statement of Donald
Kennedy). *See generally* Antler & Fox, *supra* note 1, at 592-94. Today, the children of 98%
of American women are delivered in hospitals. *See* BOSTON WOMEN'S HEALTH BOOK
COLLECTIVE, OUR BODIES, OUR SELVES 250 (2d ed. 1976).
    See also Klein v. Nassau County Medical Center, 347 F. Supp. 496, 500 (E.D.N.Y.
1972), *vacated and remanded*, 412 U.S. 925 (1973); Roe v. Ferguson, 389 F. Supp. 387,
392 (S.D. Ohio 1974), *revd. on other grounds*, 515 F.2d 279 (6th Cir. 1975).
    3. In any event, whether or not any particular medical procedure is "necessary" in a
given case is a determination to be made by a physician, not by any general hospital

II

A more serious problem is the majority's decision to uphold official action that, to me, is clearly unconstitutional.

> Though undoubtedly the States are and should be left free to reflect a wide variety of policies, and should be allowed broad scope in experimenting with various means of promoting those policies, . . . "[t]here are limits to the extent to which a legislatively represented majority may conduct . . . experiments at the expense of the dignity and personality" of the individual . . . . In this instance these limits are, in my view, reached and passed.

Poe v. Ullman, 367 U.S. 497, 555 (1961) (Harlan, J., dissenting) (quoting *Skinner v. Oklahoma,* 316 U.S. 535, 546 (1942) (Jackson, J., concurring)).

Were I writing on a clean slate, it would, I believe, suffice for me to point out that "the right of procreation without state interference has long been recognized as 'one of the basic civil rights of man . . . fundamental to the very existence and survival of the race.'" *Maher v. Roe,* 432 U.S. 464, 472 n.7 (1977) (quoting *Skinner v. Oklahoma,* 316 U.S. 535, 541 (1942)).[4] New Gotham has unquestionably interfered with that right by denying to poor women free medical care for prenatal treatment and childbirth while providing free abortions, all in the absence of any compelling governmental interest.[5]

---

policy. *See also, e.g.,* Doe v. Bolton, 410 U.S. 179, 192, 197 (1973); Roe v. Wade, 410 U.S. 113, 163 (1973); Roe v. Casey, 464 F. Supp. 487, 500 (E.D. Pa. 1978); Jaffe v. Sharp, 463 F. Supp. 222, 228 (D. Mass. 1978), *affd. sub nom.* Preterm, Inc. v. Dukakis, 591 F.2d 121 (1st Cir.), *cert. denied,* 441 U.S. 952 (1979). *See generally* Wood & Durham, *Counseling, Consulting and Consent: Abortion and the Doctor-Patient Relationship,* 4 B.Y.U. L. REV. 783 (1978).

Finally, we should accept plaintiff's construction of the hospital charter in order to avoid the constitutional difficulties examined in Part II of this opinion. *See also, e.g.,* United States v. Thirty-Seven Photographs, 402 U.S. 363, 369 (1972) (plurality opinion).

4. *See also, e.g.,* Quilloin v. Walcott, 434 U.S. 246, 255 (1978) (parent-child relationship constitutionally protected); Smith v. Organization of Foster Families for Equality & Reform, 431 U.S. 816, 843-44 (1977) (importance of biological relationship in defining "family" for purposes of due process analysis); Moore v. City of East Cleveland, 431 U.S. 494, 503 (1977) (plurality opinion) (Constitution "protects the sanctity of the family"); Paul v. Davis, 424 U.S. 693, 713 (1976) (privacy, protected by substantive aspects of fourteenth amendment but limited to those rights deemed "fundamental" or "implicit in the concept of ordered liberty," encompasses matters relating to, *inter alia,* procreation); Cleveland Bd. of Educ. v. LaFleur, 414 U.S. 632, 639-40 (1974) ("freedom of personal choice in matters of marriage and family life is one of the liberties protected by the Due Process Clause of the Fourteenth Amendment"); Stanley v. Illinois, 405 U.S. 645, 651 (1972) (essential right to conceive and raise one's children); Prince v. Massachusetts, 321 U.S. 158, 166 (1944) (private realm of family life which state cannot enter); Meyer v. Nebraska, 262 U.S. 390, 399 (1923) (liberty guaranteed by fourteenth amendment includes right to "establish a home and bring up children").

5. New Gotham has not maintained that its "overpopulation" has reached crisis

To validate such interference on the theory that it is a mere policy preference that satisfies the rational basis test is — as Mr. Justice Marshall observed in dissent in *Beal, Maher,* and *Poelker* — to employ a constitutional analysis "pull[ed] from thin air." 432 U.S. at 457. Indeed, only eleven days before the decisions in *Beal, Maher,* and *Poelker* were handed down, a majority of the Court explicitly stated that, even in the absence of an "absolute obstacle," the compelling state interest test is the proper standard for assessing the constitutionality of governmental action that implicates the right of privacy by limiting an individual's access to the means necessary for the exercise of that right.[6] As a practical matter for the indigent, moreover, no interference with

---

proportions or that its aim of improving the "quality of life" of its citizens is compelling. *See* majority opinion notes 2 & 45 *supra* and accompanying text. Nor has the city sought to establish that the persons whose reproduction might be decreased by this policy are genetically defective. *See* Buck v. Bell, 274 U.S. 200 (1927). Much of the literature examining the constitutionality of programs of population control has concluded that, as burdens on the right to procreate, such programs must advance a compelling state interest. *See, e.g.,* Gray, *Compulsory Sterilization in a Free Society: Choices and Dilemmas,* 41 U. Cin. L. Rev. 529, 547-48, 571-85 (1972); Kindregan, *State Power Over Human Fertility and Individual Liberty,* 23 Hastings L.J. 1401, 1422-23 (1972); Montgomery, *The Population Explosion and United States Law,* 22 Hastings L.J. 629, 653-59 (1971); Rabin, *Population Control Through Financial Incentives,* 23 Hastings L.J. 1353, 1386 (1972); Comment, *Population Control: The Legal Approach to a Biological Imperative,* 58 Calif. L. Rev. 1414, 1431-43 (1970); Note, *Legal Analysis and Population Control: The Problem of Coercion,* 84 Harv. L. Rev. 1856, 1880-82 (1971); Comment, *Population: The Problem, the Constitution and a Proposal,* 11 J. Fam. L. 319, 332 (1971). The compelling state interest test has likewise been invoked in analyses of programs designed to promote eugenic goals through restrictions on procreation by certain individuals or groups. *See, e.g.,* Friedman, *Legal Implications of Amniocentesis,* 123 U. Pa. L. Rev. 92, 135 (1974); Shaw, *Procreation and the Population Problem,* 55 N.C. L. Rev. 1165, 1166 (1977); Vukowich, *The Dawning of the Brave New World — Legal, Ethical, and Social Issues of Eugenics,* 1971 U. Ill. L.F. 189, 207-09; Waltz & Thigpen, *Genetic Screening and Counseling: The Legal and Ethical Issues,* 68 Nw. U. L. Rev. 696, 721-26 (1973).

   6. In Carey v. Population Servs. Intl., 431 U.S. 678 (1977), where a New York statute restricting the distribution of contraceptives was found unconstitutional, a majority of the Justices observed:

   The significance of these cases [Planned Parenthood v. Danforth, 428 U.S. 52 (1976); Doe v. Bolton, 410 U.S. 179 (1973)] is that they establish that the same test must be applied to state regulations that burden an individual's right to decide to prevent conception or terminate a pregnancy by substantially limiting access to the means of effectuating that decision as is applied to state statutes that prohibit the decision entirely. Both types of regulation "may be justified only by a 'compelling state interest' . . . and . . . must be narrowly drawn to express only the legitimate state interests at stake."

   431 U.S. at 688 (quoting Roe v. Wade, 410 U.S. 113, 155 (1973)).

   Only Justice Powell, in an opinion not joined by any other member of the Court, suggested that some less exacting standard of review applies where the state action implicates the right of privacy but does not "entirely frustrate[ ] or heavily burden[ ]" its exercise. 431 U.S. at 705 (Powell, J., concurring in part and concurring in the judgment).

individual freedom of choice regarding whether or not "to beget or bear a child"[7] could be more "absolute"[8] than the measure upheld today. For a woman in Boe's financial straits, the medical treatment she seeks is *completely* out of reach. Unless we are to exhume the utterly repudiated[9] right-privilege distinction,[10] the state action before us cannot stand.[11]

As a result of the Supreme Court's decisions in *Beal, Maher,* and *Poelker,* however, the slate upon which I write is not entirely clean, and a mere recitation of apparently well-settled constitutional principles antedating those decisions is therefore insufficient. But even conceding that some language from those opinions supports the result reached here, that support is at best superficial. The issues resolved in those cases are very different from those raised here.[12] The abortion-funding cases held simply that a state or local government may refuse to provide public funding for elective abortions; they did not indicate what result would obtain where the treatment in question relates to childbirth instead.

The error the majority makes is perhaps understandable. As a result of the Supreme Court's lengthening list of cases concern-

---

7. Carey v. Population Servs. Intl., 431 U.S. 678, 685 (1977).

8. *But see* majority opinion notes 30-32 *supra* and accompanying text.

9. Van Alstyne, *Cracks in "The New Property": Adjudicative Due Process in the Administrative State,* 62 CORNELL L. REV. 445, 446 (1977).

10. *See, e.g.,* Elrod v. Burns, 427 U.S. 347, 360-61 (1976) (plurality opinion)(citations omitted):

"[F]or at least a quarter-century, this Court has made clear that even though a person has no 'right' to a valuable governmental benefit and even though the government may deny him the benefit for any number of reasons, there are some reasons upon which the government may not rely." . . . [O]ne such impermissible reason [is that the] denial of a public benefit may not be used by the government for the purpose of creating an incentive enabling it to achieve what it may not command directly . . . . " '[T]his Court now has rejected the concept that constitutional rights turn upon whether a governmental benefit is characterized as a "right" or as a "privilege." ' "

11. One additional difficulty, which Boe does not raise and which the court therefore does not address, is the possible argument that the city's policy directive and hospital staffing practice infringe the first amendment rights of those indigent women who oppose abortion for religious reasons. Were I confronted with that question, I would again conclude that only a revival of the right-privilege distinction, *see* note 10 *supra,* could insulate such state action from otherwise certain constitutional invalidity. *See* Sherbert v. Verner, 374 U.S. 398, 406 (1963) ("to condition the availability of [governmental] benefits upon [one's] willingness to violate a cardinal principle of her religious faith effectively penalizes the free exercise of her constitutional liberties"). *Cf.* Note, *Abortion, Medicaid, and the Constitution,* 54 N.Y.U. L. REV. 120, 151-55 (1979) (first amendment problems of abortion-funding restrictions).

12. *See generally* L. TRIBE, AMERICAN CONSTITUTIONAL LAW 932 & n.70 (1978).

ing contraception[13] and abortion,[14] the concept of freedom of
choice in matters of reproduction has come to refer almost exclu-
sively to decisions *not* to bear children.[15] Clearly, however, such
freedom must encompass as well the decisions of those individuals who do wish to procreate.[16]

Mr. Justice Goldberg recognized the inseparable and com-
plementary nature of the two kinds of individual choices more
than a decade ago in his concurring opinion in *Griswold v.
Connecticut*, 381 U.S. 479 (1965), where he observed that failure
to accord constitutional protection to the private use of contraceptives by married couples[17] would not only intrude upon the
guarantees of the ninth amendment but would also establish an
unacceptable precedent for state and federal limitation of family
size despite the absence of a compelling state interest.[18] That is

---

13. *E.g.*, Carey v. Population Servs. Intl., 431 U.S. 678 (1977); Eisenstadt v. Baird,
405 U.S. 438 (1972); Griswold v. Connecticut, 381 U.S. 479 (1965). *See also* Poe v. Ullman,
367 U.S. 497 (1961); Tileston v. Ullman, 318 U.S. 44 (1943).

14. *E.g.*, Bellotti v. Baird, 99 S. Ct. 3035 (1979); Colautti v. Franklin, 439 U.S. 379
(1979); Poelker v. Doe, 432 U.S. 519 (1977); Maher v. Roe, 432 U.S. 464 (1977); Beal v.
Doe, 432 U.S. 438 (1977); Bellotti v. Baird, 428 U.S. 132 (1976); Planned Parenthood v.
Danforth, 428 U.S. 52 (1976); Connecticut v. Menillo, 423 U.S. 9 (1975) (per curiam); Doe
v. Bolton, 410 U.S. 179 (1973); Roe v. Wade, 410 U.S. 113 (1973). *See also* Singleton v.
Wulff, 428 U.S. 106 (1976).

15. The Supreme Court has heard a comparatively small number of cases directly
raising questions concerning the right to procreate, Skinner v. Oklahoma, 316 U.S. 535
(1942); Buck v. Bell, 274 U.S. 200 (1927). A number of cases focusing on other issues have
noted, in passing, rights related to childbearing. *See* note 4 *supra*.

16. The Supreme Court acknowledged this point in Maher v. Roe, 432 U.S. 464, 472
n.7 (1977), stating that "[a] woman has *at least* an equal right to choose to carry her
fetus to term as to choose to abort it" (emphasis added).

17. Justice Goldberg wrote of the "basic and fundamental . . . right of privacy in
marriage." 381 U.S. at 491. The holding in *Griswold* was subsequently extended to unmarried individuals via the equal protection clause. Eisenstadt v. Baird, 405 U.S. 438 (1972).

18. Justice Goldberg reasoned:
The logic of the dissents would sanction federal or state legislation that seems to
me even more plainly unconstitutional than the statute before us. Surely the Government, absent a showing of a compelling subordinating state interest, could not
decree that all husbands and wives must be sterilized after two children have been
born to them. Yet by their reasoning such an invasion of marital privacy would not
be subject to constitutional challenge because, while it might be "silly," no provision of the Constitution specifically prevents the Government from curtailing the
marital right to bear children and raise a family. While it may shock some of my
Brethren that the Court today holds that the Constitution protects the right of
marital privacy, in my view it is far more shocking to believe that the personal
liberty guaranteed by the Constitution does not include protection against such
totalitarian limitation of family size, which is at complete variance with our constitutional concepts. Yet, if upon a showing of a slender basis of rationality, a law
outlawing voluntary birth control by married persons is valid, then, by the same
reasoning, a law requiring compulsory birth control also would seem to be valid. In

precisely what has happened today. Just as Mr. Justice Goldberg feared, the majority here has taken "precedent" from cases limiting an individual's freedom *not* to bear children, *Beal, Maher,* and *Poelker,* to validate restrictions on the right to procreate. But "[t]he individual's freedom to . . . reproduce is 'older than the Bill of Rights.' "[19] Thus, if history and tradition are to play any role in defining those substantive rights shielded by the due process clause, *see Moore v. City of East Cleveland,* 431 U.S. 494, 503-04 (1977) (plurality opinion),[20] then surely the long-established personal right to procreate, an "intrinsic human right,"[21] should be accorded significantly greater constitutional protection than the only recently recognized "right to abort."[22]

But even if the reasoning the majority borrows from the abortion-funding cases were controlling in principle, additional difficulties would remain.

First, there is a noticeable misfit of the governmental end identified and the means selected to effectuate that goal. Even if so-called strict judicial scrutiny is not warranted in a case such

---

my view, however, both types of law would unjustifiably intrude upon rights of marital privacy which are constitutionally protected.

381 U.S. at 496-97. *See* note 5 *supra. See also* Katin, *Griswold v. Connecticut: The Justices and Connecticut's "Uncommonly Silly Law,"* 42 NOTRE DAME LAW. 680, 699 (1967).

19. Smith v. Organization of Foster Families for Equality & Reform, 431 U.S. 816, 845 (1977) (citing Griswold v. Connecticut, 381 U.S. 479, 486 (1965)).

20. A plurality of the Court explained in *Moore:*

Appropriate limits on substantive due process come not from drawing arbitrary lines but rather from careful "respect for the teachings of history [and] solid recognition of the basic values that underlie our society." *Griswold v. Connecticut,* 381 U.S., at 501 (Harlan, J., concurring). . . . Out decisions establish that the Constitution protects the sanctity of the family precisely because the institution of the family is deeply rooted in this Nation's history and tradition.

431 U.S. at 503.

A footnote at the end of that passage added, in part, the following:

In *Wisconsin v. Yoder,* 406 U.S. 205 (1972), the Court rested its holding in part on the constitutional right of parents to assume the primary role in decisions concerning the rearing of their children. That right is recognized because it reflects a "strong tradition" founded on "the history and culture of Western civilization," and because the parental role "is now established beyond debate as an enduring American tradition." *Id.* at 232.

431 U.S. at 503 n.12.

Justice Brennan, in a concurring opinion joined by Justice Marshall, also noted the significance of "tradition." 431 U.S. at 507. *See also* Bellotti v. Baird, 99 S. Ct. 3035, 3045 (1979) (plurality opinion); Parham v. J.R., 99 S. Ct. 2493, 2504 (1979); Griswold v. Connecticut, 381 U.S. 479, 493 (1965) (Goldberg, J., concurring); Poe v. Ullman, 367 U.S. 497, 542 (1961) (Harlan, J., dissenting).

21. Smith v. Organization of Foster Families for Equality & Reform, 434 U.S. 816, 845 (1977) *See also* Griswold v. Connecticut, 381 U.S. 479, 486 (1965).

22. *See* Roe v. Wade, 410 U.S. 113, 153 (1973).

as this,[23] New Gotham's intrusion into a matter of "family life" is sufficiently significant to require a court at least to "examine carefully the importance of the governmental interests advanced and the extent to which they are served by the challenged [action]." *Moore v. City of East Cleveland,* 431 U.S. 494, 499 (1977) (plurality opinion).[24]

Granting for the moment that a governmental interest in reducing crowding may be a legitimate underlying purpose, such an end is furthered only marginally by New Gotham's denial of free treatment for childbirth. Certainly, this policy will not discourage the nonindigent from reproducing.[25] And although pregnancy and childbirth today are processes ordinarily attended by medical assistance,[26] delivery of a living infant can occur outside a hospital without any medical assistance whatsoever. A woman in Boe's financial situation, determined not to abort, can in many cases give birth to her child without a physician's aid. That very real possibility not only demonstrates the ineffectiveness of the New Gotham policy but also reveals another flaw as well: Mothers carrying their pregnancies to term and delivering without medical assistance, as well as children born under such circumstances, are in much greater jeopardy of suffering some kind of serious physical complication, including death.[27] Surely New Gotham's interest in reducing overpopulation, even among the poor, is not permissibly served by increasing risks to the health

---

23. *Compare* text at majority opinion note 49 *supra with* majority opinion note 24 *supra.*

24. *See* Trimble v. Gordon, 430 U.S. 762, 767-68 (1977) (though "most exacting scrutiny" not appropriate for reviewing classification disadvantaging illegitimates, challenged state action held unconstitutional because it "bears only the most attenuated relationship to the asserted goal"); Gunther, *The Supreme Court, 1971 Term — Foreword: In Search of Evolving Doctrine on a Changing Court: A Model for a Newer Equal Protection,* 86 Harv. L. Rev. 1, 18-21 (1972).

25. Those able to afford to pay for prenatal care and medical treatment for childbirth at a private facility will not be affected in a legal or a practical way by the policy. *See* majority opinion note 1 *supra.* In some small communities, however, such restrictions on a hospital's services may have a broader impact. *See also* Poelker v. Doe, 432 U.S. 519, 524 (1977)(Brennan, J., dissenting).

26. *See* note 2 *supra* and accompanying text.

27. Increased availability and acceptance of good prenatal care as well as the greater use of hospitals are significant factors in the decreasing maternal mortality rate during pregnancy, delivery and the six-week postpartum period. A. Guttmacher, Pregnancy, Birth, and Family Planning 86-89 (1973). It is instructive to note in this context, moreover, that in "three of the states with the worst maternal and newborn [mortality] records, Mississippi, Alabama, and Arkansas, nearly one quarter of the births take place outside of the hospital." *Id.* at 87.

of those individuals evading the city's policy.[28]

One can imagine, moreover, more narrowly tailored schemes under which New Gotham's interests could be advanced — alternative policies both less onerous to individuals in Boe's class and more carefully designed to achieve the city's asserted objective.[29] For example, New Gotham could instead provide free contraceptives or counseling for family planning;[30] either service would promote the city's goal without burdening those women who are already pregnant and thus face what must appear to some as a medical and moral dilemma.[31] For those women in Boe's situation who oppose abortion but do not care to rear a child themselves, the city could limit its population by arranging for adoptive placements in less crowded locales. A number of other possibilities come to mind.[32]

Finally, I have grave reservations about another aspect of the New Gotham policy that Boe does not attack directly: the availability of abortions at any time throughout pregnancy.[33] It is true that *Roe v. Wade*, 410 U.S. 113 (1973), held only that a state, if it desired, could restrict abortions after the first trimester for reasons related to maternal health, 410 U.S. at 163, and could prohibit abortions following viability in order to preserve fetal life, 410 U.S. at 163-64; apparently, nothing in *Roe* requires states to enact such protective legislation. Still, I am troubled by the prospect of the New Gotham public hospital's performing abortions up through the final days of pregnancy.

---

28. New Gotham, of course, has not asserted nor can we infer that it intends to cure its population difficulties by increasing the infant and maternal mortality rate occurring in connection with childbirth. Nor can I believe that the majority would approve any "modest proposal" along these lines. *See also* Poelker v. Doe, 432 U.S. 519, 523-24 (1977)(Brennan, J., dissenting).

29. *Cf.* Trimble v. Gordon, 430 U.S. 762, 772-73 (1977) (though no compelling interest need be shown, Court inquires whether classification disadvantaging illegitimates "is carefully tuned to alternative considerations" or whether it "extends well beyond the asserted purposes").

30. The family planning agencies and clinics described by the majority in majority opinion note 3 *supra* provide services only for a fee.

31. Although under the privacy decisions of the United States Supreme Court, Griswold v. Connecticut, 381 U.S. 479 (1965); Roe v. Wade, 410 U.S. 113 (1973), abortion and contraception may appear to be equivalent means of birth control, abortion clearly implicates interests not implicated by contraception. *See* Carey v. Population Servs. Intl., 431 U.S. 678, 690 (1977) (contraception, unlike abortion, does not implicate, *inter alia*, interest in protecting potential life).

32. Indeed, if New Gotham's concern is one regarding the sheer number of its inhabitants, the municipal hospital could provide *free* abortions for all residents and not only those who are indigent. *See* majority opinion note 1 *supra*.

33. *See* majority opinion note 5 *supra* and accompanying text.

As a woman's pregnancy progresses beyond the point of fetal viability, an abortion becomes more and more likely to result in a live birth.[34] Given that fact and in view of the official goal of promoting population control, I see little difference between New Gotham State's legalization of post-viability abortions and a state's rescission of its criminal homicide laws. If there is any meaning at all to the fourteenth amendment's command that no state "shall deprive a person of life . . . without due process of law," then a state cannot take the latter course.[35] Although *Roe* draws a bright line between a person and a fetus for purposes of fourteenth-amendment protection, 410 U.S. at 157-59, the possibility of live births in terminations of advanced pregnancies obscures any such clear distinction between the so-called alternatives, abortion and childbirth, and thus between the constitutional implications of the two procedures.

It is for this reason, in addition to those I offered in Part I of this opinion, that I think Boe's challenge to the city's interpretation of the hospital charter is correct; at some point in pregnancy, at least after viability of the fetus, childbirth *is* a "medically necessary" procedure, for an "abortion," to the extent that term implies fetal death, no longer remains an acceptable alternative.

I would therefore strike down the challenged policy as inconsistent with both the hospital's own charter and the United States Constitution.

DANIEL, Senior Circuit Judge, concurring.

On each issue, I agree with the conclusion reached by Judge Adams joined by Judges Baker and Carson. But because those results seem extraordinary, if not ironic, I add the following thoughts that I believe must be addressed en route.

---

34. *See* Hardy, *Privacy and Public Funding: Maher v. Roe as the Interaction of Roe v. Wade and Dandridge v. Williams*, 18 ARIZ. L. REV. 903, 933-34 n.164 (1976). *Cf.* Colautti v. Franklin, 439 U.S. 379 (1979) (invalidation for vagueness of legislation imposing medical standard of care to maximize chances of fetal survival).

35. In *Roe v. Wade*, the Court suggested that the right to life accorded to persons by the fourteenth amendment requires the states to criminalize the taking of such life. *See* 410 U.S. at 156-58 & n.54. *See also* Landrum v. Moats, 576 F.2d 1320, 1325 (8th Cir.), ("The right to life is fundamental and is protected against unreasonable or unlawful takings by the procedural due process safeguards of the fifth and fourteenth amendments."), *cert. denied*, 439 U.S. 912 (1978).

* * * * * *

I

The question of "medical necessity" is, in my view, far more difficult than either the majority or the dissenting opinion intimates. It raises a number of problems that neither analysis fully explores.

The majority's complete and unquestioning reliance on the opinions in *Beal v. Doe,* 432 U.S. 438 (1977), merits initial attention. The narrow issue before the Court in *Beal* was whether Pennsylvania could, consistent with Title XIX of the Social Security Act, distinguish "medically necessary" abortions from other abortions.[1] Certainly from a lay or intuitive perspective, such a distinction is not totally unsupportable: one can easily imagine a woman seeking to terminate a life-threatening ectopic pregnancy;[2] an abortion performed under such circumstances would be meaningfully described as "medically necessary."[3] Such a case

---

1. Pursuant to the regulations challenged in *Beal,* Pennsylvania limited Medicaid assistance "to those abortions that are certified by physicians as medically necessary." 432 U.S. at 441.

2. In an ectopic pregnancy, gestation occurs in a site other than the uterine cavity, typically in a Fallopian tube. Once diagnosed, "abdominal operation is necessary at once." A. GUTTMACHER, PREGNANCY, BIRTH AND FAMILY PLANNING 125 (1973). *See* T. STEDMAN, STEDMAN'S MEDICAL DICTIONARY 1134 (4th Unabr. Lawyers' ed. 1976).

3. Title XIX of the Social Security Act speaks in terms of medical necessity in identifying those persons eligible for Medicaid assistance (persons with "insufficient . . . income and resources to meet the costs of necessary medical . . . services") and not in describing the precise kinds of medical services to be funded under the Act. 42 U.S.C. § 1396a(a)(10)(C)(i) (1976). *See* 42 U.S.C. § 1396 (1976). *Compare* Roe v. Norton, 522 F.2d 928, 933 (2d Cir. 1975), *with* 522 F.2d at 939 (Mulligan, J., concurring in part and dissenting in part), *on remand,* 408 F. Supp. 660 (D. Conn. 1975), *revd. sub nom.* Maher v. Roe, 432 .U.S. 464 (1977).

Although the Pennsylvania regulation at issue in *Beal* purportedly provided financial assistance only for those abortions deemed "medically necessary," it is unclear whether the specifications listed in the regulation in fact comport with that description. For example, abortions performed under circumstances where continued pregnancy would jeopardize the mental health of the mother appear not to be covered unless the pregnancy resulted from "statutory or forcible rape or incest." 432 U.S. at 441 n.3. If mental or psychological factors are sufficient to create medical necessity under some circumstances, however, it makes little sense to ignore such factors under other circumstances, as the Pennsylvania regulation apparently requires; on the other hand, if mental health always presents an appropriate consideration, it is unclear what a special provision for rape and incest adds to the regulation. In addition, the Pennsylvania regulation does provide funding for abortions where "[t]here is documented medical evidence that an infant may be born with incapacitating physical deformity or mental deficiency . . . ." 432 U.S. at 441 n.3. Whatever one may think of the desirability of terminating a pregnancy in such a case, it is not self-evident that such a termination is a matter of medical necessity since continuation of the pregnancy presents no immediate health threat to the mother and any perceived "threat" to the well-being of the fetus caused by the likely abnormalities is outweighed by the greater threat of fetal death posed by the abortion. *Cf.* Becker v.

is, moreover, easily distinguishable from a termination of pregnancy sought solely for reasons of maternal convenience.[4]

Given that narrow issue, the majority in *Beal* properly began its analysis by considering Pennsylvania's effort to differentiate two classes of abortions. Resolving that question should have

---

Schwartz, 46 N.Y.2d 401, 386 N.E.2d 807, 413 N.Y.S.2d 895 (1978) (rejecting child's asserted fundamental right to be born as a whole, functional human being), *revg.*, Park v. Chessin, 60 App. Div. 2d 80, 400 N.Y.S.2d 110 (1977); Ely, *The Supreme Court, 1977 Term — Foreword: On Discovering Fundamental Values,* 92 HARV. L. REV. 5, 48 n.186 (1978) (differing public opinions regarding abortions where pregnancy poses threat to mother's physical health and abortions where the baby might be born deformed).

Perhaps the Supreme Court saw Pennsylvania's goal as one of fostering only *"normal* childbirth," 432 U.S. at 446 (emphasis added), and not one of defining medical necessity. *See* Doe v. Mundy, 441 F. Supp. 447, 451 (E.D. Wis. 1977) (unsuccessful challenge to county's refusal to fund abortions where pregnancy resulted from rape or incest or when infant may be deformed). But whether or not the regulation challenged in *Beal* provides an accurate catalogue of "medically necessary abortions," I am satisfied that that term is not meaningless and is susceptible of codification. *See* Doe v. Bolton, 410 U.S. 179, 191-92 (1973).

Cf., e.g., Preterm, Inc. v. Dukakis, 591 F.2d 121, 126-27, 134 (1st Cir.) (Massachusetts's limiting Medicaid funding only to life-saving abortions unreasonable and antithetical to medical definition of medical necessity; federal "Hyde amendment" substantively alters Medicaid Act), *cert. denied,* 441 U.S. 952 (1979); Doe v. Kenley, 584 F.2d 1362, 1366 (4th Cir. 1978) ("therapeutic abortions" include all those where pregnancy poses "substantial endangerment to health"; "endangerment to life" standard ambiguous and too narrow); Zbaraz v. Quern, 572 F.2d 582, 584-85 (7th Cir. 1978) ("plain-meaning" semantic distinction between "necessary for the preservation of life" and "necessary for the preservation of health"); Doe v. Busbee, 471 F. Supp. 1326 (N.D. Ga. 1979) (reimbursement for less than all medically necessary abortions inconsistent with objectives of Title XIX; Hyde amendment does not substantively limit Title XIX); Roe v. Casey, 464 F. Supp. 487, 499-502 (E.D. Pa. 1978) (Pennsylvania cannot limit Medicaid funding only to those abortions necessary to save mother's life; Title XIX requires states to provide all medically necessary abortions); D ___ R ___ v. Mitchell, 456 F. Supp. 609 (D. Utah 1978) (reasoning in *Beal v. Doe* validates Utah's limited abortion funding for only those abortions necessary to save the life of a mother); Doe v. Mundy, 441 F. Supp. 447 (E.D. Wis. 1977) (county may choose to fund only those abortions where pregnancy threatens mother's life); Emma G. v. Edwards, 434 F. Supp. 1048, 1050 (E.D. La. 1977) (stipulation that, *inter alia,* "[t]herapeutic abortions are recognized as medically necessary procedures"); Right to Choose v. Byrne, 165 N.J. Super. 443, 454, 398 A.2d 587, 592 (Ch. Div. 1979) ("medically necessary abortions" include those where pregnancy endangers life or health); Butler, *The Right to Medicaid Payment for Abortion,* 28 HASTINGS L.J. 931, 953-61 (1977) (pre-*Beal, Maher,* and *Poelker* analysis of "medically necessary" in the abortion context); Note, *State Restrictions on Medicaid Coverage of Medically Necessary Services,* 78 COLUM. L. REV. 1491, 1495-502, 1510-16 (1978) (abortion-funding restrictions in light of analysis of "medical necessity"); Note, *Abortion, Medicaid, and the Constitution,* 54 N.Y.U. L. REV. 120, 135 (1979) (taxonomy of possible abortion-funding restrictions).

4. *See* Zbaraz v. Quern, 469 F. Supp. 1212, 1221 (N.D. Ill.) ("medically necessary" abortions constitute only one fifth of cases in which pregnant woman desires an abortion), *probable jurisdiction noted sub nom.* Williams v. Zbaraz, 100 S. Ct. 447 (1979). Judge Everett recognizes this point in his dissent, *see* dissenting opinion note 1 *supra. See also* Beal v. Doe, 432 U.S. 438, 450-51 n. * (1977) (Brennan, J., dissenting).

been the end of the matter.[5] But because of arguments raised by the plaintiffs and Title XIX's requirement of reasonableness,[6] the Court in *Beal* proceeded to compare abortions with childbirth. Noting the state's "important and legitimate interest . . . in protecting . . . human life,'"[7] the *Beal* majority shifted its focus from therapeutic versus elective abortions to elective abortions versus childbirth,[8] thereby suggesting that the latter pair somehow constitute alternative medical responses to a single condition, pregnancy.

But such a shift in focus is misleading. Nothing in *Beal* indicates that the Pennsylvania regulation was prompted by the eventual availability of alternative services for pregnant women or even that the state's interest in protecting human life played a role in the drafting of the regulation.[9] With all due deference to the Justices of the Supreme Court, the more obvious and sensible basis for upholding the Pennsylvania regulation as "reasonable" lies in the fact that, for some women, pregnancy presents no medical difficulty while, for others, the condition may be life- or health-threatening and thus may require medical treatment.[10] Pennsylvania simply undertook to provide assistance in the latter

---

5. It is unnecessary, for purposes of this analysis, to determine how the Court should have resolved the issue in *Beal,* given a clear focus on the precise question presented. *See* note 3 *supra.*

6. In challenging the statute, plaintiffs had argued that, because childbirth presents greater health risks and is costlier than abortion, the exclusion of nontherapeutic abortions from Medicaid coverage was unreasonable, in violation of the requirements of Title XIX, 42 U.S.C. § 1396a(a)(17) (1976). *See* Beal v. Doe, 432 U.S. 438, 445 (1977).

7. 432 U.S. at 445-46.

8. *See* 432 U.S. at 445-46.

As one court has observed, the Court in *Beal* "provided no direct response to [the] contentions" that the exclusion of nontherapeutic abortions from Medicaid coverage was unreasonable on both economic and health grounds. D____ R____ v. Mitchell, 456 F. Supp. 609, 618 (D. Utah 1978).

9. In its briefs, Pennsylvania did not seek to justify its regulation on this basis but invoked other grounds instead. Brief for Petitioners and Reply Brief for Petitioners, Beal v. Doe, 432 U.S. 438 (1977). *But see* Colautti v. Franklin, 439 U.S. 379 (1979) (Pennsylvania's defense of other abortion restrictions suggests goal of fetal protection); Roe v. Casey, 464 F. Supp. 487, 501 (E.D. Pa. 1978) (Pennsylvania refuses to finance nonlifesaving abortions because of "moral repugnance" felt by state legislature). Arguably, reasons related to the protection of potential life prior to viability were not offered in *Beal* because they may have appeared to have been foreclosed by Roe v. Wade, 410 U.S. 113, 150-52 (1973). *See generally* Perry, *The Abortion Funding Cases: A Comment on the Supreme Court's Role in American Government,* 66 Geo. L.J. 1191, 1196 (1978); Comment, *Equal Protection and Welfare Legislation: The Need for a Principled Approach,* 1 U. Puget Sound L. Rev. 323, 342 (1978).

10. *See* Roe v. Norton, 522 F.2d 928, 940 (2d Cir.) (Mulligan, J., concurring in part and dissenting in part), *on remand,* 408 F. Supp. 660 (D. Conn. 1975), *revd. sub nom.* Maher v. Roe, 432 U.S. 464 (1977).

category.[11] That a pregnancy presenting no medical difficulties will ultimately result in childbirth is irrelevant. The *Beal* majority thus not only obscured the relatively simple issue before it but also gratuitously invited the conclusion, articulated by Justice Brennan and then adopted by the majority in this case, that provision of abortions renders medical services related to childbirth medically "unnecessary."[12]

Though I therefore find the logic in *Beal* questionable with respect to the precise issue presented by that case, such reasoning carries considerably more force on the facts before us today. The New Gotham public hospital charter, unlike the Pennsylvania regulation, speaks not of medically necessary *abortions,* but rather of medically necessary services in general.[13] Regardless of what constitutes standard medical practice in American obstetrics today, a factor that the dissent in this case considers determinative,[14] prenatal care and medical assistance related to childbirth are certainly "unnecessary" — medically or otherwise — for any woman who is not pregnant. For each indigent pregnant woman in New Gotham who accepts the offered abortion, then, such prenatal and delivery services become not only "unnecessary" but also impossible to perform. Some such women, of course, may reject the free termination of pregnancy offered by the city. The question then becomes whether under those circumstances "medically necessary" services must include prenatal care and procedures incident to childbirth. Despite my own feeling that the New Gotham policy is unwise and perverse, I must answer that question in the negative. Considerations of fairness, akin to those underlying estoppel,[15] preclude a woman who could have voluntarily obviated all need for such services from arguing that, as a result of her choice to forgo that opportunity, those services have become "necessary."[16] Any other conclusion would drain that term of all meaning.

---

11. I put aside the question whether the Pennsylvania regulation challenged in *Beal* provides a suitable tool for attaining the presumed governmental goal. *See* note 3 *supra.*

12. *See* majority opinion notes 13-14 *supra.*

13. *See* majority opinion note 1 *supra* and accompanying text.

14. *See* dissenting opinion notes 2-3 *supra* and accompanying text

15. *See* W. PROSSER, HANDBOOK OF THE LAW OF TORTS 691 (4th ed. 1971).

16. In such cases, the continuation of pregnancy and consequent eligibility for prenatal and delivery care are voluntary, even if conception was not. *Cf.* Gilbert v. General Elec. Co., 375 F. Supp. 367, 375 (E.D. Va. 1974) (condition of pregnancy not "voluntary" simply because statistically low birth rates indicate "pregnancy can to a large extent be avoided"), *affd.,* 519 F.2d 661 (4th Cir. 1975), *revd.,* 429 U.S. 125 (1976). There may be, of course, some indigent pregnant women who do not abort because they never learn of their opportunity to do so. *See* Note, *The Abortion Alternative and the Patient's Right to*

II

Likewise, on the constitutional question, I feel compelled to join the majority, though only after considerable further examination of the issue.

The analysis in Judge Adams's opinion, although seemingly unfamiliar, is not, as Judge Everett claims, something "pull[ed] from thin air."[17] Its roots can be traced back several years to the Supreme Court's decision in *Dandridge v. Williams*, 397 U.S. 471 (1970), upholding the constitutionality of a Maryland regulation that imposed a $240 or $250 ceiling on assistance to a single family under the Aid to Families with Dependent Children program. Plaintiffs in that case had challenged the regulation as a violation of the equal protection clause on the theory that it classified families according to size and deprived members of large families of aid sufficient to meet their subsistence requirements, as determined by the state's "standard of need" formula.[18] In refuting that challenge, the Court found the system justifiable on a number of valid and rational bases asserted by the state,[19] including Maryland's desire to provide "incentives for family planning," 397 U.S. at 484.

Not only does *Dandridge* stand for the proposition that the minimally demanding rational basis test governs a state's allocation of its limited public funds,[20] but — like *Beal, Maher,* and *Poelker* — it also endorses official involvement in matters of reproductive control,[21] even without the support of a compelling state interest, so long as that official involvement falls short of

---

Know, 1978 WASH. U. L.Q. 167. One can imagine, for example, an indigent pregnant woman who, unaware of the policy directive and not desiring prenatal care, delays her initial visit to the hospital until labor has commenced. Although in such circumstances the opportunity to obviate the "need" for medical assistance related to childbirth may seem more questionable, Boe, and thus the class she represents, does not fall within this category. The mere possibility of such cases, I think, provides no answer for this lawsuit but does raise difficult questions concerning whether it is ever "too late" in a woman's pregnancy for an abortion. *See* notes 51-72 and accompanying text *infra.*

17. *See* text following dissenting opinion note 5 *supra.*

18. The Court explained the mechanics of the challenged state action, 397 U.S. at 473-75.

19. The Court stated explicitly that, since the action in question lay in the "area of economics and social welfare," it could withstand the equal protection challenge upon the showing of any "reasonable basis." 397 U.S. at 485.

20. *See* Maher v. Roe, 432 U.S. 464, 479 (1977).

21. Commentators have read *Dandridge* as a case authorizing limited governmental intrusion into individual decisions regarding family planning and procreation. Shaw, *Procreation and the Population Problem,* 55 N.C. L. REV. 1165, 1168 (1977); Note, *Legal Analysis and Population Control: The Problem of Coercion,* 84 HARV. L. REV. 1856, 1856-62 (1971). *But see* Rabin, *Population Control Through Financial Incentives,* 23 HASTINGS L.J. 1353, 1361 (1972).

imposing outright restrictions on individual choice.[22] More significantly, *Dandridge* also establishes that governmental interests in
limiting family size may be among the legitimate state objectives
satisfying the rationality standard.

This reading of *Dandridge* was invoked four years later by
Mr. Justice Powell in his concurring opinion in *Cleveland Board
of Education v. LaFleur*, 414 U.S. 632 (1974), as authority for the
proposition that "[u]ndoubtedly Congress could . . . constitutionally seek to discourage excessive population growth by limiting tax deductions for dependents." 414 U.S. at 651. Though the
means for promoting population control selected by New Gotham
differs from both the vehicle sanctioned in *Dandridge* and that
approved by Powell in *LaFleur*, the point is clear: The Constitution permits a state, for reasons less than compelling,[23] to seek to
influence individual procreative decisions, at least through less
absolute means than total prohibitions.[24] New Gotham has done

22. The inquiry in *Dandridge* was confined to *"incentives* for family planning." 397
U.S. at 484 (emphasis added). *See generally* Dixon, *The Supreme Court and Equality:
Legislative Classifications, Desegregation, and Reverse Discrimination*, 62 CORNELL L.
REV. 494, 513-14 n.102 (1977); Note, *supra* note 21, at 1858-60.

23. Some elaboration of the compelling state interest doctrine becomes necessary
here. The standard invocations of this test fail to make clear whether the compelling
character of a particular governmental interest stems from some intrinsic feature of that
interest itself, regardless of the surrounding circumstances, or whether those surrounding circumstances help determine the compelling or noncompelling nature of the interest.
The phrase "compelling state interest" suggests the former. The timetable adopted in
Roe v. Wade, 410 U.S. 113, 162-64 (1973), however, under which various state interests
mature to an ultimately compelling point as a woman's pregnancy progresses, suggests
that it is not some inherent characteristic of the interest itself that renders it compelling
but rather some additional factor. Thus, while state interests in population control may
become compelling in certain emergency situations of extreme and severe overcrowding,
defendants do not argue that such interests are compelling under the circumstances
extant in New Gotham. *See* majority opinion notes 2 & 45 *supra* and accompanying text.
Cf. Regents of the Univ. of Calif. v. Bakke, 438 U.S. 265, 314 (1978) (Powell, J.) ("interest
of diversity is compelling in the context of a university's admissions program"); Korematsu v. United States, 323 U.S. 214 (1944) (military urgency, during time of war with
Japanese Empire, renders governmental interest in security sufficiently compelling to
justify exclusion of persons of Japanese ancestry from West Coast).

24. The Court's language in Carey v. Population Servs. Intl., 431 U.S. 678 (1978),
decided immediately before the abortion-funding cases and cited by Judge Everett in his
dissent, dissenting opinion note 6 *supra*, while presenting some analytical inconsistencies,
is not necessarily to the contrary. Though the Court in that case confronted legislation
limiting access to contraceptives rather than barring their use, the statutory scheme did
prohibit the distribution of contraceptives under certain circumstances and provided
criminal penalties for violations of that prohibition. Thus, the legislation invalidated in
Carey resembles much more closely the "absolute obstacles" struck down in Roe v. Wade,
410 U.S. 113 (1973), than the positive financial incentives designed to encourage one
choice over its alternative, at issue in the abortion-funding cases and before us in the
instant appeal. It is the use of criminal sanctions that apparently renders an obstacle

no more.[25]

The analysis in *Dandridge* and *LaFleur* not only presages the reasoning adopted in the abortion-funding cases but also harmonizes with a number of suggestions offered by commentators for encouraging decreased reproduction.[26] Instead of responding to perceived problems of undue population growth by recommending strict limitations on family size, these commentators advocate programs designed to restructure the incentives and disincentives that presently seem to favor reproduction.[27] Thus, for example, such diverse laws as the tax exemptions for dependent children and prohibitions on homosexual marriages might be altered to encourage, though not to compel, decreased procreation.[28] Official adoption of such an incentive system would presumably be consistent with the language of *Dandridge* and with Justice Powell's reading thereof and, consequently, would be immune from the almost-always-fatal application of strict judicial scrutiny.[29] It would, moreover, find particularly strong and fresh support in the kind of reasoning used in *Beal, Maher,* and *Poelker,*[30] which commits such matters to majoritarian determination.[31] New Gotham's policy directive and manner of staffing

---

impermissibly "absolute" or "direct." *See* Colautti v. Franklin, 439 U.S. 379, 386 n.7 (1979). *See also* Frug, *The Judicial Power of the Purse,* 126 U. PA. L. REV. 715, 780 (1978) (denial of *all* welfare funds to those exercising protected right constitutes impermissible penalty); Hardy, *Privacy and Public Funding: Maher v. Roe as the Interaction of Roe v. Wade and Dandridge v. Williams,* 18 ARIZ. L. REV. 903, 912 n.51 (1976).

25. *See* text at majority opinion note 46 *supra.*

New Gotham is seeking not to discourage childbirth itself but rather to achieve a rate of population growth it deems desirable. *Compare* Perry, *supra* note 9, at 1196, *with* Note, *Abortion, Medicaid, and the Constitution,* 54 N.Y.U. L. REV. 120, 129-30 (1979).

26. *See* Note, *supra* note 21, at 1874-75. The author classifies such proposals as part of a "regulationist," as distinguished from "voluntarist," approach to population control, while noting the "conceptual fuzziness" of the two categories. *Id.* at 1870. Similar suggestions appear in Gray, *Compulsory Sterilization in a Free Society: Choices and Dilemmas,* 41 U. CIN. L. REV. 529, 567-71 (1972), and Rabin, *supra* note 21. *See also* Emerson, *Nine Justices in Search of a Doctrine,* 64 MICH. L. REV. 219, 232 (1965).

27. *See, e.g.,* Rabin, *supra* note 21; Note, *supra* note 21, at 1870.

28. For additional suggestions, see Barnett, *The Constitutionality of Selected Fertility Control Policies,* 55 N.C. L. REV. 357 (1977); Driver, *Population Policies of State Governments in the United States: Some Preliminary Observations,* 15 VILL. L. REV. 818 (1970); Rabin, *supra* note 21; Shepard, *Federal Taxation and Population Control,* 55 N.C. L. REV. 385 (1977); Note, *supra* note 21, at 1874 n.83. *See* Dembitz, *Should Public Policy Give Incentives to Welfare Mothers to Limit the Number of Their Children?,* 4 FAM. L.Q. 130 (1970).

29. *See* Gunther, *The Supreme Court, 1971 Term — Foreword: In Search of Evolving Doctrine on a Changing Court: A Model for a Newer Equal Protection,* 86 HARV. L. REV. 1, 8 (1972).

30. *See* text at majority opinion notes 26-36 *supra.*

31. *Beal, Maher,* and *Poelker* arguably return to the political process decisions that

its municipal hospital constitute precisely the sort of politically fashioned incentive system that such an approach suggests.

Judge Everett's effort to distinguish on the basis of history and tradition the right to prevent or terminate a pregnancy, on the one hand, from the right to bear children, on the other,[32] does not compel a different conclusion. Allowing a woman some measure of reproductive freedom, including a limited right to abort, did not begin with *Roe v. Wade,* 410 U.S. 113 (1973). As the Court's opinion in *Roe* points out, "at common law, at the time of the adoption of our Constitution, and throughout the major portion of the 19th century, . . . a woman enjoyed a substantially broader right to terminate a pregnancy"[33] than she did immediately before *Roe* was decided. In other words, given the analysis in *Roe,* historical considerations alone will not provide sufficient support for the line Judge Everett seeks to draw. But even if such a distinction were tenable, there is another reason why Judge Everett's reliance on cases like *Moore v. City of East Cleveland,* 431 U.S. 494 (1977), misses the mark: Although *Moore* did emphasize the constitutional significance of "history and tradition," it did so in the context of striking down a city's absolute prohibition of certain kinds of family living arrangements.[34] Neither *Moore* nor the other cases Judge Everett cites, however, provide that history and tradition must limit a city in its selection of policy preferences or value judgments, the kind of official action at issue here.[35]

Of course, the tacit thrust of Judge Everett's reasoning may be that the Supreme Court's language in *Moore,* together with the holdings of *Beal, Maher,* and *Poelker,* indicates some sort of withdrawal from the broad pronouncements of *Roe.* That is, perhaps the emphasis in *Moore* on traditional or "basic values"[36] and the

---

the Supreme Court had committed to individual choice in *Roe v. Wade. See* L. TRIBE, AMERICAN CONSTITUTIONAL LAW 929-32 (1978).

32. *See* text at dissenting opinion notes 12-22 *supra.*

33. 410 U.S. at 140. *See* Means, *The Phoenix of Abortional Freedom: Is a Penumbral or Ninth-Amendment Right About to Arise from the Nineteenth-Century Legislative Ashes of a Fourteenth-Century Common-Law Liberty?,* 17 N.Y.L.F. 335 (1971). *But see* Byrn, *An American Tragedy: The Supreme Court on Abortion,* 41 FORDHAM L. REV. 807, 815-27 (1973). *See generally* J. MOHR, ABORTION IN AMERICA (1978).

34. 431 U.S. at 503 (plurality opinion). Those violating the ordinance struck down in *Moore* could stand convicted of a criminal offense. *See* 431 U.S. at 496 (plurality opinion).

35. *See* dissenting opinion notes 16-22 *supra* and accompanying text. *But see* United States Dept. of Agriculture v. Moreno, 413 U.S. 528 (1973) (congressional effort to favor traditional living arrangements through food stamp program held unconstitutional).

36. Moore v. City of East Cleveland, 431 U.S. 494, 503 (1977) (plurality opinion) (quoting Griswold v. Connecticut, 381 U.S. 479, 501 (1965) (Harlan, J., concurring)).

"sanctity of the family,"[37] along with the Court's apparent "anti-abortion" rulings in the abortion-funding cases, constitutes a departure from the position embraced in *Roe*.[38] Read in that manner, *Beal, Maher,* and *Poelker* would offer no support for the result we reach here. Although a number of critics of the abortion-funding cases have indeed described them in this fashion,[39] I am reluctant to draw a conclusion that so completely contradicts the Supreme Court's own assertion that these decisions "signal[ ] no retreat from *Roe* or the cases applying it."[40] I leave to future students of the Court's recent decisions — and to the Court itself — the task of determining whether such far-reaching implications are to be read from between the lines of explicit statements to the contrary.

Nor am I persuaded by Judge Everett's effort to undercut the public hospital policy on the ground that it is not sufficiently tailored to the purpose for which it was adopted. First, as a mechanism for promoting population control, it is at least as effective as the policies upheld in *Beal, Maher,* and *Poelker* were for encouraging childbirth.[41] In those cases, as in the situation before us, the policy in question had an impact only upon the poor.[42] The

---

37. 431 U.S. at 503 (plurality opinion).

38. Perhaps Judge Everett suggests that the Court's decision in *Roe v. Wade* deviates so significantly from American tradition that "it [cannot] long survive," Moore v. City of East Cleveland, 431 U.S. 494, 501 (1977) (plurality opinion) (quoting Poe v. Ullman, 367 U.S. 497, 542 (1961) (Harlan, J., dissenting)), and that the abortion-funding cases reflect the beginning of its demise.

39. *See, e.g.,* L. TRIBE, *supra* note 31, at 933-34 n.77; Clark, *Legislative Motivation and Fundamental Rights in Constitutional Law,* 15 SAN DIEGO L. REV. 953, 1012, 1019 (1978); Perry, *supra* note 9, at 1191; Simson, *Abortion, Poverty, and the Equal Protection of the Laws,* 13 GA. L. REV. 505 (1979); Susman, *Roe v. Wade and Doe v. Bolton Revisited in 1976 and 1977 — Reviewed?; Revived?; Revested?; Reversed?; or Revoked?,* 22 ST. LOUIS U. L.J. 581 (1979); 7 CAP. U. L. REV. 483 (1978); Note, *Denial of Public Funds for Nontherapeutic Abortions,* 10 CONN. L. REV. 487, 500-07 (1978); Note, *The Supreme Court, 1976 Term,* 91 HARV. L. REV. 70, 144-45 (1977); Note, *Medicaid Funding for Abortions: The Medicaid Statute and the Equal Protection Clause,* 6 HOFSTRA L. REV. 421, 438-41 (1978); 21 How. L.J. 937, 948-49 (1978); 24 LOY. L. REV. 301, 307 (1978); Note, *Indigent Women — What Right to Abortion?,* 23 N.Y. L. SCH. L. REV. 709, 739 (1978); 52 TUL. L. REV. 179, 187-88 (1977); 13 TULSA L.J. 287 (1977).

Cf. Canby, *Government Funding, Abortions, and the Public Forum,* 1979 ARIZ. ST. L.J. 11 (suggesting analogy of the public forum to resolve difficulties of abortion-funding cases); Hardy, *supra* note 24, at 919 (suggesting, but ultimately rejecting, "hybrid" constitutional approach to require public funding of abortions).

40. Maher v. Roe, 432 U.S. 464, 475 (1977).

41. *See* Simson, *supra* note 39, at 513; Note, 6 HOFSTRA L. REV., *supra* note 39, at 441.

42. Indeed, this fact may serve to enhance the legitimacy of New Gotham's policy. Buck v. Bell, 274 U.S. 200 (1927), upheld the constitutionality of compulsory sterilization of the "feebleminded" on the theory that those who "sap the strength of the State" could

fact that other avenues for procuring the desired medical treatment were available to the nonindigent did not prompt the Court in *Beal, Maher,* and *Poelker* to question the legitimacy of the vehicle used to achieve the asserted goal.[43] Indeed, under the very relaxed standard of review applied by the Court in the abortion-funding cases, it is not clear that any means-end fit need be examined at all.[44]

And, to the extent that Judge Everett suggests that the flaw in the public hospital policy lies in its failure to encourage abortion in each New Gotham pregnancy, Supreme Court authority is clearly to the contrary. It is well established that, when a state or local government embarks upon a program of reform, it is not constitutionally compelled to "strike at all evils at the same time."[45] In other words, reform "may take one step at a time, addressing itself to the phase of the problem which seems most acute . . . ."[46] The possibility of additional or more far-reaching ways to reduce New Gotham's population does not undermine the legitimacy of the means selected.[47]

---

be required to make such "sacrifices." 274 U.S. at 207. If *Buck* remains sound, the less onerous policy directive of New Gotham, because it does only affect the indigent, could be supportable on a similar theory. *See also* Bolner & Jacobsen, *The Right to Procreate: The Dilemma of Overpopulation and the United States Judiciary,* 25 LOY. L. REV. 235, 245 (1979).

43. The Court noted in *Maher* that even indigent women desiring abortions could still seek such treatment from private sources. 432 U.S. 464, 474 (1977). *See* Beal v. Doe, 432 U.S. 438, 459 n.2 (Marshall, J., dissenting).

44. The Court merely inquired whether the "distinction drawn between childbirth and nontherapeutic abortion . . . [was] 'rationally related' to a 'constitutionally permissible' purpose." Maher v. Roe, 432 U.S. at 478.

45. San Antonio Indep. School Dist. v. Rodriguez, 411 U.S. 1, 39 (1973); Katzenbach v. Morgan, 384 U.S. 641, 657 (1966). *See* Califano v. Jobst, 434 U.S. 47, 57-58 (1977); Geduldig v. Aiello, 417 U.S. 484, 495 (1974); Dandridge v. Williams, 397 U.S. 471, 486-87 (1970).

46. Geduldig v. Aiello, 417 U.S. 484, 495 (1974); San Antonio Indep. School Dist. v. Rodriguez, 411 U.S. 1, 39 (1973).

47. Even reform undertaken on a piecemeal basis is, of course, subject to equal protection limitations. Thus, for example, a preliminary step in a broader population control program singling out blacks for decreased procreation would evoke rigorous judicial scrutiny under the equal protection clause. *See* Skinner v. Oklahoma, 316 U.S. 535, 541 (1942); Shaw, *supra* note 21, at 1166. *See also* Califano v. Westcott, 99 S. Ct. 2655, 2663 (1979) ("Congress may not legislate 'one step at a time' when that step is drawn along the line of gender"). But alleged classifications based on indigency do not trigger such stringent review. Maher v. Roe, 432 U.S. 464, 471 (1977).

Boe's plight, like that of the women challenging the restrictions in the abortion-funding cases, is that without state assistance she can afford to purchase neither an abortion nor medical care incident to childbirth. Given its discretion regarding the expenditure of its public funds, however, New Gotham could have chosen to subsidize neither choice. Clearly, Boe does not argue, nor could she, that the Constitution requires

It is of no moment, moreover, to observe that even poor women can continue to reproduce without any medical assistance whatsoever.[48] An analogous point, when made in the abortion-funding cases, carried negligible constitutional weight.[49] Indeed, the fact that even indigent women can choose to carry their pregnancies to term demonstrates the nonabsolute nature of the burden imposed upon them by the city. And, as the opinion for the majority in this case explains, it is precisely this nonabsolute nature of the burden that sustains the policy and practice in question.[50]

Essentially identical reasoning, with slight elaboration, answers Judge Everett's final point, where he questions New Gotham State's allowing abortions to be performed throughout pregnancy — a necessary condition for the effective implementation of the city's policy directive.[51]

Judge Everett's concern apparently stems from the possibility that an abortion performed during advanced pregnancy might result in a live birth. If that be the case, however, New Gotham State's lack of legislation prohibiting abortions is irrelevant, for upon birth, a "person" within the scope of the state's homicide laws has come into existence.[52] Whether or not the fourteenth amendment requires a state to impose criminal penalties for depriving such "persons" of life[53] is also irrelevant, for New Gotham

states or cities to provide medical assistance for all indigent-pregnant women. *See* 432 U.S. at 480 n.13.

48. *See* text at dissenting opinion notes 26, 27 *supra*.

49. In dissent in the abortion-funding cases, Justice Marshall predicted that the Court's holdings would result in the procurement of more unsafe and illegal abortions by the indigent. 432 U.S. at 455-56 n.1.

50. *See* majority opinion note 32 and text at majority opinion note 46 *supra*.

51. The absence of any state criminal prohibitions against abortion permits the policy directive to operate in a noncoercive manner (*i.e.*, simply to encourage abortions rather than to compel them) and simultaneously to maximize each indigent pregnant woman's opportunities to choose the result favored by the city.

52. Before birth, however, no such "person" exists. *See* Roe v. Wade, 410 U.S. 113, 157-59 (1973), and cases cited therein. *See also* Commonwealth v. Edelin, ___ Mass. ___, 359 N.E.2d 4, 12 (1976) (state manslaughter statute construed, in light of *Roe*, to apply only after live birth and only to defendant's acts in postnatal period). *Cf.* Planned Parenthood v. Danforth, 428 U.S. 52, 83-84 (1976) (criminal failure to protect liveborn infant "surely will be subject to prosecution . . . under the State's criminal statutes").

53. Although the matter is not free from uncertainty, the Court in *Roe* read the fourteenth amendment not merely to authorize governmental protection of a person's life but to "entitle" him to such protection from the state. *See* 410 U.S. 113, 159 (1973). *But see* L. TRIBE, *supra* note 31, at 929 n.61 (noting state action problem in such reasoning); Michelman, *The Supreme Court, 1968 Term — Foreword: On Protecting the Poor Through the Fourteenth Amendment*, 83 HARV. L. REV. 7, 17 (1969) ("The due process

State has not repealed its criminal homicide laws, but only its abortion prohibitions.

The problem that arises, however, is that where live births do in fact result from the abortions encouraged by the city, the single goal of the official action challenged here, population control, is not advanced. The question, as I see it, then becomes whether this incongruity of means and end renders the policy directive unconstitutional because it is irrational[54] as applied to women whose pregnancies have advanced so far that any termination might yield a live birth.

The problem is complicated by the ambiguity of the term "abortion" itself. In the more typical lawsuit where plaintiffs challenge state action alleged to restrict their freedom of choice in aborting pregnancies, a number of personal privacy-based interests can be asserted. The classic case of this variety, *Roe v. Wade,* 410 U.S. 113 (1973), considered such personal interests as the possibility of direct harm from pregnancy and the future stress, both physical and psychological, of maternity and child care.[55] A more specific focus emerged in *Planned Parenthood v. Danforth,* 428 U.S. 52 (1976), where, in overturning Missouri's spousal consent requirement, the Court emphasized the privacy interest attributable to a woman's direct and immediate physical involvement in pregnancy.[56] Theoretically, the kinds of interests recognized by the Court in those cases could be honored by a termination of pregnancy simpliciter, regardless of the fate of the fetus, or by placement of any live-born child for adoption.[57]

But as the instant case — as well as cases concerning abortions for eugenic reasons[58] — indicates, a preference for abortion

clause inveighs only against certain 'deprivations' by the 'state,' occurrences which seemingly cannot occur by mere default."); Tribe, *The Supreme Court, 1972 Term — Foreword: Toward a Model of Roles in the Due Process of Life and Law,* 87 HARV. L. REV. 1, 33 n.144 (1973). *Cf.* Landrum v. Moats, 576 F.2d 1320 (8th Cir.) (allegation that police officers, under color of state law, unreasonably deprived deceased of life presents cognizable claim that fourteenth amendment has been transgressed), *cert. denied,* 439 U.S. 912 (1978).

54. *See* notes 19-21 and accompanying text *supra.*

55. *See* 410 U.S. at 153. *See also* Bellotti v. Baird, 99 S. Ct. 3035, 3048 (1979) (plurality opinion); Doe v. Bolton, 410 U.S. 179, 192 (1973).

56. *See* 428 U.S. at 71.

57. In other words, satisfaction of the interests identified in *Roe* and *Planned Parenthood* do not require that an abortion cause fetal death. *See* Note, *Choice Rights and Abortion: The Begetting Choice Right and State Obstacles to Choose in Light of Artificial Womb Technology,* 51 S. CAL. L. REV. 877, 899-900 (1978). See also Tribe, *supra* note 53, at 27.

58. *See, e.g.,* Berman v. Allan, 80 N.J. 421, 404 A.2d 8 (1979); Becker v. Schwartz, 46 N.Y.2d 401, 386 N.E.2d 807, 413 N.Y.S.2d 895 (1978); Jacobs v. Theimer, 519 S.W.2d 846 (Tex. 1975); Dumer v. St. Michael's Hosp., 69 Wis. 2d 766, 233 N.W.2d 372 (1975).

over childbirth can be motivated by interests other than those satisfied by mere return of the woman's body to its nonpregnant state or by obviation of child-rearing responsibilities.[59] In these cases, the sole immediate purpose for which the abortion is performed is feticide. Where a pregnancy has so far advanced that its termination would produce a live fetus (then child), such a purpose cannot be served.

Significantly, the Supreme Court in its groundbreaking decision in *Roe* circumvented the issue. By adopting viability as the criterion for constitutionally acceptable state regulation undertaken to protect the fetus,[60] the Court established a foundation for prohibiting those abortions most likely to result in live births.[61] But that analysis is merely a foundation: It only permits states to take such protective action; it does not require them to do so.[62] In addition, under *Roe* and the Court's subsequent decisions in *Planned Parenthood v. Danforth,* 428 U.S. 62 (1976), and

---

In all of these cases, one issue was whether plaintiff-parents had a cause of action in tort against medical personnel who were allegedly negligent in failing to inform them of a substantial risk that a particular pregnancy might result in the birth of a defective child, where the parents claimed that they would have elected to terminate the pregnancy had they possessed such information. *See also* Gildiner v. Thomas Jefferson Univ. Hosp., 451 F. Supp. 692 (E.D. Pa. 1978) (negligent genetic testing). *Cf.* Colautti v. Franklin, 439 U.S. 379, 389 & n.8 (1979) (discerning possible conflict between time required to detect some genetic defects and the restriction of abortions where "sufficient reason to believe that the fetus may be viable").

59. *See* Delgado & Keyes, *Parental Preferences and Selective Abortion: A Commentary on Roe v. Wade, Doe v. Bolton, and the Shape of Things to Come,* 1974 WASH. U. L.Q. 203; Note, *State Protection of the Viable Unborn Child After Roe v. Wade: How Little, How Late,* 37 LA. L. REV. 270, 280 (1976); Note, *supra* note 57, at 901-11. *Cf.* note 57 *supra* (satisfaction of motivating interests).

60. 410 U.S. 113, 163-64 (1973).

61. *See* Tribe, *supra* note 53, at 26-29.

The Court's subsequent elaboration of the viability concept in Planned Parenthood v. Danforth, 428 U.S. 52 (1976), is not to the contrary. There, in upholding a Missouri statutory definition of viability as "that stage of fetal development when the life of the unborn child may be continued indefinitely outside the womb by natural or artificial life-supportive systems," 428 U.S. at 63, the Court emphasized that a determination of viability "is, and must be, a matter for the judgment of the responsible attending physician," 428 U.S. at 64, and observed that the Missouri definition actually allows greater freedom to those electing abortion than does the definition offered in *Roe,* 428 U.S. at 64. This latter point demonstrates the permissive, as distinguished from mandatory, nature of the timetable set forth in *Roe. See* 410 U.S. 113, 164-65 (1973). *See also* Colautti v. Franklin, 439 U.S. 379 (1979) (statutory requirement that person performing abortion must protect fetal life if, *inter alia,* sufficient reason to believe fetus may be viable is unconstitutionally vague).

62. The Court stated: "For the stage subsequent to viability, the State in promoting its interest in the potentiality of human life *may,* if it *chooses,* regulate, and even proscribe, abortion except where it is necessary, in appropriate medical judgment, for the preservation of the life or health of the mother." 410 U.S. at 164-65 (emphasis added).

Colautti v. Franklin, 439 U.S. 379 (1979), viability — the potential ability of the fetus to live outside the mother's womb, albeit with artificial aid[63] — is a factual determination to be predicated not upon a universal or fixed point in gestation, but rather upon individualized, fetus-by-fetus assessments.[64]

The difficulty of applying this rule to particular cases is illustrated by a recent opinion of a three-judge district court in South Carolina enjoining the criminal prosecution of a physician for illegal abortion and murder after he terminated an approximately twenty-five week pregnancy and the fetus, delivered alive, survived for twenty days, *Floyd v. Anders*, 440 F. Supp. 535 (D. S. C. 1977), *vacated and remanded per curiam*, 440 U.S. 445 (1979). The court apparently reasoned that, because the fetus could not survive outside the womb indefinitely, but only for twenty days, it was not viable;[65] thus, it held that the state could not prosecute the physician without violating the constitutional constraints of *Roe* and *Planned Parenthood*.[66]

Whether or not such reasoning is sound,[67] it highlights the difficulty of accurately assessing the viability of any individual fetus before the termination of a pregnancy (and hence the difficulty of determining whether any particular abortion will be likely in fact to advance the cause of population control).[68] To suggest, as Judge Everett does, that New Gotham cannot en-

---

63. 410 U.S. at 160.

64. *See* 410 U.S. at 160-61; Planned Parenthood v. Danforth, 428 U.S. 52, 64 (1976); Colautti v. Franklin, 439 U.S. 379, 388 (1979); Floyd v. Anders, 440 F. Supp. 535, 539 (D. S.C. 1977), *vacated and remanded per curiam*, 440 U.S. 445 (1979).

65. 440 F. Supp. at 538.

66. 440 F. Supp. at 538-39.

67. By focusing on the actual life span of the fetus, once removed from the womb, rather than its potential ability to survive, the opinion implies that viability is a determination that can be made only *after* the termination of the pregnancy in question. *See* 440 F. Supp. at 538. *Roe v. Wade*, however, defined a viable fetus as one "potentially able to live outside the mother's womb, albeit with artificial aid." 410 U.S. at 160. In a subsequent opinion, the Court explained that viability, so defined, nonetheless contemplates more than "momentary survival." Colautti v. Franklin, 439 U.S. 379, 387 (1979). *See also* Anders v. Floyd, 440 U.S. 445 (1979) (per curiam), *vacating and remanding* 440 F. Supp. 535 (D.S.C. 1977); Wynn v. Scott, 449 F. Supp. 1302, 1316 (N.D. Ill.), *appeal dismissed for want of jurisdiction sub nom.* Carey v. Wynn, 439 U.S. 8 (1978), *affd.*, 599 F.2d 193 (7th Cir. 1979).

68. Predicting the actual impact of any abortion upon population growth or control would appear to require even more difficult determinations than assessing viability. Presumably a fetus that lives for twenty days following abortion would have a *de minimis* effect on the size of New Gotham's population; such a fetus might, however, properly be classified as viable, according to the Supreme Court definition of that term in *Roe*, 410 U.S. at 160, and notwithstanding the conclusion to the contrary reached in Floyd v. Anders, 440 F. Supp. 535 (D.S.C. 1977), *vacated and remanded per curiam*, 440 U.S. 445 (1979). *See* note 67 *supra*.

courage terminations of advanced pregnancies is to ignore these vagaries inherent in the notion of viability.[69] And, to the extent that any abortion, whenever performed, increases the risk of death to the particular fetus in question,[70] New Gotham's decision to encourage abortions throughout pregnancy rather than during a more limited period of gestation is consistent with the underlying goal of promoting population control to the fullest extent possible.[71] That live births may result, even when the city successfully encourages indigent women to procure abortions, provides an additional reflection of the noncoercive and nonabsolute nature of the governmental action challenged here and of the minimal level of constitutional scrutiny against which we are to measure it.[72]

None of these efforts to respond to Judge Everett's dissent, of course, need be read to say that the action pursued by New Gotham is wise or humane, for we do not decide such cases on those grounds, *see Maher v. Roe,* 432 U.S. 464, 479 (1977). Rather, whatever the apparent infirmities of the city's course, the abortion-funding cases, together with the additional support of other Supreme Court decisions, point ineluctably to its validity.

---

69. *See* note 67 *supra. See also* Colautti v. Franklin, 439 U.S. 379, 390-93 (1979).

70. The method of abortion used becomes significant in this analysis. In Planned Parenthood v. Danforth, 428 U.S. 52, 75-79 (1976), the Court discussed a number of different methods of abortion employed after the first trimester. One of those, saline amniocentesis, almost invariably causes fetal death while another, prostaglandin instillation, stimulates premature labor, more likely resulting in a live birth. *See* Colautti v. Franklin, 439 U.S. 379, 399 (1979); Note, *supra* note 59, at 279-80.

71. *See* note 51 *supra.*

72. *See* note 50 *supra* and accompanying text.

ROE v. WADE AND THE LESSON OF THE PRE-*ROE* CASE LAW

Richard Gregory Morgan*†

The standard criticism of *Roe v. Wade*[1] is that the Supreme Court indulged in "Lochnering": the improper second-guessing of a legislative balance.[2] Rarely does the Supreme Court invite critical outrage as it did in *Roe* by offering so little explanation for a decision that requires so much. The stark inadequacy of the Court's attempt to justify its conclusions — that abortion implicates women's "privacy," that only the most important state interests may supersede that right, and that they may do so only after certain stages of pregnancy — suggests to some scholars that the Court, finding no justification at all in the Constitution, unabashedly usurped the legislative function.[3] Professor Ely, the first to cry "Lochner," could only adduce from the opinion that the Court "manufactured a constitutional right out of whole cloth and used it to superimpose its own view of wise social policy on those of the legislatures."[4] Even some who approve *Roe*'s form of judicial review concede that the opinion itself is inscrutable.[5]

---

* Law Clerk, The Honorable J. Edward Lumbard, United States Court of Appeals for the Second Circuit. A.B. 1976, University of California at Los Angeles; J.D. 1979, University of Michigan — Ed.

† Being an avid reader of authors' acknowledgments (because it's fun to see who knows whom), I have often read "I would never have completed this work without the invaluable encouragement of So-and-So." But being young, energetic, and imbued with a work ethic, I have never understood how anyone could even think of not completing a task once begun — until, for a variety of circumstances they know, I found myself unable to continue this paper without the daily support of Ginny Popper and Carl and Joan Schneider. Thanks guys.

1. 410 U.S. 113 (1973).

2. *See, e.g.,* Ely, *The Wages of Crying Wolf: A Comment on Roe v. Wade*, 82 YALE L.J. 920 (1973).

3. *See* Epstein, *Substantive Due Process By Any Other Name: The Abortion Cases*, 1973 SUP. CT. REV. 159, 184-85:

> *Roe v. Wade* is symptomatic of the analytical poverty possible in constitutional litigation . . . . Thus in the end we must criticize both Mr. Justice Blackmun in *Roe v. Wade* and the entire method of constitutional interpretation that allows the Supreme Court in the name of Due Process both to "define" and to "balance" interests on the major social and political issues of our time.

4. Ely, *supra* note 2, at 937.

5. *See* Tribe, *The Supreme Court, 1972 Term — Foreword: Toward a Model of Roles in the Due Process of Life and Law*, 87 HARV. L. REV. 1, 7 (1973) ("One of the most curious things about *Roe* is that, behind its own verbal smokescreen, the substantive judgment on which it rests is nowhere to be found.").

Critics have cried "Lochner!" before, however, and that worries Professor Ely, who fears that the specter of past mistakes may lose its awe by becoming too familiar.[6] But more was at stake in the Supreme Court's handling of *Roe* than the wrath of critics: By taking an abortion case when it did, the Court forestalled the development of one of its traditional aids for deciding difficult questions — a thoughtful lower-court case law.

Supreme Court decisions are often thought of as if they have no history, somehow beginning and ending in the Supreme Court. But they are products of a judicial system, one that traditionally adheres to certain axioms that protect and enhance the quality of Supreme Court review. One axiom posits that the Supreme Court should hesitate to decide disputes which the political branch is still actively debating. Beyond observing the well-established "political questions" doctrine, the Court respects the representativeness of government and deepens the thoughtfulness of its own deliberations if it stays out of a dispute until legislatures and executives make an initial decision.[7] A second axiom cautions that even after a dispute reaches the judicial system, the Supreme Court should still hesitate to hear a specific case until lower courts have "aged" the dispute by articulating the best arguments on both sides and discarding the unpersuasive or irrelevant.[8]

The Supreme Court completely disregarded both those axioms in *Roe*. The politically unsettled and judicially confused law of abortion in 1971 and 1972, when the Court twice heard arguments and deliberated *Roe,* should have warned it not to decide the case. By doing so, the Court thrust itself into a political debate and stunted the development of a thoughtful lower-court case law. If the Court did perceive the warnings but continued toward a decision anyway, perhaps trusting that its own consider-

---

6. Ely, *supra* note 2, at 943-44.

7. *Cf.* A. BICKEL, THE LEAST DANGEROUS BRANCH 115 (1962) ("standing" and "case and controversy" help make sound judicial decisions by letting courts see legislation's practical consequences before they decide).

8. *See* Youngstown Steel & Tube Co. v. Sawyer, 343 U.S. 937, 938 (1952) (Burton, J., dissenting from grant of certiorari):

The constitutional issue which is the subject of the appeal deserves for its solution all of the wisdom which our judicial system makes available. The need for soundness in the result outweighs the need for speed in reaching it. The Nation is entitled to the substantial value inherent in an intermediate consideration of the issue by the Court of Appeals. Little time will be lost and none will be wasted in seeking it. The time taken will be available also for constructive consideration by the parties of their own positions and responsibilities.

able wits would devise an answer the lower courts had not, the result suggests that the judicial system's axioms deserve more respect than they received. This Article, by showing briefly in Section I that the Court should not have decided an abortion case when it did, and by showing at more length in Section II that the Court could find no persuasive rationale in the pre-*Roe* cases for each of the points in its decision, argues that Roe was almost destined to be a bad opinion.

I.

In 1973, political forces were still vigorously debating abortion. Most states had prohibited abortions, except to save a woman's life, since the nineteenth century,[9] but a movement was afoot to relax that restriction. In the five years immediately preceding *Roe*, thirteen states had revised their statutes to resemble the Model Penal Code's provisions,[10] which allowed abortions not only if the pregnancy threatened the woman's life, but also if it would gravely impair her physical or mental health, if it resulted from rape or incest, or if the child would be born with grave physical or mental defects.[11] Four states had removed all restrictions on the permissible reasons for seeking an abortion before a pregnancy passed specified lengths.[12] Furthermore, as the Supreme Court noted in *Roe*, both the American Medical Association and the American Bar Association had only recently changed their official views on abortion (and not without opposition).[13] The abortion debate was not merely one of how far to relax restrictions, however. At least one of the states whose restrictive statutes were judicially invalidated had in 1972 reaffirmed its determination to prohibit abortions unless necessary to save the woman's life.[14] And since several of the pre-*Roe* constitutional challenges were raised by defendants in state abortion prosecutions,[15] it is clear that at least those states had not allowed their

---

9. See the Supreme Court's survey in *Roe* of the history of abortion and abortion laws, 410 U.S. at 138-39.

10. *See* Comment, *A Survey of the Present Statutory and Case Law on Abortion: The Contradictions and Problems*, 1972 U. ILL. L.F. 177, 180.

11. MODEL PENAL CODE § 230.3 (Proposed Official Draft 1962).

12. *See* Comment, *supra* note 10, at 181.

13. 410 U.S. at 143, 146.

14. *See* Abele v. Markle, 351 F. Supp. 224, 226 (D. Conn. 1972), *vacated and remanded*, 410 U.S. 951 (1973).

15. YWCA v. Kugler, 342 F. Supp. 1048 (D.N.J. 1972), *cert. denied*, 415 U.S. 989, *affd. without opinion*, 493 F.2d 1402 (3d Cir. 1974); Rosen v. Louisiana State Bd. of

abortion statutes to lapse into desuetude.[16] In short, the political process in many states had yet to decide on abortion. But *Roe*'s sweeping rejection of Texas's statute voided almost every other state's as well.[17]

Especially given the absence of a firm constitutional footing for deciding the question, the Court could sensibly have refrained from stepping into the debate when it did. Of course, the Court might never decide anything if it always waited for the last political word, and had *Roe* been a soundly reasoned opinion, the Court would surely never have been criticized for being a bit hasty. Indeed, because several states had liberalized their abortion statutes, some might argue that the Court should nudge the rest of the nation toward recognizing the right those states had found. But the second traditional axiom should still have warned the Court not to decide *Roe:* the dispute had not sufficiently steeped in the lower courts. Allegations that abortion statutes violated a constitutional right of privacy were new to the courts. As late as mid-1968, the New Jersey Supreme Court flatly rejected two defendants' claim that the state statute's exception for abortions with "lawful justification" included abortions to end unwanted pregnancies: "It is beyond comprehension that the defendants could have believed that our abortion statute envisioned lawful justification to exist whenever a woman wanted to avoid having a child. The statutes of no jurisdiction in this country permit such an excuse for an abortion."[18] The court's construction of "lawful justification" was undoubtedly correct; the significant point is that the court gave no hint of even considering that a right of privacy might justify such an excuse. The landmark case of *People v. Belous*,[19] apparently the first case to consider a right-

---

Medical Examiners, 318 F. Supp. 1217 (E.D. La. 1970), *vacated and remanded*, 412 U.S. 902 (1973); Babbitz v. McCann, 310 F. Supp. 293 (E.D. Wis.), *appeal dismissed per curiam*, 400 U.S. 1 (1970); United States v. Vuitch, 305 F. Supp. 1032 (D.D.C. 1969), *revd.*, 402 U.S. 62 (1971); People v. Belous, 71 Cal. 2d 954, 458 P.2d 194, 80 Cal. Rptr. 354 (1969), *cert. denied*, 397 U.S. 915 (1970); State v. Barquet, Fla., 262 So. 2d 431 (Fla. 1972); People v. Nixon, 42 Mich. App. 332, 201 N.W.2d 635 (1972), *remanded*, 389 Mich. 809, *revd.*, 50 Mich. App. 38, 212 N.W.2d 797 (1973) (per curiam).

16. *See generally* A. BICKEL, *supra* note 7, at 148. Indeed, even after Babbitz v. McCann, 310 F. Supp. 293 (E.D. Wis.), *appeal dismissed per curiam*, 400 U.S. 1 (1970), declared Wisconsin's restrictive abortion statute unconstitutional, the state attorney general continued to threaten prosecution. Babbitz v. McCann, 320 F. Supp. 219, 221 (E.D. Wis. 1970), *vacated*, 402 U.S. 903 (1971).

17. *See* 410 U.S. at 118; Ely, *supra* note 2, at 920.

18. State v. Moretti, 52 N.J. 182, 194, 244 A.2d 499, 505-06, *cert. denied*, 393 U.S. 952 (1968).

19. 71 Cal. 2d 954, 458 P.2d 194, 80 Cal. Rptr. 354 (1969), *cert. denied*, 397 U.S. 915 (1970).

of-privacy challenge to an abortion statute and certainly the first reported case to endorse one,[20] was decided only in September 1969, less than two years before the Supreme Court decided to hear *Roe*.[21] Between 1970 and 1972, a flurry of constitutional challenges hit the courts, but of the seventeen courts that decided right-of-privacy claims, twelve were three-judge district courts whose judgments allowed direct appeal to the Supreme Court.[22] Thus, when the Court had *Roe* before it and looked, as the axiom has it, to the lower-court deliberations,[23] it found not one federal decision that had received intermediate appellate consideration, and only four decisions of state supreme courts,[24] none of which offered particularly illuminating analysis.

In general, three years is hardly time enough for the judicial system to evolve sound analysis for most constitutional issues, and for so emotionally charged an issue as abortion,[25] three years

---

20. *See* Comment, *supra* note 10, at 184.

21. The Supreme Court decided on May 3, 1971 to hear arguments on jurisdiction and the merits. 402 U.S. 941 (1971).

22. Decisions by three-judge district courts: Abele v. Markle, 351 F. Supp. 224 (D. Conn. 1972), *vacated and remanded,* 410 U.S. 951 (1973); Crossen v. Attorney Gen., 344 F. Supp. 587 (E.D. Ky. 1972), *vacated and remanded,* 410 U.S. 950 (1973); YWCA v. Kugler, 342 F. Supp. 1048 (D.N.J. 1972), *cert. denied,* 415 U.S. 989, *affd. without opinion,* 493 F.2d 1402 (3d Cir. 1974); Abele v. Markle, 342 F. Supp. 800 (D. Conn. 1972), *vacated and remanded,* 410 U.S. 951 (1973); Poe v. Menghini, 339 F. Supp. 986 (D. Kan. 1972); Corkey v. Edwards, 322 F. Supp. 1248 (W.D.N.C. 1972), *vacated and remanded,* 410 U.S. 950 (1973); Doe v. Scott, 321 F. Supp. 1385 (N.D. Ill. 1971), *vacated and remanded,* 410 U.S. 950 (1973); Steinberg v. Brown, 321 F. Supp. 741 (N.D. Ohio 1970); Doe v. Bolton, 319 F. Supp. 1048 (N.D. Ga. 1970), *modified and affd.,* 410 U.S. 179 (1973); Rosen v. Louisiana State Bd. of Medical Examiners, 318 F. Supp. 1217 (E.D. La. 1970), *vacated and remanded,* 412 U.S. 902 (1973); Roe v. Wade, 314 F. Supp. 1217 (N.D. Tex. 1970), *affd. in part and revd. in part,* 410 U.S. 113 (1973); Babbitz v. McCann, 310 F. Supp. 293 (E.D. Wis.), *appeal dismissed per curiam,* 400 U.S. 1 (1970). Decision by one-judge district court: United States v. Vuitch, 305 F. Supp. 1032 (D.D.C. 1969), *revd.* 402 U.S. 62 (1971). Decisions by state supreme courts: People v. Belous, 71 Cal. 2d 954, 458 P.2d 194, 80 Cal. Rptr. 354 (1969), *cert. denied,* 397 U.S. 915 (1970); Cheaney v. State, 259 Ind. 138, 285 N.E.2d 265 (1972), *cert. denied,* 410 U.S. 991 (1973); Rogers v. Danforth, 486 S.W.2d 258 (Mo. 1972) (en banc); State v. Munson, 86 S.D. 663, 201 N.W.2d 123 (1972), *vacated and remanded,* 410 U.S. 950 (1973).

23. Of course one way in which the Supreme Court "looks" at lower-court decisions is through the parties' and amici briefs. The briefs submitted to the Court for *Roe* are generally susceptible to all the criticisms levelled at the lower courts, leaving the Supreme Court, like T.S. Eliot's self-possessed gallant, "really in the dark."

24. *See* note 22 *supra.*

25. The emotions surrounding abortion were not lost on the courts. Although the Supreme Court professed "to resolve the issue by constitutional measurement, free of emotion and of predilection," 410 U.S. at 116, not all the lower-court judges could have said the same. *See, e.g.,* Rosen v. Louisiana State Bd. of Medical Examiners, 318 F. Supp. 1217, 1229 (E.D. La. 1970), *vacated and remanded,* 412 U.S. 902 (1973) ("This problem involves the condition of pregnancy and its likely consequence, the first entrance of a new

was very little time indeed. The Court could justifiably have let the dispute simmer longer in the lower courts. And technically, the Court could have done so. In *Roe*, both parties appealed the lower-court decision to the Supreme Court: Jane Roe from the denial of an injunction against enforcement of the statute, and District Attorney Wade from the grant of a declaratory judgment that the statute was unconstitutional.[26] But as the Court acknowledged, its own cases "are to the effect that § 1253 does not authorize an appeal to this Court from the grant or denial of declaratory relief alone."[27] Thus, only Roe's complaint from the denial of an injunction was properly before the Court on appeal. Nonetheless, the Court held that "those decisions do not foreclose our review of both the injunctive and declaratory aspects of a case of this kind when it is properly here, as this one is, on appeal under § 1253 from specific denial of injunctive relief, and the arguments as to both aspects are necessarily identical."[28] Even if the arguments as to both aspects were strictly speaking identical (which they probably were only if the Court wished them to be), the Court still did not have to decide the constitutional question. It could have stayed the direct appeal on the injunction until the appeal on the declaratory judgment had progressed to the Court through the court of appeals, as technically that appeal should have done.[29] The reason for doing so would have been clear: a decision on the injunction should logically await a decision on constitutionality (the declaratory judgment issue) and a decision on constitutionality should await a fuller consideration by the courts of appeals. Instead, worried that "[i]t would be destructive of time and energy for all concerned were we to rule other-

---

player, 'mewling and puking,' onto the world stage. Shakespeare, As You Like It, Act ii, sc. 7, 1, 139."); Byrn v. New York City Health & Hosps. Corp., 31 N.Y.2d 194, 286 N.E.2d 887, 335 N.Y.S.2d 390 (1972) (dissent of Burke, J., who condemned New York's liberal abortion statute by dismissing women's "self-created problem" of injuries from illegal abortions, 31 N.Y.2d at 207, 286 N.E.2d at 893, 335 N.Y.S.2d at 398, by decrying "the massacre of the innocents," 31 N.Y.2d at 209-10, 286 N.E.2d at 894, 335 N.Y.S.2d at 400, and by lamenting, "The deeper disease in this legislation is the widening gap between the American self-image of a country that values *human life* and the reality of a growing preoccupation of the hedonists with a competitive drive for *La Dolce Vita*." 31 N.Y.2d at 211, 286 N.E.2d at 895, 335 N.Y.S.2d at 402 (emphasis original)), *appeal dismissed*, 410 U.S. 949 (1973).

26. 410 U.S. at 122.
27. 410 U.S. at 123.
28. 410 U.S. at 123.
29. Interestingly, the Court dismissed for want of jurisdiction the defendant's appeal from the grant of a declaratory judgment in *Roe*'s companion case, Doe v. Bolton, 410 U.S. 179, 187 (1973).

wise,"[30] the Court reached out to grab the abortion question and thereby impaired its ability to construct a sound opinion, something much more valuable than time and energy.[31]

II.

Even though abortion was a new issue to the courts, and even though no federal court of appeals had considered it, the Supreme Court might still have been justified in hearing *Roe,* for it had been decided by a three-judge district court, and theory has it that "[t]here is little to be gained by delaying important litigation of that sort that initially commands an extraordinary district court of three judges — at least one of them a circuit judge — for review by three other judges on a court of appeals."[32] In this instance, however, that theory proved false, and had done so even before the Supreme Court heard rearguments of *Roe.*[33] The district court cases failed to develop any adequate analysis for deciding the constitutionality of abortion statutes; indeed, most of them never honestly acknowledged the competing interests involved. There is some indication that a sounder case law might have evolved if given time.[34] But that was prevented by *Roe,* where the Supreme Court, without offering any sound reason of its own, took each step of its decision in the face of the inability of the lower courts that considered those steps to reach a reasoned conclusion. In 1973 the Court could not find a rationale, but decided anyway. That smacks distinctly of a legislative process.

A.   *"This right of privacy . . . is broad enough . . . ."*

As do most discussions of the right of privacy, the Supreme Court's began by conceding that "[t]he Constitution does not explicitly mention any [such] right."[35] A long line of cases, however, has recognized in several amendments "a guarantee of certain areas or zones of privacy," and "make[s] it clear that the right has some extension to activities relating to" marriage, procreation, contraception, family relations, child rearing, and edu-

---

30. 410 U.S. at 123.
31. *See* note 8 *supra.*
32. 17 C. WRIGHT, A. MILLER & E. COOPER, FEDERAL PRACTICE AND PROCEDURE: JURISDICTION § 4040, at 78 (1969).
33. The last of the important pre-*Roe* cases, Abele v. Markle, 351 F. Supp. 224 (D. Conn. 1972), *vacated and remanded,* 410 U.S. 951 (1973), was announced on September 20, 1972. The Supreme Court heard reargument on October 11, 1972.
34. *See* text at notes 86-88 and 113-29 *infra.*
35. 410 U.S. at 152.

cation.[36] A less informative phrase than "has some extension to" is hard to imagine, but the Court gives no more information than that before declaring, "This right of privacy . . . is broad enough to encompass a woman's decision whether or not to terminate her pregnancy."[37] The Court then lists several detriments that might befall women if they were altogether denied the choice of abortion.[38] The opinion leaves ambiguous whether the Court meant this list somehow to prove that abortion fits within "privacy," or only to suggest the variety of considerations that will surround the exercise of that right,[39] but it does make clear that these potential detriments do not imply any "unlimited right to do with one's body as one pleases."[40]

The inadequacy of that explanation is obvious. It does not explain why the right of privacy, just because it extends to some matters of sex and family, extends to abortion; nor what kind of "privacy" abortion involves (especially given that the Court later distinguished this "privacy" from that involved in all the other activities to which the right extends[41]); nor why the list of detriments brings abortion within the right, if that is what the list means to do; nor why the right apparently extends to women who incur none of these detriments (especially if it is the detriments that warrant extending the right).[42] But like the right of privacy itself, *Roe*'s inadequacy inheres in a long line of cases. The pre-*Roe*, lower-court decisions that struck down abortion statutes for impairing the right of privacy wholly neglected legal analysis. In virtually all the cases, the proponents of abortion argued the same simplistic theory — that abortion involves both family and

---

36. 410 U.S. at 152-53.

37. 410 U.S. at 153.

38. 410 U.S. at 153.

39. Professor Ely guesses that the Court's "conclusion is thought to derive from the passage that immediately follows it." Ely, *supra* note 2, at 932. Professor Tribe seems to agree that avoiding these detriments is the gravamen of this right of privacy. Tribe, *supra* note 5, at 10. But neither mentions the paragraph's last sentence, which immediately follows the catalog of detriments: "All these are factors the woman and her responsible physician necessarily will consider in consultation." 410 U.S. at 153. That sentence suggests that the Court simply meant by the catalog to guide the considerations of the physicians in whom it places so much trust ("The abortion decision in all its aspects is inherently, and primarily, a medical decision, and basic responsibility for it must rest with the physician." 410 U.S. at 166), not that the catalog somehow proves that abortion implicates privacy. As Professor Ely said, "Confusing signals are emitted . . . ." Ely, *supra* note 2, at 922.

40. 410 U.S. at 154.

41. 410 U.S. at 159.

42. *See* Ely, *supra* note 2, at 923 n.26.

sex, and that *Griswold v. Connecticut*[43] and *Eisenstadt v. Baird*[44] place a zone of privacy around such matters[45] — and most of the courts agreed without a second thought.

The first case to declare an abortion statute unconstitutional, *People v. Belous,*[46] exemplifies the lower courts' response to this theory. The opinion's entire explanation for including abortion within the right of privacy runs:

> The fundamental right of the woman to choose whether to bear children follows from the Supreme Court's and this court's repeated acknowledgment of a "right to privacy" or "liberty" in matters related to marriage, family, and sex . . . . That such a right is not enumerated in either the United States or California Constitutions is no impediment to the existence of the right.[47]

No "impediment," perhaps, but the absence of any explicit right or privacy within the Constitution should have suggested to the court that it do more to support its holding than simply assert that the right exists and that a right of abortion follows from it.[48] That arguments can be made to defend extending the right of privacy to abortion is beside the point, for arguments can be made against it too. The point is that the *Belous* court, like many of the lower courts and like the Supreme Court itself in *Roe,* never even acknowledged that arguments exist. Once *Belous* was decided, however, precedent existed — albeit of dubious value — and in a follow-the-leader style a second court cited *Belous* to support its decision,[49] a third court cited *Belous* and the second,[50] and so on until the Supreme Court cited them all.[51] Yet the most the Supreme Court could say was that those cases generally

---

43. 381 U.S. 479 (1965).

44. 405 U.S. 438 (1972).

45. *See, e.g.,* Abele v. Markle, 351 F. Supp. 224, 227 (D. Conn. 1972), *vacated and remanded,* 410 U.S. 951 (1973); Steinberg v. Brown, 321 F. Supp. 741, 745 (N.D. Ohio 1970); Doe v. Bolton, 319 F. Supp. 1048, 1054 (N.D. Ga. 1970), *modified and affd.,* 410 U.S. 179 (1973).

46. 71 Cal. 2d 954, 458 P.2d 194, 80 Cal. Rptr. 354 (1969), *cert. denied,* 397 U.S. 915 (1970).

47. 71 Cal. 2d at 963, 458 P.2d at 199-200, 80 Cal. Rptr. at 359-60 (citations omitted).

48. *Cf.* Ely, *supra* note 2, at 928 n.58 (The Supreme Court's "inability to pigeonhole confidently the right involved is not important in and of itself. It might, however, have alerted the Court to what *is* an important question: whether the Constitution speaks to the matter at all." (emphasis original)).

49. Babbitz v. McCann, 310 F. Supp. 293, 300 (E.D. Wis.), *appeal dismissed per curiam,* 400 U.S. 1 (1970).

50. Roe v. Wade, 314 F. Supp. 1217, 1222 (N.D. Tex. 1970), *affd. in part and revd. in part,* 410 U.S. 113 (1973).

51. 410 U.S. at 154.

"reached the same conclusion,"[52] that they "agreed that the right of privacy, however based, is broad enough to cover the abortion decision."[53] Just how they reached that conclusion the Court necessarily left unexplained.

Those courts that did attempt an explanation, *Doe v. Scott*[54] for instance, usually drew the analogy between contraception and abortion:

> We do not agree with the defendants that the choice whether to have a child is protected before conception but is not so protected immediately after conception has occurred. A woman's interest in privacy and in control over her body is just as seriously interfered with by a law which prohibits abortions as it is by a law which prohibits the use of contraceptives.[55]

Although less cryptic than *Belous*, this is hardly more persuasive. Certainly abortion statutes interfere with women's interests as seriously as do restrictions on the use of contraceptives. But why does a right to resist interference with the use of contraceptives equal a right to resist interference with abortion? If because women may control their own bodies, as *Scott* suggests, then the analogy reads into *Griswold* a rationale that simply is not there.[56] If for some other reason, then what? The analogy to contraception is not a complete argument for placing abortion within the right of "privacy."[57] It is, nonetheless, about the only argument the pre-*Roe* courts made.

One case, *Abele v. Markle*,[58] did try something slightly different. The court still relied on the questionable reading that *Griswold* and *Eisenstadt* apply to abortion, but in describing women's interests it said:

---

52. 410 U.S. at 154.

53. 410 U.S. at 155.

54. 321 F. Supp. 1385 (N.D. Ill. 1971), *vacated and remanded*, 410 U.S. 951 (1973).

55. 321 F. Supp. at 1390 (footnote omitted).

56. *See* Ely, *supra* note 2, at 929-30, 929 n.68. The Supreme Court expressly rejected in *Roe* the theory of unimpairable bodily control, 410 U.S. at 154, and characterized *Griswold* as a case about "marital intimacy," 410 U.S. at 159; but even before *Doe v. Scott*, at least one court had already refused (although without explanation) to read into *Griswold* a theory of bodily control. Doe v. Bolton, 319 F. Supp. 1048, 1055 n.2 (N.D. Ga. 1970), *modified and affd.*, 410 U.S. 179 (1973).

57. *See* Epstein, *supra* note 3, at 170.

58. 342 F. Supp. 800 (D. Conn. 1972), *vacated and remanded*, 410 U.S. 951 (1973). There are two cases entitled *Abele v. Markle*. The first, 342 F. Supp. 800 (D. Conn. 1972), struck down the restrictive abortion statute Connecticut had originally passed in 1860. The second, 351 F. Supp. 224 (D. Conn. 1972), struck down the substantially identical statute Connecticut passed in response to the first *Abele* decision. *See* text at note 113 *infra*.

The decision to carry and bear a child has extraordinary ramifications for a woman. Pregnancy entails profound physical changes. Childbirth presents some danger to life and health. Bearing and raising a child demands difficult psychological and social adjustments. The working or student mother frequently must curtail or end her employment or educational opportunities. The mother with an unwanted child may find that it overtaxes her and her family's financial or emotional resources. The unmarried mother will suffer the stigma of having an illegitimate child. Thus, determining whether or not to bear a child is of fundamental importance to a woman.[59]

The similarity between this list and the Supreme Court's in *Roe* is obvious.[60] Unfortunately, even assuming that the Court consciously adopted this particular argument (and without a word-by-word borrowing, an assumption is all that is warranted), what the Court meant by "privacy" remains a mystery, for this argument leaves unanswered why the state may regulate any number of decisions with equally "extraordinary ramifications."[61]

Finally, another of the pre-*Roe* cases, *Doe v. Bolton*,[62] not only failed to offer any rationale, but tossed off its conclusion so cavalierly that one wonders whether the court really knew what it meant: "For whichever reason, the concept of personal liberty embodies a right to privacy which apparently is also broad enough to include the decision to abort a pregnancy." And in footnote 2: "We see no connection between this theory and the claimed right of a woman 'to use her body in any way she wishes' read into Griswold by some."[63] That is no way for a court to expound a Constitution.

Given this complete failure of the lower courts to argue persuasively for extending the right of privacy to abortion, it is hardly surprising that the Supreme Court had nothing to justify its decision. The lower courts offered it no guidance, nor did the proponents in *Roe,* whose briefs argued more expansively but relied largely on the inconclusive arguments that had proved successful thus far.[64] In short, the pre-*Roe* cases forged a trail that the Supreme Court followed as if dutifully. That *is* surprising. Lower courts help to prepare disputes for Supreme Court review, but the Court obviously need not follow lower courts that cannot

59. 342 F. Supp. at 801-02 (footnote omitted).
60. *Compare* 342 F. Supp. at 801-02 *with* 410 U.S. at 153.
61. *See* Ely, *supra* note 2, at 932 n.81.
62. 319 F. Supp. 1048 (N.D. Ga. 1970), *modified and affd.,* 410 U.S. 179 (1973).
63. 319 F. Supp. at 1055 n.2.
64. Brief for Appellants at 91-124, Roe v. Wade, 410 U.S. 113 (1973).

articulate persuasive reasons for doing so. And yet the Court did just that.

B. *"Where certain 'fundamental' rights are involved . . . ."*

In the course of its curiously dim elucidation of privacy, the Supreme Court said, "These decisions make it clear that only personal rights that can be deemed 'fundamental' or 'implicit in the concept of ordered liberty' . . . are included in this guarantee of personal privacy."[65] With just that label — "fundamental" — the Court ordained the demands of its review: only "compelling state interests" would justify abridging the right.[66] Irritated by the Court's reliance on equal protection precedent in this due process case, and presumably by the offhanded manner in which the Court found so disputed a right as abortion "implicit in . . . ordered liberty," Justice Rehnquist dissented, "Unless I misapprehend the consequences of this transplanting of the 'compelling state interest test,' the Court's opinion will accomplish the seemingly impossible feat of leaving this area of the law more confused than it found it."[67] But in fact, *Roe* left this area only *as* confused as it found it. The pre-*Roe* cases that found the right of privacy broad enough to include abortion had already distorted the concept of fundamental rights.

Identifying those rights that are "fundamental," in that they are "implicit in the concept of ordered liberty," is a difficult task in itself, but it rightly demands of courts especial clarity and persuasiveness, because of the extraordinary protection a right once deemed fundamental acquires against legislative encroachment. Thus Justice Harlan wrote:

> Each new claim to Constitutional protection must be considered against a background of Constitutional purposes, as they have been rationally perceived and historically developed . . . . The decision of an apparently novel claim must depend on grounds which follow closely on well-accepted principles and criteria. The new decision must take "its place in relation to what went before and further [cut] a channel for what is to come."[68]

And thus it is incredible that without a hint of explanation the court in *People v. Belous* announced "[t]he *fundamental* right

---

65. 410 U.S. at 152 (citation omitted).
66. 410 U.S. at 155.
67. 410 U.S. at 173.
68. Poe v. Ullman, 367 U.S. 497, 544 (1961) (Harlan, J., dissenting) (citation omitted).

of the woman to choose whether to bear children."[69] If the court
had convincingly shown that a right of abortion follows from the
Supreme Court's privacy cases, it would have taken the first step
toward showing that right fundamental. It was content instead to
apply the label, and the courts that followed it were content to
march in lockstep behind. *Babbitz v. McCann,* for example, cred-
ited *Belous* with showing that a right of abortion "is a fundamental liberty that is implicit in the penumbrae of the Bill of Rights,
and is supported, by analogy, in many past decisions."[70] Then the
lower-court *Roe v. Wade* relied on *Belous* and *Babbitz,*[71] and *Doe
v. Scott* relied on all three,[72] plus the lower-court *United States
v. Vuitch,* which never said a word about fundamental rights.[73]
The misuse of the fundamental rights concept became unmistak-
able in the lower-court *Roe,* which said, "Freedom to choose in
the matter of abortions has been accorded the status of a
'fundamental' right in every case coming to the attention of this
Court . . . ."[74] Merely counting judicial votes for bestowing
super-protection is exactly what courts are not supposed to do.
But that is what the lower courts and the Supreme Court did.

C. *"The appellee . . . argue[s] that the fetus is a
'person' . . . ."*

To respond to Texas's argument that "the fetus is a 'person'
within the language and meaning of the Fourteenth Amendment,"[75] the Supreme Court listed each use of "person" in the
Constitution, adroitly adduced that "in nearly all these instances, the use of the word is such that it has application only postnatally,"[76] and concluded, "All this, together with our observation . . . that throughout the major portion of the 19th century
prevailing legal abortion practices were far freer than they are
today, persuades us that the word 'person,' as used in the Fourteenth Amendment, does not include the unborn."[77] Professor

---

69. 71 Cal. 2d 954, 963, 458 P.2d 194, 199, 80 Cal. Rptr. 354, 359 (1969) (emphasis
added), *cert. denied,* 397 U.S. 915 (1970).

70. 310 F. Supp. 293, 300 (E.D. Wis.), *appeal dismissed per curiam,* 400 U.S. 1 (1970).

71. 314 F. Supp. 1217, 1222 (N.D. Tex. 1970), *affd. in part and revd. in part,* 410
U.S. 113 (1973).

72. 321 F. Supp. 1385, 1390 (N.D. Ill. 1971), *vacated and remanded,* 410 U.S. 950
(1973).

73. 305 F. Supp. 1032, 1035 (D.D.C. 1969), *revd.,* 402 U.S. 62 (1971).

74. 314 F. Supp. at 1222.

75. 410 U.S. at 156.

76. 410 U.S. at 157.

77. 410 U.S. at 158.

Ely, evidently touched by the irony of the Court's sudden allegiance to the letter of the Constitution, found "[t]he canons of construction employed here . . . most intriguing when they are contrasted with those invoked to derive the constitutional right to an abortion."[78]

The irony appeared in pre-*Roe* case law as well. Although most of the lower courts, including those that upheld abortion statutes, never addressed this issue, two courts faced it squarely when purported guardians ad litem alleged that abortions unconstitutionally deprive fetuses of life. In both *McGarvey v. Magee-Womens Hospital,* where the guardian claimed that even Pennsylvania's traditional restrictive statute was unconstitutional for allowing abortions without "some form of judicial process,"[79] and *Byrn v. New York City Health & Hospitals Corp.,* where the guardian argued that New York's liberal statute was unconstitutional for ever allowing abortions except to save the woman's life,[80] the courts found that the fourteenth amendment does not include fetuses, and they therefore emphatically disclaimed any authority to disturb the legislative balances.[81] Both courts are to be praised for their restraint, but it is ironic that in the midst of judicial legislation to expand abortion, the two courts asked to restrict it invoked judicial restraint. That is especially ironic because had the courts wished to expand fetal protection, they could arguably have relied, given the generally low level of analysis in the pre-*Roe* cases, on the earlier anti-abortion decision in *Steinberg v. Brown.*[82] Casually relying on the defendant's biology and Webster's dictionary, the court in *Steinberg* had decided that life begins at conception and that "[o]nce human life has commenced, the constitutional protections found in the Fifth and Fourteenth Amendments impose upon the state the duty of safeguarding it."[83] Of course, *Steinberg*'s effort to draw fetuses within the fourteenth amendment by deciding from scanty evidence when life begins had itself been judicial legislation (although paradoxically it supported the balance it second-guessed). As a whole, the pre-*Roe* courts, like the Supreme Court, seem to

78. Ely, *supra* note 2, at 926.

79. 340 F. Supp. 751, 752 (W.D. Pa. 1972), *affd.,* 474 F.2d 1339 (3d Cir. 1973).

80. 31 N.Y.2d 194, 286 N.E.2d 887, 335 N.Y.S.2d 390 (1972), *appeal dismissed,* 410 U.S. 949 (1973).

81. *McGarvey:* 340 F. Supp. at 754; *Byrn:* 31 N.Y.2d at 203, 286 N.E.2d at 890, 335 N.Y.S.2d at 395.

82. 321 F. Supp. 741 (N.D. Ohio 1970).

83. 321 F. Supp. at 746-47.

have found second-guessing a handy resort when needed, but not the kind of girl one wants to marry.

   To bolster its decision that a fetus is not a "person," the Supreme Court said, "Indeed, our decision in *United States v. Vuitch . . .* inferentially is to the same effect, for we there would not have indulged in statutory interpretation favorable to abortion in specified circumstances if the necessary consequence was the termination of life entitled to Fourteenth Amendment protection."[84] That statement is a bit disingenuous, for the Court in *Vuitch* expressly — which is more than "inferentially" — declined to discuss any aspect of the privacy arguments made by the appellee.[85] That notwithstanding, the Court can surely apply interpretative glosses to its own opinions, and this gloss had the advantage of being ready-made. In strikingly similar language, *Abele v. Markle* had previously said, "Surely the Court would have withheld even tacit approval of abortions in such circumstances if the consequence was the termination of a life entitled to fourteenth amendment protection."[86] In this instance, then, the traditional axiom was at work: the lower court identified and articulated an argument that aided Supreme Court review. Unfortunately, *Abele*'s gloss on *Vuitch* was a rather minor point; but still more unfortunately, the Court settled for plucking it out of a much larger argument. *Abele* held that "person" does not include a fetus and specifically referred to *Vuitch* in the course of arguing that a state cannot almost totally abridge women's constitutional rights by asserting an interest in fetuses which have no constitutional rights.[87] That theory is debatable, and even *Abele* stated it tentatively,[88] but it was one step toward a more

---

   84. 410 U.S. at 159.

   85. Interestingly, the Supreme Court not only avoided discussing the arguments, it conspicuously avoided even using the word "privacy":

   Appellee has suggested that there are other reasons why the dismissal of the indictments should be affirmed. Essentially, these arguments are based on this Court's decision in *Griswold v. Connecticut* . . . . Although there was some reference to these arguments in the opinion of the court below, we read it as holding simply that the statute was void for vagueness . . . . Since that question of vagueness was the only issue passed upon by the District Court it is the only issue we reach here.

402 U.S. 62, 72-73 (1971) (citation omitted). Neither the district court nor the appellee, however, had been reluctant to invoke the right of privacy. *See* United States v. Vuitch, 305 F. Supp. 1032, 1035 (D.D.C. 1969), *revd.*, 402 U.S. 62 (1971); Brief for Milan M. Vuitch, M.D., at 40-44, United States v. Vuitch, 402 U.S. 62 (1971).

   86. 351 F. Supp. 224, 228 (D. Conn. 1972), *vacated and remanded*, 410 U.S. 951 (1973).

   87. 351 F. Supp. at 228-30.

   88. 351 F. Supp. at 230.

precise definition of the state interest necessary to abridge constitutional rights than the conclusory tags "rational" and "compelling." By deciding *Roe* too soon, the Supreme Court afforded itself only the minor point, precluded any judicial debate of *Abele*'s theory, and pinned itself to an obfuscating method with " 'compelling' points."[89]

D. *"We need not resolve the difficult question of when life begins . . . ."*

Having decided that the Constitution does not protect fetuses, the Supreme Court turned to Texas's statutory claim: "Texas urges that, apart from the Fourteenth Amendment, life begins at conception and is present throughout pregnancy, and that, therefore, the State has a compelling interest in protecting that life from and after conception."[90] In response, the Court quickly abjured any attempt to decide when life begins,[91] noting instead that this question yields a "wide divergence of thinking,"[92] and that "[i]n areas other than criminal abortion, the law has been reluctant to endorse any theory that life, as we recognize it, begins before live birth."[93] How those observations lead to the conclusion that states may protect fetuses only after viability is a mystery. The critics have particularly dismissed this portion of *Roe* as the merest dissemblance of a rationale.[94] And the Court's dissembling at this point undercut the purported purpose of its opinion: to discern the relative weights of the interests involved.[95] By busying itself with the question of what a fetus *is* — "life," "potential life," a "person," a person "in the whole sense" — the Court avoided admitting that *something* hangs in the balance against women's rights and thus avoided the real question of whether states may protect fetuses, as nothing more than fetuses, and at what cost to women.[96]

This avoidance was the legacy of the pre-*Roe* cases. The courts that struck down abortion statutes for abridging women's right of privacy essentially denied that a fetus is anything at all.

---

89. 410 U.S. at 163.

90. 410 U.S. at 159.

91. 410 U.S. at 159.

92. 410 U.S. at 160.

93. 410 U.S. at 161.

94. *See, e.g.,* Ely, *supra* note 2, at 924-26; Epstein, *supra* note 3, at 180-85; Tribe, *supra* note 5, at 3-5.

95. 410 U.S. at 162, 165.

96. *See* Ely, *supra* note 2, at 933.

As Professor Ely said, "a fetus may not be a 'person in the whole
sense,' but it is certainly not nothing."[97] The lower courts pre-
tended otherwise. In *People v. Belous,* the court said:

> It is next urged that the state has a compelling interest in the
> protection of the embryo and fetus and that such interest warrants
> the limitation on the woman's constitutional rights. Reliance is
> placed upon several statutes and court rules which assertedly show
> that the embryo or fetus is equivalent to a born child. However,
> all of the statutes and rules relied upon require a live birth or
> reflect the interest of the parents.
>
> In any event, there are major and decisive areas where the
> embryo and fetus are not treated as equivalent to the born child.[98]

Satisfied that a fetus is not equivalent to a born child, the *Belous*
court thought its task complete. But why must a fetus be
"equivalent to a born child" before the state may protect it? A
fetus is a fetus. The court never considered the straightforward
question "Can the state protect a fetus?" without regard to
whether a fetus is like something else the state protects elsewhere.[99] And because it failed to do so, the court never honestly
faced the question abortion raises.

The other courts were no more honest. The lower court in *Roe
v. Wade* said, "To be sure, the defendant has presented the Court
with several compelling justifications for state presence in the
area of abortions . . . . Concern over abortion of the 'quickened'
fetus may well rank as . . . such [an] interest."[100] The court did
not say, however, what distinguishes a quickened from an unquickened fetus that the state may protect one but not the other.
If the court thought an unquickened fetus is nothing, then it was
blinking at facts. If the court thought the fetus is something, but
is too insubstantial to count, then it needed to explain why. In
Doe v. Scott[101] and *Abele v. Markle,*[102] the courts insinuated that
all of what hangs in the balance is something grotesque, by lamenting fetuses that would be born gravely defective or that resulted from rape. Those situations are undeniably tragic, but

97. Ely, *supra* note 2, at 931.

98. 71 Cal. 2d 954, 967-68, 458 P.2d 194, 202-03, 80 Cal. Rptr. 354, 362-63 (1969)
(footnotes omitted), *cert. denied,* 397 U.S. 915 (1970).

99. *See* Epstein, *supra* note 3, at 175.

100. 314 F. Supp. 1217, 1223 (N.D. Tex. 1970), *affd. in part and revd. in part,* 410
U.S. 113 (1973).

101. 321 F. Supp. 1385, 1391 (N.D. Ill. 1971), *vacated and remanded,* 410 U.S. 950
(1973).

102. 342 F. Supp. 800, 804 (D. Conn. 1972), *vacated and remanded,* 410 U.S. 951
(1973).

invoking them does not honestly characterize all fetuses. Yet the
Scott and *Abele* courts, rapt in their discomfort, allowed themselves to avoid admitting that anything not grotesque was at
stake. In *Doe v. Bolton,* the court acknowledged that "[o]nce
conception takes place and an embryo forms, for better or for
worse the woman carries a life form with the *potential* of independent human existence."[103] That potentiality, the court said,
grants to the state "a legitimate area of control,"[104] so long as the
controls "do not restrict the reasons for the initial decisions" to
abort.[105] That assessment of the fetus differs only superficially
from *Belous*'s or the lower-court *Roe*'s. By leaving unexplained
the limit on the state's interest, the court denied that anything
counterbalances the woman's right just as effectively as *Belous*
and *Roe* did when they diverted themselves with questions about
what a fetus is or resembles. One court, *Babbitz v. McCann,* at
least tried to be honest: "For the purposes of this decision, we
think it is sufficient to conclude that the mother's interests are
superior to that of an unquickened embryo, whether the embryo
is mere protoplasm, as the plaintiff contends, or a human being,
as the Wisconsin statute declares."[106] Why the woman's interests
prevail, however, is unexplained.

In sum, the resort to questions like "Is a fetus a person?" "To
what extent do other statutes protect fetuses?" and "Is a fetus
alive?" did more to divert the courts from their analytic duties
than to answer the question before them. One of the last pre-*Roe*
cases, *Abele v. Markle,* realized that fact, and dismissed in a
footnote the comparisons to other statutes.[107] Perhaps if the Supreme Court had allowed the abortion dispute to brew longer,
more courts would have faced the question and offered guidance
when the Court finally decided a case. That it rushed into this
darkness to decide *Roe,* only to fail to add new illumination,
simply adds to the impression that the Court should have heeded
the traditional axioms.

The Court concluded its discussion of Texas's statutory
claim by remarking, "In short, the unborn have never been recog-

103. 319 F. Supp. 1048, 1055 (N.D. Ga. 1970) (emphasis original), *modified and affd.,*
410 U.S. 179 (1973).
104. 319 F. Supp. at 1055.
105. 319 F. Supp. at 1056.
106. Babbitz v. McCann, 310 F. Supp. 293, 301 (E.D. Wis.), *appeal dismissed per
curiam,* 400 U.S. 1 (1970).
107. Abele v. Markle, 351 F. Supp. 224, 226 n.5 (D. Conn. 1972), *vacated and
remanded,* 410 U.S. 951 (1973).

nized in the law as persons in the whole sense."[108] This regrettable sentence first appeared in *Byrn v. New York City Health & Hospitals Corp.*[109] After noting that fetuses may acquire some rights even before birth, the *Byrn* court said, "But unborn children have never been recognized as persons in the law in the whole sense."[110] In context, the import of this sentence is quite clear. The *Byrn* court meant that even if fetuses receive some protection, they have never received all the protection people receive after birth. The Supreme Court, by using the sentence to end the entire section on Texas's interests, and by prefixing to it "In short," which clearly signals that a summary definitive statement should follow, managed to obscure what little meaning the sentence has. The traditional axiom recommends that the Court use lower-court arguments to its benefit; in this instance the Court adopted the argument so cryptically that it lost any potential benefits.

E.   *"[W]e do not agree that, by adopting one theory of life . . . ."*

Having decided in section IX that a fetus is neither a fourteenth amendment "person," nor a "person in the whole sense," the Supreme Court opened section X with, "In view of all this, we do not agree that, by adopting one theory of life, Texas may override the rights of the pregnant woman that are at stake."[111] This is a curious statement. If read out of context, it would seem to suggest that *Roe* is a case about the limits of state authority to regulate activity by deciding metaphysical questions. For according to this statement, the Court did not object to Texas's end — prohibiting abortions — but to its means — "adopting one theory of life." But that suggestion seems untenable if the statement is read in context, for nothing preceding it in the opinion discussed what theories a state may or may not endorse in the course of regulation, nor did the opinion say anything about states adopting theories when it subsequently announced its schema of permissible regulation. What, then, is the phrase, "by adopting one theory of life" doing there? One fairly plausible answer is that the phrase was meant to conceal some doctrinal sleight of hand. The Court surely wanted to avoid explicitly inval-

---

108. 410 U.S. at 162.
109. 31 N.Y.2d 194, 286 N.E.2d 887, 335 N.Y.S.2d 390 (1972), *appeal dismissed*, 410 U.S. 949 (1973).
110. 31 N.Y.2d at 200, 286 N.E.2d at 888, 335 N.Y.S.2d at 392.
111. 410 U.S. at 162.

idating Texas's legislative goal, even if that is what the Court was doing. Conveniently for the Court, Texas's brief justified protecting fetuses from the moment of conception by arguing that that is when life begins and that the state has a duty to protect life.[112] Thus, although objecting to the goal, the Court could attack the means — verbally if not analytically. Obviously, the sleight of hand was not very deft.

There may be a second, less cynical explanation for the phrase. By looking to the nature of Texas's interest — one that adopted a theory of life — the Supreme Court might have been suggesting a rationale similar to the unique theory developed in *Abele v. Markle*.[113] That theory grew from a legislative-judicial dialogue that may well have continued had the Supreme Court not decided *Roe*. In April 1972, a three-judge district court struck down Connecticut's restrictive abortion statute,[114] with one of the two majority judges expressly declining to decide how he would have voted had the state persuasively shown that an interest in protecting fetuses originally motivated the statute's enactment.[115] One month later, the Connecticut General Assembly enacted a substantially identical statute with a new first section declaring, "The public policy of the state and the intent of the legislature is to protect and preserve human life from the moment of conception . . . ."[116] When this new statute was challenged, the *Abele* court responded by considering "whether the state has power to advance such a purpose" by abridging a constitutional right.[117] In the course of its consideration, the court, rather than attaching or withholding the label "compelling," attempted the difficult task of articulating the nature of a compelling state interest:

> A compelling state interest has generally been one where the nature of the interest was broadly accepted, with dispute remaining only as to whether the state could constitutionally advance that interest by the specific means being challenged.
>
> . . . No decision of the Supreme Court has ever permitted anyone's constitutional right to be directly abridged to protect a state interest which is subject to such a variety of personal judgments [as is Connecticut's interest in protecting life from concep-

---

112. Brief for Appellee at 31, Roe v. Wade, 410 U.S. 113 (1973).

113. 351 F. Supp. 224 (D. Conn. 1972), *vacated and remanded,* 410 U.S. 951 (1973).

114. Abele v. Markle, 342 F. Supp. 800 (D. Conn. 1972), *vacated and remanded,* 410 U.S. 951 (1973).

115. 342 F. Supp. at 810 (Newman, J., concurring).

116. 351 F. Supp. at 226.

117. 351 F. Supp. at 227.

tion on] . . . . Such an interest cannot acquire the force of a
governmental decree to abridge an individual's constitutional
right. To uphold such a statute would permit the state to impose
its view of the nature of a fetus upon those who have the constitutional right to base an important decision in their personal lives
upon a different view.

. . . .
. . . Of course, legislation is not rendered unconstitutional
simply because it advances a social policy about which people
differ. Normally it is the legislative function to resolve such differences. But where a state interest subject to such variety of view-
points is asserted on behalf of a fetus which lacks constitutional
rights, and where the assertion of such an interest would accomplish the virtually total abridgment of a constitutional right of
special significance, in these circumstances such a state interest
cannot prevail.[118]

Pursuant to this test, the *Abele* court again struck down Connecticut's statute, but also suggested the type of abortion statute this
test would allow:

If a statute sought to protect the lives of all fetuses which
could survive outside the uterus, such a statute would be a legislative acceptance of the concept of viability . . . . [T]he state interest in protecting the life of a fetus capable of living outside the
uterus could be shown to be more generally accepted and, therefore, of more weight in the constitutional sense than the interest
in preventing the abortion of a fetus that is not viable.[119]

The Supreme Court's otherwise inexplicable discussion of
state interests in *Roe* can be read, with some imagination, to
suggest a similar argument.[120] Texas claimed just what Connecti-

---

118. 351 F. Supp. at 230-31 (citations omitted).
119. 351 F. Supp. at 232 (footnote omitted).
120. Of course, the Court cited in *Roe* all the lower court decisions, 410 U.S. at 154-
55, but it seems clear that the Court was particularly familiar with *Abele,* for part "A" of
Roe's § IX contains striking verbal and organizational parallels to *Abele*'s part "A."
Organizationally, both opinions marshalled the same evidence to argue that a fetus is not
a fourteenth amendment "person": that other constitutional uses of "person" do not apply
to fetuses, *compare* 410 U.S. at 157 *with* 351 F. Supp. at 229 n.8; that courts which had
addressed the issue had held that fetuses are not "persons," *compare* 410 U.S. at 158 *with*
351 F. Supp. at 228; and that *United States v. Vuitch* had implied that fetuses are not
"persons," *compare* 410 U.S. at 159 *with* 351 F. Supp. at 228. No other lower-court opinion
adduces the same three points. Verbally, *Roe* echoed *Abele*'s language three times: (1)
it described *Vuitch*'s implication with similar words, *see* text at notes 84-86 *supra;* (2) its
statement of the first claim it considered — "that the fetus is a 'person' within the
language and meaning of the Fourteenth Amendment," 410 U.S. at 156 — resembled
Abele's "The initial inquiry is whether the fetus is a person, within the meaning of the
fourteenth amendment . . . ," 351 F. Supp. at 228; and (3) its reference to "those few
cases where the issue was squarely presented," 410 U.S. at 158, resembled *Abele*'s reference to the two courts in which "[t]he issue has been squarely faced." 351 F. Supp. at

cut had: that "life begins at conception and is present throughout
pregnancy, and that, therefore, the State has a compelling interest in protecting that life from and after conception."[121] The Court
said two things in response. First: "It should be sufficient to note
briefly the wide divergence of thinking on this most sensitive and
difficult question."[122] Unfortunately, the Court left ambiguous
exactly what the wide divergence of thinking suffices to show.
Perhaps this survey of opinion suffices to show that "the judiciary, at this point in the development of man's knowledge, is not
in a position to speculate" about when life begins.[123] The survey
also suffices to show, however, that Texas's state interest rests on
a theory that many people, including no doubt many pregnant
women, sincerely reject. Second: "In areas other than criminal
abortion, the law has been reluctant to endorse any theory that
life, as we recognize it, begins before live birth . . . ."[124] Professor
Ely is surely right that if the Court was trying to show why Texas
may not protect fetuses before viability, then "the bodies of doctrine to which the Court adverts . . . tend to undercut rather
than support its conclusion."[125] If, on the other hand, the Court
was trying to suggest that a compelling state interest may not
depend on a premise so widely disputed as that life begins at
conception, then revealing that no other doctrines or statutes
endorse that premise does support its conclusion. Finally, like the
Abele court, the Supreme Court designated viability as "the
'compelling' point."[126] It explained: "This is so because the fetus
then presumably has the capability of meaningful life outside the
mother's womb. State regulation protective of fetal life after viability thus has both logical and biological justifications."[127] While
the Court does not appear to suggest that it selected viability
because Texas's interest would then be "more generally accepted,"[128] which is how *Abele* decided on viability, it does seem

---

228. Of course the verbal and organizational parallels do not prove much, especially the
verbal ones, for judges borrow language from each other like brothers borrow socks: con-
stantly, if not openly. But they do suggest that the Supreme Court knew more about *Abele*
than its holding.

121. 410 U.S. at 159; Brief for Appellee, *supra* note 112.

122. 410 U.S. at 160.

123. 410 U.S. at 159.

124. 410 U.S. at 161.

125. Ely, *supra* note 2, at 925.

126. 410 U.S. at 163.

127. 410 U.S. at 163.

128. Abele v. Markle, 351 F. Supp. 244, 232 (D. Conn. 1972), *vacated and remanded*,
410 U.S. 951 (1973).

to find significant that by viability Texas may justify its interest
in fetal life with more than just one debatable theory chosen from
among many. By the time a fetus is viable, logic and biology
dictate that the fetus, if not alive, is at least almost alive. Therefore, to read a bit into the opinion, Texas's interest would no
longer depend on a widely disputed premise, and by the *Abele*
test could be "compelling."

This reading of *Roe* is purely speculative. Indeed, seeing
Abele's theory in *Roe* is like finding the hidden object drawn into
a puzzle-picture: one must know to look for it.[129] Even if *Roe* does
contain fine shadings of *Abele,* the opinion still leaves many questions unanswered. The best that can be said is equivocal: It is
heartening to think that some rationale lurks behind *Roe,* but
equally disheartening that after taking *Roe* too soon for that rationale to develop further, the Court would not say whether it
used the rationale or not, and if not, then what rationale it did
use.

F.   *"Each grows in substantiality as the woman approaches
term . . . ."*

Immediately after rejecting Texas's claim to protect fetuses
from the moment of conception, the Court granted that the state
yet had "important and legitimate" interests in protecting
women's health and fetuses' potential life.[130] "Each [interest]
grows in substantiality as the woman approaches term and, at a
point during pregnancy, each becomes 'compelling.' "[131] For the
interest in protecting women's health, "the 'compelling' point"
was approximately the end of the first trimester, "because of the
now-established medical fact . . . that until the end of the first
trimester mortality in abortion may be less than mortality in
normal childbirth."[132] Thus, abortions within the first trimester
are "free of interference by the State."[133] For the interest in protecting potential life, "the 'compelling' point" was viability, be-

---

129. Once one begins looking, however, one finds in *Roe* a great many more references
to beliefs, theories, and the divergence of thinking than one might have suspected were
there. The opinion's first page-and-a-half, for instance, mentions attitudes, views, and
thinking six times. 410 U.S. at 116-17. And, of course, the Court included its much-
maligned survey of "medical and medical-legal history" to show "what that history reveals about man's attitudes" toward abortion. 410 U.S. at 117.

130. 410 U.S. at 162.
131. 410 U.S. at 162-63.
132. 410 U.S. at 163.
133. 410 U.S. at 163.

cause as already mentioned, "the fetus then presumably has the capability of meaningful life outside the mother's womb."[134]

The Supreme Court must have been well acquainted with differentiating compellingness of state interests according to length of pregnancy, for most of the pre-*Roe* courts had done it. With the exception of *Abele*, however, none of the lower courts had protected the right to abortion so zealously as did the Supreme Court. In assessing states' interests in women's health, for example, the lower courts had often relied solely on statistics about the relative risks in abortion and childbirth to justify their decisions that those interests no longer warranted prohibiting abortions in the first trimester.[135] But all the lower courts had expressly conceded that even in the first trimester the state could regulate who may perform abortions and where.[136] As to interests in protecting fetuses, the courts had generally found those uncompelling during "early" pregnancy,[137] or before quickening.[138] While the courts had rarely specified when "early" pregnancy

---

134. 410 U.S. at 163.

135. *See, e.g.,* YWCA v. Kugler, 342 F. Supp. 1048, 1074 (D.N.J. 1972), *cert. denied,* 415 U.S. 989, *affd. without opinion,* 493 F.2d 1402 (3d Cir. 1974); Babbitz v. McCann, 310 F. Supp. 293, 301 (E.D. Wis.), *appeal dismissed per curiam,* 400 U.S. 1 (1970); People v. Belous, 71 Cal. 2d 954, 965, 458 P.2d 194, 200-01, 80 Cal. Rptr. 354, 360-61 (1969), *cert. denied,* 397 U.S. 915 (1970). The statistical studies most frequently cited were by Christopher Tietze. That name became so familiar in the pre-*Roe* cases and in the *Roe* briefs, that when the Supreme Court cited three Tietze studies among the five named sources that wholly supported the decision not to allow any state regulation during the first trimester, 410 U.S. at 149 n.44, 163, one begins to think that the due process clause of the fourteenth amendment enacts Dr. Christopher Tietze's Abortion Statistics.

136. Abele v. Markle, 342 F. Supp. 800, 804 (D. Conn. 1972), *vacated and remanded,* 410 U.S. 951 (1973); YWCA v. Kugler, 342 F. Supp. 1048, 1075-76 (D.N.J. 1972), *cert. denied,* 415 U.S. 989, *affd. without opinion,* 493 F.2d 1402 (3d Cir. 1974); Doe v. Scott, 321 F. Supp. 1385, 1391 (N.D. Ill. 1971) (decision that a state interest in women's health is uncompelling limited to abortions "by licensed physicians in a licensed hospital"), *vacated and remanded,* 410 U.S. 950 (1973); Doe v. Bolton, 319 F. Supp. 1048, 1056 (N.D. Ga. 1970), *modified and affd.,* 410 U.S. 179 (1973); Roe v. Wade, 314 F. Supp. 1217, 1223 (N.D. Tex. 1970), *affd. in part and revd. in part,* 410 U.S. 113 (1973); Babbitz v. McCann, 310 F. Supp. 293, 302 (E.D. Wis.), *appeal dismissed per curiam,* 400 U.S. 1 (1970); People v. Belous, 71 Cal. 2d 954, 965, 458 P.2d 194, 201, 80 Cal. Rptr. 354, 360-61 (1969) (decision that state interest in women's health is uncompelling limited to "a hospital therapeutic abortion"), *cert. denied,* 397 U.S. 915 (1970).

137. Abele v. Markle, 342 F. Supp. at 804 ("within an appropriate period after conception"); Doe v. Scott, 321 F. Supp. at 1391 ("the early stages"); Doe v. Bolton, 319 F. Supp. at 1055 (exactly what *Bolton* held is difficult to discern — indeed, after two months the court issued an explanatory supplemental opinion — but the plaintiffs alleged a right to terminate "an unwanted pregnancy in its early stages," and the court apparently accepted that); United States v. Vuitch, 305 F. Supp. at 1035 ("early stages").

138. YWCA v. Kugler, 342 F. Supp. at 1075; Roe v. Wade, 314 F. Supp. at 1223; Babbitz v. McCann, 310 F. Supp. at 299.

ends, none of them except *Abele*[139] had indicated in any way that
it stretches to viability.

More important than the timing of when interests become
compelling, however, is the fact that none of the courts — lower
or Supreme — adequately justified differentiating by length of
pregnancy at all. None of them explained why relative risks
"should provide the only constitutionally relevant measure of
permissible state regulation"[140] to protect the mother's health.
And, as seen before, most of them never honestly faced the task
of balancing states' interests in fetuses against women's interests
in abortion,[141] much less articulated why the state interest was
"compelling" in late pregnancy but not in early. Thus, when the
Supreme Court drafted what Professor Ely called its
"commissioner's regulations."[142] it went beyond any balance of
interests it or the lower court had explained, and beyond what
any lower court (except *Abele*) had thought necessary. To be sure,
the Court was not wholly without models for its selection of viability as "the 'compelling' point": the statutes of Alaska, Hawaii,
and New York allowed abortions for any reason before viability.[143]
But the Court could not really have patterned its decision after
them — that would have been judicial legislation.

CONCLUSION

Roe and the pre-*Roe* cases share many of the same faults,
and not coincidentally. In the face of the lower courts' confusion,
and the inadequacy of most of their attempts to evolve a constitutional analysis for the abortion cases, the Supreme Court was
doubtless tempted to ignore the traditional axioms of Supreme
Court review, to seize the problem and resolve it itself. *Roe* should
serve as a reminder that quick resolution is not always the wisest
choice, for *Roe* is an opinion uninformed by any thoughtful lower-
court analysis. The *Abele* court's attempt to grapple with the
difficult issues suggests that more thoughtful analysis was in the
offing. Unfortunately, the Supreme Court did not wait to enjoy
those benefits.

---

139. 351 F. Supp. at 232.
140. Tribe, *supra* note 5, at 4.
141. *See* text at note 106 *supra*.
142. Ely, *supra* note 2, at 922.
143. *See* Comment, *supra* note 10, at 181.

PART II

THE POLITICS OF ABORTION

ABORTION AND THE PRESIDENTIAL ELECTION OF 1976: A MULTIVARIATE ANALYSIS OF VOTING BEHAVIOR

Maris A. Vinovskis* †

During the 1960s and 1970s, the American public was deeply split over civil rights, the war on poverty, and Vietnam. Analysts frequently divided the electorate into new categories such as the "New Liberals" and the "Silent Majority" as issue-oriented politics polarized the nation. Yet by the mid-1970s, most of the controversies of the previous decade had faded or disappeared entirely. The end of the war in Vietnam, Watergate, increasing inflation, and domestic energy shortages turned most Americans inward and away from the larger social debates of the 1960s.

Today, concern about inflation, unemployment, energy, and foreign policy alternatives has largely replaced the discussion of new domestic social programs. One possible exception to the lack of interest in social questions today is the debate over abortion. As the "pro-life" and "pro-choice" groups continue their battles within Congress and among the voters, many observers, particularly those in the news media, see abortion as one of the most divisive and important controversies of the 1970s.[1] In fact, following the widely publicized defeats of prominent pro-choice politicians such as Senator Dick Clark of Iowa and Representative Donald Fraser of Minnesota in 1978, many analysts are predicting

---

* Associate Professor, Department of History, University of Michigan; Associate Research Scientist, Center for Political Studies, Institute for Social Research, University of Michigan. B.A. 1965, Wesleyan University; M.A. 1966, Ph.D. 1975, Harvard University. — Ed.

† Funds for this project were provided by a fellowship from the Rockefeller Foundation. The analysis and opinions expressed in this paper are, of course, solely my own and do not reflect in any way the position or the views of the Foundation. I am also indebted to Sally Brower and Mary Vinovskis for preparing and programming the data.

Portions of this analysis were presented at the annual meeting of the National Abortion Rights Action League in Washington, D.C., February 1978, and at the National Right to Life Convention in St. Louis, Missouri, July 1978.

1. The choice of words used to describe the opposing sides of the abortion debate is in itself controversial. For example, the use of the term "pro-life" to designate those who are against abortions is resented by their opponents because it implies that those who favor abortions are "anti-life." Rather than taking sides on this matter, I shall use the terms commonly utilized by each faction for itself. Thus, those groups opposing abortions will be referred to as "pro-life" while those favoring abortions will be designated as "pro-choice."

that abortion will be one of the major factors in federal and state elections in 1980. As Anthony Lewis of the *New York Times* recently observed:

> Over the last few years political analysts have noted the significance of the single-issue voter: the person who cares only about a candidate's views on gun control, for example, or busing, or capital punishment. It is clear now, I think, that one such issue is likely to have the largest impact on American politics for the longest time. That is abortion.[2]

Despite the widespread public interest in the role of the abortion controversy in American politics today, no one has attempted to analyze systematically its impact on the electorate.[3] Some national opinion surveys have asked voters whether or not they would be influenced by a candidate's position on abortion, but they have not attempted to ascertain its relative importance, compared to other considerations, in the final deliberations of the electorate. In an effort to provide a more systematic study of the role of abortion in American politics today, this Article analyzes the campaign to elect the President of the United States in 1976. In particular, it studies the coverage of abortion by the news media, its importance in public opinion polls taken during the campaign, and its relative impact on voters on November 2, 1976, using multivariate analysis and survey research data.

I. Abortion and the Presidential Campaign of 1976

Repeated efforts to liberalize state abortion statutes during the 1960s culminated in changes in Colorado's restrictive abortion law in 1967. Seventeen other states followed suit and liberalized their abortion statutes before January 1973, when the Supreme Court declared almost all of the existing state laws against abortion unconstitutional.[4] Yet those early efforts to abolish restric-

---

2. *Cited in* Minneapolis Tribune, Nov. 17, 1978, at 10A.

3. The study of population policy in general and of abortion in particular has been rather limited to date — particularly empirical efforts to analyze popular or legislative voting behavior. For collections of essays on population policy and abortion, see POPULATION AND POLITICS: NEW DIRECTIONS IN POLITICAL SCIENCE RESEARCH (R. Clinton ed. 1973); POPULATION POLICYMAKING IN THE AMERICAN STATES (1974); RESEARCH IN THE POLITICS OF POPULATION (1972); POLITICAL ISSUES IN U.S. POPULATION POLICY (1974); ABORTION AND SOCIAL JUSTICE (1972); ABORTION IN THE SEVENTIES: PROCEEDINGS OF THE WESTERN REGIONAL CONFERENCE ON ABORTION, DENVER, COLORADO, FEBRUARY 27-29, 1976 (1977); ABORTION: NEW DIRECTIONS FOR POLICY STUDIES (1977).

4. On the early developments in the efforts to liberalize abortion laws in the United

tions on abortions also mobilized strong opposition from various local pro-life groups. On the eve of the Supreme Court decision, the voters in Michigan overwhelmingly defeated an attempt to liberalize that state's abortion law.[5] Thus, though a definite trend toward easing restrictions on abortions developed during the late 1960s and early 1970s, those efforts were encountering increasingly more determined and better organized opposition.

The debate over abortion did not play a very prominent role in the presidential election of 1972. Although Richard Nixon raised the topic at several points in the campaign and sent a letter to Cardinal Terence Cooke of New York supporting the effort to repeal New York's liberalized abortion law, he did not try to make it one of his major issues. Other controversies such as the war in Vietnam captured the headlines and the attention of the electorate and contributed more to Nixon's landslide victory over George McGovern than their differences over abortion.[6]

The Supreme Court decisions in *Roe v. Wade*[7] and *Doe v. Bolton*[8] on January 23, 1973, catapulted abortion to front-page attention. The pro-choice position suddenly became part of the Constitution. While most pro-choice activists basked in the afterglow of their victory or turned their efforts to other social issues, the pro-life forces suddenly faced the formidable task of trying to

---

States, see J. MOHR, ABORTION IN AMERICA: THE ORIGINS AND EVOLUTION OF NATIONAL POLICY, 1800-1900 (1978); L. LADER, ABORTION (1966); L. LADER, ABORTION II: MAKING THE REVOLUTION (1973); P. MARX, THE DEATH PEDDLERS: WAR ON THE UNBORN (1971); Potter, *The Abortion Debate*, in THE SURVIVAL EQUATION: MAN, RESOURCES, AND HIS ENVIRONMENT 91 (1971); P. Leahy, The Anti-Abortion Movement: Testing a Theory of the Rise and Fall of Social Movements (unpublished Ph.D. dissertation, Department of Social Science, Syracuse University 1975); Vinovskis, Jones, & New, *Determinants of Legislative Voting Behavior on Population Policy: An Analysis of the Massachusetts House of Representatives in 1970 and 1971*, in POPULATION POLICYMAKING IN THE AMERICAN STATES 239 (1974).

5. Cathy Abernathy of the Department of History at the University of Michigan has been doing research on the politics of abortion in Michigan during the referendum campaign in 1972 (unpublished paper, Ann Arbor, Michigan). For an example of a detailed state analysis of the politics of abortion, see P. STEINHOFF & M. DIAMOND, ABORTION POLITICS: THE HAWAII EXPERIENCE (1977).

6. On the 1972 election, see Miller, Miller, Raine, & Brown, *A Majority Party in Disarray: Policy Polarization in the 1972 Election*, 170 AM. POLITICAL SCI. REV. 753 (1976); Popkin, Gorman, Phillips, & Smith, *Comment: What Have You Done For Me Lately? Toward an Investment Theory of Voting*, 170 AM. POLITICAL SCI. REV. 179 (1976); Steeper & Teeter, *Comment on "A Majority Party in Disarray,"* 70 AM. POLITICAL SCI. REV. 806 (1976); RePass, *Comment: Political Methodologies in Disarray: Some Alternative Interpretations of the 1972 Election*, 17 AM. POLITICAL SCI. REV. 814 (1976); Miller & Miller, *Ideology in the 1972 Election: Myth or Reality—A Rejoinder*, 17 AM. POLITICAL SCI. REV. 832 (1976).

7. 410 U.S. 113 (1973).

8. 410 U.S. 179 (1973).

reverse the Court's decision on abortion. Thus, *Roe* caused a role reversal that shifted political initiative on the abortion issue from the pro-choice group to the pro-life camp. The first major test of the political impact of the Supreme Court decision came in the congressional elections of 1974. Though some pro-life groups targeted several congressmen whom they regarded as particularly pro-choice, a candidate's position on abortion proved relatively unimportant in most races. A detailed survey of the issues in the contests for the House and Senate during 1974 revealed that in the vast majority of the electoral contests, abortion was not a major campaign topic.[9]

As the country prepared for the 1976 elections, the abortion issue received more discussion, and political observers began to wonder whether the attitudes of American voters toward abortion had changed as the result of the Supreme Court decision. Frequently, the public shifts its opinion on an issue after the Supreme Court declares it to be either constitutional or unconstitutional; one might have expected such a shift after *Roe v. Wade.* To ascertain any shifts in public opinion on abortion between the 1972 and 1976 elections, we used the data from the American National Election surveys for 1972 and 1976.[10] Since the exact wording of the questions about abortion can affect the level of support for or opposition to abortions, comparisons based on different surveys can be very misleading.[11] The comparison between 1972 and 1976, however, should be valid since the same question was asked in both years. Each respondent in 1972 and 1976 was shown a page with the following statements:

1. Abortion should never be permitted.
2. Abortion should be permitted only if the life and health of the woman are in danger.

---

9. Rosoff, *Support of Abortion Political Suicide?,* 7 Fam. Plan. Perspec. 13 (1975). Her findings are confirmed by my investigation of the campaign literature of candidates for the House, Senate, and state governors for 1974.

10. The data used in this essay were made available by the Inter-University Consortium for Political and Social Research. The data for the CPS 1976 American National Election Study were originally collected by the Center for Political Studies of the Institute for Social Research, the University of Michigan, under a grant from the National Science Foundation. Neither the original collectors of the data nor the Consortium bear any responsibility for the analysis or interpretations presented here.

11. The influence of the exact wording used in questions about abortion on the level of support or opposition to abortions has already been extensively documented. For example, see Blake, *Abortion and Public Opinion: The 1960-1970 Decade,* 171 Science 540 (1971); Blake, *The Abortion Decisions: Judicial Review and Public Opinion,* in Abortion: New Directions for Policy Studies 51 (1977).

3. Abortion should be permitted if, due to personal reasons, the woman would have difficulty in caring for the child.

4. Abortion should never be forbidden, since one should not require a woman to have a child she doesn't want.

7. Other

The results of these surveys indicate that only a small percentage of the public in both years felt that abortions should never be permitted or never be forbidden (*see* figure 1). The great majority of people agreed that abortions should be permitted, but only under certain circumstances.

The Supreme Court in *Roe* held that prior to the end of the first trimester, the abortion decision and its effectuation must be left to the medical judgment of the pregnant woman's attending physician. In the second trimester the state may, if it chooses, regulate and proscribe abortions, except where it is necessary for the preservation of the life or health of the mother. In other words, during the first six months of the pregnancy, the woman is free to have an abortion for any reason though the state may limit that choice in the second trimester if it so chooses.

FIGURE 1

ATTITUDE OF AMERICAN VOTERS TOWARD ABORTIONS
IN 1972 AND 1976

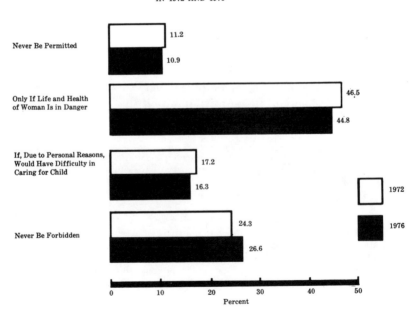

Although the great majority of people agreed with the Supreme Court's decision to permit abortions (only 11.2% in 1972 and 10.9% in 1976 felt abortions should never be permitted), more than half of the respondents also answered either that abortions should be forbidden or that they should only be allowed if the life and health of the woman are in danger (57.7% in 1972 and 55.6% in 1976). Thus, while the public accepted the Supreme Court's liberalization of abortions, it did not agree with the extent of the freedom the Court granted women to obtain abortions.

Attitudes toward abortion changed very little between 1972 and 1976. Though the percentage of Americans who felt that abortions should never be forbidden increased from 24.3% in 1972 to 26.6% in 1976 and the proportion who felt it should never be permitted dropped from 11.2% to 10.9%, that shift is small enough that it might be simply the result of sampling error rather than any actual change in attitudes. Since there was apparently so little change in the attitudes of Americans toward abortions between 1972 and 1976, and since an overwhelming majority favored abortions if the life or health of the woman were in danger, one might have expected that abortion would not be a major campaign topic in 1976 any more than it was in either 1972 or 1974. Yet, at least among some voters, the abortion debates were among the most divisive of the 1976 campaign, and they even captured the headlines momentarily. Why?

One reason for the emergence of abortion as a campaign issue in 1976 was that the pro-life forces launched several organized efforts to force politicians to take a position on abortion even though most presidential aspirants would have preferred to avoid the matter altogether. On November 20, 1975, in a highly unusual move, the National Council of Catholic Bishops overwhelmingly adopted a "Pastoral Plan for Pro-Life Activities." The Pastoral Plan was addressed to "all Church-sponsored or identifiable Catholic national, regional, diocesan and parochial organizations and agencies" and called upon them to support a "comprehensive pro-life legislative program" that included the passage of a constitutional amendment for the protection of the unborn child. The Bishops' Plan was unique not only for its legislative agenda, but also for its attempt to organize political support at the local levels during the 1976 election. The Plan stated:

> This effort at persuasion is part of the democratic process, and is carried on most effectively in the congressional district or state from which the representative is elected. . . . Thus it is absolutely

necessary to have in each congressional district an identifiable, tightly-knit and well organized pro-life unit. This unit can be described as a public interest group or a citizens' lobby. No matter what it is called:

(a) its task is essentially political, that is, to *organize people* to help persuade the elected representatives; and (b) . . . it is focused on passing a constitutional amendment.[12]

Throwing the weight of the National Council of Catholic Bishops behind the efforts to pass a constitutional amendment to limit abortions gave the pro-life forces an important boost toward legitimizing their activities and placing the abortion issue in the forefront of potential campaign topics for 1976. Furthermore, the unprecedented and dramatic political conduct of the bishops generated controversy that received additional media coverage. For example, the liberal *National Catholic Reporter* issued a highly critical editorial about the Pastoral Plan:

If the bishops have created a Catholic party, and only time will tell, they have unleashed a fearsome thing. The Catholic Church — and its bishops — will have moved into the upper reaches of national politics as an identifiable political lobby/party of massive proportions. Such proportions, given the 48 million Catholic population in this country, could yet rival or counterbalance the largest political parties or lobbies in this country: the Republican party, the Democratic party, and the AFL-CIO. . . . The National Conference of Catholic Bishops may have signaled a major change in the makeup of U.S. policies.[13]

Although no cohesive, national Catholic party or lobby ever materialized during the 1976 election, the National Conference of Catholic Bishops did play a prominent role in the election, particularly in the later stages, by raising the question of whether the normally Democratic Catholic vote would go to Jimmy Carter, whose position on abortion leaned more toward pro-choice than that of Gerald Ford. By threatening to tie Catholic support to the abortion issue rather than to some other problem such as unemployment or housing, the Pastoral Plan helped to push the abortion controversy into the presidential campaign.

While the National Conference of Catholic Bishops sought to mobilize support for a constitutional amendment against abortions, other pro-life groups coalesced behind the candidacy of Ellen McCormack in the Democratic primaries. Running as a

---

12. *Cited in* Planned Parenthood-World Population Washington Memo, Dec. 15, 1975, at 2 (emphasis original).

13. *Cited in id.* at 3.

zealous "right-to-life" advocate, McCormack took advantage of the new federal matching campaign funds for presidential candidates who were able to raise at least $5000 in twenty states. Though McCormack's candidacy made little headway among most voters, her presence in primaries such as New Hampshire and Massachusetts forced other candidates to deal with abortion. Few people regarded her as a serious presidential candidate, but most viewed her campaign as an opportunity to publicize the movement for a constitutional amendment on abortion. As Jay Bowman, head of Georgia's Right-to-Life Committee, put it, "she's not a serious candidate, but she can get equal time [on television] for the pro-life message and she can get the Federal government to pay for the ads."[14]

In the aftermath of the first presidential primary, the cause of pro-life groups gained an identifiable target. Jimmy Carter, a relatively unknown candidate, emerged as the winner of the Democratic primary in Iowa. After his victory, several other Democratic candidates accused him of "waffling" on such issues as abortion, capital punishment, amnesty for Vietnam war evaders, and his own political record, an accusation that was to stay with Carter throughout the campaign. The Iowa primary directed national attention toward abortion because Carter was accused of deliberately misleading Iowa voters about his stand on abortion. Indeed, Carter campaigned in Iowa by emphasizing his personal opposition to abortion. In a statement for the Des Moines diocesan newspaper, the *Catholic Mirror,* he argued that "no active government should ever contribute to abortions. We should do all we can to minimize abortions and to favor a national statute that would restrict the practice of abortion in our country."[15]

Carter's statements were interpreted by many pro-life activists in Iowa as indication of his support for a constitutional amendment to limit abortions; on this assumption, many of these activists supported Carter in the primary caucuses. Just a few days before the primary, however, some Catholic leaders suddenly realized that Carter did not really support a constitutional amendment. In Sioux City, Monsignor Frank J. Brady announced that, "I was misinformed that Governor Carter favored a constitutional amendment to reverse the Supreme Court's deci-

---

14. *Cited in* Newsweek, Feb. 9, 1976, at 23.
15. *Cited in* Planned Parenthood-World Population Washington Memo, Feb. 13, 1976, at 1.

sion on abortion."[16] Many people in the pro-life movement felt
that Carter had deliberately misled them in Iowa, and this contributed to their animosity towards him later in the campaign.

Following Carter's unexpected but impressive victory in
Iowa, the news media and the other candidates forced him to
explain his position on abortion. In a statement to *Newsweek,*
Carter clarified his stand:

> I think abortion is wrong. It should not be encouraged by the
> government. The government should take a positive role in pre-
> venting unwanted pregnancies through education and family-
> planning programs. I do not favor a constitutional amendment to
> give states local option-authority without knowing the specifics at
> this time. I might support a Federal statute minimizing abortions
> beyond the first thirteen weeks of pregnancy.[17]

Thus, though Carter reiterated his personal opposition to abortion, he did not favor a constitutional amendment prohibiting
abortions. Instead, he tried to leave the door open for some type
of federal statute to limit abortions, but most observers doubted
the constitutionality of any such act.

Carter's difficulties with abortion soon forced other presidential aspirants to state their own positions. On the Democratic
side, Senator Birch Bayh became the candidate most identified
with the pro-choice position. As pro-life groups shifted their attack from Carter to Bayh, Carter was able to direct his attention
to other issues.[18] Though several of the other Democratic candidates, especially George Wallace in the Florida primary, sought
support from the pro-life forces, most observers felt that Ellen
McCormack had cornered most of that support.

On the Republican side, Ronald Reagan pursued and received the support of many pro-life activists by endorsing a constitutional amendment to restrict abortions.[19] Though Reagan
was momentarily embarrassed by the fact that he had signed the

---

16. *Cited in id.* at 2.
17. Newsweek, Feb. 2, 1976, at 18.
18. Throughout the primaries, most of the editorial praise or support for presidential
candidates in the pro-life *National Right to Life News* was either for Ellen McCormack
or Ronald Reagan while Birch Bayh received a disproportionate amount of the criticism.
During the early Democratic primaries, Carter received less scrutiny and attention than
many of the other Democratic contenders.
19. As the Republican convention was about to convene, Ronald Reagan singled out
abortion as one issue on which he planned to challenge Ford before the Republican Platform Committee. New York Times, Aug. 9, 1976, at 12. Rather than trying to make this a
source of major contention between Reagan and himself, Ford's supporters accepted
Reagan's position on abortion in the Republican platform.

liberalized abortion law in California, he repudiated his earlier behavior and wholeheartedly embraced the pro-life cause. President Ford, on the other hand, sought to find a middle ground. Rather than agreeing to a constitutional amendment to restrict abortions, he favored one to put the entire question back into the hands of the states. In a CBS television interview with Walter Cronkite, Ford summarized:

> I'm in a moderate position in that area. I do not believe in abortion on demand. I do not agree with the Supreme Court's decision in 1973. I do not agree that a constitutional amendment ·is the proper remedy. I think we should recognize that there are instances when abortion should be permitted. Illness of the mother, rape or other unfortunate things that might happen. So there has to be some flexibility. I think the Court decision went too far, I think the constitutional amendment goes too far. If there was to be some action in this area, it's my judgment that it ought to be on the basis of what each individual state wishes to do under the circumstances. Again, I should add that even though I disagree with the Court's decision, I have taken an oath of office and I will, of course, uphold the law as interpreted by the Court, but I think there is a better answer.[20]

After Carter's victory in Iowa, the news media began to speculate at great length about the importance of the abortion issue. For example, in early February *Newsweek* proclaimed abortion as "1976's Sleeper Issue" while a *New York Times* headline claimed that "Abortion Is Big Issue in Primaries in Massachusetts and New Hampshire."[21] The results of the New Hampshire and Massachusetts primaries, however, temporarily deflated the importance of abortion in the campaign. Despite the predictions that Ellen McCormack might do very well in both primaries, she received only about one percent of the vote in New Hampshire and 3.5% in Massachusetts. Even more telling were the results of a *New York Times*/CBS poll of Massachusetts Democrats on primary day, which indicated that only seven percent of the Democratic voters thought abortion was an important issue and that only forty percent of that seven percent cast their ballots for Ellen McCormack.[22]

After the New Hampshire and Massachusetts primaries, the news media turned their attention away from abortion. Though

---

20. *Cited in* Planned Parenthood-World Population Washington Memo, Feb. 13, 1976, at 2.
21. Newsweek, Feb. 9, 1976, at 21; New York Times, Feb. 4, 1976, at 53.
22. New York Times, Mar. 4, 1976, at 18.

the topic still surfaced from time to time, it did not generate as much concern from candidates and reporters as it had following the Iowa primary. Even when the Democratic Convention passed a resolution against a constitutional amendment and the Republican platform called for an amendment restricting abortions, the media showed little interest. But while the news media downplayed the abortion issue immediately after the conventions, the pro-life forces redoubled their efforts. Carter acknowledged that abortion was the most discussed subject in the letters he received and that most of the writers felt that the Democratic party platform on abortion was too liberal.[23] Nevertheless, it was only when the Catholic bishops reentered the picture that the abortion issue suddenly recaptured the country's attention.

On August 31, Carter met with six Roman Catholic bishops at the Mayflower Hotel in Washington. He expected to use the meeting to establish a better working relationship with those church leaders, and he had been led to believe that the meeting would permit productive discussion with the Catholic prelates of social issues besides abortion. Unfortunately his strategy backfired as Archbishop Joseph L. Bernardin of Cincinnati, President of the National Conference of Catholic Bishops, refused to discuss other issues until they resolved the abortion question. As a result, when Archbishop Bernardin emerged from the meeting, he announced that he and his colleagues "continued to be disappointed" with Carter's abortion stance.[24]

Although supporters of the pro-life movement were not satisfied with Ford's compromise position and had fought for a Reagan victory, Ford's post-convention campaign nevertheless benefited from the movement's negative reactions to Carter. After Ford met with the six Catholic bishops on September 10, Archbishop Bernardin said the group was "encouraged" though "not totally satisfied" by the President's position on abortion.[25] By their public comments, the leaders of the National Conference of Catholic Bishops again stirred the abortion controversy toward the surface of the campaign stew.

The news media quickly picked up on Carter's difficulties with the Catholic bishops over abortion. For example, the

---

23. New York Times, July 25, 1976, at 30.

24. For details on the meeting with the bishops, see M. SCHRAM, RUNNING FOR PRESIDENT: A JOURNAL OF THE CARTER CAMPAIGN 250-53 (1977).

25. U.S. NEWS & WORLD REPORT, Sept. 20, 1976, at 15-18; NEWSWEEK, Sept. 20, 1976, at 16-18.

Newsweek headline on the campaign ran: "On Abortion, the Bishops v. the Deacon."[26] Speculation was rampant over whether Carter would be able to hold traditionally Democratic voters when Ford's position on abortion seemed much more acceptable. Carter's difficulties with the abortion issue were evident at several campaign stops when pro-life demonstrators heckled him and prevented him from speaking.[27]

In September 1976, just as abortion was being revived as a major campaign issue, the *New York Times* and CBS conducted another survey of the national electorate. Voters were asked, "Do you favor an amendment to the Constitution which would make abortions illegal, or do you oppose such a change in the law?" Contrary to the image projected by the pro-life demonstrations, the majority of Americans opposed such an amendment (*see* figure 2): Only 32% of the electorate favored a constitutional amendment to declare abortions illegal, while 58% opposed it.[28]

FIGURE 2

ATTITUDE OF VOTERS ON AN AMENDMENT TO THE
CONSTITUTION WHICH WOULD MAKE ABORTIONS ILLEGAL,
SEPTEMBER 1976

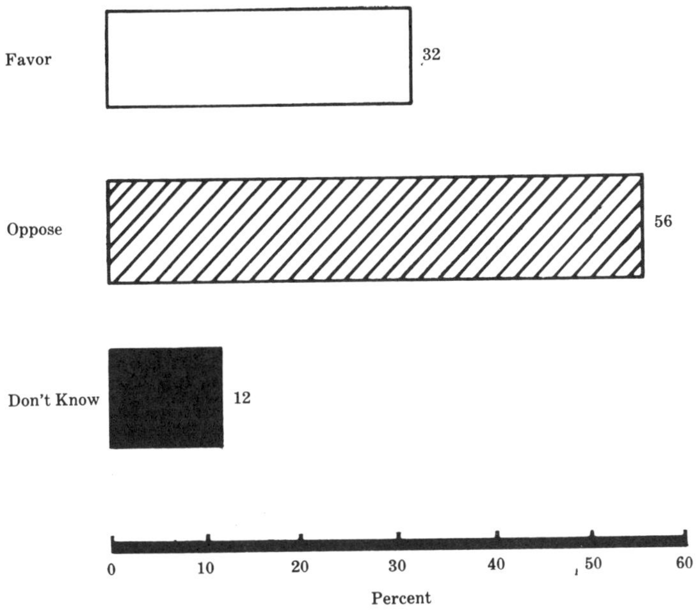

Favor   32

Oppose   56

Don't Know   12

0   10   20   30   40   50   60

Percent

26. NEWSWEEK, Sept. 20, 1976, at 11.
27. *See* U.S. NEWS & WORLD REPORT, Sept. 20, 1976, 15-18; NEWSWEEK, Sept. 20, 1976, at 11-12, 16-18.
28. New York Times, Sept. 10, 1976, at 19.

Even more interesting from the perspective of the presidential campaign, however, was the unexpected discovery that the controversy over a constitutional amendment was basically nonpartisan (*see* figure 3). Although 45% of those opposed to an amendment supported Carter, 47% of those favoring a constitutional amendment also supported him.

FIGURE 3

PRESIDENTIAL PREFERENCES OF VOTERS BY THEIR
POSITION ON A CONSTITUTIONAL AMENDMENT WHICH
WOULD MAKE ABORTIONS ILLEGAL, SEPTEMBER 1976

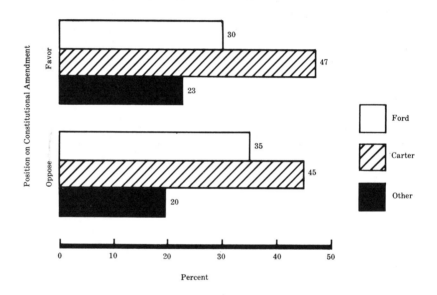

Following the survey's release, the abortion controversy once again subsided as reporters and the news media concluded that both pro-life and pro-choice activism had relatively little impact on voters. Despite the continued efforts of the pro-life groups, abortion never regained the attention and importance that it enjoyed in the media following the Iowa primary and the denunciation of Carter's position by the Catholic bishops.

II. ABORTION AS A DETERMINANT OF VOTING BEHAVIOR IN THE PRESIDENTIAL ELECTION

On November 2, American voters elected Carter by the closest electoral margin in sixty years. Although Carter won 51% of the popular vote to Ford's 48%, the electoral count was so close that a switch of fewer than 8000 votes in Ohio and Hawaii could have given Ford a 270 to 268 victory in the Electoral College. On the other hand, a shift of only 70,000 votes in eight other states would have given Carter a sizable 337 to 201 margin.

Given the closeness of the election, it was inevitable that "Monday-morning quarterbacks" would second-guess the importance of various events and issues in the campaign. Most observers concluded that abortion was not a significant factor in the election; pro-choice commentators were particularly quick to proclaim that the "election . . . shows abortion not a major issue."[29] Because pro-choice forces had not been especially visible or effective during the race, they were content to declare the issue politically unimportant rather than try to claim a major victory from Carter's election. Moreover, Carter's willingness to place statutory restrictions on abortions prevented pro-choice supporters from placing too much emphasis on his victory. The pro-life supporters, however, now faced an unhappy predicament: on the one hand, they wanted to emphasize the importance of abortion in electoral politics; on the other hand, the candidate they had so vehemently opposed had just won. John Mackey of the Ad Hoc Committee in Defense of Life described it:

> *HAD FORD PULLED IT OFF* there is no doubt that abortion would have been labelled a *major* factor — it *was* a big reason for Carter's amazingly narrow win, and showed in such states as Indiana, New Jersey, and Connecticut. But in politics it's winner-take-all, and Carter's victory is a sharp setback to the anti-abortion movement (even though it won impressive victories in lesser races).[30]

The issue still remains unresolved: Did the voters' positions on abortion influence their decisions to vote for Carter or Ford? The news media and many other observers flip-flopped through the campaign over whether abortion was a major factor, concluding in the final weeks that it was not particularly important. The abortion activists were split throughout the campaign — most pro-choice observers downplayed the political impact of the issue while their pro-life counterparts emphasized it — even after Carter's narrow victory.

We can test for the relative importance of the abortion issue by using the survey data available from the American National Election Survey on American voting behavior from November 2, 1976. Using a preelection questionnaire administered to 2248 re-

---

29. Planned Parenthood-World Population Washington Memo, Nov. 12, 1976, at 4.
30. Lifeletter, Nov. 3, 1976, at 1.

spondents and a postelection one that was given to 1909 respondents, that survey offers clues to whether the abortion issue was an important factor in determining voter behavior. The question on abortion in that survey is the one we examined earlier — voters were given four statements on abortion and asked to indicate their personal preference for one of them.

One might simply cross-tabulate the respondents' answers about abortion with the way they voted to see whether one's position on abortion influenced one's vote. In fact, this simple statistical procedure is the one most commonly employed in the few efforts to assess the relationship between abortion and voting behavior. It is inadequate, however, because it does not permit us to ascertain the relative importance of one's position on abortion, compared to such other factors as one's party identification, attitude on other issues, or religious orientation. For example, we may find that pro-choice voters were more apt to support Carter, not so much because of his specific position on abortion, but because of his more liberal overall image compared to Ford. Thus, we need to control for the possible effects of other factors in trying to determine the role of abortion in the final decision to vote for Carter or Ford.

Our data set consists of the responses of all persons in the postelection survey who voted for either Carter or Ford and who answered the question on abortion. The dependent variable (the one to be explained) is the vote on the presidency. As independent variables we selected twelve different factors that may have influenced voters — age, sex, race, marital status, education, family income, religion, index of liberalism, identification, region of the country, size of the community, and attitude on abortion. Though the bulk of our analysis relied upon those independent variables, we also included in some calculations a series of variables measuring voters' attitudes on other social and economic issues, to see how well those other factors predicted voting behavior compared to one's position on abortion.

All of the data were analyzed using multiple classification analysis (MCA). Since many of the readers of this Article may not be familiar with multiple classification analysis, I will try to provide a brief introduction to this technique. MCA is a form of multiple regression analysis with dummy variables. The predictive value of each dummy variable is expressed as an adjusted deviation from the grand mean (overall average) of the dependent variable (whom a person votes for). For example, MCA answers the question: how much of the vote for Carter is associated with someone being Catholic, while controlling for such other variables as the voter's age, sex, and the size of the community. Similarly, it also provides an approximate answer to the question: *Ceteris paribus,* what is the effect of one's religion on whether one votes for Carter? Multiple classification analysis "controls" for other variables by assuming that, as it looks at one class of a predictor variable, the distribution of all other predictor variables will be the same in that class as in the total population, thus "holding constant" their effects. Although traditional multiple regression programs also do this, MCA has three advantages: it does not require variables to be interval variables, it does not require or assume linearity and thus can capture discontinuities in the direction of association, and finally, it is more descriptive because it calculates the gross effects of a predictor class — the actual mean of the class — as well as the mean after adjusting for the influence of other variables.[31]

Our analysis reveals that one's position on abortion was not a good predictor, by itself, of whether one voted for Ford or Carter. In fact, voters did not divide in any consistent pattern for Carter or Ford on the basis of their own attitudes on abortion. While over fifty percent of those who said either that abortions should never be permitted or that they should never be forbidden voted for Carter, less than fifty percent of those who qualified their support for or opposition to abortion supported him (see the unadjusted percentages in figure 3). Furthermore, the weakness of attitudes on abortion as a predictor, by itself, of voting behavior is confirmed by the fact that less than one half of one percent of the variation in voting can be explained by the abortion variable (see eta^2 in table A2 in the appendix).

The relationship between attitudes on abortion and voting behavior became only slightly more consistent after we used MCA to control for the effects of the other independent variables. The results — the adjusted percentages in figure 4 — indicate that taking into account other possible determinants of voting behavior, voters who favored allowing abortions were more apt to vote for Carter than for Ford. For example, after controlling for

---

31. There are various issues associated with the use of multiple classification analysis that need to be considered before using this procedure. For an excellent and well-written introduction to multiple classification analysis, see F. ANDREWS, J. MORGAN, J. SONQUIST, & L. KLEM, MULTIPLE CLASSIFICATION ANALYSIS: A REPORT ON A COMPUTER PROGRAM FOR MULTIPLE REGRESSION USING CATEGORICAL PREDICTORS (2d ed. 1973).

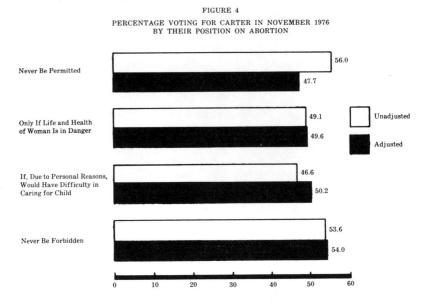

FIGURE 4

PERCENTAGE VOTING FOR CARTER IN NOVEMBER 1976
BY THEIR POSITION ON ABORTION

the other factors, only 47.7% of the voters who felt abortions should never be permitted voted for Carter, while 54.0% of those who thought abortions should never be forbidden voted for him. But although controlling for other factors reveals a consistent and expected relationship, it still does not show abortion to be a major determinant of voting behavior in 1976. In fact, the voter's attitude on abortion was the weakest of all predictors.[32] The two strongest predictors were an individual's party identification and index of liberalism (see the beta weights in table A2).[33]

We calculated one final measure of the relative importance of abortion in 1976. In the postelection portion of the American National Election Survey, each voter was asked: "What do you think are the most important problems facing this country?" The first three responses of each interviewee were recorded. While

---

32. Since so much attention was focused on whether Carter would be able to maintain the Catholic vote, it is interesting to observe that 58.1% of the Catholics supported him rather than Ford. However, after controlling for the effects of the other variables, Carter did not receive more support from Catholics than from the rest of the population (see table A1).

33. For an analysis of the 1976 election and a comparison of the relative importance of issues in 1972 and 1976, see A. Miller & W. Miller, Partisanship and Performance: "Rational" Choice in the 1976 Presidential Election (unpublished paper presented at the American Political Science Association Meeting, Washington D.C., September 1977); W. MILLER, & T. LEVITAN, LEADERSHIP & CHANGE: PRESIDENTIAL ELECTIONS FROM 1952 TO 1976 at 189-240 (1976); G. POMPER, THE ELECTION OF 1976: REPORTS AND INTERPRETATIONS (1977).

18.9% of all the items mentioned dealt with inflation and 24.2% with unemployment, less than one tenth of one percent mentioned abortion — once again suggesting that only a very small minority of the 1976 electorate considered abortion an important issue.

III. Conclusion

Abortion was never a very important concern of voters during the 1976 presidential campaign. Yet it managed to capture the headlines in the weeks after the Iowa primary and in September after Archbishop Bernardin publicly denounced Carter's stance on abortion. But by the end of the campaign, even the news media, which had been eagerly exploiting the abortion issue earlier, acknowledged that it simply was not a major campaign issue. On November 2, when voters pulled the levers in polling booths across the country, very few of them decided to vote for either Ford or Carter on the basis of the candidates' positions on abortion.

The pro-life movement attempted — and failed — to make a candidate's position on abortion a crucial factor in the election. Despite their dedication and intense efforts, its supporters were not able to mobilize the American public — not even those who basically agreed with them — on behalf of candidates who favored a constitutional amendment to restrict abortions. Yet they succeeded in temporarily convincing the news media that abortion was a major issue in the campaign. Furthermore, they were able to force the presidential aspirants to take a position on abortion, typically one that was to some extent critical of the Supreme Court decision. Thus, although unsuccessful, the pro-life forces were more active and visible than their pro-choice counterparts throughout the campaign.

There are several reasons why abortion became a campaign issue even though most Americans did not perceive it to be a major national problem. The pro-life movement was very effective in mobilizing volunteers and staging demonstrations. Although these demonstrators were always a small minority of the electorate, they managed to attract the news media. In addition, Ellen McCormack's campaign generated considerable publicity for the pro-life cause even though it ultimately drew few votes. The Catholic bishops and their Pastoral Plan were also important. By appearing to make their acceptance or rejection of a presidential aspirant depend almost entirely on the candidate's position on abortion, the bishops lent credibility and support to the pro-life efforts. Fourth, the emergence of fewer major campaign issues in 1976 than in 1972 made it much easier for a relatively unimportant but highly visible issue like abortion to capture public attention. Finally, and perhaps most importantly, the news media were particularly prone to exaggerate the importance of the abortion issue in American presidential politics. Until the public opinion polls and the election returns conclusively demonstrated the weakness of abortion as a campaign issue, the news media were quite willing to depict it as a major factor.

Although it is hazardous to speculate on the role of the abortion issue in future presidential elections, I will venture some tentative observations based upon this statistical analysis as well as my assessment of trends in both the pro-life and pro-choice movements since 1976. It is likely that in 1980 both the pro-choice and pro-life groups will be much better organized and better financed than in either 1972 or 1976. Furthermore, after some of the successes of the pro-life effort in the 1978 congressional campaigns, the movement has exhibited an increasing tendency to participate in electoral politics at all levels. Similarly, the pro-choice forces, in large part reacting to the activities of their opponents, seem to be more actively involved in politics. Nevertheless, there is still no indication whatsoever that the American public will perceive the abortion issue as any more important in 1980 than in 1972 or 1976. Since the politicians as well as the news media have now had an opportunity to evaluate the limited impact of abortion on two different presidential campaigns, perhaps abortion will not have the same high visibility in the news media and in the presidential campaign efforts in 1980 as in 1976.

On the other hand, although it is likely that abortion will not play a major role in the presidential campaign of 1980, it probably will be more important in state and local elections, where the organized efforts of dedicated activists can be more influential. Even at the state and local levels, however, most voters probably will not decide solely because of the candidates' positions on abortion, yet the presence of pro-choice or pro-life activists will likely be more effective in these elections than in the presidential election. Compared with the 1976 results that I have documented in this Article, I suspect that in 1980 abortion will be much more of a state and local issue, and much less of a presidential issue.

APPENDIX

TABLE A1

PERCENTAGE VOTING FOR CARTER FOR PRESIDENT,
NOVEMBER 2, 1976, CLASS MEANS, ADJUSTED MEANS, NET
DEVIATIONS, AND NUMBER OF CASES
(1 = CARTER / 0 = FORD)

	Class Mean	Adjusted Mean	Net Deviation	Number of Cases
Age:				
18-29	51.9	47.5	— 3.1	267
30-39	49.3	53.5	+ 2.9	241
40-49	47.2	50.0	— .6	210
50-59	54.0	52.9	+ 2.3	223
60-69	48.9	52.8	+ 2.2	205
70 and Up	52.0	46.3	— 4.3	147
Sex:				
Male	50.4	52.0	+ 1.4	569
Female	50.8	49.5	— 1.1	724
Race:				
White	46.5	49.3	— 1.3	1172
Black	94.9	63.2	+12.6	102
Other	63.3	59.4	+ 8.8	19
Marital Status:				
Married	47.7	51.2	+ .6	882
Never Married	52.4	48.6	— 2.0	130
Divorced or Separated	62.7	48.1	— 2.5	119
Widowed	55.1	51.1	+ .5	162
Education:				
8 Grades or Less	65.9	52.8	+ 2.2	170
9-11 Grades	61.8	50.1	— .5	150
High School Graduate	50.7	51.0	+ .4	452
Some College	47.1	50.7	+ .1	276
BA or Advanced Degree	36.8	48.5	— 2.1	245
Family Income:				
0-$4999	65.0	54.9	+ 4.3	170
$5000-$9999	59.0	52.2	+ 1.6	243
$10,000-$14,999	50.5	52.0	+ 1.4	285
$15,000-$19,999	48.9	46.9	— 3.7	166
$20,000-$24,999	45.4	49.5	— 1.1	169
$25,000 and Up	29.2	42.7	— 7.9	183
No Information	55.4	58.8	+ 8.2	77

	Class Mean	Adjusted Mean	Net Deviation	Number of Cases
Religion:				
Presbyterian	35.7	50.8	+ .2	78
Lutheran	39.7	46.5	− 4.1	124
Methodist	42.3	49.2	− 1.4	149
Baptist	50.9	46.8	− 3.8	112
Southern Baptist	60.2	52.1	+ 1.5	110
Other Protestant	45.3	51.0	+ .4	297
Roman Catholic	58.1	50.6	0	322
Jewish	71.3	56.5	+ 5.9	32
Other Religion	48.5	48.4	− 2.2	14
None or No Preference	68.0	61.7	+11.1	55
Index of Liberalism:				
Liberal	84.1	62.9	+12.3	104
Slightly Liberal	72.6	60.1	+ 9.5	124
Moderate	51.9	52.6	+ 2.0	346
Slightly Conservative	26.2	39.3	−11.3	196
Conservative	16.5	36.8	−13.8	213
Other	66.2	56.4	+ 5.8	310
Party Identification:				
Strong Democrat	91.2	84.1	+33.5	219
Weak Democrat	74.7	71.6	+21.0	292
Independent-Democrat	75.6	70.8	+20.2	145
Independent-Independent	42.0	40.1	−10.5	133
Independent-Republican	14.7	21.3	−29.3	139
Weak Republican	21.2	26.0	−24.6	201
Strong Republican	3.3	13.0	−37.6	164
Region of Country:				
Northeast	54.7	53.4	+ 2.8	281
Central	47.1	53.2	+ 2.6	411
South	53.4	46.5	− 4.1	382
West	46.9	49.2	− 1.4	219
Degree of Urbanization:				
Under 2500	51.4	52.2	+ 1.6	408
2500-9999	43.7	49.0	− 1.6	251
10,000-49,999	45.5	50.1	− .5	273
50,000-349,999	53.0	48.9	− 1.7	214
350,000 and Up	65.5	52.2	+ 1.6	147
Attitude on Abortion:				
Never Permitted	56.0	47.7	− 2.9	127
Only If Life of Woman Is in Danger	49.1	49.6	− .4	206
Permitted for Personal Reasons	46.6	50.2	− .4	206
Never Forbidden	53.6	54.0	+ 3.4	354
Other	49.2	46.5	− 4.1	50
Total	50.6			1293

TABLE A2

PERCENTAGE VOTING FOR CARTER FOR PRESIDENT,
NOVEMBER 2, 1976, ETA^{2}S, BETAS, AND R^2

	Eta^2	Beta
Age	0	.0544
Sex	0	.0252
Race	.0686	.0786
Marital Status	.0068	.0230
Education	.0307	.0250
Family Income	.0393	.0850
Religion	.0272	.0627
Index of Liberalism	.1871	.1793
Party Identification	.4103	.5307
Region of Country	.0026	.0604
Degree of Urbanization	.0137	.0295
Attitude on Abortion	.0005	.0020

$R^2 = .4421$ Note: The Eta^{2}s and R^2 have been adjusted
for the degrees of freedom.

PUBLIC SUPPORT FOR PRO-CHOICE ABORTION POLICIES IN THE NATION AND STATES: CHANGES AND STABILITY AFTER THE *ROE* and *DOE* DECISIONS†

Eric M. Uslaner*
Ronald E. Weber**

"The Supreme Court," according to the legendary Mr. Dooley, "follows the election returns."[1] In 1973, the Court's two landmark decisions, *Roe v. Wade*[2] and *Doe v. Bolton*,[3] struck down statutes in the forty-six states where abortions were not permitted under any circumstances or were allowed only to save the life of the woman during the first three months of pregnancy. There had been a considerable increase in the level of support for the pro-choice position among the public in the few years preceding *Roe* and *Doe*. But did the decisions themselves lead to even more public support for that position? What variations do we find among the states and where has the increase in public support for the pro-choice position seemed the most dramatic? Finally, what has been the impact of the abortion controversy on the political process?

We shall examine these questions here and suggest some tentative answers. First, we shall consider the available national poll evidence. Second, we shall examine variations in political opinion on abortion policies in the states. Finally, we shall examine the abortion controversy as it has affected legislative decision making and electoral politics. When we consider the variations among the states, we shall present estimates of state public opinion on abortion policy through a computer simulation technique,

† The support of the General Research Board of the Graduate School, University of Maryland — College Park and the Office of Research and Advanced Studies, Indiana University is gratefully appreciated. We are also grateful to John Mulligan of the *Providence Journal and Bulletin*. The Political Science Laboratory and Data Archive at Indiana University provided the necessary staff support for the data analysis.

* Associate Professor of Government and Politics, University of Maryland — College Park. B.A. 1968, Brandeis University; M.A. 1970; Ph.D. 1973, Indiana University. — Ed.

** Professor of Political Science, Louisiána State University. B.A. 1964, Macalester College; Ph.D. 1969, Syracuse University. — Ed.

1. *Quoted in* R. CLAUDE, THE SUPREME COURT AND THE ELECTORAL PROCESS at xiv (1970).

2. 410 U.S. 113 (1973).

3. 410 U.S. 179 (1973).

developed by the second author and refined jointly by us, which permits us to get approximate figures on state opinions from national surveys.

We cannot establish any causal relationship between increasing support for the pro-choice position and the Court's 1973 rulings. The level of public support was increasing in the late 1960s and early 1970s. As we shall see below, it is not evident that a majority (or even a plurality) supported the pro-choice position by 1973. Even by early 1974, the margin of preference for that position was small enough to have resulted only from sampling error in the Gallup surveys.

We would not expect a leveling-off of the increase in public support for the pro-choice position after the *Roe* and *Doe* decisions, which altered "the law of the land." One of the critical characteristics of political leadership is the ability to elicit support from the public on controversial issues. Presidents have come to rely upon this "rallying around the flag" by the public almost as a requisite for making bold policy initiatives, particularly on foreign policy.[4] Once an initiative has been taken, public support increases dramatically. Presidents often reach their highest levels of popularity in the polls following such bold decisions, even if those decisions are later viewed as quite wrong.[5] A bad idea becomes a good one once it has been adopted as national policy. The Cambodian incursion of 1970 provides one of the most striking examples of public response to presidential leadership. A Gallup poll taken shortly before the action showed only seven percent supporting such a move. After President Nixon ordered the incursion, the support level rose to fifty percent.[6]

We shall consider below the reasons why there has not been a similar increase in support for the pro-choice position. But we turn first to an examination of the national poll data.

National Abortion Opinion Polls

There is a vast amount of public opinion data on abortion policy. Unfortunately, few comparisons across these data sets can be made because of differences in question wording. Some questions are as direct as: Should abortions be legal during the first

4. *See* J. MUELLER, WAR, PRESIDENTS, AND PUBLIC OPINIONS 53, 211 (1973).

5. *Id.*

6. *See* J. SPANIER & E. USLANER, HOW AMERICAN FOREIGN POLICY IS MADE 94 (2d ed. 1978).

three months of pregnancy? Others cite the *Roe* and *Doe* rulings of the Court. Still others concentrate on the conditions under which the respondent might support legal abortions. Yet another group involves the question of a constitutional amendment to prohibit abortions. Clearly, we cannot draw inferences across all of these questions.

There is some consistency among sets of questions. Perhaps the most useful for overall comparison is a series of similar Harris questions asked from June 1972 to March 1979 and presented in Table 1 below. Before 1973, the surveys asked respondents whether they would favor legalized abortions during the first four months of a pregnancy; beginning in 1973, the questions mentioned the Court action and asked whether the respondent agreed or disagreed with the decisions permitting abortions during the first three months of pregnancy. Aside from the mention of the Court, the later questions were very similar to the earlier ones. We see in the table a drop in support for the pro-choice position in August 1972 and a sharp rise in support after *Roe* and *Doe* in April 1973. Comparing the April 1973 to the June 1972 responses, however, we find little evidence of a shift, and hence we cannot dismiss the possibility that the August survey had more error in it than the June survey. We see minor increments in support for the pro-choice position until August 1976, when the percentage favoring that alternative reached almost sixty percent and the size of the undecided group almost doubled. The August 1977 survey almost completely restored the balance found in the April 1976 poll. Finally, the most recent survey indicates that the pro-choice position now has the strongest level of public support (sixty percent) that it has had since the *Roe* and *Doe* decisions. The Harris results thus suggest that there has been some incremental rise in support for the pro-choice position, but that the Court decisions did not set off a steady increase in support for legalized abortions. Particularly in light of the 1973 change in question wording (specifically citing the Court's decisions), we would have expected a much larger increase in support for the pro-choice position if there were a process of legitimization at work; furthermore, we would also have expected a more *continuous* growth of support for that position.

TABLE 1

TRENDS IN PUBLIC OPINION ON ABORTION LEGALIZATION, 1972-1979
(Harris Polls)

		Favor	Oppose	Not Sure
June	1972[a]	48%	43%	9%
August	1972[a]	42	46	12
April	1973[b]	52	41	7
May	1975[c]	54	38	8
April	1976[c]	54	39	7
August	1976[c]	59	28	13
August	1977[c]	53	40	7
March	1979[c]	60	37	3

Sources: DeBoer, *The Polls: Abortion*, 41 PUB. OPINION Q. 554 (1978); ABC
News—Harris Survey, March 5, 1979.[d]

[a]The question was: Do you favor or oppose allowing legalized abortions to
take place up to four months of pregnancy?

[b]The question was: The U.S. Supreme Court recently decided that state laws
which made it illegal for a woman to have an abortion up to three months of
pregnancy were unconstitutional, and that the decision on whether a woman
should have an abortion up to three months of pregnancy should be left to
the woman and her doctor to decide. In general, do you favor or oppose the
U.S. Supreme Court decision making abortions up to three months of
pregnancy legal?

[c]Slightly different question: In 1973, the U.S. Supreme Court decided that . . . .

[d]We wish to thank ABC-News, Washington, D.C., for making this release
available to us.

Further evidence on the possible impact of the Supreme
Court decisions on public attitudes toward the legalization of
abortion is provided in Table 2. In a series of annual national
surveys conducted from 1972 to 1977, the National Opinion Research Center (NORC), posed questions about the legalization of
abortion in six hypothetical situations. The results indicate
rather clearly that support for the legalization of abortion in each
of the six circumstances increased between the spring of 1972 and
the spring of 1973. In addition, the pattern of responses prevailing
just after the Court decisions in *Roe* and *Doe* continued in the
next four yearly surveys (1974 through 1977). After the Court
decisions, almost half of the public supported the most liberal
pro-choice option — legal abortion for a mother who wants no
more children or a woman who is unmarried and does not wish
to marry. Overall, the NORC series of questions suggests that the
Court decisions had an impact on public opinion on abortion and
that the public is very close to supporting legalization of abortion
in the most liberal of circumstances.

TABLE 2

TRENDS IN PUBLIC OPINION ON ABORTION, 1972-1977

Reason for Abortion	Response	1972	1973	1974	1975	1976	1977
Defect in the	Yes	74%	82%	83%	80%	82%	83%
baby	No	20	15	14	16	16	14
	DK	6	3	3	4	2	3
Mother wants	Yes	37	46	45	44	45	44
no more children	No	56	51	50	52	52	51
	DK	7	3	5	4	3	5
Mother's health	Yes	82	91	90	88	89	88
threatened	No	12	8	7	9	9	9
	DK	6	1	3	3	2	3
Family is	Yes	45	52	52	51	51	52
very poor	No	47	45	43	44	45	45
	DK	8	3	5	5	4	3
Pregnancy	Yes	73	81	83	80	80	80
result of rape	No	19	16	13	16	16	16
	DK	8	3	4	4	4	4
Mother wants	Yes	40	47	48	46	48	47
to remain single	No	52	49	48	49	48	48
	DK	8	4	4	5	4	5

Sources: National Opinion Research Center (NORC), *General Social Survey* 1972, 1973, 1974, 1975, 1976, 1977. This table compiles responses to the question: "Please tell me whether or not you think it should be possible for a pregnant woman to obtain a legal abortion if . . . . 1) there is a strong chance of serious defect in the baby? 2) she is married and does not want any more children? 3) the woman's health is seriously endangered by the pregnancy? 4) the family has a very low income and cannot afford any more children? 5) she became pregnant as a result of rape? 6) she is not married and does not want to marry the man?"

The Harris and NORC survey findings that the public became more pro-choice in the wake of the Court decisions are generally reinforced by a set of Gallup (American Institute of Public Opinion) surveys asking virtually identical questions to the Harris questions from 1969 until 1974. The Gallup surveys, however, suggest that the movement of the public toward legalizing abortion was already under way just before the announcement of the Court decisions in *Roe* and *Doe*. The three Gallup surveys were taken in November 1969, December 1972,[7] and March 1974.

7. AIPO 861 was administered in early December 1972, and not in January 1973, as is often noted.

These Gallup polls showed a sharp increase in support for the pro-choice position from 1969 to December 1972 (a month before the *Roe* and *Doe* decisions), and considerably less change from 1972 to 1974. In 1969, 40% of the respondents favored legal abortions, compared to 50% opposed and 10% with no opinion. The respective figures for late 1972 were 46%-45%-9%. There was hardly a clear plurality favoring the pro-choice position; the 1% margin could easily have been due to sampling error. However, there did seem to be a substantial increase in support for legal abortions across most major demographic variables. These data are presented in Table 3 below. In 1974, there was a barely noticeable shift of one percent toward the pro-choice position (46-47), with 9% unsure. There were few dramatic changes in support levels from 1972 to 1974, despite the fact that the Court decisions had "legitimized" legal abortions during the first three months of pregnancy.[8]

TABLE 3

TRENDS IN PUBLIC OPINION ON ABORTION LEGALIZATION, 1969-1974
Percent Favoring Pro-Choice Position in Gallup Polls

	11/69	12/72	3/74	Change: 1969-1972	Change: 1972-1974	Change: 1969-1974
National	40	46	47	+6	+1	+7
College	58	63	67	+5	+4	+9
High School	37	44	44	+7	0	+7
Grade School	31	30	25	−1	−5	−6
Under 30 years	46	55	55	+9	0	+9
30-49 years	39	48	44	+9	−4	+5
50 and over	38	39	43	+1	+4	+5
Protestants	40	45	48	+5	+3	+8
Catholics	31	36	32	+5	−4	+1
Men	40	49	51	+9	+2	+11
Women	40	44	43	+4	−1	+3

Sources: Gallup Opinion Index (February 1973 and April 1974)

---

8. A preliminary analysis of the responses in the Center for Political Studies (University of Michigan) 1972 and 1976 national surveys to an identical question on the circumstances under which legalized abortions should be permitted reveals a pattern of no aggregate change in public attitudes on abortion before and after the Supreme Court decisions. In both 1972 and 1976, about 41% preferred the pro-choice position under the circumstances posed in the survey. However, a cross-tabulation of the responses to the same question by members of a panel of individuals who were interviewed in both 1972 and 1976 indicates that a substantial amount of change in opinion on abortion legalization occurred in the period that included the Court decision. A total of 40% of the panel

Examining Table 3 in some greater detail, we find that between 1969 and 1974 there were marked increases in most demographic groups' support for abortion. The largest increase reported in that table is for men (+11%), compared to a very modest rise of 3% for women. Nine percent gains were registered for college-educated respondents and those under thirty, while Protestants increased their support by 8%. There was a drop in support only among respondents who had finished only grade school, while Catholic support did not change much in the aggregate over the entire time span. When we consider the relative magnitudes of the changes over the six-year period, we find that the most dramatic shifts occurred from 1969 to 1972, before the Court decisions. Only the age group of fifty and older and the college educated group registered gains of as much as 4% from 1972 to 1974; support among those with a grade school education dropped 5%, while that among the 30- to 49-year-olds, like that among Catholics, dropped 4%. These changes are relatively modest compared to the shifts found between 1969 and 1972. All of the increase in support among high school graduates and those under thirty came in the earlier period. Of the ten demographic groups considered in Table 2, eight had larger shifts (up or down) in the earlier period than in the later years. Thus, it does seem that the Court's decisions "followed the election returns" — or at least the poll data. Indeed, an amicus curiae brief was filed by pro-choice forces in the *Roe v. Wade* case, and Justice Brennan specifically cited changing public opinion in his concurring opinion.

The abortion issue did not play a major role in electoral politics in the late 1960s and early 1970s. In fact, the *Roe* and *Doe* decisions took many politicians by surprise. In following public opinion, however, the Court could not have been oblivious to the rising level of public support for abortion among the traditionally middle-of-the-road groups in the electorate. This "silent majority" (also called "the unpoor, the unblack, and the unyoung") became significantly more pro-choice in the early 1970s. Comparing the Gallup poll results in Table 3 with other demographic breakdowns from Harris polls in June 1972 and February 1973, we note that the greatest increases in support for the pro-choice position came from the following groups: younger voters (before the Court decisions); older voters (after the Court decisions); resi-

---

changed opinion on the proper circumstances under which legalized abortions should be permitted, with about half of the 40% moving in the pro-choice direction and the other half going in the pro-life direction.

dents of the Midwest and the South, and particularly residents of small towns; whites; middle-income workers; men; the college educated; Protestants and Jews; and Republican identifiers. Not all of these groups were part of any "silent majority"; nor were these groups the strongest supporters of legalized abortions. What is important about them is that they had the greatest *increases* in support. The poor, the blacks, the independent voters, the city dwellers, the suburbanites, the affluent, and those residing on the two coasts already had strong majorities supporting the pro-choice position and hence were not seriously affected by the Court's decisions. But the groups listed above were moving toward a new center on abortion policy and the Court not only followed national opinion, it stepped out considerably in front of it.

Two groups' opinions are particularly noteworthy: those of women and Catholics. The Gallup and Harris polls cited above indicate that men have been more supportive of abortion than women from the mid-1960s to the late 1970s.[9] On this issue, the women's movement does not reflect the views of most American women. Nevertheless, the gap between male and female support for at least some abortions seems to be narrowing. Women are now as likely as men to support abortions during the first trimester for many reasons that have been included in polls: when the life of the woman is endangered, when the pregnancy has been caused by rape or incest, when the woman might suffer physical damage from the pregnancy, when the woman's mental health is endangered, and when the woman cannot afford to support the child. Women are somewhat more supportive of abortion than men if there is a chance that the baby might be deformed. Yet most women maintain that life begins at conception and the differences between male and female beliefs on that issue are both large (15-20%) and stable over time.[10]

It is hardly surprising to note that Catholics have been less supportive of legalized abortions than most other demographic groups. The Gallup surveys summarized in Table 3 do show an increase in support for the pro-choice position between 1969 and 1972 of a magnitude equal to that found for Protestants. After *Roe*

---

9. *See* DeBoer, *The Polls: Abortion,* 41 PUB. OPINION Q. 553 (1978); Blake, *The Abortion Decisions: Judicial Review and Public Opinion,* in ABORTION: NEW DIRECTIONS FOR POLICY RESEARCH 51 (1977); Manier, *Abortion and Public Policy in the U.S.: A Dialectical Examination of Expert Opinion,* in ABORTION: NEW DIRECTIONS FOR POLICY RESEARCH 1 (1977); *Gallup Opinion Index,* July 1975, and April 1978.

10. Blake, *supra* note 9, at 65.

and *Doe,* many Catholics reverted to their former opposition, no doubt reinforced by the strong stand taken by the Church on the Court decisions. The bulk of Catholic opposition seems to come, not surprisingly, from Catholic women, whose objections to abortions have been strong and consistent.[11] Catholic men have become somewhat more pro-choice, but remain much less so than non-Catholic males. In 1974, white Catholic men were 12% less supportive of abortion whenever the parents do not want another child than white non-Catholic men. The gap between white Catholic and non-Catholic women was about the same (13%), but the level of opposition among both groups of white women was higher than it was for white men.

Judith Blake wonders whether what she calls a basically "conservative" public opinion on most aspects of abortion policy may undermine the legitimacy of the Court and of the pro-choice activists themselves.[12] The Court misrepresented public opinion, she maintains, undermining the legitimacy of the decision and of any efforts by the bureaucracy to implement it. While *Roe* and *Doe* clearly followed the *trend* in the early 1970s, they went far beyond the actual level of public support for abortion.

The abortion policies of *Roe* and *Doe* have not been legitimized. We have not seen substantial increases in public support for abortion after the Court decisions; instead, we have witnessed a hardening of positions by many who were opposed to abortions. The issues have become increasingly salient rather than resolved.

We have examined the patterns of support for and opposition to abortion within the national public, but we need to turn to variations across the fifty states. The states will be the major battlegrounds for abortion policy in the 1980s.

Variations in Abortion Opinions Among the States

To obtain a survey sample that would give results within 3% of the true population's opinions at least 95% of the time, we would need to interview approximately 1500 people. This would amount to interviewing 75,000 respondents to make generalizations about each of the fifty states. We must rule out such an approach on at least two grounds: (1) the cost would simply be prohibitive, and (2) even if we could gather the data, the number of cases obtained for the nation would be extremely difficult to

---

11. *Id.* at 67.
12. *Id.* at 80-81.

analyze (the computer time alone needed for analysis would be astronomical). It is important, nevertheless, to study abortion policies at the state level because that is where most decisions are made. We also want to study all fifty states, not just a subset. There do not appear to be any satisfactory criteria for selecting a "representative" sample of states. Virtually without fail, studies of selected states include the home state of the investigation — it may be interesting, but it rarely is representative.

In 1960, Pool, Abelson, and Popkin made the first attempt to estimate public opinion state by state from national surveys. Working under contract with the Democratic party, they dubbed themselves the "Simulmatics" project.[13] Their approach assumed that an individual's vote or attitude is basically determined by the social groups and political party with which that individual identifies. They created a set of 480 "voter-types," from which they constructed "synthetic electorates" for the states. Their approach assumed that the difference between Maine and New York is not truly a difference between inhabitants of the two states as such, but a difference in the proportions of different voter-types who make up each state.[14] Overall, the Simulmatics team had considerable success in predicting the outcome of the 1960 election and was only somewhat less successful in the Johnson landslide four years later.

These results led Weber and his associates to develop a more general computer simulation approach to estimate constituency opinion in the states.[15] The National Center for Health Statistics of the Public Health Service simultaneously developed a similar model in 1968 to create synthetic state estimates of disability from data in the National Health Survey.[16] Weber's model was similar to that of the Simulmatics project, although it used 960 different voter-types.[17] The initial simulations employed region, occupation, size of place of residence, race, sex, age, and religion as the demographic determinants of the voter-types. A revision of the simulation methodology for the 1970s replaced sex and

13. I. POOL, R. ABELSON, & S. POPKIN, CANDIDATES, ISSUES, AND STRATEGIES: A COM-PUTER SIMULATION OF THE 1960 AND 1964 ELECTIONS (1965).

14. *Id.* at 40-41.

15. R. WEBER, PUBLIC POLICY PREFERENCES IN THE STATES (1971); Weber, Hopkins, Mezey, & Munger, *Computer Simulation of State Electorates,* 36 PUB. OPINION Q. 549 (1972).

16. NATIONAL CENTER FOR HEALTH STATISTICS, SYNTHETIC STATE ESTIMATES OF DISABILITY (1968).

17. R. WEBER, *supra* note 15; Weber, Hopkins, Mezey & Munger, *supra* note 15.

occupation with education and income as demographic variables. Both versions used a simple additive cross-tabulation approach with a "control" for region. The simulations were validated with state data on education (earlier work) and election results (both simulations). Overall, the various statistical criteria in the validation were well met; the earlier work accounted for slightly more than half of the variance in state-level voting returns, while the revised simulation accounted for approximately 70% of the variation in election results.[18] The same method is then used to estimate public opinion within the states.

The simulation methodology has met with fairly widespread acceptance and has been used in work other than our own.[19] Here, we report state estimates of public opinion on abortion policy for 1969 and 1972 (see Table 4). The estimates are least reliable for Arizona, Idaho, Nevada, Utah, and Wyoming, which have large Mormon populations. We cannot estimate the division of Mormon opinions directly from the original survey data; hence, Mormons are included along with all other Protestants in the estimation of state-wide opinion. We have, however, refined estimates for the five states with large Mormon populations by making an assumption about the distribution of Mormon opinion on abortion legalization and then adjusting the opinion estimates, depending upon the size of the Mormon population in each state. We assumed that Mormons as a group are very strongly opposed to abortion.

---

18. Montjoy, Weber, & Maggiotto, Estimating Constituency Opinion (unpublished mimeo).

19. Hinckley, *Incumbency and the Presidential Vote in Senate Elections: Defining Parameters of Subpresidential Voting,* 64 AM. POLITICAL SCI. REV. 836 (1970); Sutton, *The States and the People: Measuring and Accounting for 'State Representativeness',* 5 POLITY 451 (1973); Rose, *National and Local Forces in State Politics: The Implications of Multi-Level Policy Analysis,* 67 AM. POLITICAL SCI. REV. 1162 (1973); Hopkins, *Opinion Publics and Support for Public Policy in the American States,* 18 AM. J. POLITICAL SCI. 167 (1974); Fry, *An Examination of the Relationship Between Selected Electoral Characteristics and State Redistributive Efforts,* 18 AM. J. POLITICAL SCI. 421 (1974); Sullivan & Minns, *Ideological Distance Between Candidates: An Empirical Examination,* 20 AM. J. POLITICAL SCI. 439 (1976); A. SCHNEIDER, OPINIONS AND POLICIES IN THE AMERICAN STATES: THE ROLE OF POLITICAL CHARACTERISTICS 3 (Sage Professional Papers in American Politics 1976); Cook, *Public Opinion and Federal Judicial Policy,* 21 AM. J. POLITICAL SCI. 247 (1977); Kritzer, *Political Correlates of the Behavior of Federal District Judges: A 'Best Case' Analysis,* 40 J. POL. 25 (1978); Erikson, *Constituency Opinion and Congressional Behavior: A Reexamination of the Miler Stokes Representation Data,* 22 AM. J. POLITICAL SCI. 511 (1978). Sutton & Wilson, *Opinion-Policy Congruence: State Regimes and State Regime Differences,* 5 POL. METHODOLOGY 127 (1978).

TABLE 4

ESTIMATED POLICY PREFERENCES BY STATE ON ABORTION ON DEMAND IN FIRST
THREE MONTHS OF PREGNANCY (1969 AND 1972)

	1969			1972		
State	Favor %	Oppose %	No Opinion %	Favor %	Oppose %	No Opinion %
ALABAMA	.247	.667	.085	.272	.633	.096
ALASKA	.532	.364	.103	.695	.261	.045
ARIZONA	.478	.396	.128	.600	.341	.060
ARKANSAS	.231	.677	.092	.250	.649	.102
CALIFORNIA	.533	.354	.114	.669	.277	.055
COLORADO	.516	.369	.116	.657	.286	.057
CONNECTICUT	.447	.441	.113	.489	.415	.096
DELAWARE	.449	.441	.110	.495	.402	.103
FLORIDA	.402	.484	.114	.349	.532	.119
GEORGIA	.252	.666	.081	.284	.622	.094
HAWAII	.508	.365	.127	.645	.306	.050
IDAHO	.406	.473	.122	.517	.416	.067
ILLINOIS	.398	.492	.110	.403	.514	.082
INDIANA	.390	.497	.113	.401	.507	.092
IOWA	.386	.500	.114	.395	.511	.093
KANSAS	.395	.493	.111	.408	.499	.093
KENTUCKY	.338	.530	.133	.280	.595	.124
LOUISIANA	.216	.693	.091	.237	.679	.084
MAINE	.442	.442	.116	.490	.404	.106
MARYLAND	.422	.477	.101	.388	.505	.108
MASSACHUSETTS	.433	.444	.113	.478	.425	.097
MICHIGAN	.380	.509	.112	.388	.526	.086
MINNESOTA	.384	.503	.113	.395	.517	.088
MISSISSIPPI	.223	.686	.091	.232	.669	.099
MISSOURI	.379	.502	.119	.375	.530	.094
MONTANA	.474	.402	.124	.602	.335	.064
NEBRASKA	.387	.500	.113	.396	511	.093

TABLE 4

ESTIMATED POLICY PREFERENCES BY STATE ON ABORTION ON DEMAND IN FIRST
THREE MONTHS OF PREGNANCY (1969 AND 1972)

	1969			1972		
State	Favor %	Oppose %	No Opinion %	Favor %	Oppose %	No Opinion %
NEVADA	.494	.396	.111	.635	.312	.053
NEW HAMPSHIRE	.442	.445	.113	.494	.407	.099
NEW JERSEY	.472	.418	.109	.514	.392	.094
NEW MEXICO	.459	.407	.134	.583	.360	.057
NEW YORK	.525	.374	.102	.556	.349	.095
NORTH CAROLINA	.358	.514	.128	.302	.574	.124
NORTH DAKOTA	.347	.531	.122	.346	.560	.094
OHIO	.398	.491	.111	.408	.505	.086
OKLAHOMA	.399	.485	.115	.358	.523	.120
OREGON	.490	.388	.122	.617	.317	.066
PENNSYLVANIA	.459	.427	.114	.498	.401	.101
RHODE ISLAND	.414	.467	.120	.452	.456	.092
SOUTH CAROLINA	.350	.518	.133	.286	.590	.124
SOUTH DAKOTA	.353	.527	.120	.351	.551	.098
TENNESSEE	.365	.506	.129	.309	.567	.124
TEXAS	.393	.487	.120	.354	.534	.112
UTAH	.297	.592	.111	.391	.550	.059
VERMONT	.419	.465	.115	.466	.428	.106
VIRGINIA	.386	.496	.117	.343	.539	.118
WASHINGTON	.501	.381	.118	.638	.300	.062
WEST VIRGINIA	.423	.443	.135	.450	.432	.118
WISCONSIN	.373	.510	.117	.379	.534	.087
WYOMING	.477	.404	.118	.608	.330	.062

Sources: AIPO 793 (November, 1969) and AIPO 861 (December, 1972). The
question wording was: "Would you favor or oppose a law which
would permit a woman to go to a doctor to end pregnancy at any
time during the first three months?"

As was true for the national public opinion data on abortion policy presented in Table 3, the state public opinion estimates in Table 4 indicate that support for abortion increased in most states between 1969 and 1972. In some states, particularly in the West and the Northeast, the increase was fairly dramatic. In other states, such as those in the Midwest and Deep South, very little movement occurred in either direction. Only in some of the Border South states was there any decline in support for abortion. Less than half the states showed plurality support for abortion in either year, but the number of states supporting abortion legalization increased from 16 in 1969 to 22 in 1972. And no state that supported abortion in 1969 showed less support in 1972.

Abortion Policy and Politics

The *Roe* and *Doe* decisions did not produce a consensus supporting the new "law of the land." Instead, they provoked more activity by both supporters and opponents of abortion. A constitutional amendment prohibiting abortions has been proposed, but has not made much progress. The *Roe* and *Doe* decisions did force virtually all states to reconsider their abortion policies. With outright prohibition of abortions no longer a feasible alternative, the legislatures had to choose among a more limited range of options. The rather complex set of statutes that emerge from these restrictions has defied easy classification. We are still working on scaling procedures to reduce this complexity so that generalizations can be made across the states.

Once abortions could not be banned outright, the center of debate changed. Many abortions for poor women were funded by Medicare and Medicaid programs; abortion opponents sought to cut off such funding, and several states have taken steps in that direction. The fight to deny federal funds for abortions has occupied a great deal of time in the last two Congresses, stalling appropriations bills for the Department of Health, Education, and Welfare for months. The pro-life groups lobbied strenuously on behalf of the efforts of Representatives Henry Hyde (R., Ill.) and Edward Beard (D., R.I.) to forbid federal funding of abortions, and their message was clearly heard in the House of Representatives. The Senate adopted a considerably more pro-choice position, and prolonged periods of stalemate led to a series of compromises that permit continued federal funding for many abortions.

What effect has lobbying had on legislative policy? No causal connection is discernible, but there are some indications that these groups have not been as effective as one would expect. Maris Vinovskis and his associates studied two proposals for abortion law reform and one bill about contraceptive information to develop an index of legislative voting on population policies for the lower house of Massachusetts. They found in analyzing roll calls for the 1970 and 1971 sessions that the legislator's religious affiliation and index of liberalism on other issues were the most important determinants of liberalism on population policies.[20] Richardson and Fox, in two studies of a Western Mountain state, report that the religion of legislators was the most powerful predictor of voting on abortion, dwarfing all of the demographic variables used as surrogates for constituency opinion and all other traits of the members; as one might expect, Mormons and Catholics were the more pro-life, while Protestants and Jews tended to be pro-choice.[21] At the national level, a study by Vinovskis indicates that demographic features of the constituency display very weak relationships to legislators' voting on abortion policies in the House of Representatives.[22] Instead, the members' general liberalism is the strongest, and their religion the second strongest, determinant of House voting on abortion funding. Furthermore, a study by *Congressional Quarterly* indicates that members from heavily Catholic constituencies are not significantly more likely to vote against abortion funding than those from other constituencies; nor is there any strong concern for the political consequences of voting one's conscience.[23] Our own conversations with observers both on and off Capitol Hill (including members) also suggest that the decision on abortion funding is an intensely personal one and is not easily altered by the lobbying of groups on either side.

If the legislative process is not as susceptible to interest-group pressure as we might have expected on such a volatile issue,

20. Vinovskis, Jones, & New, *Determinants of Legislative Voting Behavior on Population Policy: An Analysis of the Massachusetts House of Representatives in 1970 and 1971*, in POPULATION POLICYMAKING IN THE AMERICAN STATES 239 (1974).

21. Richardson & Fox, *Religious Affiliation as a Predictor of Voting Behavior on Abortion Reform Legislation*, 11 J. SCI. STUD. RELIGION 347 (1972); Richardson & Fox, *A Longitudinal Study of the Influence of Selected Variables on Legislators' Voting Behavior on Abortion Reform Legislation*, 14 J. SCI. STUD. RELIGION 159 (1975).

22. Vinovskis, *Interview on Abortion Politics*, 1978, ZERO POPULATION GROWTH NATL. REP. (August, 1978) at 4-5.

23. *Abortion: How Members Voted in 1977*, 36 CONG. Q. WEEKLY REP. 258 (1978).

can these groups make their voices heard in elections? Pro-life groups have become increasingly active in electoral politics in recent years, endorsing some candidates and working for the defeat of others. Such groups have been given responsibility for the defeat of Senator Dick Clark (D., Iowa) by a relative political neophyte, Roger Jepsen, in 1978. Other defeats have occurred in primaries, most notably the bids of Representative Donald Fraser for the Democratic nomination for Senator in Minnesota and State Senator Minnette Doderer for the Democratic nomination for Lieutenant Governor in Iowa in 1978. All three candidates had been heavy favorites before the elections. There were claims of pro-life victories in other, less certain races as well. However, as with Environmental Action, which biennially selects the most vulnerable "Dirty Dozen" in the Congress as targets for defeat, it is difficult to determine how much contribution the pro-life groups make in any specific election.[24] The fourth-place showing of the new Right-to-Life party in the state of New York, dislodging the Liberals from that position, was perhaps one of the most remarkable achievements of the 1978 campaign: the party had not contested state elections before and had only one candidate running in 1978, and the pro-life position had been embraced just as warmly by the third-place Conservative party. The new party's strength was not sufficient, however, to deny reelection to Governor Hugh Carey, a Catholic supporter of state funding for abortions.

One should not discount the effects that pro-choice groups might have had in recent elections, although they are not as well organized or as electorally active as the pro-life groups. It can hardly be denied that the pro-choice groups (both on their own and through other organizations in the women's movement) considerably helped the successful reelection bids of Carey and Indiana Senator Birch Bayh, the latter in 1974.

In many respects the abortion controversy of the 1970s is similar to the busing disputes of the late 1960s and early 1970s. Both the pro-life and anti-busing movements began in reaction to decisions of the Supreme Court. Both activated many people

---

24. Representative James Cleveland, one of the "Dirty Dozen" in 1978, has filed a suit against Environmental Action, claiming that there are at least 100 members of Congress with environmental voting records similar to his. The New Hampshire Republican charged that he was selected because he appeared to be electorally vulnerable (he won anyway) and that the environmental lobby could thus claim a "victory" if he lost, regardless of what might have contributed to the outcome.

who previously had been at the periphery of either electoral or group politics. The two movements each caught on quickly and developed a strong national base. And both groups aroused strong sentiments through the populist appeals of politicians. The anti-busing movement rapidly waned in strength; today, it is virtually nonexistent. Is the pro-life movement ultimately headed in the same direction?

It is difficult to give an answer to the question. For all of the similarities in the groups (including the probability of a high degree of overlapping support), some critical differences remain. While both groups have been successful in some electoral contests and neither has been particularly successful in ousting *incumbents* they have opposed, the anti-busing movement depended much more heavily upon electoral politics than has the pro-life movement. In one sense, the political fortunes of the anti-busing movement rose and fell with those of former Governor George C. Wallace of Alabama. Relatively few other Democrats followed Wallace's line on busing and many of the Republicans who did so lost office in the Watergate landslide of 1974. Busing was no longer a political issue after the paralysis of Wallace in 1972 and the defeat of the anti-busing Republicans in 1974. The pro-life movement has become more active in electoral politics, but its real strength to date has been organizational. The anti-busing movement had a dispersed constituency; if there was no busing in an area, or if busing had won general civic acceptance (as in Jacksonville and Seattle), there was no anti-busing movement to speak of. The busing issue also proved to be of limited appeal as a long-standing concern. Eventually, even the citizens of Boston and Louisville realized that local politics and even school board politics were based upon more fundamental issues than busing. That "law of the land" might not be popular, but at least it is generally accepted.

The pro-life movement, on the other hand, developed in communities all across the country. The support of many religious denominations not only added to the legitimacy of the movement, but also provided critical organizational resources. Perhaps the linkage with religious denominations has been the reason why the pro-life movement, unlike the anti-busing crusade, has not been dominated by a single political leader or even a group of leaders. Neither Hyde nor Beard has become a national political figure. In fact, Beard's tactics in Congress almost got him into serious trouble with President Carter. Although Carter wanted to curb government financing of abortions, he also wanted a Health, Education, and Welfare appropriations bill passed and chastised Beard for his narrow view. Beard's opponent used this episode quite effectively — even in a heavily Catholic and pro-life political district — and almost pulled off a major upset. The Congressman later apologized and promised to become a more "responsible" legislator.[25] The example of Beard's close call with his own electorate may suggest that voters are reluctant to put single-issue candidates into office, even while the same voters organize into a multiplicity of such groups to promote policies.

If this perspective is correct, it appears that the pro-life groups may face a most interesting paradox. The best chance of success for these groups is to work through organizations designed to affect policy formation, while the most dangerous course is through continued electoral action. The development of a national Right-to-Life party might isolate the movement from its support in the Democratic and Republican parties and might encourage leaders to step forward as potential heirs to the Wallace mantle of "new right" populism. But the paradox is that the pro-life groups have had only limited success in the policy-making arena and have been most successful in some electoral situations. In order to have greater policy success, the movement might well deduce that it should step up its electoral activities to replace pro-choice legislators. Such a strategy would seem to have much potential for disrupting the bipartisan support the organizations have developed in Congress and many statehouses, and thus would probably ensure the pro-life movement a fate similar to that of the anti-busing movement. Whether the pro-life movement adopts that strategy may well determine the future relationship of the abortion issue to the more traditional economic and social issues that divide the nation.

---

25. *Same Face, New Man Returning to Capitol,* Providence Evening Bulletin, Nov. 8, 1978.

THE POLITICS OF ABORTION IN THE HOUSE OF REPRESENTATIVES IN 1976

Maris A. Vinovskis* †

The halls of the United States Congress have reverberated throughout our history with noisy and emotional debates over divisive issues. Slavery, voting rights for women, and military involvement in Vietnam typify the problems that have frequently made political service difficult. Most representatives and senators are pragmatic politicians who feel very uncomfortable with any issue that divides the electorate into widely divergent factions that are unwilling or unable to compromise. Such issues can disrupt the normal conciliatory proceedings of Congress, creating hostility and bitterness among people who usually expect politeness, if not friendship, from their political opponents. After the Supreme Court legalized abortions in January 1973, members of the House and Senate found themselves with another volatile issue, one so fundamental that it drives antagonists to brand each other "murderers" and "baby-killers."

The battle over federal funds for abortions and the attempts to pass a constitutional amendment to prohibit all abortions have become annual events that most members of Congress privately dread but publicly welcome. As "pro-life" and "pro-choice" constituents descend upon their elected officials each year, representatives are forced to face an issue that has no easy legislative solution.[1] Despite the intensity and disruptiveness of these con-

---

* Associate Professor, Department of History, University of Michigan; Associate Research Scientist, Center for Political Studies, Institute for Social Research, University of Michigan. B.A. 1965, Wesleyan University; M.A. 1966, Ph.D. 1975, Harvard University. — Ed.

† Funds for this project were provided by a fellowship from the Rockefeller Foundation. The analysis and opinions expressed in this paper are, of course, solely my own and do not reflect in any way the position or the views of the Foundation. I am also indebted to Sally Brower and Mary Vinovskis for preparing and programming the data.

Portions of this analysis were presented at the annual meeting of the National Abortion Rights Action League in Washington, D.C., February 1978 and at the National Right to Life Convention in St. Louis, Missouri, July 1978.

1. The choice of words used to describe the opposing sides of the abortion debate is in itself controversial. For example, the use of the term "pro-life" to designate those who are against abortions is resented by their opponents because it implies that those who favor abortions are "anti-life." Rather than taking sides on this matter, I shall use the terms commonly utilized by each faction for themselves. Thus, those groups opposing abortions will be referred to as "pro-life" while those favoring abortions will be designated as "pro-choice."

frontations, there have been no thorough and independent analyses of this phenomenon. Instead, most information on the abortion controversy in Congress has come from the understandably biased pens of the activists on both sides. Representatives and other policy makers are forced to make their decisions without fully understanding the political dynamics of the issue.

This Article will try to remedy that lack of analysis by investigating the enactment by the House of restrictions on federal abortion funding. I will first describe the debates that preceded three important votes on abortion; I will then analyze those votes using multivariate statistical analysis.

I. The Controversy over the Hyde Amendment

During the debates on abortion in the late 1960s and early 1970s, Congress tried to remain aloof. In part, this reflected a feeling that abortion was a state matter and that federal intervention was unwarranted. Congress did declare in 1970 that abortions were not to be considered a form of family planning under Title X of the Public Health Service Act. No efforts were made, however, to prohibit the use of federal Medicaid funds for abortions in states, such as New York, with liberalized abortion laws.

The Supreme Court's sweeping decision in *Roe v. Wade*[2] persuaded pro-life activists to shift their efforts from the state to the federal level, and in particular to Congress. Legislators introduced bills in both houses of the 93d Congress to promote the pro-life position, including proposals to permit individuals and institutions to refuse to perform abortions on grounds of conscience, to restrict federal funding of abortions, and to amend the Constitution to prohibit abortions. While a few of these efforts succeeded (individuals and institutions were exempted from performing abortions if abortions conflict with their consciences), most of these bills failed to pass either in the House or in the Senate, and amendments died in House-Senate conference. For example, the Senate passed a ban on the use of Labor-HEW funds for abortions except when "such abortions are necessary to save the life of the mother," but the House rejected it. In general, senators in the 93d Congress were more willing than representa-

---

On the early developments in the efforts to liberalize abortion laws in the United States, see sources cited in Vinovskis, *Abortion and the Presidential Election of 1976: A Multivariate Analysis of Voting Behavior*, 77 Mich. L. Rev. 1750, 1751 n.4 (1979).

2. 410 U.S. 113 (1973).

tives to restrict or prohibit abortions, though most members of both chambers were disinclined to expend much time or energy on either side of the issue.[3]

As the 94th Congress convened early in 1975, few observers expected it to enact any additional abortion legislation. The House seemed unwilling to budge from its determined opposition to restrictions on federal abortion funding and to a constitutional amendment limiting abortions. Most pro-life activists expected the Senate to lead the fight to restrict abortions, but early in the session those hopes were dashed. On April 10, 1975, the Senate reversed its position of the previous year by voting 54 to 36 to table Senator Dewey F. Bartlett's (R.-Oklahoma) amendment to bar federal funding of abortions under the Social Security Act.[4]

Although 1975 was a rather disappointing year for the pro-life movement, its supporters looked forward to the federal and state campaigns in 1976 to elect officials more favorable to a constitutional amendment against abortions than those currently in office. The decision of the National Conference of Catholic Bishops to organize pro-life activity in each congressional district stimulated new efforts within Congress itself to force each senator and representative to take a public stand on abortion. Though most pro-life leaders still had little hope of passing a constitutional amendment in either the House or the Senate in 1976, they were determined to obtain at least a roll-call vote on abortion in both chambers.[5]

The first major confrontation occurred in the Senate. On April 28, 1976, Senator Jesse A. Helms (R.-North Carolina) introduced a constitutional amendment to guarantee unborn children the right to life. In order to overcome the unwillingness of the Senate Judiciary Committee to report out any anti-abortion constitutional amendments, he introduced his measure as a Senate Resolution (S.J. Res. 178) — "With respect to the right of life guaranteed in this Constitution, every human being, subject to the jurisdiction of the United States, or of any State, shall be deemed, from the moment of fertilization, to be a person and entitled to the right of life."[6] Following a bitter and emotional

---

3. On the developments in the 93d Congress, see Rosoff, *Support of Abortion Political Suicide?*, 17 FAM. PLAN. PERSPEC. 13 (1975).

4. 121 CONG. REC. 9823 (1975).

5. On the efforts of the pro-life groups in the 1976 elections, see Vinovskis, *supra* note 1.

6. 122 CONG. REC. 11,556 (1976).

debate, the Senate voted, 47 to 40, to table the Helms resolution.[7] The pro-life Senators had suffered another defeat, but they were elated by the unexpected closeness of the vote. Eleven senators who had voted to table the Bartlett amendment the previous year, including such prominent leaders as Senator Edward M. Kennedy (D.-Massachusetts), now voted against tabling. One pro-life observer put it:

> A SENATE "DEFEAT" THAT WAS A STUNNING VICTORY, a whole new political situation, with all the pro-abortion contenders knocked out — a growing and organized abortion vote — it all adds up to the best news anti-abortion Americans have had since the nationwide struggle against abortion-on-demand started more than three years ago.[8]

Following the success of the pro-life forces in obtaining a roll-call vote on abortion in the Senate, they tried to bring a similar measure to the floor of the House. As in the Senate, their attempts to offer an anti-abortion constitutional amendment were stymied whenever they were referred to one of the committees,[9] so pro-life representatives sought alternative means of getting their colleagues recorded on a roll-call abortion vote. Despite rumors that pro-life representatives might try to attach an abortion amendment to one of the appropriations bills, observers were startled when, on June 24, Representative Henry J. Hyde (R.-Illinois) offered an amendment to the Labor-HEW appropriations bill for fiscal 1977:

> None of the funds appropriated under this Act shall be used to pay for abortions or to promote or encourage abortions.[10]

In support of his amendment, Hyde relied on the standard pro-life arguments. He contended that a human being is created at conception, a human that has at least the right to life.

> I think in the final analysis, you must determine whether or not the unborn person is human. If you think it is animal or vegeta-

7. Id. at 11,580.
8. Lifeletter, May 11, 1976, at 1 (emphasis original).
9. Throughout the debates on the Hyde amendment, pro-choice representatives argued that an appropriations bill was not the proper vehicle for dealing with abortion; instead, they suggested that the matter be resolved in a debate and vote on a constitutional amendment to prohibit abortions. Most of these pro-choice advocates, however, were quite willing to see the anti-abortion constitutional amendments bottled up in the Subcommittee on Civil and Constitutional Rights and made no effort to bring those measures to the floor in order to provide a focus for the abortion debate other than the Labor-HEW appropriations bill.
10. 122 CONG. REC. 20,410 (1976).

ble then, of course, it is disposable like an empty beer can to be crushed and thrown out with the rest of the trash.

. . . .

> And if you believe that human life is deserving of due process of law — of equal protection of the laws, then you cannot in logic and conscience help fund the execution of these innocent defenseless human lives.[11]

While some representatives opposing the Hyde amendment defended all abortions, others stressed the unfairness of denying abortions only to poor women. Representative Daniel J. Flood (D.-Pennsylvania), Chairman of the Labor-HEW Appropriations Subcommittee and a supporter of a constitutional amendment to prohibit abortions, pleaded with his colleagues to reject the Hyde amendment:

> I oppose this amendment, and I will tell you why. Listen. This is blatantly discriminatory; that is why.
> The Members do not like that? Of course they do not. It does not prohibit abortion. No, it does not prohibit abortion. It prohibits abortion for poor people. That is what it does. That is a horse of a different rolling stone. That is what it does. It does not require any change in the practice of the middle-income and the upper-income people. Oh, no. They are able to go to their private practitioners and get the service done for a fee. But, it does take away the option from those of our citizens who must rely on medicaid — and other public programs for medical care.[12]

The argument that the Hyde amendment discriminates against poor women was to be repeated through the debates in Congress. Even the supporters of the Hyde amendment acknowledged that it was not the best way to deal with the issue, but they felt it was the only workable strategy at that time — especially since the pro-choice forces refused to allow a constitutional amendment to be placed before the full House for a vote. As Representative Robert E. Bauman (R.-Maryland) put it:

> The gentleman [from Pennsylvania] raises an interesting, but I think answerable, point on the grounds that this would discriminate against poor people. The answer is that we have not been able to pass a constitutional amendment that would permit the right to life, regardless of poverty or wealth. But I do not understand that the child of a poor parent has any less right to live than the child of a rich parent. If we could protect the right to life for all children, we would do it. But the fact of the matter is, under

---

11. *Id.*
12. *Id.*

medicaid and other programs that are financed in this bill, the Federal Government has been paying for more than 300,000 abortions annually at a cost of $40 to $50 million.

I think the unborn children whose lives are being snuffed out, even though they may not be adults have a right to live, too, regardless of the mistaken and immoral Supreme Court decision. I do not think the taxpayers of the United States have any obligation to permit their money to be used in this manner for federally financed abortions. That is the only issue here today.[13]

Given the highly emotional nature of this issue, one might have expected a prolonged and bitter debate over abortion. Yet the initial discussions in the House over the Hyde amendment were unusually short. Perhaps this reflected the fact that many representatives were caught off-guard and were unprepared to join in the debate. Or perhaps most representatives were reluctant to take a strong public position on abortion in an election year, when few of them expected the Hyde amendment to require a roll-call vote, much less to pass.[14] But the popular expectations were wrong. By a vote of 207 to 167, the House accepted the Hyde amendment — a stunning and unexpected victory for the pro-life movement. Later that same day, Representative Bella S. Abzug (D.-New York) tried to reverse the earlier decision because she claimed that "[a] good number of Members who voted on this amendment indicated to us that they had not really understood the depth or the breadth of this amendment."[15] But by a vote of 199 to 165, the House upheld the Hyde amendment.

The stunned pro-choice groups regrouped and concentrated their lobbying on the Senate. The pro-life organizations, sensing victory, redoubled their efforts and besieged the senators with telephone calls and telegrams. On June 28, the struggle reached its climax. Senator Robert W. Packwood (R.-Oregon) moved to delete the Hyde amendment from the House version of the Labor-HEW appropriations bill.[16] After an attempt to table Packwood's motion failed by a vote of 55 to 27, the Senate voted 57 to 28 to strike the Hyde amendment from the bill. Compared to the nar-

---

13. *Id.* at 20,411.

14. When Representative Bauman had tried to attach an amendment to the Labor-HEW appropriations bill for fiscal 1976 that would have ended federal funding of abortions, he was defeated on a voice vote. When he called for a recorded vote on the issue, he failed to muster the necessary 20 votes to obtain a roll-call vote. Planned Parenthood-World Population Washington Memo, July 11, 1975, at 2-3.

15. 122 CONG. REC. 20,423 (1976).

16. *Id.* at 20,881.

row pro-choice victory over the Helms constitutional amendment two months earlier, the defeat of the Hyde amendment was much more decisive. In part, the larger margin reflected the unwilling-ness of some senators to accept the language that would not have permitted federal funds for abortions when the life of the mother was endangered. The stage was now set for a confrontation be-tween representatives and senators over a politically and emo-tionally explosive issue that most members of both chambers privately wished had never arisen during an election year.

Congress had faced a similar situation in 1974. In that year, however, it was the Senate that had attached an anti-abortion amendment to the Labor-HEW appropriations bill and the House that had rejected it. When the House-Senate conferees met, they had agreed to drop the amendment and rationalized their deci-sion by stating that

> an annual appropriation bill is an improper vehicle for such a controversial and far-reaching legislative provision whose implica-tions and ramifications are not clear, whose constitutionality has been challenged, and on which no hearings have been held. The rules and traditions of both the House and the Senate militate against the inclusion of legislative language in appropriations bills.[17]

Yet 1976 was quite different from 1974. Abortion had rarely been mentioned in congressional campaigns in 1974, but it was highly visible in both the presidential and congressional contests in 1976.[18] In the summer and fall of 1976, most politicians were uncertain about the importance of the abortion issue to voters.[19] Furthermore, during the deliberations of the 93d Congress, mem-bers did not hear much about abortion from their constituents; members of the 94th Congress, however, were bombarded with mail and petitions from both sides.[20] The House-Senate conferees in 1976 no longer felt they could duck the abortion issue by simply arguing that such a rider was not germane to an appropriations bill.

The House-Senate conferees were under great pressure to settle their differences on the Labor-HEW appropriations bill for fiscal 1977 quickly, as fiscal 1976 was about to end and new funds

---

17. H.R. REP. No. 1489, 93d Cong., 2d Sess. 20 (1974).

18. Rosoff, *supra* note 3.

19. Vinovskis, *supra* note 1.

20. During the fall of 1976, I visited the offices of 25 representatives and discussed the abortion issue with the congressmen or their staffs. Most of them indicated that their mail from the pro-life forces was much heavier than that from the pro-choice side.

would be needed to keep these agencies in operation. Nevertheless, neither the House nor the Senate conferees felt that they could back down, since their colleagues were afraid of antagonizing supporters over the abortion issue just before the election. Therefore, though the conferees could resolve seventy-five of the seventy-six amendments in disagreement between them, they were unable to settle their differences on abortion; as a result, the Hyde amendment was sent back to both chambers for reconsideration.

When the House took up the Labor-HEW appropriations bill on August 10, it readily accepted the conference report by a vote of 279 to 100.[21] Though some thought that the House might recede from its insistence on the Hyde amendment, it soon became evident that the pro-life camp would not only maintain its majority, but would even increase it. Representative Flood, for instance, reversed his previous opposition to the Hyde amendment:

> I was concerned that this amendment might be interpreted as prohibiting medicaid funds from being used to terminate pregnancies, which might be necessary in some cases to save a mother's life. This would be unfair to people who are unable to pay the very high costs of medical care which prevail today. I have been persuaded that this problem would not be as serious as it might appear, and that the therapeutic and medical services that might be necessary and advised could be paid for by State, local, or private funds.[22]

While pro-life speakers tried to minimize the Hyde amendment's termination of federal funds for poor women whose lives were endangered by their pregnancies, the pro-choice spokesmen emphasized it. When Representative Joel M. Pritchard (R.-Washington) moved to concur with the Senate version of the Labor-HEW appropriations bill, which did not restrict federal funds for abortions, he appealed to those representatives who favored abortions in some instances but were politically afraid of the pro-lifers in their districts.

> Then there is a third group in this House who, I believe, think that abortions are all right in some cases, but they are very, very worried about voting at this time, just several months before the election.
> Some may feel that this vote will not be recorded or will not be known. Even though they admit that in their districts the ma-

21. 122 CONG. REC. 26,780 (1976).
22. Id. at 26,782.

jority of people support abortion and allowing women to make this decision — they also realize that a very hard and very skillful minority is working very hard — which is their right — and they are afraid that they will be punished at the polls.[23]

Following a much longer and more spirited debate than the one two months before, the House defeated Pritchard's motion by a vote of 223 to 150. The 73-vote difference on Pritchard's motion signaled a sizable increase in House support for the pro-life position and made any attempts to compromise the issue with the Senate more difficult. On August 25, however, the Senate rejected the Hyde amendment and insisted on its own version of the bill by a vote of 53 to 35.[24] Nevertheless, pro-choice strength in the Senate eroded, as five senators switched from a June 28 pro-choice vote to an August 28 pro-life vote.

With the House and Senate again deadlocked, the conferees reconvened to seek a compromise that would be acceptable to a majority in both houses. The stalemate was finally broken when Representative Silvio O. Conte (R.-Massachusetts) persuaded his fellow House conferees to accept a revised version of the amendment, one he hoped would appease the senators:

> None of the funds contained in this Act shall be used to perform abortions except where the life of the mother would be endangered if the fetus were carried to term.[25]

At first, the senators were reluctant to accept Conte's wording. Senator Edward W. Brooke (R.-Massachusetts), one of the leaders of the pro-choice effort in the Senate, offered several changes to weaken the Conte proposal even further. But Brooke's efforts were in vain and the Senate conferees accepted Conte's amendment by a vote of 10 to 5.[26] On September 16, the House took up the Labor-HEW appropriations bill again. Since both houses had already accepted the conference report on everything except the Hyde amendment, the only issue before the House was the disagreement over abortion. Representative Flood urged his colleagues to accept the compromise wording drafted by Conte as the only reasonable way to settle the impasse and enact the $56 billion appropriations bill for fiscal 1977, whose start was only

---

23. *Id.*

24. *Id.* at 27,680.

25. *Id.* at 30,895.

26. For details of the struggles among the House-Senate conferees, see Planned Parenthood-World Population Washington Memo, Aug. 27, 1976, at 1-2; National Right to Life News, October 1976, at 12.

fifteen days away.[27] The House ultimately accepted the conference report by a vote of 256 to 114.[28] The next day, the Senate
concurred by a vote of 47 to 21.[29] Thus, the long and bitter battle
over abortion had finally ended with a major victory for the pro-
life movement.

II. PATTERNS OF VOTING ON THE HYDE AMENDMENT IN THE HOUSE OF REPRESENTATIVES

Throughout the debate over the Hyde amendment in 1976,
analysts of Capitol Hill maneuvering tried to account for its unexpected success in the House of Representatives. Their explanations of the voting behavior of the representatives were often col-
ored by their own views on abortion. For example, while pro-
choice analysts emphasized the importance of religion in determining a representative's vote, with Catholic representatives allegedly spearheading the antiabortion effort, pro-lifers denied the
importance of religion and pointed to the Protestant representatives who supported the Hyde amendment.

One reason for the difficulty in assessing the relative importance of various factors in congressional voting is that all of the
analyses of the Hyde amendment have relied on a simple cross-
tabulation of the data. These analyses calculate the percentage
of Republicans and Democrats voting for the Hyde amendment
or the proportion of Roman Catholics, Protestants, and Jews supporting it, but they do not try to estimate the relative importance
of each of these factors after controlling for the effects of the other
characteristics of the representatives and their constituents.[30] By
failing to use multivariate techniques, most studies of congressional voting on the Hyde amendment are too limited to provide
an accurate explanation of the voting pattern.

In this analysis I examine the determinants of representatives' votes on the Hyde amendment on June 24, August 10, and
September 16, 1976. The dependent variable in each case is
whether a representative supported or opposed the Hyde amendment on that particular roll-call vote.[31] To compute independent

27. 122 CONG. REC. 30,895-96 (1976).
28. *Id.* at 30,901.
29. *Id.* at 30,997.
30. For example, see Eccles, *Abortion: How Members Voted in 1977,* CONG. Q., Feb. 4, 1978, at 258.
31. In order to include as many representatives on each roll-call vote as possible, those who supported the Hyde amendment included not only those who voted for it, but

variables, we assembled data on about 100 different factors for each representative, but narrowed our final set of predictors to eleven. Four of the independent variables describe the representatives' personal characteristics: age, education, sex, and religion. Three variables describe representatives' political lives: their party affiliation, the political situation in their district as of October 9, 1976, and their index of voting on other issues in the House. The last four independent variables describe the constituents of the representatives' home districts: the percentage of the population living in urban or suburban areas, the percentage of constituent families with annual income less than $3,000, the percentage of constituents who are black, Spanish, or Indian, and the region of the country. Though we used additional independent variables in some of the analyses, these eleven variables were the core of the investigation.[32]

To avoid the limitations of looking at only one or two variables at a time to explain the vote on the Hyde amendment, we used multiple classification analysis (MCA). Multiple classification analysis permits us to analyze the relative importance of each of the independent variables while controlling for the effects of the other variables. Multiple classification analysis also allows us to examine the relationship between each subcategory of an independent variable (such as the subcategories "Methodists" and "Catholics" of the independent variable "religion") and the vote on the Hyde amendment after taking the other factors into consideration.[33]

---

also those who were paired for or announced for it (though the latter two were usually very few in number). Similarly, those who opposed the Hyde amendment included not only those who voted against it, but also those who were paired against or announced against it. Unfortunately, since we did not have enough information on the personal, political, and constituent characteristics of all representatives, a few of them were not included in the analysis even though we know how they voted on the Hyde amendment. Several additional runs with the missing data were made to see whether any serious biases were introduced by these procedures; the results indicate that the MCA runs reported in this paper are representative of general pattern of actual voting behavior on the Hyde amendment.

On June 24 there were two roll-call votes on the Hyde amendment. Since the second one was an attempt by Representative Abzug to convince her colleagues to reconsider their previous vote (though very few of them actually changed their vote), we used the second vote; if, however, a representative had not participated at all on the second roll-call vote, his position on the first roll-call vote was used.

32. Many of the other independent variables, such as whether a representative was black or white, could not be used in the final MCA runs because there was such a large overlap between it and some other independent variable.

33. For a more thorough discussion of the use of multiple classification analysis, see my description of it in any other essay in this collection. Vinovskis, *supra* note 1, at 1764-65.

We will consider the relationship between each of the eleven independent variables and the vote on the Hyde amendment for the three different occasions that produced a roll-call vote in the House. As I noted above, the pro-life forces steadily gained strength, from 54% on June 24 to 58% on August 10 to 69% on September 16. Part of the difference between the first two and the last, of course, may be explained by the changes in the language of the amendment to permit federal funding of abortions when the life of the mother is endangered. The changes in voting over that period, however, may also reflect a decision of pro-choice representatives to accommodate themselves to the pressure from the pro-life activists in their districts. Therefore, in the balance of this Article I will discuss each explanatory variable individually and note any exceptional changes in predictive power between votes.

Our first independent variable was the age of the representative. In the general population, young adults are usually more pro-choice than older Americans.[34] Among the representatives, the pattern is more complex. Representatives under forty or over seventy were the most likely to support the Hyde amendment, but votes varied little with age until representatives passed seventy. This pattern held even after we controlled for the effects of the other independent variables (see figure 1). Overall, the age of the representatives was only a moderate predictor of their voting behavior (see the beta weights in tables 2, 4, and 6 in Appendix A).

Among the general population pro-life and pro-choice Americans show significant differences in level of education. The more educated one is, the more likely one is to support the pro-choice position. Thus, while 74% of those with a grade school education disapproved of the legalization of abortions for mothers who simply want no more children, only 42% of those with a college education disapproved.[35]

Any relationship between education and support for the Hyde amendment in Congress is complicated by the fact that almost every representative has either attended or graduated from college. Therefore, we subdivided the representatives by whether they had had at least some college training or a B.A., legal training beyond a B.A., other education beyond a B.A., or

34. Blake, *The Abortion Decisions: Judicial Review and Public Opinion*, in ABORTION: NEW DIRECTIONS FOR POLICY STUDIES 51 (1977).
    35. *Id.*

FIGURE 1

ADJUSTED PERCENTAGE OF REPRESENTATIVES
VOTING TO PROHIBIT FEDERAL FUNDS FOR
ABORTIONS BY AGE OF REPRESENTATIVE

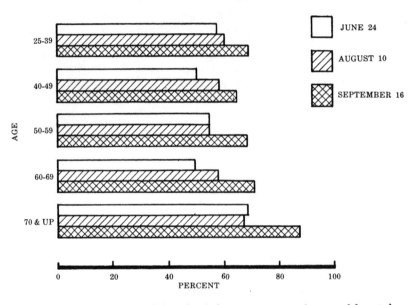

whether the educational level of the representative could not be ascertained. One might hypothesize that those representatives who had training beyond the B.A. would be less likely to support the Hyde amendment and that those with some legal training would be the least likely to support it since the constitutionality of the amendment was being questioned.

Representatives with education beyond a B.A. were indeed less likely to support the Hyde amendment than those with just some college training or a B.A. — even after we controlled for the other variables (see figure 2). Although in some situations legally trained representatives were more apt to oppose the Hyde amendment than those with nonlegal education beyond the B.A., in other situations the reverse was true — probably indicating that the constitutionality of the Hyde amendment was never as questionable to all lawyer-representatives as the pro-choice supporters implied during the debates on abortion. After controlling for other factors, the educational level of a representative usually was not as good a predictor of voting behavior as age.

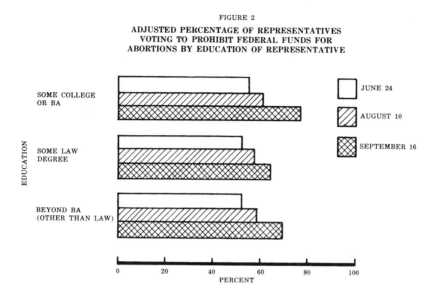

FIGURE 2

ADJUSTED PERCENTAGE OF REPRESENTATIVES
VOTING TO PROHIBIT FEDERAL FUNDS FOR
ABORTIONS BY EDUCATION OF REPRESENTATIVE

One frequent complaint from the pro-choice people through-out the debates on the Hyde amendment was that a legislative body composed almost entirely of men was making decisions that denied women the right to decide whether or not to have an abortion. They portrayed the Hyde amendment as the imposition of male values on powerless poor women. Several representatives and senators clearly implied that if Congress had a higher proportion of female members, the Hyde amendment would have been defeated. Thus, Representative Pritchard observed: "Finally, Mr. Speaker, if we had had 17 men and the rest of them were women, then both of us know that there would be a different discussion made today on this decision."[36]

In the general population women are actually more negative about abortions than men, though the difference is quite small.[37] In the House, however, female representatives were much more apt to vote against the Hyde amendment than their male counterparts. For example, 55.3% of male representatives supported the Hyde amendment on June 24 and only 27.8% of female representatives endorsed it. Yet after we controlled for the effects of the other variables, the differences between male and female representatives were considerably narrower (see figure 3). In other

36. 122 CONG. REC. 30,900 (1976).
37. Blake, *supra* note 34.

words, though female representatives were more likely to vote against the Hyde amendment than male representatives, it was due to many factors other than gender. As a result, it is not clear that if more women were elected to the House, especially from the more conservative districts, they would be any more likely to oppose restrictions on federal funding of abortions than the men who occupy those seats today.

Women are powerful in both the pro-life and pro-choice movements. One of the difficulties some pro-choice advocates have encountered on the Hill is that many male representatives feel rather uncomfortable with female activists who do not outwardly conform to the more traditional role of women in our society.[38] As a result, though women are prominent and active in both movements, those in the pro-life effort, who tend to accept a more traditional image and role for women in society, are often more personally acceptable to their congressmen than their counterparts in the pro-choice group.

FIGURE 3

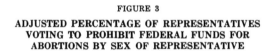

ADJUSTED PERCENTAGE OF REPRESENTATIVES
VOTING TO PROHIBIT FEDERAL FUNDS FOR
ABORTIONS BY SEX OF REPRESENTATIVE

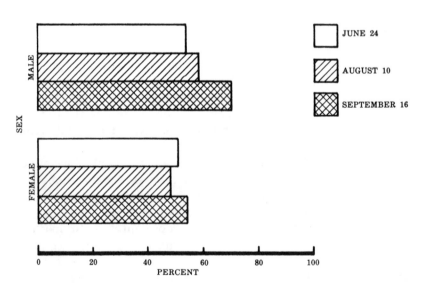

38. When I discussed the relative effectiveness of the lobbyists from the pro-choice and pro-life sides with 25 congressional offices, most of the respondents, including those who voted against the Hyde amendment, felt that the tactics of the pro-lifers were more effective; several people mentioned that pro-choice lobbyists were often handicapped because they did not fit the stereotype of the traditional American woman.

One of the most controversial aspects of the debates over abortion is the role of religion in promoting pro-life activities — particularly the involvement of the Catholic Church. On the one hand, most pro-choice activists stress the importance of the Catholic Church and clergy in mobilizing support for the pro-life efforts. The most extreme pro-choice activists see the entire anti-abortion effort directed and financed by the Catholic Church with only token Protestant and Jewish participation. On the other hand, pro-lifers are very uneasy and often quite resentful whenever the religious issue is raised. Some deny the active participation of the Catholic Church while others try to justify its involvement. In any case, most pro-life supporters feel that the importance of the Catholic Church has been deliberately exaggerated by their pro-choice opponents to discredit and discourage any further pro-life activity among Catholics and to rally Protestant and Jewish support for the pro-choice side.

During the debates on the Hyde amendment in the 94th Congress, the Catholic Church and many of its clergymen were actively encouraging their parishioners to support efforts to restrict or prohibit abortions. Following the guidelines of the "Pastoral Plan for Pro-Life Activities" adopted by the National Conference of Catholic Bishops in November 1975, the Church hoped to organize Catholics in every congressional district who could persuade their officials to support pro-life positions.[39] Rather than trying to deny the involvement of the Catholic Church in pro-life efforts, Monsignor James McHugh, Director of the pro-life activities for the National Conference of Catholic Bishops, defended it: "I think every church has a right to use its political muscle and its political expertise to try to persuade the rest of the society to adopt the views that they find consonant with their faith and belief, and consonant with the political philosophy of the country itself."[40] But McHugh did go on to deny that the Catholic Church tries to engage directly in any political activity:

> We encourage those things happening, but we do not consider that those are uniquely the role of the church. The church stops . . . in the public policy area with pronouncements, with encouragement, with clarifying issues, with perhaps even testifying before Congress. But we do not think that the church or her agencies

---

39. Vinovskis, *supra* note 1.
40. Transcript of CBS News program, "The Politics of Abortion" (aired April 22, 1978), at 16.

should be involved in this congressional district activity, in this election of candidates, in this endorsement of one candidate over another. We enumerated those things because those are the kinds of activity that we feel citizens themselves should engage in, and we were certainly trying to encourage our Catholic citizens to work into the political order.[41]

The pro-choice spokespeople agree with McHugh's statement that the Catholic Church is trying to influence its parishioners to support efforts such as the Hyde amendment, but they strongly disagree with his contention that the Church and its clergymen have stopped short of direct political involvement such as soliciting contributions or distributing pro-life literature.[42] In any case, the real question is not whether the Catholic Church and its supporters participated in the efforts to enact the Hyde amendment, directly or indirectly, but whether they were influential — particularly among the Catholic representatives.

Catholic representatives were much more likely to support the Hyde amendment than their Protestant or Jewish counterparts. For example, 74.7% of Catholic representatives endorsed the Hyde amendment on June 24 and only 51.2% of the Presbyterian, 57.1% of the Methodist, 55.3% of the Baptist, 42.5% of the Episcopalian, and 10.5% of the Jewish representatives voted for it. Thus, as the pro-choice side has argued, representatives of different religions showed significant differences in level of support for the Hyde amendment.[43]

But did the differences between Catholic and non-Catholic representatives on the Hyde amendment disappear after we controlled for the effects of the other variables? Did the religion of a representative really influence his vote, or were the patterns described above merely coincidental? After we controlled for the effects of other attributes of the representatives, the differences in voting behavior between Catholic and non-Catholic representatives not only persisted, but substantially increased (see figure 4). Catholic representatives were much more likely to vote for

---

41. *Id.* at 17.

42. For example, see Planned Parenthood-World Population Washington Memo, Sept. 17, 1976, at 1-3; National Abortion Rights Action League Newsletter, Sept. 1976, at 8-7.

43. Though we do have the religious affiliations of the representatives, we do not have any information on other aspects of their religious orientations. For example, it would be useful to know which representatives consider themselves evangelical or even which ones regularly attend church. If we had additional information about religious beliefs and practices, religion might be an even better predictor of voting behavior on the Hyde amendment than simply knowing their religious affiliations.

restricting federal funds for abortions than Protestant or Jewish representatives. In fact, after controlling for the effects of the other variables, religion was the second best predictor of how someone voted on the Hyde amendment.

FIGURE 4

ADJUSTED PERCENTAGE OF REPRESENTATIVES
VOTING TO PROHIBIT FEDERAL FUNDS FOR
ABORTIONS BY RELIGION OF REPRESENTATIVE

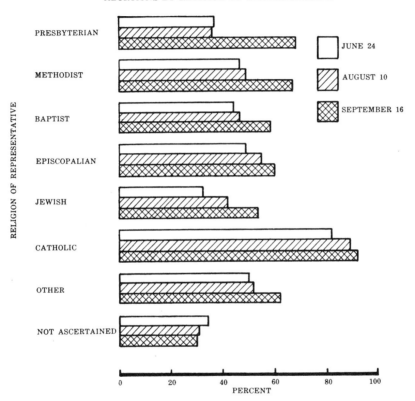

Though this analysis confirms the existence of a link between religion and support for the Hyde amendment it must be interpreted in light of another fact — there are not enough Catholic representatives in the House or Senate to account alone for the success of the Hyde amendment. On June 24, Catholics constituted only about one third of those who voted for the Hyde amendment. If the Protestant representatives had not split almost equally on the issue, the Hyde amendment would never have passed; only the Jewish representatives were solidly opposed to the Hyde amendment and they are too few to offset the strong support from Catholic representatives. Moreover, although the religious affiliation of a representative is unquestionably a major predictor of how that person voted on the Hyde amendment in 1976, it is still not clear what effect pressure from the Catholic Church had. Our analysis cannot explain whether the greater likelihood of Catholic representatives voting for the Hyde amendment was due to their personal religious values and convictions about abortion or to a special respect for the views of the National Conference of Catholic Bishops.

So far we have considered the effects of four personal characteristics of the representatives on their votes on the Hyde amendment; now we turn to some political factors — their political affiliation, their political prospects as of October 9, 1976, and their index of liberalism on other issues as measured by the percentage of times they voted with the recommendations of the Americans for Democratic Action. Many representatives, particularly those in the pro-choice camp, lamented that the Hyde amendment had become such a controversial political issue and urged their colleagues to vote on the basis of its moral and health implications rather than its political consequences. As Representative Pritchard put it: "I do not believe that the majority of the Members favor this amendment. This is not a time to be political, it is a time to be concerned with the health of this Nation."[44] Nevertheless the political consequences of voting for or against the Hyde amendment were never far from the thoughts of most representatives.

Party affiliation appears to be a very strong predictor of how representatives voted on the Hyde amendment. Though Republicans in the general population tend to be more pro-choice than Democrats, Republican representatives were much more likely to vote to restrict federal funding of abortions than their Democratic counterparts. While 73.6% of the Republican representatives voted for the Hyde amendment, only 43.9% of the Democrats supported it. Given that large difference in support, some commentators have seen this as a party issue, particularly since the party platforms and presidential nominees in 1976 also divided along party lines on the abortion issue.[45] Yet after we controlled for the effects of the other variables, the differences between Republicans and Democrats not only disappeared, but on two of the

---

44. 122 CONG. REC. 26,783 (1976).
45. See Vinovskis, supra note 1.

three roll-call votes Democrats were now slightly more likely to favor the Hyde amendment than Republicans (see figure 5). Though party affiliation by itself seemed to be a strong predictor of voting behavior on abortion, after we controlled for other factors it became relatively unimportant.

FIGURE 5

ADJUSTED PERCENTAGE OF REPRESENTATIVES VOTING TO PROHIBIT FEDERAL FUNDS FOR ABORTIONS BY POLITICAL AFFILIATION OF REPRESENTATIVE

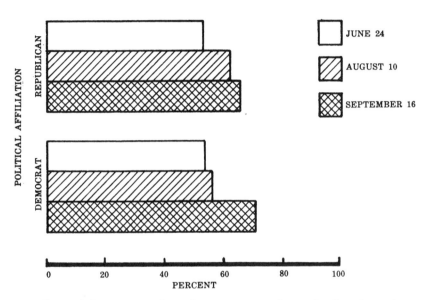

One might suspect that the representatives who faced particularly difficult reelection battles would be more concerned about the political effects of their Hyde amendment votes than those who were not running for reelection or who did not face stiff reelection fights. To evaluate the political situation of each representative, we relied upon the evaluation of the House campaigns as of October 9, 1976, in the *Congressional Quarterly*, which is acknowledged by most Capitol Hill observers as one of the most accurate surveys of congressional campaigns.[46]

First, we classified the representatives by whether or not they were running for reelection as of October 9, 1976. Among those who were not returning, we distinguished those who had decided

---

46. CONG. Q., Oct. 9, 1976, Supplement.

to abandon electoral politics completely from those who were seeking another office, had already been defeated in a primary, or had died in office by October 9. We hypothesized that those who had decided to retire completely from electoral politics would be less likely to be influenced by outside pressure groups than those who had left the House for another position, had been running for reelection earlier and then lost their primary, or had died in office (there were very few representatives who had lost in a primary fight for reelection or died in office). One must be rather careful in drawing general conclusions from the few individuals not returning. The incumbents seeking reelection were subdivided into three categories — those whose reelection seemed assured, those whose reelection was likely but not certain, and those whose reelection was in considerable doubt as of October 9. An overwhelming percentage of House members up for reelection were from safe districts and therefore we expected them to be more politically able to vote their individual consciences on the Hyde amendment than their colleagues facing difficult reelection campaigns.

When we controlled for the effects of other variables, the representatives leaving the House usually were much more likely to oppose the Hyde amendment than those who were running for reelection (see figure 6). Even those who were leaving the House to seek another elected office were more likely to oppose restrictions on federal funding of abortions than those who were engaged in difficult reelection fights — particularly on the votes of June 24 and September 16. In every situation, the representatives who were retiring from electoral politics altogether opposed the Hyde amendment more than any of their colleagues.

After we controlled for the effects of the other variables, we found representatives seeking reelection from safe districts more likely to support the Hyde amendment than their colleagues, though the differences were not very sizable. The puzzling thing about the results is that the two sets of representatives supposedly the most immune from outside pressure, those retiring from electoral politics altogether and those in safe districts, responded in opposing ways to the Hyde amendment. Perhaps this is a function of a small number of cases we have for the representatives who are retiring from politics altogether, which may have produced statistically unstable results. Or perhaps even though outside observers considered a district safe, the representative running for reelection was still very concerned about pro-choice and

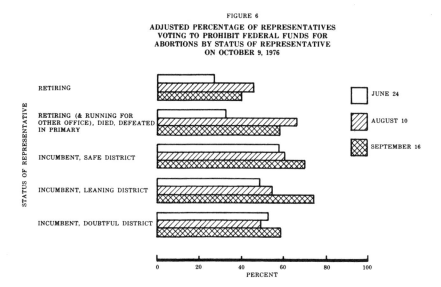

FIGURE 6

ADJUSTED PERCENTAGE OF REPRESENTATIVES
VOTING TO PROHIBIT FEDERAL FUNDS FOR
ABORTIONS BY STATUS OF REPRESENTATIVE
ON OCTOBER 9, 1976

pro-life activists since any drop in the 1976 margin of victory might encourage a more formidable opponent to run in 1978.[47]

While most commentators on the Hyde amendment have studied the religious and political affiliations of the representatives, few have speculated about the association between their pattern of voting on other issues and the way they voted on cutting federal funds for abortions. From time to time, the pro-choice side has chided pro-life representatives for not supporting federally funded family planning programs or for not voting additional money for helping teenage mothers, but not even these pro-choice critics have seen the abortion battle as one between conservatives and liberals. In fact, many pro-choice activists expect support from conservatives since both groups should be able to agree on the necessity of removing any government interference with what they see as part of the private lives of women.

To test whether there is a relationship between voting for the Hyde amendment and one's position on other issues, it is useful to have a measure of voting behavior that identifies a representative's place on the political spectrum. We used as our index of liberalism the percentage of times representatives voted with the

---

47. Congressmen from safe districts are often very concerned about future challenges to them. For an excellent discussion of the way representatives perceive their constituents and reelection campaigns, see R. FENNO, HOME STYLE: HOUSE MEMBERS IN THEIR DISTRICTS (1978).

recommendations of the Americans for Democratic Action (removing, of course, the vote on the Hyde amendment from the roll-
call votes used to compute the ADA index). We also used several
other indices of political orientation, including those put out by
the AFL-CIO Committee on Political Education, the National
Farmers Union, the Chamber of Commerce, and the Americans
for Constitutional Action, in different MCA runs and we had
results very similar to those produced by using the ADA index.[48]

The addition of an index of liberalism produced dramatic
results: A representative's index of liberalism was the single best
predictor of voting behavior on the Hyde amendment. Even after
controlling for other factors, representatives who voted with the
recommendations of the ADA less than twenty-five percent of the
time were three or four times as likely to vote for the Hyde
amendment as those who agreed with the ADA position at least
seventy-five percent of the time (see figure 7). Thus, despite what
one might infer from the remarks of the news media and Capitol
Hill observers, a representative's overall liberalism is a much
better predictor of the vote on restricting federal funds for abortions than any other variable, including the representative's religious affiliation.

This conservative-liberal split on abortion funding places
many pro-life representatives in an awkward position. On the one
hand, they argue that abortions should not be used as a substitute
for family planning and that pregnant women should be helped
by private and public agencies to care for their unborn child so
that they will not need to resort to an abortion. In fact, the pro-
life position stresses the value of the mother and her child in our
society and seeks to encourage couples to have children rather
than abortions. On the other hand, since pro-life representatives
tend to be more conservative than their pro-choice counterparts,
they are reluctant to vote for higher federal spending for programs
designed to prevent unwanted pregnancies or to assist pregnant
women. On the same day that the House first enacted the Hyde
amendment, it rejected an amendment by Representative James
H. Scheuer (D.-New York) to increase family planning funds
under Title X of the Public Health Service Act.[49] Those representatives who voted for the Hyde amendment were much
more likely to vote against the Scheuer amendment than

48. These indices are available in Cong. Q., Feb. 5, 1977, at 222.
49. 122 Cong. Rec. 20,396 (1976).

FIGURE 7

ADJUSTED PERCENTAGE OF REPRESENTATIVES
VOTING TO PROHIBIT FEDERAL FUNDS FOR
ABORTIONS BY PERCENTAGE OF VOTES WITH ADA

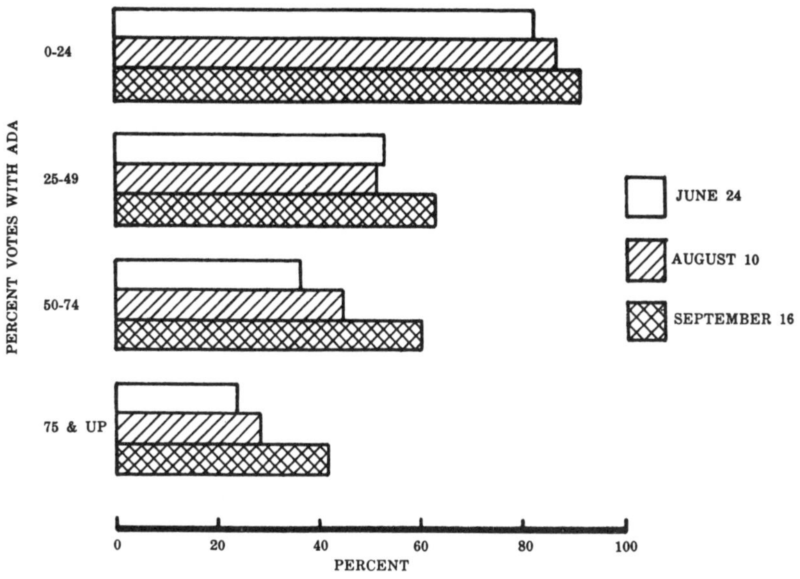

those who opposed the Hyde amendment, after we controlled for the effects of the other variables.[50] Thus, many pro-life representatives had to explain to their constituents why they opposed higher levels of funding for family planning programs at the same time that they were cutting off federal funds for abortions for poor women who did not want any more children.

Finally, we considered the impact of some of the characteristics of constituents in a congressional district on the way that representative voted on the Hyde amendment. Unfortunately, some of the constituents' characteristics that may be most influential — such as the religious affiliation of the voters — are not tabulated at the level of the congressional district. But we do have information at the district level from the 1970 census on the percentage of constituents living in urban or suburban areas, the percentage of families with incomes less than $3000, the percentage of voters who are black, Spanish, or Indian, and the region

50. Based on my unpublished MCA investigation of the determinants of voting on the Scheuer amendment.

of the country in which the district is situated.[51] Therefore, we analyzed the significance of those factors.

Representatives from rural areas were more likely to support the Hyde amendment than representatives from the urban areas. While 63.3% of the representatives who had less than twenty-five percent of their constituents in urban or suburban areas voted for the Hyde amendment on June 24, only 45.3% of those with at least seventy-five percent of their constituents in urban or suburban areas voted for it. These differences, however, largely disappeared when we controlled for the effects of the other variables (see figure 8).

FIGURE 8

ADJUSTED PERCENTAGE OF REPRESENTATIVES
VOTING TO PROHIBIT FEDERAL FUNDS FOR
ABORTIONS BY PERCENTAGE OF CONSTITUENTS
LIVING IN URBAN/SUBURBAN AREAS

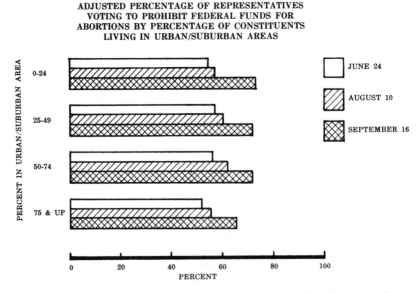

Since the Hyde amendment ended federally funded abortions for poor women, one might expect that representatives with a high proportion of low-income constituents would have been more likely to oppose it. Though this was generally true, we were surprised to find that after we controlled for the effects of the other variables, the strongest support for the Hyde amendment on June 24 and August 10 came from those districts with at least twenty percent of their families having a yearly income of less than $3000 (see figure 9). This variable, like the previous one, was

---

51. The census information was obtained from M. BARONE, G. UJIFUSA, & D. MATTHEWS, THE ALMANAC OF AMERICAN POLITICS (1975).

not a particularly strong predictor of voting behavior, but what predictive value it had runs counter to what intuition suggests. Personal and political considerations of representatives seem to have overridden financial needs of constituents in determining the pattern of voting for the Hyde amendment.

FIGURE 9

ADJUSTED PERCENTAGE OF REPRESENTATIVES
VOTING TO PROHIBIT FEDERAL FUNDS FOR
ABORTIONS BY PERCENTAGE OF CONSTITUENT
FAMILIES WITH INCOMES LESS THAN $3000

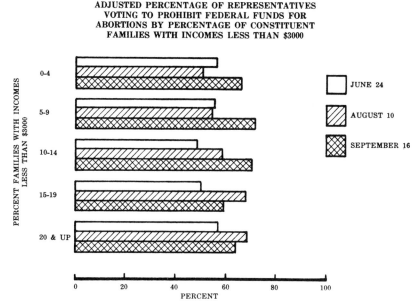

The higher the proportion of nonwhite constituents, the more likely the representative was to vote against the Hyde amendment. Though controlling for the effects of the other factors compressed the differences somewhat, the general pattern remained the same (see figure 10). Compared to other variables, this one was a moderately strong predictor of voting behavior on the Hyde amendment.

During the debates on restricting federal funds for abortions, pro-life advocates often charged those who favored abortions for poor black women with genocide. As Representative Hyde argued:

> All of us should have a particular sensitivity to the concept of the word genocide. In New York City, last year for every 1,000 minority births, there were 1,304 minority abortions. That is one way to get rid of the poverty problem, get rid of poor people. Let us call that pooricide.[52]

---

52. 122 CONG. REC. 26,785 (1976).

FIGURE 10

**ADJUSTED PERCENTAGE OF REPRESENTATIVES
VOTING TO PROHIBIT FEDERAL FUNDS FOR
ABORTIONS BY PERCENTAGE OF CONSTITUENTS
WHO ARE BLACKS, SPANISH, OR INDIANS**

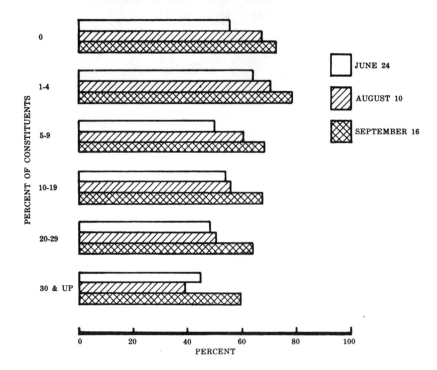

Nevertheless, though the pro-life activists openly appealed for support from the black representatives and those with a high proportion of nonwhite constituents, they failed to make any significant inroads. The black representatives rejected attempts to end federal funding of abortions as discriminatory against poor women — many of whom were black. As Representative Parren J. Mitchell (D.-Maryland) observed:

> Clearly then, if the proponents of this legislation are against abortion then it is not appropriate for them to prohibit the access to abortions for only one class of people. I abhor this type of victimization. This legislation will only approve inequities in the constitutional rights of our citizens and increase the disparity that already exists among white and black, rich and poor, the economically and socially advantaged and disadvantaged.[53]

---

53. *Id.* at 26,784.

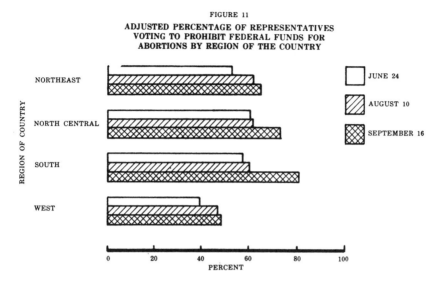

FIGURE 11

ADJUSTED PERCENTAGE OF REPRESENTATIVES
VOTING TO PROHIBIT FEDERAL FUNDS FOR
ABORTIONS BY REGION OF THE COUNTRY

Overall, the eleven independent variables could account for about one third of the variation in voting behavior on the Hyde amendment. Compared to other attempts to exlain voting patterns using multiple classification analysis and as many independent variables, this is a reasonable and satisfactory level of explanation, particularly since information on some potentially important factors such as the religious affiliation of constituents was unavailable to us.

III. CONCLUSION

When the 94th Congress reconvened in January 1976, almost no one predicted that the pro-life forces would succeed in passing an amendment to the Labor-HEW appropriations bill to cut off federal funds for abortions except when the life of the mother was endangered. Perhaps even more surprising was that the leadership and impetus for this effort came from the House of Representatives rather than the Senate, since in the 93d Congress the House had been firmly opposed to most pro-life legislation. It is difficult to explain the sudden success of the pro-life effort in the House. Though many representatives genuinely thought that the Supreme Court had gone too far in its legalization of all abortions in the first six months, subject only to state health regulations in the second trimester, most of them did not feel very strongly about the abortion issue. In fact, many representatives acknowledged the complexity of the abortion question and privately admitted that they wished Congress had never become embroiled in the Hyde amendment controversy. Yet a small group of persuasive zealots in the House was able to force their reluctant colleagues to take a recorded stand on abortion in an election year.

The success of the pro-life movement is certainly related to the uncertainty of most representatives and most other observers about the importance of the abortion controversy to the electorate. Though most representatives were not in any real danger of being defeated for reelection, they did not want to take any chances by triggering an emotional pro-life crusade against themselves in their districts. The pro-life forces were particularly effective at the local level, thanks in part to the active support and encouragement of the National Conference of Catholic Bishops through its Pastoral Plan for Pro-Life Activities. Some of the success of the pro-lifers at the grass-roots level reflected the inability of their pro-choice counterparts to mount an equally effective political effort at the level of the congressional district, partly because the pro-choice advocates concentrated their attention more on national than local lobbying and partly because they had great difficulty in arousing their followers to wage as fervent a fight on abortion as the pro-lifers did.

When the representatives placed their plastic cards in the voting slots to record their votes on the Hyde amendment, they were certainly aware of the political pressures from both sides. Furthermore, they overestimated the political saliency of the abortion issue by assuming that the emotional intensity among the activists in some way reflected the feelings of the general public on abortion. Though these outside pressures in an election year were undoubtedly necessary ingredients for the pro-life victory in the House, they still do not explain why some representatives responded positively to the Hyde amendment while others chose to oppose it.

The personal values and attitudes of representatives about abortion certainly played a major role in their final decisions. This analysis suggests that representatives who generally tended to be more conservative on other social issues or who were brought up as Catholics were much more likely to favor restricting federal funds for abortions than those who were generally more liberal or raised in a Protestant or Jewish environment. Since most representatives did not care enough about abortion to make it their personal crusade in the House in 1975, one is led to suspect that while personal values and characteristics predisposed representatives to respond in certain ways once the abortion issue was forced upon them, left to themselves they would have never pushed to cut off federal funds from abortions.

APPENDIX A

TABLE No. 1

VOTE IN THE HOUSE OF REPRESENTATIVES ON THE AMENDMENT
TO PROHIBIT USE OF FEDERAL FUNDS TO PAY FOR OR
TO PROMOTE ABORTIONS, JUNE 24, 1976
(1 = SUPPORTED AMENDMENT / 0 = OPPOSED AMENDMENT)

	Class Mean	Adjusted Mean	Net Deviation	Number of Cases
Age of Representative:				
25-39	55.8	58.0	+ 4.1	52
40-49	52.3	51.5	— 2.9	109
50-59	54.2	55.1	+ 1.2	118
60-69	50.0	49.6	— 4.3	74
70 and Above	75.0	68.9	+15.0	16
Education of Representative:				
Some College or BA	62.5	55.5	+ 1.6	96
Some Law Degree	50.5	53.0	— .9	200
Beyond BA				
(Other Than Law)	46.6	52.3	— 1.6	58
Not Ascertained	73.3	63.5	+ 9.6	15
Sex of Representative:				
Male	55.3	54.1	+ .2	351
Female	27.8	51.2	— 2.7	18
Religion of Representative:				
Presbyterian	51.2	37.0	—16.9	43
Methodist	57.1	46.9	— 7.0	56
Baptist	55.3	44.1	— 9.8	38
Episcopalian	42.5	48.7	— 5.2	40
Jewish	10.5	32.4	—21.5	19
Catholic	74.7	82.1	+28.2	91
Other	47.9	50.2	— 3.7	73
Not Ascertained	22.2	34.9	—19.0	9
Party Affiliation of Representative:				
Republican	73.6	53.4	— .5	125
Democrat	43.9	54.2	+ .3	244
Status of Representative on October 9, 1976:				
Retiring	38.9	27.8	—26.1	18
Retiring (but running for other office), Died, or				
Defeated in Primary	28.6	33.7	—20.2	1
Incumbent, Safe District	56.5	58.0	+ 4.1	253
Incumbent, Leaning District	50.8	49.4	— 4.5	59
Incumbent, Doubtful or				
Unsure District	60.0	53.4	— .5	25

	Class Mean	Adjusted Mean	Net Deviation	Number of Cases
Percentage of Times Voting with Americans for Democratic Action:				
0-24	78.4	82.6	+28.7	139
25-49	51.7	52.7	— 1.2	60
50-74	44.6	36.6	—17.3	92
75 and Above	23.1	24.2	—29.7	78
Percentage of Constituents Living in Urban/Suburban Areas:				
0-24	63.3	54.5	+ .6	60
25-49	60.8	57.7	+ 3.8	51
50-74	64.7	56.3	+ 2.4	68
75 and Above	45.3	51.9	— 2.0	190
Percentage of Constituent Families with Incomes Less Than $3000:				
0-4	60.7	57.2	+ 3.3	28
5-9	51.1	56.3	+ 2.4	180
10-14	51.2	48.8	— 5.1	82
15-19	59.3	50.4	— 3.5	54
20 and Above	64.0	57.3	+ 3.4	25
Percentage of Constituents Who Are Blacks, Spanish, or Indians:				
0	67.6	55.7	+ 1.8	34
1-4	63.0	64.1	+10.2	92
5-9	51.6	50.6	— 3.3	64
10-19	58.3	53.7	— .2	72
20-29	37.8	49.1	— 4.8	45
30 and Above	41.9	45.1	— 8.8	62
Region of Country:				
Northeast	49.5	52.7	— 1.2	91
North Central	67.0	60.6	+ 6.7	106
South	61.3	57.4	+ 3.5	106
West	27.3	39.4	—14.5	66
Total	53.9			369

TABLE No. 2

VOTE IN THE HOUSE OF REPRESENTATIVES ON THE AMENDMENT
TO PROHIBIT USE OF FEDERAL FUNDS TO PAY FOR OR
TO PROMOTE ABORTIONS, JUNE 24, 1976:
ETA^{2}S, BETAS, AND R^2

	Eta^2	Beta
Age of Representative	.0095	.0852
Education of Representative	.0118	.0462
Sex of Representative	.0114	.0125
Religion of Representative	.0840	.3385
Party Affiliation of Representative	.0773	.0078
Status of Representative, October 9, 1976	.0069	.1602
Percentage of Times Voting with Americans for Democratic Action	.1743	.4798
Percentage of Constituents Living in Urban/Suburban Areas	.0246	.0454
Percentage of Constituent Families with Incomes Less Than $3000	.0081	.0694
Percentage of Constituents Who Are Blacks, Spanish, or Indians	.0265	.1327
Region of Country	.0716	.1478

R^2 = .3222

Note: The Eta^{2}s and R^2 have been adjusted for the
degrees of freedom.

TABLE No. 3

VOTE IN THE HOUSE OF REPRESENTATIVES ON MOTION
TO DELETE AMENDMENT PROHIBITING USE OF FEDERAL FUNDS
TO PAY FOR OR TO PROMOTE ABORTIONS, AUGUST 10, 1976
(1 = OPPOSED MOTION / 0 = SUPPORTED MOTION)

	Class Mean	Adjusted Mean	Net Deviation	Number of Cases
Age of Representative:				
25-39	59.3	61.3	+ 2.9	59
40-49	59.1	59.3	+ .9	115
50-59	54.8	55.6	— 2.8	126
60-69	58.1	57.7	— .7	74
70 and Above	77.8	66.5	+ 8.1	18
Education of Representative:				
Some College or BA	68.0	60.9	+ 2.5	100
Some Law Degree	55.0	57.3	— 1.1	211
Beyond BA (Other Than Law)	52.3	58.5	+ .1	65
Not Ascertained	68.8	56.9	— 1.5	16
Sex of Representative:				
Male	59.9	58.9	+ .5	374
Female	27.8	48.0	—10.4	18
Religion of Representative:				
Presbyterian	52.4	36.2	—22.2	42
Methodist	62.3	48.7	— 9.7	61
Baptist	57.5	47.4	—11.0	40
Episcopalian	51.3	55.7	— 2.7	39
Jewish	15.0	42.4	—16.0	20
Catholic	79.2	89.1	+30.7	101
Other	51.9	52.9	— 5.5	79
Not Ascertained	20.0	31.0	—27.4	10
Party Affiliation of Representative:				
Republican	81.3	62.6	+ 4.2	128
Democrat	47.3	56.4	— 2.0	264
Status of Representative on October 9, 1976:				
Retiring	64.7	46.7	—11.7	17
Retiring (but running for another office), Died, or Defeated in Primary	58.8	66.3	+ 7.9	17
Incumbent, Safe District	57.7	60.4	+ 2.0	267
Incumbent, Leaning District	60.3	55.3	— 3.1	63
Incumbent, Doubtful or Unsure District	57.1	48.6	— 9.8	28

	Class Mean	Adjusted Mean	Net Deviation	Number of Cases
Percentage of Times Voting with Americans for Democratic Action:				
0-24	84.9	87.1	+28.7	146
25-49	51.5	51.7	— 6.7	66
50-74	51.0	45.9	—12.5	96
75 and Above	26.2	28.1	—30.3	84
Percentage of Constituents Living in Urban/Suburban Areas:				
0-24	71.2	57.9	— .5	59
25-49	68.5	61.0	+ 2.6	54
50-74	69.3	62.3	+ 3.9	75
75 and Above	48.0	56.5	— 1.9	204
Percentage of Constituent Families with Incomes Less Than $3000:				
0-4	60.6	51.5	— 6.9	33
5-9	54.0	55.1	— 3.3	189
10-14	59.8	59.2	+ .8	92
15-19	67.3	68.0	+ 9.6	55
20 and Above	65.2	69.2	+10.8	23
Percentage of Constituents Who Are Blacks, Spanish, or Indians:				
0	76.9	67.2	+ 8.8	39
1-4	68.7	70.9	+12.5	99
5-9	59.4	61.1	+ 2.7	64
10-19	61.0	55.7	— 2.7	77
20-29	41.7	51.7	— 6.7	48
30 and Above	40.0	39.7	—18.7	65
Region of Country:				
Northeast	57.4	61.8	+ 3.4	94
North Central	69.3	60.9	+ 2.5	114
South	64.9	60.1	+ 1.7	111
West	32.9	47.6	—10.8	73
Total	58.4			392

TABLE No. 4

VOTE IN THE HOUSE OF REPRESENTATIVES ON MOTION
TO DELETE AMENDMENT PROHIBITING USE OF FEDERAL FUNDS
TO PAY FOR OR TO PROMOTE ABORTIONS, AUGUST 10, 1976:
ETA^{2}S, BETAS, AND R^2

	Eta^2	Beta
Age of Representative	.0090	.0545
Education of Representative	.0090	.0309
Sex of Representative	.0161	.0461
Religion of Representative	.0929	.3858
Party Affiliation of Representative	.1018	.0566
Status of Representative, October 9, 1976	.0011	.0906
Percentage of Times Voting with Americans for Democratic Action	.2021	.4772
Percentage of Constituents Living in Urban/Suburban Areas	.0410	.0490
Percentage of Constituent Families with Incomes Less Than $3000	.0099	.1095
Percentage of Constituents Who Are Blacks, Spanish, or Indians	.0508	.2152
Region of Country	.0619	.1059

R^2 = .3790

Note: The Eta^{2}s and R^2 have been adjusted for the
degrees of freedom.

TABLE No. 5

VOTE IN THE HOUSE OF REPRESENTATIVES
ON THE CONFERENCE COMMITTEE AMENDMENT TO PROHIBIT USE
OF FEDERAL FUNDS TO PAY FOR OR TO PROMOTE ABORTIONS EXCEPT
WHERE LIFE OF MOTHER WOULD BE ENDANGERED, SEPTEMBER 16, 1976
(1 = SUPPORTED AMENDMENT / 0 = OPPOSED AMENDMENT)

	Class Mean	Adjusted Mean	Net Deviation	Number of Cases
Age of Representative:				
25-39	67.9	69.2	+ .1	56
40-49	67.6	65.8	— 3.3	108
50-59	66.7	68.6	— .5	117
60-69	71.2	71.0	+ 1.9	66
70 and Above	93.8	87.8	+18.7	16
Education of Representative:				
Some College or BA	79.8	76.7	+ 7.6	94
Some Law Degree	64.8	65.3	— 3.8	196
Beyond BA (Other Than Law)	63.2	69.4	+ .3	57
Not Ascertained	81.3	70.5	+ 1.4	16
Sex of Representative:				
Male	70.6	69.8	+ .7	347
Female	37.5	54.5	—14.6	16
Religion of Representative:				
Presbyterian	80.6	68.1	— 1.0	36
Methodist	76.8	66.5	— 2.6	56
Baptist	69.2	58.6	—10.5	39
Episcopalian	55.0	60.1	— 9.0	40
Jewish	31.6	53.6	—15.5	19
Catholic	87.1	92.1	+23.0	93
Other	58.6	62.1	— 7.0	70
Not Ascertained	20.0	30.0	—39.1	10
Party Affiliation of Representative:				
Republican	82.0	65.7	— 3.4	122
Democrat	62.7	70.9	+ 1.8	241
Status of Representative on October 9, 1976:				
Retiring	60.0	41.0	—28.1	15
Retiring (but running for another office), Died, or Defeated in Primary	57.1	58.5	—10.6	14
Incumbent, Safe District	68.9	71.2	+ 2.1	254
Incumbent, Leaning District	75.9	74.0	+ 4.9	58
Incumbent, Doubtful or Unsure District	68.2	59.1	—10.0	22

	Class Mean	Adjusted Mean	Net Deviation	Number of Cases
Percentage of Times Voting with Americans for Democratic Action:				
0-24	90.9	91.6	+22.5	132
25-49	63.1	63.2	− 5.9	65
50-74	65.5	60.2	− 8.9	87
75 and Above	41.8	46.3	−22.8	79
Percentage of Constituents Living in Urban/Suburban Areas:				
0-24	81.8	73.8	+ 4.7	55
25-49	73.6	72.2	+ 3.1	53
50-74	81.4	72.0	+ 2.9	70
75 and Above	59.5	65.8	− 3.3	185
Percentage of Constituent Families with Incomes Less Than $3000:				
0-4	68.8	67.1	− 2.0	32
5-9	65.9	72.1	+ 3.0	173
10-14	72.1	71.0	+ 1.9	86
15-19	72.9	59.0	−10.1	48
20 and Above	75.0	64.0	− 5.1	24
Percentage of Constituents Who Are Blacks, Spanish, or Indians:				
0	81.1	72.1	+ 3.0	37
1-4	77.4	78.0	+ 8.9	93
5-9	67.7	68.1	− 1.0	65
10-19	70.1	67.6	− 1.5	67
20-29	56.1	64.1	− 5.0	41
30 and Above	58.3	59.9	− 9.2	60
Region of Country:				
Northeast	62.0	65.0	− 4.1	92
North Central	80.0	73.5	+ 4.4	110
South	81.2	80.7	+11.6	101
West	40.0	48.2	−20.9	60
Total	69.1			363

TABLE No. 6

VOTE IN THE HOUSE OF REPRESENTATIVES
ON THE CONFERENCE COMMITTEE AMENDMENT TO PROHIBIT USE
OF FEDERAL FUNDS TO PAY FOR OR TO PROMOTE ABORTIONS EXCEPT
WHERE LIFE OF MOTHER WOULD BE ENDANGERED, SEPTEMBER 16, 1976:
ETA^2S, BETAS, AND R^2

	Eta^2	Beta
Age of Representative	.0032	.0951
Education of Representative	.0160	.1033
Sex of Representative	.0189	.0682
Religion of Representative	.1182	.3220
Party Affiliation of Representative	.0363	.0544
Status of Representative, October 9, 1976	.0076	.1529
Percentage of Times Voting with Americans for Democratic Action	.1547	.3890
Percentage of Constituents Living in Urban/Suburban Areas	.0409	.0743
Percentage of Constituent Families with Incomes Less Than $3000	.0053	.0990
Percentage of Constituents Who Are Blacks, Spanish, or Indians	.0198	.1341
Region of Country	.1001	.2368

$R^2 = .3255$

Note: The Eta^2s and R^2 have been adjusted for the degrees of freedom.

Index

About the Editors

Carl E. Schneider is a graduate of Harvard College and the University of Michigan Law School. He was editor-in-chief of the *Michigan Law Review.*

Maris A. Vinovskis is associate professor of history at the University of Michigan and associate research scientist at the Center for Political Studies of the Institute for Social Research.